T0305386

Value for Money

Scrivener Publishing
100 Cummings Center, Suite 541J
Beverly, MA 01915-6106

Publishers at Scrivener
Martin Scrivener (martin@scrivenerpublishing.com)
Phillip Carmical (pcarmical@scrivenerpublishing.com)

Value for Money

How to Show the Value for
Money for All Types of Projects
and Programs in Governments,
Nongovernmental Organizations,
Nonprofits, and Businesses

**Patricia Pulliam Phillips,
Jack J. Phillips, Gina Paone,
and Cyndi Huff Gaudet**
With the Assistance of Kylie McLeod

Scrivener
Publishing

WILEY

This edition first published 2019 by John Wiley & Sons, Inc., 111 River Street, Hoboken, NJ 07030, USA
and Scrivener Publishing LLC, 100 Cummings Center, Suite 541J, Beverly, MA 01915, USA
© 2019 Jack J. Phillips and Patricia P. Phillips
For more information about Scrivener publications please visit www.scrivenerpublishing.com.

ROI Institute®, ROI Methodology®, Certified ROI Professional® are registered to ROI Institute, Inc. and
are used by others only with written permission of Jack and Patti Phillips.

Wiley Global Headquarters
111 River Street, Hoboken, NJ 07030, USA

For details of our global editorial offices, customer services, and more information about Wiley products
visit us at www.wiley.com.

Library of Congress Cataloging-in-Publication Data

ISBN 978-1-119-32265-8

Cover image: Office Meeting - Rawpixelimages, Currency Map - Tudor Antonel Adrian |
        Dreamstime.com
Cover design by Kris Hackerott

Set in size of 11pt and Minion Pro by Exeter Premedia Services Private Ltd., Chennai, India

10 9 8 7 6 5 4 3 2 1

Praise for Value for Money

--

"There are very few constants in healthcare. Two of them – the push for greater quality and productivity – are comprehensively addressed by the authors. And in so doing, the direct connection between resource investment – time and money – and the return on those investments is concisely and profoundly made."

Ross Mitchell
Vice President, External and Government Affairs
Brookwood Baptist Health

"*Value for Money* is a must read, must have for every leader at every level who wants to understand the science of showing value in their organization. The insights, learning, and practical impact of the examples provided throughout the book are timeless and will shape our understanding of ROI for decades to come. If you want to know about the monetary impact of your program, follow the principles outlined in *Value for Money*."

Dr. Brad Shuck
Associate Professor
University of Louisville

"This book is a roadmap for all types of businesses, no matter whether profit or nonprofit, to find their way to true success. I personally have experienced the incredible impact ROI Institute makes of optimizing expendable resources to have the needed outcomes with greater impact. It is a must-read for anyone who wants to be successful and dynamic in their work and life."

CH (BG) Charles R. Bailey, Ret.
Deputy General Secretary
General Board of Higher Education and Ministry
The United Methodist Church

"The publication of this book comes at a critical moment. Being in a position to clearly show value for money in non-for-profit, governmental and multi-lateral institutions has become critical for the survival of high impact programs for the well-being of the most vulnerable amongst us.

For as long as I have known Gina, she has been concerned about performance – not only the performance of individuals, but also of groups and Organisations. Her professional endeavours and dedication to making this world a better place for everyone, together with her first-hand knowledge of what it means to demonstrate value for money for donors, makes her an exceptionally powerful contributor to this arena."

Michéle Pagé
Head of Human Resources
Organisation for Economic Cooperation and Development (OECD)

"*Value for Money* provides easy to grasp tools and concepts for anyone involved with program or project budgets. As a 30-year professional involved with programs and project budgets ranging from several thousand to several hundred million dollars, I can attest to the growing need to show value from a variety of data points. This book fulfills this growing need perfectly and should be on every program or project manager's desk!"

Col. Garry L. Thompson
United States Army

"We live in a world where almost every sector in society is increasingly being asked to be more accountable, and to be able to demonstrate a return on investment. The NGO, Public and Multi-lateral sectors are not immune from this accountability landscape, where constituents, beneficiaries, donors and a range of other stakeholders are demanding demonstrable efficiencies and results. Building on a wealth of previous work in the area, *Value for Money* is the definitive guide for organizations and individuals grappling with this issue, from the Enhanced Logic Model to articulating shared responsibilities, to providing practical tools and templates – this book sets the standard, and will define how we think about demonstrating value for the next generation."

Michael Emery
Director of Human Resources
United Population Fund

"Kudos to the authors for providing a logical, systematic project evaluation framework that incorporates both financial and key nonfinancial elements affecting an investment decision."

Hank Walker
Partner, Andrade/Walker Consulting
Former CEO of a large Catholic health system

"There is no more important measure than business impact, yet many business professionals I encounter struggle with how to align their projects to business objectives. Jack and Patti Phillips not only use their years of experience in measuring impact, but also their vast network of contacts to arrive at 12 easy steps anyone can follow. If you want to produce real results, this book is a must read."

Kevin Oakes
CEO
Institute for Corporate Productivity (i4cp)

"Having worked in the public sector for over 15 years for the United Nations and partnered with Jack and Patti Phillips of ROI Institute, USA, to develop two key measurement courses for the UN System on the ROI Methodology, it is evident, as highlighted in *Value for Money,* that there continues to be a global demand to show "value" and "results", particularly in programs aimed at growing human capital. As noted in the book, the global financial crises, donor fatigue, and reduced resources reinforces the need to view financial contributions as an investment that must be accounted for with tangible results showing clear outcomes. "Value for Money" is a useful and practical guide that helps us to reassess the impact of our work in bringing about tangible results for organizational change."

Mariama Daramy-Lewis
Chief, Human Resources and Training Section
United Nations Environment Programme*

*The views expressed herein are those of the author and do not necessarily reflect the views of the United Nations or the UN Environment Programme.

Contents

Praise for Value for Money   v

Foreword   xxv

Preface   xxvii
    Value is Changing…   xxvii
    Need for a New Approach   xxviii
    The ROI Methodology: The Enhanced Logic Model   xxix
    We Can't Measure Our Way to Success   xxx
    Flow of the Book   xxxi

Acknowledgements   xxxv

Authors   xxxviii

1   The Value Evolution   1
    The Value Shift   4
        Types of Values   5
        The Importance of Monetary Values   6
        The "Show Me" Generation   6
        The New Definition of Value   7
    Why Now?   8
        Program Failures   8
        Budget Constraints   9
        Project and Program Costs   9
        Donors are More Demanding   10
        Measurement at the Impact Level Is No Longer Optional   11
        Process Improvements Use   12
        Managers' New Business Focus 12
        Case Study   12
        Globalization   13
        The Growth of Project Management   14
        Evidence-Based or Fact-Based Management   14
        Mistrust of Institutions   15

Benchmarking Limitations 15
The Executive Appetite for Monetary Value 16
Challenges Along the Way 16
Preparation and Skills 17
Fear of ROI 17
Time Commitment 17
Power and Politics 18
Misleading Hype 18
Sustainability 19
Final Thoughts 19

2 Six Ways to Show Value for Money **21**
Six Ways to Show Value for Money 25
#1 - Actual ROI Calculation 27
#2 - Focus on Impacts and Intangibles 28
#3 - Meeting Expectations 29
#4 - The Payoff of Improved Behaviors 29
#5 - Cost-Effective Approach 30
#6 - Cost of Not Implementing the Program 31
Conclusion 32
Barriers to Showing Value for Money 32
We Don't Make Widgets 32
Because there are No Profits, ROI is Not Possible 33
ROI is Just Not Appropriate for the Public Sector 34
We Don't Have the Resources 35
This is too Complicated 36
No One is Asking for this 37
Final Thoughts 38

3 Needed: An Enhanced Logic Model **39**
A Review of Models 42
Definition 42
Logic Model Elements 44
Other Models 45
Concerns about Current Models 47
Lack of Focus on Benefit-Cost Analysis 47
Lack of Emphasis on Attribution 49
Confusion on Outcomes and Impact 49
Little Focus on the Chain of Value of a
Particular Program or Project 50
Unclear Timing of Data Collection 51
Needs Assessments versus Activities 52

Lack of Focus on Results   52
Inability to "Show the Money"   54
Not CEO- and CFO-Friendly   56
Managing Resources for Evaluation   57
Lack of Focus on Process Improvement   58
The Inability to Influence Investment   59
How Does Your Current Model Stack Up?   60
Focus of Use   61
Standards   61
Types of Data   61
Dynamic Adjustments   62
Connectivity   62
Approach   63
Conservative Nature   63
Simplicity   63
Theoretical Foundation   63
Acceptance   64
Requirements for the Value for Money: A Measurement Process   64
ROI Methodology   65
Terminology: Projects, Solutions, Participants   66
Final Thoughts   67

4   Introducing the ROI Methodology   69
Types of Data   70
Input   70
Reaction and Planned Action   72
Learning   73
Application and Implementation   73
Impact   74
Return on Investment   74
The Initial Analysis   75
Using Design Thinking to Deliver and Measure Results   77
The ROI Process Model   78
Plan the Evaluation   78
#1 - Start with Why: Align Programs with the
Business   78
#2 - Make it Feasible: Select the Right Solution   81
#3 - Expect Success: Design for Results   81
Collect Data   82
#4 - Make it Matter: Design for Input,
Reaction, and Learning   82

#5 - Make it Stick: Design for Application
and Impact 83
Analyze Data 83
#6 - Make it Credible: Isolate the Effects of
the Program 83
#7 - Make it Credible: Convert Data to
Monetary Value 84
#8 - Make it Credible: Identify Intangible Benefits 84
#9 - Make it Credible: Capture Costs of Projects 85
#10 - Make it Credible: Calculate the Return
on Investment 85
Optimize Results 86
#11 - Tell the Story: Communicate Results to
Key Stakeholders 86
#12 - Optimize the Results: Use Black Box
Thinking to Increase Funding 86
Operating Standards and Philosophy 87
Implementing and Sustaining the Process 87
Benefits of this Approach 88
Aligning with Business 89
Validating the Value Proposition 89
Improving Processes 89
Enhancing the Image and Building Respect 90
Improving Support 90
Justifying or Enhancing Budgets 90
Building Productive Partnerships 91
Final Thoughts 91

5   **Start with Why: Align Programs with the Business** **93**
Impact Measures are Critical 96
The Challenge 97
Begin with the End in Mind 97
It's a Change 97
It Requires Discipline 98
Avoid Paralysis by Analysis 98
The Alignment Model 98
Payoff Needs 99
Key Questions to Ask 102
Obvious versus Not-So-Obvious Payoffs 102
Reasons for New Programs 104
The Costs of the Problem 105

Case Study 107
The Value of Opportunity 107
To Forecast or Not to Forecast 108
Case Study 108
Business Needs 109
Determining the Opportunity 109
Identifying the Business Measure—Hard Data 110
Output 110
Quality 110
Cost 110
Time 112
Case Study 112
Defining the Business Need—Soft Data 113
Leadership 114
Work Climate/Satisfaction 114
Client Service 114
Employee Development/Advancement 114
Initiative/Innovation 114
Image/Reputation 115
Using Tangible versus Intangible—A Better Approach 115
Finding Sources of Impact Data 115
Identifying All the Measures 116
What Happens if You do Nothing? 117
Case Study 117
Final Thoughts 118

6   Make It Feasible: Select the Right Solution   119
Performance Needs 122
The Performance Dialogue 122
Examine the Data and Records 123
Initiate the Discussion 123
Case Study 123
Use Benchmarking from Similar Solutions 124
Use Evaluation as the Hook 124
Involve Others 125
Discuss Disasters in Other Places 125
Use Analysis Techniques 125
Keep it Sensible 126
Case Study 127
Learning Needs 131
Subject-Matter Experts (SMEs) 131

Job and Task Analysis 131
Observations 132
Demonstrations 132
Tests 132
Management Assessment 133
Case Study 133
Preference Needs 134
Key Issues 134
Case Study 135
Matching Solutions to Needs 135
Some Solutions are Obvious 135
Solutions Can Come in Different Sizes 136
Some Solutions Take a Long Time 136
Solutions Should be Tackled with the Highest Priority
Items First 136
The Matrix Diagram 136
Selecting Solutions for Maximum Payoff 138
Short-Term versus Long-Term Costs 138
Consider Forecasting ROI 138
Time Needed for Implementation 138
Avoid Mismatches 139
Verifying the Match 139
Tackling Multiple Solutions 140
Final Thoughts 140

7 Expect Success: Design for Results **141**
The Power of Expectations 144
Case Study 144
Keep it Sensible 146
Defining the Success of Programs 147
Designing for Results at Each Level 149
Level 0, Input 149
Level 1, Reaction 150
Level 2, Learning 150
Level 3, Application 150
Level 4, Impact 150
Case Study 151
Level 5, ROI 151
Use Empathy 151
Developing Objectives at Multiple Levels 152
Case Study 152
Reaction Objectives 153

Learning Objectives 154
Application Objectives 155
Impact Objectives 157
Return on Investment (ROI) Objectives 158
Case Study 158
The Power of Objectives 160
Application/Impact Objectives Drive Programs 160
Application/Impact Objectives Enhance
Design and Development 160
Application/Impact Objectives Improve
Facilitation 160
Application/Impact Objectives Help Participants
Understand What Is Expected 161
Impact Objectives Excite Sponsors and Donors 161
Application/Impact Objectives Simplify Evaluation 161
All Levels of Objectives Inform the Stakeholders 162
Defining Roles and Responsibilities 162
Analysts 163
Designer 163
Developer 163
Program Owner 164
Facilitator 164
Participants 164
Sponsor or Donor 165
Managers of Participants/Significant Others 165
Evaluator 165
Other Stakeholders 165
Planning the Evaluation 166
Evaluation Purpose 166
Feasibility of Outcome Evaluations 167
Data Collection Plan 167
ROI Analysis Plan 167
Project Plan 171
Final Thoughts 172

8   Make It Matter: Design for Input, Reaction, and Learning 173
Communicating with Results in Mind 174
Announcements 175
Brochures 175
Case Study 175
Correspondence 176
Workbooks and Participant Guides 176

Changing the Role of Participants	177
The Necessity	177
Defining Roles	177
Documenting the Roles	178
Creating Expectations	178
Identifying Impact Measures Before Participating in the Program	179
Case Study	179
Involving Managers or Significant Others	181
Think ROI	181
ROI Review	182
Case Study	182
Actions to Take	183
Design Input for Results	183
Target Audience	183
Case Study	184
The Need	184
Case Study	185
Timing and Duration	185
Motivation	186
Readiness	186
Conclusion	187
Design Reaction for Results	187
Topics to Measure	188
Case Study	189
Measuring Reaction	191
Case Study	192
Using Reaction Data	192
Forecasting ROI at this Level	192
Design Learning for Results	193
The Learning Style	194
Sequencing and Time	194
Activities	194
Data Collection for Input, Reaction, and Learning	194
Questionnaires and Surveys	194
Measuring with Tests	196
Measuring with Simulation	196
Timing of Data Collection	197
Early, Detailed Feedback	198
Pre-Program	198
Collecting at Periodic Intervals	198

	For Long Programs with Multiple Parts	199
	Final Thoughts	199
9	**Make It Stick: Design for Application and Impact**	**201**
	Data Collection for Application and Impact	204
	Questionnaires and Surveys	204
	Improving the Response Rate for Questionnaires and Surveys	204
	Interviews	209
	Focus Groups	210
	Observations	210
	Action Plans	211
	Set Goals and Targets	212
	Define the Unit of Measure	212
	Place a Monetary Value on Each Improvement	214
	Implement the Action Plan	214
	Isolate the Effects of the Program	214
	Provide a Confidence Level for Estimates	215
	Collect Action Plans	215
	Summarize the Data and Calculate the ROI	215
	Performance Contract	217
	Monitoring Business Performance Data	219
	Existing Measures	219
	Case Study	220
	Developing New Measures	221
	Selecting the Appropriate Method for Each Level	222
	Type of Data	222
	Participants' Time for Data Input	222
	Manager (or Significant Other) Time for Data Input	223
	Cost of Method	223
	Disruption of Normal Work Activities	223
	Accuracy of Method	223
	Utility of an Additional Method	224
	Cultural Bias for Data Collection Method	224
	Timing of Data Collection	224
	Collecting Application Data	224
	Collecting Impact Data	225
	Built-In Application Tools	226
	Improvement Plans and Guides	227
	Application Tools/Templates	227
	Job Aids	227

Case Study   228
Involving the Participants' Manager or Significant Other   230
    The Most Influential Group   230
    Pre-Program Activities   231
    During the Program Activities   232
    Post-Program Activities   232
    Reinforcement Tools   232
    Case Study   233
Final Thoughts   235

10 Make It Credible: Isolate the Effects of the Program   237
The Importance of Pinpointing the Contribution   240
    Reality   240
    Myths   240
Preliminary Issues   242
    Review Chain of Impact   242
    Identify Other Factors   243
Quantitative and Research Isolation Methods   244
    Case Study   244
    Experimental Design   246
    Trend Line Analysis   249
    Mathematical Modeling   252
    Calculating the Impact of Other Factors   253
Qualitative Isolation Methods   254
    Participants' Estimate of Impact   255
    Steps to Measure Attribution Using Estimates   258
    Manager's Estimate of Impact   259
    Customer Estimates of Program Impact   260
    Internal or External Expert Estimates   260
    Estimate Credibility: The Wisdom of Crowds   261
    Case Study   261
Select the Method   263
Final Thoughts   264

11 Make It Credible: Convert Data to Monetary Value   265
The Importance of Monetary Value   267
    Value Equals Money   267
    Money Makes Impact More Impressive   268
    Converting to Monetary Values is Similar to Budgeting 268
    Monetary Value is Vital to Organizational Operations 269
    Monetary Values Are Necessary to Understand
        Problems and Cost Data   269

Key Steps in Converting Data to Money   270
Standard Monetary Values   272
    Converting Output Data to Money   273
    Case Study   274
    Calculating the Cost of Inadequate Quality   276
    Case Study   278
    Converting Employee Time Savings Using Compensation   279
    Case Study   280
    Finding Standard Values   281
When Standard Values are Not Available   281
    Using Historical Costs from Records   282
        Time   282
        Availability   282
        Access   282
        Accuracy   283
    Using Input from Experts   284
    Using Values from External Databases   285
    Linking with Other Measures   286
    Using Estimates from Participants   288
    Using Estimates from the Management Team   289
    Using Program Staff Estimates   289
Selecting the Technique   290
    Choose a Technique Appropriate for the Type of Data   290
    Move from Most Accurate to Least Accurate   290
    Consider Source Availability   291
    Use the Source with the Broadest Perspective on the Issue   291
    Use Multiple Techniques When Feasible   291
    Apply the Credibility Test   292
    Consider the Short-Term/Long-Term Issue   292
    Consider an Adjustment for the Time Value of Money   294
Final Thoughts   295

12 Make It Credible: Identify the Intangibles   297
Why Intangibles are Important   299
    Intangibles are the Invisible Advantage   300
    We are in the Intangible Economy   301
    More Intangibles are Converted to Tangibles   302
    Case Study   302
    Intangibles Drive Programs and Investments   303
Measuring and Analyzing Intangibles   304
    Measuring the Intangibles   304

Converting to Money	307
Case Study	307
Case Study	310
Identifying and Collecting Intangibles	311
Analyzing Intangibles	312
Final Thoughts	313
13 Make It Credible: Capture Costs of the Program and Calculate ROI	**315**
The Importance of Costs and ROI	319
Fundamental Cost Issues	320
Fully Loaded Costs	320
Case Study	321
Costs Reported without Benefits	322
Develop and Use Cost Guidelines	323
Sources of Costs	323
Prorated versus Direct Costs	324
Employee Benefits Factor	325
Specific Costs to Include	325
Initial Analysis and Assessment	326
Development of Program Solutions	326
Acquisition Costs	326
Implementation Costs	326
Case Study	327
Maintenance and Monitoring	327
Support and Overhead	328
Evaluation and Reporting	328
Cost Tabulation in Action	328
Problem and Solution	328
Program Description	329
Selection Criteria	330
Program Administration	331
The Drivers of Evaluation	331
Program Costs	332
The ROI Calculation	333
Benefit/Cost Ratio	334
ROI Formula	335
Case Study	336
Monetary Benefits	337
Misuse of ROI	338
Social Return on Investment	339

ROI Objectives   340
Whose ROI?   340
Other ROI Measures   342
    Payback Period (Breakeven Analysis)   342
    Discounted Cash Flow   342
    Internal Rate of Return   343
Final Thoughts   343

14 Tell the Story: Communicate Results to Key Stakeholders   345
The Presentation   346
Reaction and Learning   347
Application   348
Business Impact   348
ROI   350
Intangibles   351
Conclusion and Recommendations   351
Reflection   352
The Importance of Communicating Results   352
    Communication is Necessary to Make Improvements   352
    Communication is Necessary to Explain the Contribution   353
    Communication is a Politically Sensitive Issue   353
    Different Audiences Need Different Information   353
    Case Study   354
Principles of Communicating Results   355
    Communication Must be Timely   355
    Communications Should be Targeted to
        Specific Audiences   355
    Media Should be Carefully Selected   356
    Communication Should be Unbiased and Modest in Tone   356
    Communication Must Be Consistent   356
    Make the Message Clear   356
    Testimonials Must Come from Respected Individuals   357
    The Audience's Bias of the Program Will Influence the
        Communication Strategy   357
The Process for Communicating Results   357
Step 1: Analyze Reason for Communication   359
Step 2: Plan for Communication   359
Step 3: Select Audience   360
Step 4: Develop Reports   363
Step 5: Select Media   363
    Meetings   363

Interim and Progress Reports	366
Routine Communication Tools	366
Case Study	367
Email and Electronic Media	369
Program Brochures and Pamphlets	369
Case Studies	370
Step 6: Present Information	370
Routine Feedback on Program Progress	371
Storytelling	373
Presentation of Results to Senior Management	374
Case Study	376
Step 7: Analyze Reaction	378
Final Thoughts	379

**15 Optimize Results: Use Black Box Thinking to
Increase Funding** **381**

Process Improvement is the Key: Black Box Thinking	383
The Aviation Industry	384
The Healthcare Industry	384
Failures in Programs	386
Making Adjustments in Programs	387
The Fear of Results	387
You Can Always Make it Better	388
When Do You Discontinue the Program?	388
The Timing of Changes	390
Level 0, Input	390
Level 1, Reaction Measures	390
Level 2, Learning Measures	391
Level 3, Application Measures	391
Level 4, Impact Measures	392
Making the Adjustments	392
Increasing ROI	393
Addressing Costs	393
Addressing the Monetary Benefits	395
Timing of Assessments	395
Influencing Allocation	396
Investment versus Cost	396
Competition for Funding	398
Anxiety and Downturns Translate into Cost Reduction	399
Final Thoughts	400

16 Forecast the ROI   **401**

The Importance of Forecasting ROI   407

Expensive Programs   407

High Risks and Uncertainty   407

Case Study   408

Post-Program Comparison   409

Compliance   410

The Trade-Offs of Forecasting   411

Pre-Program ROI Forecasting   413

Basic Model   413

Basic Steps to Forecast ROI   414

Sources of Expert Input   417

Securing Input   418

Conversion to Money   419

Estimate Program Costs   419

Case Study   420

Forecasting with a Pilot Program   422

ROI Forecasting with Reaction Data   423

Case Study   424

Use of the Data   426

Forecasting Guidelines   427

Final Thoughts   429

17 Make It Work: Sustaining the Change to a
Results-Based Process   **431**

Overcoming Resistance   433

Assess the Climate   434

Develop Roles and Responsibilities   434

Identifying a Champion   434

Developing the Champion   435

Establishing a Task Force   435

Assigning Responsibilities   436

Establish Goals and Plans   436

Setting Evaluation Targets   437

Developing a Plan for Implementation   438

Revise Guidelines and Procedures   438

Prepare the Team   440

Involving the Team   440

Teaching the Team   440

Initiate ROI Studies   441

Prepare the Management Team 442
Remove Obstacles 443
    Dispelling Myths 443
    Delivering Bad News 444
    Using the Data 444
Monitor Progress 445
Final Thoughts 446

References **447**

Appendix A **459**

Appendix B **467**

Appendix C **471**

Index **473**

Foreword

I discovered the ROI Methodology eight years ago in a partnership agreement between ROI Institute and my training and consulting institute, "Arab Institute for Marketing and Sales"

(AIMS), which was founded 17 years ago. To date, more than 90,000 professionals have been involved in our programs. We conducted several ROI Certification programs to develop human resources experts in measuring the return on investment. We have obtained consulting contracts, including one with Mobily, one of the largest communications companies in Saudi Arabia. I have also read several books from ROI Institute on measurement, monetary benefits, and return on investment, written by Jack and Patricia Phillips.

In my view, calculating the return on investment requires courageous stakeholders as well as an efficient skillful environment and a credible, scalable methodology.

I write this foreword today in Granada (Spain) where one-fifth of 100 young leaders (male and female) graduates receive a European Fellowship on managing the nonprofit organizations, in cooperation with the Euro Arab Foundation and the University of Granada. I have spent more than thirty years working with charities and nonprofits inside Saudi Arabia and outside Saudi Arabia in the Philippines, Pakistan, Jordan and Albania. I found that our business relies on trust.

Over the past fifteen years, the Kingdom of Saudi Arabia has had a big leap in the third sector, nonprofits, which achieved a growth of 100%. In Saudi Arabia, there are currently 950 nonprofit organizations. Annually, these organizations spend about one billion dollars in the social, economic, and human rights of the disabled, elderly, women, and children. The government spends more than 9 billion dollars for the same groups through the social security fund.

The role of the third sector has shifted from the role of pastoralism to empowerment and development, especially after the launch of the vision of the Kingdom of Saudi Arabia 2030 under the leadership of His Royal Highness Prince Mohammed bin Salman. The vision emphasized the role of the third sector to achieve the role of the goals of the vision and increase its participation in the gross national product from 0.05% to 3%.

This book arrives in a favorable historical moment where the entire environment in the state and society accepts and drives towards accounting and anti-corruption. We are asking, where do we place our resources? What is our role in development?

We must be honest with ourselves if we want to protect future generations that are the center of the concept of comprehensive development. The environment is favorable and the leaders are ready, now the methodology is present in this book. We were honored to host Jack Phillips in Riyadh this year with a seminar on the return on investment in nonprofit organizations. I was pleased with the large turnout which means that the environment is favorable. Now, we have decided to launch a forum on the measurement of return on investment in nonprofit projects. We expanded the subject to include the government sector as well as social responsibility programs in the private sector. We will have several events and workshops to suit the needs of Saudi Arabia, as well as providing courses to graduate specialists in measuring return on investment.

The book is a success. It begins with defining the terms, addresses the major questions, applies academic knowledge, and then guides readers to a roadmap for implementation. Additionally, the book explores the problems that will confront you and shows how to overcome them. ROI Institute and the book's authors have created a great resource which will set the standard in measuring the impact.

We must expand the scope of application and adapt to the environment. We must simplify the procedures and present the results to expand towards change for the better. When we know the results and take the most important steps to maximize the impact, yield will increase, and costs will be reduced, while achieving fairness and equity in distribution.

As for me, I will translate the book into Arabic. I have embarked on that task now.

Dr. Yousef O. Alhuzaim
General Secretary
Princess Alanood Foundation
July 2018

Preface

Value is Changing…

Bill and Melinda Gates, cofounders of the world's largest foundation, dedicated their 2017 annual letter to Warren Buffett. He donated the largest amount of money in the history of the Gates Foundation. In a cordial way, Buffett had asked the Gateses to describe the results of this contribution—essentially, he was asking for the *value for money*.

In their annual letter, the Gateses began with Buffett's correspondence to them. They then showed the return on his investment. Essentially, the annual letter was Warren Buffett's ROI for the roughly $30 billion investment in the Gates Foundation. The letter focused on the impacts of their various grants and initiatives. For one initiative, they actually showed the financial return on investment. This single act of responsibility and accountability portrays what is happening across the public and social sectors. Foundations, nonprofits, governments, nongovernmental organizations, religious institutions, universities, associations, and others are being held to higher levels of accountability than ever before.

Chaplains in hospital settings are being asked to show the value they deliver to healthcare organizations, otherwise, they face a reduction in numbers. The United Methodist Church is stepping up to this challenge by preparing chaplains to show the value of what they do in terms that funders can understand. This often means value for money and, in some cases, the financial ROI.

The president of the University of Malaysia Putra is asking the head of the library to show the ROI for all of the database subscriptions. Subscriptions represent an almost $20 million investment each year. "After all, isn't all of this information on the Internet?" asked the president. This prompted the head of the library to show the ROI of having the database from the perspective of the students and faculty.

The largest foundation in Saudi Arabia, and one of the largest in the Middle East, is planning a conference for nonprofits. The theme of the conference is "Measuring the ROI for Non-Profits." Part of the plans for this conference is to not only teach and show examples of how and why to measure ROI, but to also offer ROI Certification for nonprofit leaders so they can build internal capability to show value for money for the contributions they receive.

Various government agencies are facing tremendous accountability issues. The IT function within the Social Security Administration in the United States has been asked to show the ROI for major IT projects. Otherwise, its $1.3 billion investment would be in jeopardy. One intelligence agency is being asked to show the impact and ROI of a master's degree program offered to high-potential employees on agency time, paid by the agency.

Alberta Health Services, the largest provincial health system in Canada, has challenged its Healthy Living group to show the impact and ROI of their various programs. Demonstrating such results comes with the prospect of allocating more funds into the preventive-type programs that they advocate and organize.

These, and hundreds of other examples, show what is happening in the public sector. Accountability is required in areas unaccustomed to demonstrating value beyond the activities they offer. This is caused, in part, by four major trends:

1. Budgets are constrained, reduced, and tightly monitored, more so than any time in the past.
2. There is more competition for funding within an organization than ever before, and the competition frequently makes a compelling case for portions of budgets other than their own.
3. Organizations are moving from activities to results and on to fact-based outcomes, and sometimes to the financial ROI.
4. Donors and funders are requesting more accountability for their contributions. For government, it's the taxpayers. For foundations, charities, and nonprofits, it's the donors. And for businesses, it's shareholders and top executives.

These trends are a reality for many organizations and will likely continue. In fact, we anticipate that they will become even more pronounced.

Need for a New Approach

Moving toward fact-based outcomes is a challenge to all organizations as they attempt to show the value for the money that they receive. This book shows six ways to show value for money; some of the ways are closely related or interconnected. Of the six ways, the most credible is the ROI calculation. This is accomplished by following steps in cost-benefit analysis, an economic theory grounded in public finance. Development of the ROI metric follows standards and assumptions that meet financial officer approval.

ROI is not always necessary for public sector programs. Although, in theory, it can be accomplished, only a small number of projects deserve this level of analysis. This book describes how to take the analysis all the way through to the ROI calculation. A few shortcuts are possible, which creates a basis for some of the other ways to show the value. While the ultimate demonstration of value for money is ROI, it is reserved for specific types of projects.

The ROI Methodology: The Enhanced Logic Model

The classic logic model has served organizations quite well for many years, particularly those in the public sector. This book presents an enhanced version of the logic model, responding to needs not addressed with, and concerns about, the classic logic model. Although this classic model has been successful, times have changed, and the accountability needs have shifted. The model presented here, the ROI Methodology, addresses these needs and the needs for measurement and evaluation across the spectrum of organizations. Chapter 3 in this book is devoted to why a new evaluation system is needed.

The ROI Methodology has been evolving for some time. Initially, it was developed in the business sector to help executives see value for money in terms they could understand, appreciate, and support. Along the way, it attracted the attention of governments—with 26 federal governments adopting and using this methodology. Many nongovernmental organizations (NGOs) have adopted it, such as the United Nations, which started using this method with a UN General Assembly resolution in 2008. Nonprofits are using it, including charities, foundations, associations, and religious organizations. Approximately 300 healthcare organizations are now using the process, sparked in part by the book *Measuring ROI in Healthcare* (McGraw-Hill, 2013). About 150 universities are using it to show the value of their internal processes as well as external outreach programs and services. Grant writers are now suggesting that if you can wrap ROI around your proposal and deliver impact and ROI data to the organization providing the grant money, you double your chances of receiving the grant. John White, one of the premier grant writers in the United States, agrees [1]. The ROI Methodology has been very successful and has become the most used evaluation system in the world.

This book responds to a need for a system that tackles these widespread applications head-on, with the emphasis on the public arena while not losing sight of the business applications. This book attempts to do what no other book has attempted: present a methodology that crosses boundaries of different functional areas and professional fields, types of organizations, cultures, and countries to have one system that can be used in those environments. The ROI Methodology is a proven process in those areas already, and this book brings that experience and focus to readers.

This will be a book that can help those who are measuring the success of any type of project, program, initiative, system, procedure, event, or process in these types of organizations:

- Publicly traded businesses
- Privately held businesses
- Governments (federal, state, and local level)
- Nongovernment organizations
- Nonprofits
- Universities
- Community colleges and technical institutes
- K-12 school systems
- Foundations
- Charities
- Trusts
- Networks and alliances
- Associations
- Religious organizations

The ROI Methodology is a flexible, versatile process that can withstand the scrutiny of critics, while providing CEO and CFO friendly data through a process that is user-friendly.

Whether it is a development program in East Africa, an economic development activity for Oman, a cultural event in Brussels, a military operation in South Africa, a UN peacekeeping mission in Lebanon, a women's initiative in Brazil, a medical procedure in Canada, or a faith-based initiative in the United States, this process will be useful for delivering and demonstrating value for money.

We Can't Measure Our Way to Success

Many of us in the measurement and evaluation profession have suggested, encouraged, and supported more measurement and evaluation. We, the authors of this book, have tackled this in different ways and through different media channels. Our premise has been that when evaluators measure at the business level, they also make adjustments and improve programs. However, four challenges have prevented the needed change: 1) fear of the outcomes, which prevents program owners from making needed adjustments; 2) the task of measurement appears impossible, as it will be difficult to collect needed data; 3) exposing concern of a flawed system that no one wants to correct; and 4) resources needed to measure, underscoring a lack of funds to support the effort.

We don't mean to imply that others haven't addressed this issue; they have. However, current systems still fall short of what is actually needed. Many great books have been developed to address part of these issues. For example, several books are available on aligning programs to the business at the beginning, selecting the right solution, writing objectives at multiple levels, and developing programs with impact in mind, as well as many books on measurement and evaluation. Some of the books have attempted to tackle several of these issues in more detail at the same time.

It is time to tap into the good work from other fields and bring those concepts into the accountability process. Excellent contributions have been made in systems thinking, change management, design thinking for innovation, process optimization, expectation management, and work culture. These contributions, with many books to support them, hold the key to rethinking projects and programs to make them successful. The goal is to design for success, with that success defined as credible data connecting programs to the business impact measures.

We are proposing to tweak what has been done and bring in important concepts from other fields, in particular design thinking, from the innovation field. This approach has five elements:

1. A logical flow to the process, with eight simple steps
2. A focus on designing for results throughout the process
3. Shared responsibilities along the way
4. Tools, templates, and support throughout the process
5. Educational programs to ease implementation

Flow of the Book

This comprehensive book includes 17 chapters presenting a logical flow of information about this enhanced logic model. It is divided into six parts. The first part sets the stage by explaining why this is even needed in today's climate. The first chapter recaps the evolution of accountability—how it has changed in all types of organizations, with particular emphasis on the public sector. Chapter 2 describes six ways to show the value for money. This is a huge request these days, and it can be tackled in different ways. However, it is usually built around the framework of the ROI Methodology presented in this book. Chapter 3 makes the case for an enhanced logic model, built on a classic logic model that has served us quite well. There is a need for an enhanced version of this, which is what we offer in this book. The fourth chapter presents the system—the ROI Methodology—and all of the parts of it. It is a quick reference chapter that not only explains how we've addressed all the needs for an enhanced logic model, but also explores the parts of it and how they are interconnected, as well as the benefits of using it.

Part two addresses planning for evaluation and results. This includes three chapters that represent the first three steps to design for results. The first chapter (Chapter 5) focuses on clarifying why a program is being implemented. This involves business alignment and connecting the project or program to the business needs at the outset. Chapter 6, *Make it Feasible,* explores selecting the right solution to achieve business alignment. This chapter explains a new role in many organizations, performance consulting. Chapter 7 is perhaps one of the most powerful chapters and focuses on expecting success, which comprises four major parts. The first is to define the success of programs overall. That becomes the desired success with a goal of designing programs to achieve success. The second is to set objectives at multiple levels, including impact and sometimes ROI. The third is to be sure that the expectation for success permeates all of the stakeholders so they know what they have to do to make this program successful at the impact level. Lastly, it introduces the planning tools to plan an impact and ROI evaluation of a program.

Part three concerns data collection spanning two chapters. Chapter 8 focuses on making it matter to the individual, organization, community, or society to ensure that the program is important, needed, and relevant. This addresses collecting data for input to the program, reactions to the program, and the learning needed to make it work. Chapter 9 explores making it stick—ensuring that the program is properly implemented and driving the desired impact. This ensures that everyone involved is doing what they need to do in order to make the program successful. They are taking actions, such as using technology, following a procedure, conducting interviews…doing things with corresponding impact. The chapter also discusses the various ways of collecting data from these actions.

Part four addresses data analysis with four chapters. This is one of the most comprehensive portions of the book. It is designed to help readers make results credible enough so that a chief financial officer (CFO), top executive, or donor can understand, believe, and support the results that are delivered. Part four includes four major chapters. Chapter 10 discusses the attribution issue, detailing the different ways to determine how much of the impact results are connected to the program. This is a powerful and critical chapter. Chapter 11 focuses on converting data to money, which often appears to be more difficult than it actually is, even in the public sector. At least 10 ways are detailed to show you how to locate or calculate the money. Chapter 12 explores those hard to value measures that will ultimately represent intangible benefits of programs. These intangibles need to be connected to the program from the beginning, with credible data collected throughout the process. Intangibles are powerful—many programs are initiated based on intangibles, and you don't want to lose that point in your analysis. Chapter 13 focuses on cost and ROI. All the costs that should be included in the project or program, including both direct and indirect costs, are detailed here. These become the standards for this methodology. Then the three ways the ROI is calculated are detailed, including the classic benefits-cost ratio that has been used for hundreds of years, to the ROI calculation, which is more of a business term and dates back at least 400 years (and is now the most-used way to show the value for both capital and noncapital expenditures). The pay-back period is also detailed, showing how long it would take to get the money back from the investment.

Part five focuses on reporting results and involves two chapters. Chapter 14 addresses how to communicate the data to various target audiences, ensuring that they understand and use the data appropriately. Storytelling is introduced as a way to present the results in a compelling way. The next chapter (Chapter 15) discusses using the data to make improvements and even justify future expenditures. Essentially, this step is optimizing the return of investment, leading to more allocation of funds to the program.

Lastly, part six, with two chapters, focuses on sustaining the process. Chapter 16 covers forecasting, which considers program value from another perspective. These days, funders may ask for a forecast of the ROI before contributing to a program. This chapter fully explores this issue. The last chapter, Chapter 17, explains how to implement this methodology into your organization so that it becomes a sustainable, routine process.

Collectively, these 17 chapters provide a critical reference to show the value for money in any type of program, project, or setting.

Acknowledgements

First, we want to acknowledge and applaud the great work of our clients whom we have served over the 25 years since ROI Institute was founded. We moved into a variety of new countries, cultures, organizations, and functional areas, not because it was part of our business development strategy, but because several innovative and forward-thinking executives from these different areas could see the potential of this methodology to show the value for money in their situations. They asked for this and were patient with us as we experimented, made adjustments, and made it successful for them. To those client groups we give tremendous credit for this book.

We also want to thank all of the ROI Institute team members, our collection of international partners (spanning 70 countries), and our associates across the United States. We learn a lot from them and, in many cases, they have brought us into new environments, cultures, countries, and opportunities to apply this methodology.

We also want to thank the ROI Institute staff. While our staff is busy organizing consulting activities, teaching assignments, speaking engagements, and research efforts, they all realize that the business thrives and builds on the books that ROI Institute authors write. As we often say, we would not have a business without our books, but books are not our business. This is a major book for us, and we thank all the staff who helped us make it better. We particularly want to thank Kylie McLeod, our Communications Coordinator, who has taken this project on with a vengeance to get it done in a short period of time with a very professional effort. Kylie, we thank you for your great efforts and look forward to the many great projects you have in front of you in the future.

From Patti: This book is a long time coming. We have waited for the right opportunity to develop it. Given our work with nonprofit, nongovernmental, intergovernmental, religious, educational, and private sector organizations has reached the level it has, this the right time. We could not have done it without a team working along-side us. Many thanks to our co-authors, Gina and Cyndi, for sharing your experience and expertise, and for your friendship. And a big thank you to Kylie, Hope, Staci, and Andy for making things happen for us while we're out doing what we do best. You guys rock!

And a special thanks to Jack. It was May 20, 1997, at Chappy's deli, when I first met Jack. There, a planned one-hour meeting stretched to four hours. It was during that conversation I first learned of his ROI Methodology -- a process he developed in 1973 and perfected over the years through application and research. While its application began in the training and human resources industries, we have expanded its use well beyond. Our work in the nonprofit and nongovernmental sectors is some of our most inspiring. Through this work, while we help change organizations, we hope that in some small way we are helping change the world.

Jack's constant effort to drive ROI is why the concept has reached ubiquity in disciplines that disregarded it in the past. He is the reason that every marketing piece alludes to ROI; why practitioners and their functions are lauded for their efforts to demonstrate ROI; and why measurement, evaluation, ROI, and accountability are the norms not novelties. Jack is my inspiration, my husband, and above all else, my friend. Because he laid the groundwork, I, along with many others, have a platform on which to stand and be heard. All I can say is, *thank you, Jack, for all that you have done and all that you do. The past 21 years have been a journey like none other and I look forward to the next 21! I love you.*

From Jack: Thanks to Patti for being the driving force for our work in governments, nongovernmental organizations, and nonprofits. Her heart is always in the right place when working with these agencies. She is a tenacious consultant, outstanding researcher, a keynote presenter with a strong message, and one of the best writers I know. Her facilitation sets the example for all of our global facilitators. Above all, she's my best friend, a lovely spouse, and curious explorer. Thanks for all you do…for everyone – family, friends, and professional colleagues. For this book, I am particularly grateful for Gina and Cyndi joining us as co-authors. They bring unique perspectives and much experience from the public sector, an important thrust for this book.

From Gina: The last few years have been full of life changing moments and opportunities and I am so grateful to have had the chance to work with Jack and Patti on this book. This has been the culmination of the past 15 years of a professional learning relationship and more importantly a deep lasting friendship. Thank you, Jack and Patti, for allowing me to grow and change with your direction and leadership - you are both so very special to me. I also would like to thank my family. My husband Stefano for allowing me the space and time and support to do what I have done through the past several years, you sustain me, you support me, "ti voglio bene." To my children, Matteo and Alessandra, there is not a day that your names are not mentioned out loud - I am so proud of the adults that you have become. Thank you to the rest of my family and friends; you have always encouraged me. To my mother, Elena, my mentor and my confidant and the life moments and learnings that we have shared, you are truly an amazing woman. Finally, to my father, John, to the moments we had and the moments we missed and now you are with me all the time, you are everywhere.

From Cyndi: Gratitude is an intentional, daily choice, the choice to look around and acknowledge the many opportunities that have come my way. I appreciate being able to partner and collaborate with the *best of the best* in Jack and Patti, and I'm incredibly grateful for their continued support and generosity to lifelong learners. I stand on the shoulders of all the amazing role models who have shaped and influenced my work. Thanks to my colleagues at Southern Miss who always inspire me to work hard, have fun and make a difference. The love and support from my husband, Robert, and our children and grandchildren has allowed me to pursue my passion, which makes for a happy life.

 **Patti P. Phillips, PhD** is president and CEO of ROI Institute, Inc., the leading source of ROI competency building, implementation support, networking, and research. She helps organizations implement the ROI Methodology in over 60 countries. Patti serves as a member of the Board of Trustees for the United Nations Institute for Training and Research (UNITAR); chair of the People Analytics Board at the Institute for Corporate Productivity (i4cp); Principal Research Fellow for The Conference Board; board chair of the Center for Talent Reporting; and ATD CPLP Certification Institute Fellow. Patti also serves as faculty on the UN System Staff College in Turin, Italy, the Escuela Bancaria y Comercial in Mexico City, Mexico, and The University of Southern Mississippi's PhD in Human Capital Development program. Her work has been featured on *CNBC*, *EuroNews*, and over a dozen business journals.

Patti's academic background includes a B.S. in Education from Auburn University, a Master's in Public and Private Management from Birmingham-Southern College, and PhD in International Development from The University of Southern Mississippi.

She facilitates workshops, speaks at conferences, and consults with organizations worldwide. Patti is author, coauthor, or editor of over 75 books and dozens of articles on the topic of measurement, evaluation, and ROI. Patti can be reached at patti@roiinstitute.net.

Jack J. Phillips, PhD, is a world-renowned expert on accountability, measurement and evaluation, and chairman of ROI Institute. Through the Institute, Phillips provides consulting services for Fortune 500 companies and workshops for major conference providers throughout the world. Phillips is also the author or editor of more than 100 books and more than 300 articles.

His expertise in measurement and evaluation is based on more than 27 years of corporate experience in five industries (aerospace, textiles, metals, construction materials, and banking). Phillips has served as training and development manager at two Fortune 500 firms, senior HR officer at two firms, as president of a regional federal savings bank, and management professor at a major state university.

Jack has received several awards for his books and work. On three occasions, Meeting News named him one of the 25 Most Powerful People in the Meetings and Events Industry, based on his work on ROI. The Society for Human Resource Management presented him an award for one of his books and honored a Phillips ROI study with its highest award for creativity. The Association for Talent Development gave him its highest award, Distinguished Contribution to Workplace Learning and Development for his work on ROI. His work has been featured in the *Wall Street Journal*, *BusinessWeek*, and *Fortune* magazine. He has been interviewed by several television programs, including *CNN*. Jack served as President of the International Society for Performance Improvement for 2012–2013 and was honored with the prestigious Thomas F. Gilbert Award in 2018. In 2017, Jack received the Brand Personality Award from Asia Pacific Brands Foundation for his work as an international consultant, author, teacher, and speaker.

Jack has undergraduate degrees in electrical engineering, physics, and mathematics; a master's degree in decision sciences from Georgia State University; and a PhD in human resource management from the University of Alabama. He has served on the boards of several private businesses – including two NASDAQ companies – and several nonprofits and associations, including the Association for Talent Development and the National Management Association. He is chairman of ROI Institute, Inc., and can be reached at (205) 678-8101, or by e-mail at jack@roiinstitute.net.

Gina Paone joined the International Monetary Fund in February 2011, after nearly 11 years with the United Nations World Food Programme based in Rome, Italy, and 10 years in the private sector in a marketing capacity based in Toronto, Canada. She is currently the Division Chief, Talent Acquisition and Operations at the International Monetary Fund.

Ms. Paone holds a bachelor's degree in Business Administration from the University of Western Ontario in London, Ontario, Canada, and a master's in Organizational Development from Pepperdine University in Malibu, California.

She is married with two children and lives in Washington, D.C.

Dr. Cyndi Huff Gaudet is Director of the School of Interdisciplinary Studies and Professional Development at The University of Southern Mississippi Gulf Coast Campus. Cyndi is a scholar-practitioner whose passion is developing people through academic programs of excellence. She championed the development and implementation of the MS and PhD in Human Capital Development at Southern Miss, programs designed to prepare senior learning leaders who can strategically lead and manage talent in organizations. Her research agenda to help organizations implement a systematic approach for developing human capital has been disseminated through professional conference presentations, numerous publications, and earned national awards of research recognition.

Cyndi's commitment to excellence and innovation resulted in awards, including the *NASA Public Service Group Achievement Award, U.S. Department of Labor Recognition of Excellence—Educating America's 21st Century Workforce, Southern Growth Policies Board Innovator in Workforce Development, LSU School of Human Resource Education and Workforce Development Alumnus Award of Excellence, Gulf Coast Women of Achievement Woman of the Year Award, University Commencement Grand Marshal, College of Science and Technology Outstanding Research Award, Southern Miss Distinguished Professor of e-Learning, You Rock! Professor of the Year,* and the *Students' Choice Award.*

Dr. Gaudet's consulting services for organizational learning and development, leadership development, talent management, training, executive coaching, and strategic planning span public and private sector organizations. Gaudet holds ROI Certification from ROI Institute, a BS and MEd from Southern Miss and a PhD in Human Resource Education and Workforce Development from Louisiana State University.

1

The Value Evolution

In July 2017, an unlikely group convened on the campus of Birmingham-Southern College to learn how to show the value of what they do. Although this task is not all that unusual, the audience may surprise you. The United Methodist Endorsing Agency (UMEA), a division of the General Board of Higher Education and Ministry (GBHEM), hosted this Return on Investment (ROI) Workshop for 57 senior chaplains, spiritual care managers, and faith community leaders. Here's an excerpt of an article about the program published by The United Methodist Church [1].

> Over the last several years, a major paradigm shift has occurred in how organizational systems understand and value spiritual care. For many organizations, value and relevance are primarily centered on the bottom line. Although monetary value is a critical concern, it is the comparison of this value with the program/project costs that captures the attention of stakeholders—translating into ROI.
>
> "Show me the money" is the familiar response from many business leaders and investors. Sometimes this is an appropriate response. At

other times, it is misguided, especially when it comes to understanding the impact and value of chaplaincy and spiritual care. As Jeffrey Parkkila, senior chaplain at Westminster Retirement Community, Winter Park, Florida, stated, "I have struggled to find the language to communicate with the corporate world the needs of ministry and the value of spiritual care. This ROI training gives me a platform to communicate our value."

Realizing that measures not subject to monetary conversion are also important, if not critical to most programming and projects, participants learned that a balanced profile of success is required, which must include qualitative and quantitative data as well as financial and non-financial outcomes.

John Callanan, senior chaplain with United Methodist Homes of the Greater New Jersey Conference reflected, "My CEO has been pleading with me to demonstrate value, now I have a process to demonstrate the impact of pastoral care and bring the pastoral care department into greater accountability."

Stephen Brinkley, senior chaplain of the Trauma Center at Orlando Regional Medical Center commented, "Business language is a new language for me—yet, my health system is challenging me to translate the value of ministry in a new way. Failure to do so on my part jeopardizes the future of chaplaincy."

Jack and Patti Phillips engaged the workshop participants in learning a new language by embracing the ROI Methodology. The methodology offers a balanced approach to measurement that captures five levels of outcome data.

When chaplains and spiritual care leaders engage the process, the ROI model provides alignment, connecting needs assessment with evaluation, thereby empowering the translation of ministry's value and impact within organizational systems.

Invigorated by what she was learning, Linda Stetter, director of Spiritual Care, St. Mary Corwin Medical Center, Pueblo, Colorado, stated, "I can now quantify my ministry. This methodology empowers Spiritual Care to not be perceived as a cost center—but an organizational contribution center! This is great news!"

Jeffrey Uhler, chaplain at the Aurora Medical Center, Milwaukee, Wisconsin, added, "Last evening I received a message from my supervisor about a conversation she was having with management pertaining to the addition of chaplaincy staff. Management's feedback to her, 'You'll need an ROI plan.' Today, chaplaincy received good news—we have learned a methodology to give management just what they asked for, the ability to demonstrate ROI. I am excited!"

Bruce Fenner, endorsing agent for The United Methodist Church and director of endorsement at UMEA noted that the evaluations of this leadership development workshop were the highest of any program ever offered by the endorsing agency for its constituents. He attributes this to the outstanding leadership, clarity of vision, practical instruction, and applicability of the material for this time of our lives. "We were fortunate to have Jack and Patti Phillips bring their leadership. They are world-renowned experts in the field of measurement," noted Fenner. "If we, as clergy working in specialized ministry, are to be relevant in this increasingly secular culture and workforce, there is a pressing need to learn a new language in ministry—the language of business. Business leaders do not typically understand the pastoral care world, nor are they going to learn our language. Rather, we must become bilingual if spiritual care is to have value and impact in broader organizational systems. There is nothing better suited to get us on our way than what we experienced from ROI Institute."

This program underscores how the need for results has shifted, even in unexpected settings. No organization or profession can escape the need for accountability and even "business results." The good news about this group is their attitude about this task and the progress they are making. Chaplaincy groups are showing the impact of their work, and a publisher has agreed to publish their case studies and stories. An important professional community had stepped up to this challenge.

While "show me the money" is not a new request for business, top leaders of all types of organizations want value for their investments. It is relatively new to the public sector. While "showing the money" is the ultimate report of value for many, organization leaders recognize that value lies in the eye of the beholder; therefore, the method used to show the money must also show the value as perceived by all stakeholders. Just as important, organizations need a methodology that provides data to help improve investment decisions. This book presents an approach that does both: it captures the value that organizations receive for investing in programs and projects, and it develops needed data to improve those programs in the future.

This chapter presents the evolution of value—moving from activity-focused value to the ultimate value, return on investment (ROI). This chapter also describes issues and challenges faced by those seeking a technique to show the money.

The Value Shift

"Show me the money" represents the newest value statement. In the past, program success was measured by activity or input, such as number of people involved, programs implemented, actions taken, money spent, days to complete. Little consideration was given to the impacts derived from these activities and inputs. Today the value definition has shifted: value is defined by results versus activity. More frequently, value is defined as monetary benefits compared with costs to calculate the financial ROI. Figure 1.1 reveals the many applications of this concept. These examples

1   The British Columbia Interior Health System calculated the ROI for a new procedure for colorectal surgery.

2   The Ministry of Education in Dubai calculated the ROI for implementing a model classroom program.

3   A major U.S. city calculated the ROI for investing in housing to reduce the number of homeless citizens on the streets.

4   The Australian Capital Territory Community Care agency forecast the ROI for the implementation of a client relationship management (CRM) system.

5   Horizon Home, a comprehensive shelter and protection system for abused and battered women, developed the ROI for the services provided to clients.

6   The state of Alabama developed the ROI for a recidivism program for drug related offenders.

7   A major city calculated the ROI for a new disciplinary system and selection system to reduce unplanned absenteeism and bus delays.

8   The Healthy Living Group in a Canadian government healthcare system developed the ROI for a smoking cessation program for citizens under the age of 35.

9   The UN Women agency measured the ROI for a micro financing program to increase economic empowerment of women, especially of those who are most excluded.

10   A large insurance company developed the forecast and actual ROI for a work at home program for two job groups.

11   A major hotel chain calculated the financial value and ROI of its coaching program.

12   An NGO has developed the impact and ROI for a new law to make domestic violence illegal in Kazakhstan.

13   A refugee services agency conducted ROI studies on two of its major programs: employment and vocation services.

14   The Singapore Defense Science and Technology Agency (DSTA) is measuring the ROI on team effectiveness.

15   The Danish Postal Service calculated the ROI for a project to improve employee engagement.

16   A large U.S. bank calculated the ROI for sponsoring a major sports event.

17   The World Food Programme (Rome, Italy) developed the ROI for a leadership development program for country directors.

18   A major U.S. defense department agency calculated the ROI for a master's degree offered to high potential employees inside the agency.

Figure 1.1 A Variety of ROI Applications – The Possibilities are Endless. (*Continued*)

19	The Association for Talent Development calculated the ROI for the annual conference, from participant perspective and exhibitor perspective.
20	The United Nations Security Department calculated the ROI for providing police training in Kuala Lumpur, Malaysia.
21	Novartis, a Swiss-based pharmaceutical, developed the ROI for a management development program.
22	A package delivery company developed the ROI for the replacement of keys with a fob in courier vehicles.
23	Laboratory Systems, a small 13-person company in Ireland, calculated the ROI for new product development.
24	Innova Energy developed the ROI for a stress reduction program.
25	A large Canadian bank calculated the ROI for networking among its senior leaders.
26	A large international consulting firm calculated the ROI for a social media system designed to manage the knowledge of their consultants.
27	The U.S. Air Force calculated the ROI for implementing new procedures to prevent an intrusion into a database.
28	The Institute for Clergy Excellence calculated the ROI in a program to address the burn out among clergy.
29	Sprint/Nextel developed the ROI for a diversity program.
30	A large European software company calculated the ROI for a virtual business development conference for the sales team.

Figure 1.1 A Variety of ROI Applications – The Possibilities are Endless.

span the globe and types of organizations, with most of them in the public sector.

From education and business, to government, healthcare, and public policy, organizations are showing value by using the comprehensive evaluation process described in this book. Although this methodology to "show the money" had its beginnings in the 1970s, it has expanded in recent years to become the most comprehensive and far-reaching approach to demonstrating the value for money.

Types of Values

Value is determined by stakeholders' perspectives, which may include organizational, spiritual, personal, and social values. Value is defined by consumers, taxpayers, and shareholders. Capitalism defines value as the economic contribution to shareholders. The global reporting initiative (GRI), established in 1997, defines value from three perspectives: environmental, economic, and societal.

Even as projects, processes, and programs are implemented to improve the social, environmental, and economic climates, the monetary value is often sought to ensure that resources are allocated appropriately and that investments reap a return. No longer is it enough to report the number of programs offered, the number of participants or volunteers trained, or the dollars generated through a fundraising effort. Stakeholders at all levels—including executives, administrators, politicians, shareholders, managers and supervisors, taxpayers, project designers, and participants—are searching for outcomes, and in many cases, the monetary values of those outcomes.

"Strive not to be a success, but rather to be of value." – Albert Einstein

The Importance of Monetary Values

Many people are concerned that too much focus is placed on economic value. But it is economics, or money, that allows organizations and individuals to contribute to the greater good. Monetary resources are limited, and they can be put to best use—or underused or overused. Organizations and individuals have choices about where they invest these resources. To ensure that monetary resources are put to best use, they must be allocated to programs, processes, and projects that yield the greatest return.

For example, if a program is implemented to improve outcomes, and it does improve outcomes, we can assume that the initiative was successful. But if the initiative cost more than the outcome gains are worth, has value been added to the organization? Could a less expensive process have yielded similar or even better results, possibly reaping a positive ROI? Questions like these are, or should be, asked on a routine basis. No longer will activity suffice as a measure of results. A new generation of decision makers is defining value in a new way.

The "Show Me" Generation

Figure 1.2 illustrates the requirements of the new "show me" generation. "Show me" implies that stakeholders want to see impact data (i.e., outcome numbers and measures). This accounted for the initial attempt to see value in programs. This evolved into "show me the money," a direct call for financial results. But this alone does not provide the needed evidence to ensure that projects add value. Often, a connection between programs and value is assumed, but that assumption soon must give way to the need to show an actual connection. Hence, "show me the real money" was an attempt at establishing credibility. This phase, though critical, still left stakeholders with an unanswered question: "Do the monetary benefits linked to the program outweigh the costs?" This question is the mantra

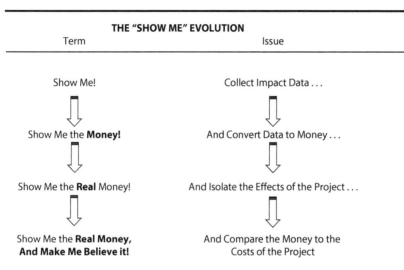

Figure 1.2 The "Show Me" Evolution.

for the new "show me" generation: "Show me the real money and make me believe it." But this new generation of project sponsors also recognizes that value is more than just a single number: value is what makes the entire organization system tick—hence the need to report value based on people's various definitions.

The New Definition of Value

The changing perspectives on value and the shifts that are occurring in organizations have all led to a new definition of value. Value is no longer defined as a single number; rather, its definition is comprised of a variety of data points. Value must be balanced with quantitative and qualitative data, as well as financial and nonfinancial perspectives. The data sometimes reflect tactical issues, such as activity, as well as strategic issues, such as financial impact. Value must be derived using different time frames and not necessarily represent a single point in time. It must reflect the value systems that are important to stakeholders. The data representing value must be collected from credible sources, using cost-effective methods; and value must be action oriented, compelling individuals to make adjustments and changes.

The processes used to calculate value must be consistent from one project to another. Standards must be in place so that results can be compared. These standards must support conservative outcomes, leaving assumptions to decision makers.

The ROI Methodology presented in this book meets all these criteria. It captures six types of data that reflect the issues contained in the new definition of value: reaction and perceived value, learning and confidence, application and implementation, impact and consequences, return on investment, and intangible benefits.

Why Now?

In the past decade, a variety of forces have driven additional focus on measuring the impact of programs, including the financial contribution and ROI. These forces have challenged old ways of defining program success.

Program Failures

A recent *New York Times* analysis revealed that McKinsey and Company, a top consulting firm, entered into a consulting contract to help Eskom, a South American state-owned electric utility, improve its performance. Power blackouts were common, maintenance was being deferred, a major boiler exploded, and the company was on the verge of insolvency. In 2015, McKinsey thought it could help with a large contract with a potential value of $700 million. This contract is now under investigation by the authorities who claim that the contract was illegal and that "it is far from clear that the flailing power company is much better off than it was before." Also, McKinsey has worked with the state-owned rail and port agency, Transnet, since 2005. Still, Transnet "remained an underachiever, its ports inadequate, its freight rail system moribund." In a statement, McKinsey said, "We are embarrassed by these failings, and we apologize to the people of South Africa, our clients, our colleagues and our alumni, who rightly expect more of our firm [2]."

Almost every organization encounters unsuccessful projects—projects that go astray, costing far too much and failing to deliver on promises. Project disasters occur in business organizations as well as in government, NGOs, and nonprofit organizations. Some project disasters are legendary. Some are swept into closets and covered up, but they are there, and the numbers are far too large to tolerate [3]. The endless string of failures has generated increased concerns about measuring project and program success—before, during, and after implementation.

The critics of these projects suggest that the failure could be avoided if: (1) the project is based on a legitimate need from the beginning; (2) adequate planning is in place at the outset; (3) data are collected throughout the project to confirm that the implementation is on track; and (4) an impact study is conducted to detail the project's contribution. Unfortunately, these steps are sometimes unintentionally omitted, not fully understood, or purposely ignored; hence, greater emphasis is being placed on the processes of accountability. This book attempts to show how these four elements come together to create value-adding projects and programs.

Budget Constraints

The prevailing economic model relies on a continual expansion of the size of the budget for projects and programs. A world in which things simply go on as usual is already inconceivable. The modern economy is structurally reliant on economic growth for its stability. When growth falters—as it did dramatically during the financial crisis—politicians panic. Businesses struggle to survive. People lose their jobs and sometimes their homes. A spiral of recession looms. Governments have less money. NGO funding suffers. Nonprofits lose donors or donor money. All types of projects and programs are trimmed or eliminated [4].

Even in times of uncertainty, budgets are scrutinized and reduced. The key is to keep as much of the budget as possible or increase it in the face of uncertainty. To do this, you need to show the value for money with credible data. The challenge for us is to create the conditions under which this is possible. It is the most urgent task of our time.

Project and Program Costs

The costs of projects and programs continue to grow. As costs rise, the budgets for these projects become targets for others who would like to have the money for their own projects. What was once considered a mere cost of doing business is now considered an investment, and one to be wisely allocated. For example, consider the field of learning and development in the United States. Learning and development is, of course, necessary, particularly to introduce new skills and technology to employees, but 20 years ago it was regarded by some company executives as a frivolous expense. These days, the annual direct cost of organizational learning and development is estimated to be over $150 billion in the United States. A few large organizations spend as much as $1 billion every year on operational learning and development. With numbers like these, learning and development is no longer considered a frivolous expense; rather, it is regarded as an investment, and many executives expect a return on major programs.

The same is true for information technology (IT). Years ago, it seemed a necessary but minor part of most organizational structures. Not so today. Consider, for example, FedEx. Casual observers may not regard FedEx as a high-tech company. It apparently consists of trucks and airplanes moving packages. Yet FedEx handles and keeps track of more than 125 million packages per day, coordinating the work of 400,000 employees, and operating 664 airplanes and more than 170,000 vehicles in more than 220 countries [5]. Seconds and minutes count with FedEx. A technology glitch could amount to a public relations disaster [6]. Because of the importance of IT, the company gives it an annual budget of more than $1 billion, a significant amount that attracts the attention of many executives.

Donors are More Demanding

There are over 1.4 million nonprofits in the United States, more than 500,000 of which have been created in the last 10 years! Yet according to the Urban Institute, there are only 1,100 different "types" of nonprofit programs (such as hunger relief, after school, arts and culture, housing, elder care, etc.). Simple math tells us, on average, there are over 1,000 nonprofits for each type of problem. Donors have a huge range of choices competing for their charitable instincts. That's a lot of people trying to do the same thing! [7]. There are hundreds of choices for where we can donate funds and get the same warm glow. The differentiator is the results…the impact of the nonprofit.

The Bill and Melinda Gates Foundation is probably the best example of how donor behavior has changed. When this foundation makes a grant, it requires value for money in several ways. When donors give money to the foundation, they are prepared to show the value for money. Their largest donor is Warren Buffett, one of the richest people on the planet and probably the most astute investor.

Bill and Melinda addressed their 2017 annual letter to Warren Buffett, who in 2006 donated the bulk of his fortune to their foundation to fight disease and reduce inequity [8]. Ten years later, in 2016, Buffet asked them to reflect on what impact his gift had on the world. In his letter, he stated:

> I also believe it's important that people better understand why success in philanthropy is measured differently from success in business or government. Your letter might explain how the two of you measure yourselves and how you would like the final scorecard to read. Your foundation will always be in the spotlight. It's important, therefore, that it be well understood. And there is no better way to this understanding that personal and direct communication from the two whose names are on the door.

Their response to Buffet captures the value for money:

> Ten years ago, when we first got word of your gift to the foundation, we were speechless. It was the biggest single gift anyone ever gave anybody for anything. We knew we owed you a fantastic return on your investment. Of course, philanthropy isn't like business. We don't have sales and profits to show you. There's no share price to report. But there are numbers we watch closely to guide our work and measure our progress. Our goals are shared by many other organizations working to save and improve lives. We're all in this together. So, most of the numbers we look at don't focus just on how we as a foundation are doing, but on *how the world is doing*—and how we see our role. Warren, your gift doubled the foundation's resources. It's allowed us to expand our work in US education, support smallholder farmers, and create financial services for the poor. But in this letter, we're going to tell you about our work in global health—because that was the starting point of our philanthropy, and it's the majority of what we do. We'll tell the story through the numbers that drive our work.

They went on to report the success of Buffet's investments. The focus was on impact but occasionally ventured into ROI. For example: "And for every dollar spent on childhood immunizations, you get $44 in economic benefits. That includes saving the money that families lose when a child is sick, and a parent can't work." This focus is needed in all types of public sector organizations.

Measurement at the Impact Level Is No Longer Optional

A consistent and persistent trend in accountability is evident in organizations across the globe: almost every function, process, project, or initiative is judged based on higher standards than in the past. Various functions in organizations are attempting to show their worth by capturing and demonstrating the value they add to the organization. They compete for funds; therefore, they have to show value. For example, the research and development function must show its value in monetary terms to compete with mainstream processes, such as sales and production, which for more than a century have shown their value in direct monetary terms.

Funders need to know whether programs are really producing change or just trying to change. "I don't know" becomes a very expensive proposition when people are attaching economic value to actual results. Organizations will no longer be able to duck the measurement question by citing the complexity of their work.

Process Improvements Use

The use of ROI and the need to show monetary value have increased because of the organizational improvement processes that have dominated many organizations, particularly in North America, Europe, and Asia. These process improvement efforts (with labels such as business process improvements, reengineering, Six Sigma, Lean processes, and analytics) have elevated the need to show value in three important ways. First, these processes themselves often create or enhance a measurement culture within organizations. Second, these processes have been successful at adding real value to the organization. Third, the quest to show the value of these processes has created the need to show their actual monetary impact, up to and including ROI.

Managers' New Business Focus

In the past, managers of many support functions in government, nonprofit, and private organizations had no business experience. Today, things have changed. Many of these managers have a business background, a formal business education, or a business focus. These new, enlightened managers are more aware of bottom-line issues in the organization and are more knowledgeable of operational and financial concerns. They often take a business approach to their processes, with ROI being a part of that strategy. Because of their background, ROI is a familiar term. They have studied the use of ROI in their academic preparation, where the ROI Methodology was used to evaluate purchasing equipment, building new facilities, or buying a new company. Consequently, they understand and appreciate ROI and are eager to apply it in other areas.

Case Study

The Impact Hiring Initiative at FSG is making strides in helping employers explore innovative best practices in hiring, retention, and advancement of people who are faced with systemic barriers to employment. The concept of impact hiring focuses on establishing talent practices that create business improvements through hiring and developing individuals such as opportunity youth, formerly incarcerated individuals, and people with disabilities.

"A lot of what we're doing focuses on frontline workers and entry level jobs," said Nicole Trimble, Executive Director of the Impact

Hiring Initiative. "Historically, companies have seen these jobs and people as expendable."

That mindset is changing. Companies are reaching out to the Impact Hiring Initiative because they need help attracting talent, filling roles, and handling high turnover.

Kim Shin, an Associate Director at FSG, said, "This needs to move from a community engagement initiative to a business and HR strategy. Looking at inclusive hiring this way will make it a long-term, lasting practice."

The Impact Hiring Initiative offers nine-month-long Innovation Labs that provide employers an opportunity to recognize the business value of impact hiring. These labs include consulting support, peer-to-peer learning, and a communication platform for sharing employment innovations. They are also a space for employers to pilot and test new strategies.

The next step for the Impact Hiring Initiative team is to conduct an ROI study on tracked data from pilot programs explored in the Innovation Labs. They plan to share this case study with other companies in the future to help organizations implement these types of talent strategies and to show how inclusive hiring helps both businesses and the community.

"The ROI is absolutely necessary, as are data and analytics – but those things alone don't change behavior. We have to integrate these quantitative measures with a heart and mind shift," Trimble said. "In order to have employers invest in people who don't look like them, don't have the same background, and haven't had the same life experience, we have to help break down the barriers between them."

Globalization

Over the last 200 years, a period equal to just one-tenth of 1 percent of our existence as a species, humans have experienced high rates of population growth, technological progress, and increases in standards of living. The world's population has grown six fold, per person material output has increased about tenfold, and we live, on average, three times as long as people did 200 years ago. This unprecedented growth in human economic activity has been accompanied by the expansion of international economic activity. Humans have become increasingly interdependent, to the point where most people today could not survive were it not for jobs performed, goods produced, and income spent in other parts of the world.

This economic growth, coupled with instant communication, creates a level playing field across the globe. Success and failures are known quickly, putting pressure on leaders to transform learning from success and failures. When an economic and social miracle occurs in one country, like Singapore, other countries want similar improvements. When a country's economic and social system collapses, like Greece, other countries try to prevent the same default. Both of these scenarios bring new programs and often with increased accountability [9].

The Growth of Project Management

Few processes in organizations have grown as much as project management. Just two decades ago it was considered a lone process attempting to bring organizational and management structure to projects. Today, the Project Management Institute, which offers three levels of certification for professional project managers, has more than 500,000 members in 204 countries [10]. Jobs are being restructured and designed to focus on projects. Many project managers are being asked to show the ROI for their projects. Also, with the growing use of project management solutions, tools, and processes, a corresponding need to show the accountability for investing so heavily in this process has developed.

Evidence-Based or Fact-Based Management

Recently there has been an important trend to move to fact-based or evidence-based management. Although many key decisions have been made using instinctive input and gut feelings, more managers are now using sophisticated and detailed processes to show value. Smart decisions must be based on more than gut feelings or the blink of an eye. With a comprehensive set of measures, including financial ROI, better decisions regarding people, projects, and processes are possible.

When taken seriously, evidence-based management can change how every manager thinks and acts. It is a way of seeing the world and thinking about the craft of management. Evidence-based management proceeds from the premise that using better, deeper logic and facts to the extent possible helps leaders do their jobs better. It is based on the belief that facing the hard facts about what works and what doesn't work and understanding and rejecting the total nonsense that often passes for sound advice, will help organizations perform better [11]. This move to fact-based management makes expanding measurement to include ROI easier.

Mistrust of Institutions

When there is lack of trust, increased accountability is needed. The public has a mistrust of institutions of all types. While a lack of trust is a concern in business (especially banks and financial institutions), it is a persistent problem with governments, nongovernment organizations (NGOs), and even nonprofits. In 2011, Gallup reported that Americans' approval of Congress was at an all-time low of 13 percent [12].

What may be a surprise is the distrust of nonprofits and charities. In the 1970s, public concern about fundraising and administrative costs in charities grew. By the end of the 1970s, 20 states and numerous county and local governments had adopted laws or ordinances limiting charity solicitations to organizations that could prove a sizable portion of the collection went for charitable purposes rather than for salaries and administrative costs. Many of these were subsequently rendered unconstitutional by US Supreme Court rulings. Things deteriorated further for charities after the attacks on September 11, 2001, when the media and others jumped all over the Red Cross for the speed and manner with which it distributed donations to victims. The *Chronicle of Philanthropy* reported in 2002 that a whopping "forty-two percent of Americans said they had less confidence in charities now than they did before the attacks because of the way charities handled donations."

Six years later, things hadn't improved. A March 2008 survey by the Organizational Performance Initiative at the Wagner School of Public Service also found that Americans remained skeptical of charitable performance and that estimates of charitable waste remained disturbingly high. Only 17 percent felt charities did a "very good job" running programs and services [13].

Benchmarking Limitations

Executive and managers have been obsessed with benchmarking. They have used benchmarking to compare every type of process, function, and activity. Unfortunately, benchmarking has its limitations. First, the concept of best practices is sometimes an elusive issue. Not all participants in a benchmarking project or report necessarily represent the best practices. In fact, they may represent just the opposite: benchmarking studies usually involve organizations willing to pay to participate. Second, the measures could be the wrong measures. What is needed by one organization may not always be needed by another. A specific benchmarked measure or process may be limited in its actual use. Consider, for example, the most benchmarked question for nonprofits and charities: "What percentage of my donation goes to the mission versus overhead?" They want the amount going to the mission (cause) to be very high and the amount going to overhead to be very low. While it makes sense, a little reflection and analysis reveals that this question is flawed in several ways.

1. It makes us think that overhead is not part of the mission, but it is an important part of the charity or nonprofit.
2. It reveals nothing about the quality of the charity's work.
3. It's an input measure, not an impact measure.
4. The way it's calculated can be misleading [14].

Finally, the benchmarking data are often devoid of financial aspects, reflecting few if any measures of the actual financial contributions with ROI values. Therefore, managers have asked for more specific internal processes that can show these important measures.

The Executive Appetite for Monetary Value

Providing value for money is receiving increased interest in the executive suite. Top managers who watch budgets continue to grow without appropriate accountability measures are frustrated, and they are responding to the situation by turning to ROI. Top executives now demand ROI calculations and monetary contributions from programs and services where they were not previously required. For years, managers and department heads convinced executives (and donors) that their processes could not be measured and that the value of their activities should be taken on faith. Executives no longer buy that argument; they demand the same accountability from these functions as they do from the sales and production areas of the organization. These major forces are requiring organizations to shift their measurement processes to include the financial impact and ROI.

Challenges Along the Way

The journey to increased accountability and the quest to show monetary value, including ROI, are not going unchallenged. This movement represents a tremendous cultural shift for individuals, a systemic change in processes, and often a complete rethinking of the initiation, design, development, delivery, and maintenance of processes in organizations.

Preparation and Skills

Although interest in showing the value and measuring ROI is now heightened and much progress has been made, these are still issues that challenge even the most sophisticated and progressive functions. The problem often lies in the lack of preparation and skills that are needed to conduct these types of analyses. The preparation for most jobs in these areas often lacks the required skill building. Rarely do the curricula in degree programs or the courses in a professional development program include processes and techniques to show accountability at this level. Consequently, these skills must be developed by the organization, using a variety of resources, so that they are in place for successful implementation.

Fear of ROI

Few topics stir up emotions to the degree that ROI does. Some program owners suggest that the conclusion behind the ROI value is simple: if it is negative, executives will kill the program; if it is extremely positive, they do not believe it. The potential for this response from executives causes some professionals to avoid the issue altogether. A familiar reaction emerges: "If my project or program is not delivering value, the last thing I want to do is publish a report for my principal sponsor." Unfortunately, if the project is not delivering value, the sponsor probably already knows it, or at least someone in the organization or community does. The best thing to do is to be proactive and to show the value for money using a systematic, credible process.

Then there is the fear of abuse of the data. Will the data be used to punish the program owner, reward participants, or improve processes? Ideally, results should be used to improve processes with positive feedback when appropriate. The challenge is to ensure that data are not misused or abused. The fear of ROI can be minimized when the individuals involved understand the process, how it is designed and delivered, and the value that it can bring from a positive perspective.

Time Commitment

Thorough analysis takes time. Many practitioners and some sponsors are restless and do not want to take the time to do the appropriate analyses. In a fast-paced work environment where decisions are often made quickly and with little input or data, some executives question the time and the effort involved in this type of analysis. What must be shown, however, is that this effort is necessary and appropriate, and will ultimately pay off. When the process is implemented, the individuals involved usually see that the value of the increased effort and activity far outweighs the cost of the time.

Power and Politics

Having appropriate data represents power to many individuals. How that power is used is important. If used for constructive purposes, data are perceived as valuable. If data are used for destructive or political purposes, they may be seen as less valuable. The important issue is that if the information is based on credible facts, then it generates power. If it is based on opinions or gut feelings, then the person who provides those opinions is more influential than the opinions themselves. Essentially, facts create a level playing field for decision-making. As one executive from a high-technology company said, "If a decision is based on facts, then anyone's facts are equal as long as they are relevant; however, if it must be based on opinions, then my opinion counts a lot more." This underscores the power of having credible data for making decisions [15].

Misleading Hype

Claims abound about success and the use of data to support an idea, project, or program. When the facts are examined, however, they often reveal something completely different. For example, some use return on expectations (ROE), suggesting that this is an impact. Further analysis reveals that this is usually only reaction data. Others use social return on investment (SROI) as a substitute for ROI. Unfortunately, many times this is only intangible data with no financial information.

Tremendous claims, ads, and success stories are presented to promote a concept or idea. Exaggerated statements in marketing campaigns add to the confusion. For example, SAP ran a series of ads claiming that companies that use their software are more profitable than those that do not. An independent research unit found the opposite to be true. SAP then refused to show how they arrived at the conclusion.

Projects and programs are evaluated in a variety of ways, and few accepted standards, rules, and processes exist with which to validate those assumptions and claims. A systematic process with conservative, accepted standards can create a credible story of program success.

Sustainability

The final challenge is sustaining such a radical shift in accountability. The implementation of the ROI Methodology must consist of more than just conducting one or two studies to show the value of the project or program. It must represent a complete change in processes so that future projects and programs focus on results. This change will require building capability, developing consistent and compelling communication, involving stakeholders, building the process into projects, creating expectations, and using data for process improvements. This is the only way to sustain any change for the long term; otherwise, it becomes a one-shot or short-term project opportunity.

> *"Progress always involves risk. You can't steal second base and keep your foot on first." – Frederick B. Wilcox*

Final Thoughts

So what? What does all this mean? This chapter makes the case for having a more comprehensive, credible process to show the value for money. Many important stakeholders are demanding, requiring, or at least suggesting more accountability up to and including the monetary value. "Show me the money" has become a common request—and is being made now more than ever. A variety of forces have created this current focus on results, leaving program planners with only one recourse: to step up to the accountability challenge, create a process that can make a difference, develop data that please a variety of important stakeholders, and use a process that makes projects and programs better in the future. That is the intent of the process described in this book.

2

Six Ways to Show Value for Money

Sarah Robertson provides counseling services at food banks in Canada. As a counselor for the Catholic Family Services, she helps individuals who are having financial problems and cannot afford to pay for food [1].

Sarah helps them understand their situation and plots a path for improvement. Sometimes the citizens need a job, or their spouse needs a job, or perhaps a better job. Maybe there is a serious medical problem that is preventing employment that requires care through the provincial health system. Although the government provides healthcare, citizens still have to pay some fees. Also, a medical problem takes time away from work. A family member may have an addiction and needs help to overcome the addiction. Perhaps a spouse is headed for incarceration or is currently incarcerated. Perhaps the family needs legal assistance. Any of these situations can mean disaster for a low to middle-income family. Sarah provides essential counseling for these unfortunate citizens of the province, with the aim of resolving their "presenting issue."

Sarah was somewhat surprised when a representative of the provincial government, who funds her particular program, visited her and asked about results. When she asked for clarification on the kind of results desired, she was asked very directly, "Could you show the ROI of the counseling?" She responded, "What's ROI?"

The government representative explained, "It is return on investment. We are investing in this counseling program and we want to know how your program is actually adding value to the provincial government. Is it reducing cost? Is it avoiding cost? Is it adding tax revenue? If so, can you tell us how much and let's compare it to the cost of your counseling to see if it is a good investment for us." She responded that she had no idea but would find out.

The government representative continued, "We know this is a valuable and needed service. However, because we are having a budget shortfall related to a reduction in oil prices, we must cut some budgets. We are trying to understand which ones to reduce. Although we would like to fund every program, we cannot. We want to fund the programs that represent a good investment for the province. If you can show data to support this, it would help us justify continuing to fund your program."

Sarah was shocked and somewhat dismayed by the request. She quickly found some information on ROI. Luckily, she found an ROI certification near her in another province in Canada, enrolled, and began to develop her skills to show the ROI for her process.

Sarah was depressed. She had almost no data about this program except for the data she provided to the government indicating how many people were counseled, the type of counseling provided, and the number of counseling sessions conducted. Of course, she provided an invoice for her services. Beyond that, she had no data, but she was optimistic. Perhaps she could find some way to do this.

About a month after the government visit, Sarah attended the ROI Certification and began to understand the ROI process more completely, and with some discussions with her colleagues, she began to reach some conclusions. First, she needed to send the government the reaction data that she had collected. In an existing data collection process, she asked the participants detailed information about "Why are you involved in these sessions? Are the counseling sessions helpful? Are the sessions useful? Is the information important to your survival? Is this something that you will use?" This is valuable information that begins to show the value of this counseling from the participant's perspective.

Sarah also realized that she needed to have learning measures. Participants must learn two major points as they take part in the counseling sessions. First, they must understand clearly how they got into the present situation (i.e., what caused them to need to come to the food bank for food?). Second, they must know what to do to improve the situation and ultimately find a path to independence. She can easily capture this data at the end of the first two sessions (e.g., session 1, what got them into the process; session 2, develop a plan to address the issues).

Sarah also began to realize that she needed follow-up information on actions. As part of the process, she always develops an action plan with each person. The plan is based on the participants' situation, detailing what they must do to overcome their problem. In every case, there were specific actions that they must take, advice they should seek, other agencies they must visit, or employers they should interview. The important point is that an action plan is in place. With some improvements and adjustments, she could easily use this information for application data. She thought the government would view this as important data.

Action is not enough; Sarah needed the impacts. In every case, there is a potential positive impact coming from the counseling as individuals are securing jobs (or a better job), being released from jail (or prevented from going to jail), getting their child off an addiction, correcting a medical problem, or resolving a legal issue. Whatever the situation, there is a consequence with a major impact on the person and on the government system.

Sarah thought that if there was an impact, it could be caused by many other factors. For example, if someone gets a job and she has helped with tips, advice, coaching, contacts, and appointments, there are other factors that caused that person to get the job. However, part of the cause of job success goes to this program and that is the important point. What she learned during the ROI certification program is that there is always a way to isolate the effects of the program on the impact data. She felt comfortable that she could do this credibly with some help. She also felt comfortable that all the data were available directly from the individual, system, or some agency. This would be extremely valuable information for the government, particularly if she isolated the effects of her counseling on the impact data.

Recognizing that this is not what the government had asked for, she moved to the next level, ROI, which means that impact data must be converted to money. After some discussion and questioning, she realized that for almost every consequence there was either a cost prevented, or money added. For example, if someone gets a job, that person now has a reduction or elimination of unemployment benefits, which is a cost avoidance. That individual will also now pay taxes, and so the taxes are revenue for the province. If a person is prevented from going to jail (or they get out of jail earlier), those days of incarceration can be attributed to this program and represent a standard cost that is available from the province. When someone has a medical problem, the provincial government pays for almost all of it. If it is corrected, a cost is avoided. If addiction is stopped, a cost is avoided. In almost every one of the outcomes, there is some cost avoided to the provincial government. She felt comfortable that these values were available and could be obtained with minimal effort.

Obviously, the fees the government is paying for counseling represent the cost to the government, but she quickly realized that is not all of the cost. It is also the cost of the counseling room, because after all, the government is furnishing the facility. All the costs, indirect and direct, would need to be included, which she says should be not that difficult. Then the benefit-cost ratio and the standard ROI calculation could be developed, which was the data that the government requested.

Sarah was a little concerned because she said the benefit of the counseling, in her mind, is not just the money, but the impact the program has on the lives of these families. If the counseling works, they regain their self-esteem and dignity, family relationships are improved, quality of life is enhanced, and they feel good about their government helping them in a time of need— "these kinds of measures you cannot convert to money," she said. "And they are important intangibles." The key is to connect them to this program, which is easily accomplished.

Sarah concluded that she could have a complete set of data, measuring reaction, learning, application, impact, ROI, and the intangibles. This would provide the government the data it needed.

Unfortunately, before Sarah Robertson could complete her study, she received notice from the provincial government that her program had been cancelled. She explained to the representative that she was working on an ROI study that should be completed in a month. The representative explained, "It's too late . . . The decision has been made. It was a difficult decision . . . But we have to cut budgets. We just don't have the revenue, and we don't have any data about the success of this program."

Sarah was upset and angry. "How could the government be so cruel?" she asked. "Is everything about money?" She planned to challenge the decision but felt that it would probably be a waste of time.

On top of this frustration was the reality that she must find another job. As a contract employee, she must replace this lost contract with another one, and in this environment, it would be difficult. In addition, she worried about the people who come to the food bank. "Will someone be there to help them? Probably not," she concluded.

———————————————— × ————————————————

This sad, but true, story reveals several issues about the value for money question. This is sad because the counseling program is probably driving some important impacts, according to Sarah. If she had some impressive impacts, the value for money request would probably not have surfaced.

There are lessons for both the funder and the recipient. Funders need to push the evaluation value chain to a higher level, probably to the impact level instead of the number of people served and the costs, which are input. The recipients of funds should be proactive and push the evaluation to a level that the client needs. This is usually the impact level.

Six Ways to Show Value for Money

We were surprised when the Refugee Project at the Department of Family Services in the state of Florida asked for our assistance in showing the ROI for all of their efforts to integrate refugees into this country. As we gathered more detail from the agency, we found that they were responding to requests from funders of this project to show more value for money. For this particular requestor, the value for money meant the financial ROI—the return on investing in this project.

In ROI Institute's five-day ROI Certification workshop, participants are learning how to measure the success of their projects all the way to the impact and ROI. The session begins with an introduction of individuals and an explanation of why they are there. One person from the Police Department of the City of Ottawa indicated that she was there to learn how to show the value for money. She added that her job title was Coordinator, Value for Money and that she wanted to show the value received from the various sources of funding.

These two examples are not isolated situations. There is a tremendous push for organizations to show value for money.

> *"Rule #1: Never lose money. Rule #2: Never forget Rule #1."*
> *– Warren Buffett*

In an era of tight, reduced, and heavily scrutinized budgets, the value of the programs is important. In today's climate, many executives and administrators want to see value for money. Whether in the government (at the city, county, state, or federal level), nongovernment organizations (NGOs), nonprofits, or businesses, the issue of value for money is now a part of many procurement processes and the basis for new program approvals. This chapter outlines the different ways to address this critical issue, which has become an absolute must for anyone implementing programs or projects.

While several potential approaches are available to address the value for money issue, the first step is to identify the different types of outcome data that are possible. When a new program is implemented, it is possible to measure results at different levels, as shown in Figure 2.1.

These levels are important, universal, and form the basis for a logical flow of data as programs are implemented. Participants' time and financial resources are tabulated at level zero. The outcomes of the program are categorized in five levels: how participants reacted to the program; what they learned to make the program successful; how they actually used the program concepts, materials, and processes; the impact of the program on the organization, community, or individual; and the financial ROI calculation.

The most important data set are impact measures. The good news is that four categories of impact data are available internally in every work unit and externally for every program: output, quality, cost, and time. In government, output of the unit is one measure such as forms processed, inspections made, or licenses issued. For a healthcare program, the outputs are patients discharged, ER visits, patients processed through MRI, and improvement in health status. For international development programs, output is jobs secured, income increases, and improvement in poverty rates. In business, output is production, sales, new accounts, and the number of projects completed. In a university, output is the number of graduates, placement rates, and salary of graduates.

Level	Typical Measures	Issue
0 Input	Volume, cost, and time	How many people are involved, their time and cost?
1 Reaction	Relevance, importance, and necessity	How did they react to the program?
2 Learning	Skills and knowledge acquisition	Did participants learn how to make the program successful?
3 Application	Extent of use of the program content, frequency of use, and success with use	Did participants implement the program? Was it successful?
4 Impact	Productivity, patient outcomes, quality, cost, time, crime rates, satisfaction, image, jobs secured, and stress	What was the impact, the consequence of the application?
5 ROI	Benefit cost ratio and roi, expressed as a percent	What was the payoff for investing in this program?

Figure 2.1 Types of Possible Data Categories.

Quality measures, such as mistakes, errors, rework, and waste, are available in every organization. Time measures include the time for activities, processes, tasks, and procedures and are also available everywhere. The final category, costs, are everywhere as well, which makes up the budget for the work unit or program.

Objectives are usually set for every level. At Level 4, the impact can be either tangible (when it can be converted to money), or intangible (when it is not converted to money). The decision to convert or not is based on whether there is available time or resources to do it credibly. With this basic understanding of the types of data, let's focus on the different ways to show value for money.

#1 - Actual ROI Calculation

The most credible approach involves an actual ROI calculation, which is covered thoroughly in this book. Although most programs should not be evaluated at this level, a few need to be pushed to this level of accountability. With this approach, one or more impact measures are improved by implementing the program. The measures selected are in performance records, operating reports, public databases, or other documents that detail the impact. These measures should be converted to money.

For example, in the Internal Revenue Service (IRS), a work-at-home program was implemented for business tax examiners. The result showed that productivity (cases examined per month) increased as a result of this program. A new medical procedure for colon cancer surgery reduced infections, readmissions, and length of stay, yielding a high ROI. A defense department intelligence agency implemented a master's degree program in information science for high-potential employees, fully paid for by the agency with the provision that the employees would take the program on agency time. The result was a dramatic drop in turnover of high potentials, yielding a positive ROI. In New York State, a supervisor-training program was developed and yielded a positive ROI. A UN security police intervention in Malaysia reduced complaints from citizens and reduced crime rates in four categories, yielding a positive ROI. In a large metropolitan area, the city bus system implemented a new selection system and disciplinary procedure to address bus driver unplanned absenteeism and bus delays, resulting in a very positive ROI. These and many other examples occur routinely. Governments, NGOs, nonprofits, and businesses are showing the actual ROI calculation for investing in new programs.

To accomplish this, the program should have clearly defined impact objectives with participants working toward those objectives. In most cases, the measures improve and the amount of improvement is tracked. Then, the effects of the program on that improvement are isolated from other influences. The portion of the improvement connected to the program is converted to monetary values and compared to the fully loaded cost of the program to calculate the ROI. This is the financial value for money and represents the ultimate value for money and the basis of this book.

#2 - Focus on Impacts and Intangibles

For many organizations, the executives and sponsors are satisfied if impact is measured and the amount of the improvement is attributed (or isolated) to the program. In most of the studies and examples presented in this book, the impact is enough value for money. For the food bank/counseling program in the opening story, presenting credible data on the impacts should be enough to satisfy the government representative. The ROI would probably not be needed in that situation. In the city bus driver example presented earlier, showing the improvement in unplanned absenteeism and bus delays would be enough for most sponsors.

Nonprofits should measure their impact to demonstrate value for money created for donors and stakeholders and to influence the resource allocation decisions of prospective stakeholders. Measuring impact is about demonstrating that a nonprofit is making a meaningful contribution to outcomes—both social and economic—that donors and other stakeholders highly value. Measurement enables you to quantify and communicate the degree of value (outcomes) created by the program. If a particular government agency or a corporation really values the program, they will want to know how much impact was produced, not just that the strategy was "effective" as reported by a researcher.

In short, the purpose of measurement in most public-sector programs is to show not only that you are "making a difference" but also what difference you are making. To be sure, stakeholders in the social capital market are concerned about effectiveness [2].

Intangible impacts are also powerful. By definition, an intangible benefit is a measure that cannot be converted to money credibly with a minimum amount of resources. Many programs drive key intangibles such as image, engagement, trust, collaboration, health status, citizen satisfaction, happiness, team effectiveness, cooperation, alliances, climate change, and empowerment. These important intangibles add tremendous value to an organization or community. It's often the intangibles that make the best places to work, the most innovative organizations, the most admired organizations, and the most sustainable organizations.

For some executives, these intangibles represent value for the money that was invested in programs to drive them. The important issue is to have program participants indicate the extent to which the program has influenced each particular intangible measure.

#3 - Meeting Expectations

Another way to consider value for money is the extent to which the program met expectations of the sponsor or other stakeholder groups. Some program planners, organizers, and owners use ROE (return on expectation), ROA (return on anticipation), ROP (return on potential), and ROO (return on objectives). Expectations are usually developed with clearly defined objectives. Objectives can be set at the reaction level (this should be important to our agency), learning level (participants must be able to use this procedure), application level (participants must use the new system every time), impact level (citizen complaints are reduced by 20 percent), or ROI level (realize a 10 percent ROI). The evaluation data reveals if these objectives were met. We prefer to label this as meeting the objectives.

For some executives, this represents value for money. However, when results are pitched as ROE, ROA, ROP, or ROO, this can create the illusion that it's a higher level of evaluation. For example, the supporters of ROE suggest that this is an impact. However, it could be reaction, learning, or application data. The word "return," when used to present results, can create confusion with executive and financial officers. The finance and accounting team think that they own this term, with concepts of return on investment (ROI), return on equity (ROE), return on assets (ROA), and return on capital employed (ROCE). Using these same terms creates confusion with this very important group—and it's not necessary. Call it what it is…we met our objectives at these levels.

#4 - The Payoff of Improved Behaviors

Sometimes internal programs have competencies or behaviors detailed in learning and application objectives. These competencies may represent a significant portion of a participant's job or responsibilities. It is possible to use a concept called utility analysis where the value is placed on improved behavior and competencies based on the salary of the participants [3].

Here's how it works. Let's consider a situation where a manager in a nonprofit is participating in a leadership development program. This participant has a salary of $50,000 per year, and the leadership competencies covered in the leadership development program represent 30 percent of the participant's job. In essence, 30 percent of the salary, or $15,000, can be influenced with these competencies. We determine the extent to which competencies have improved, comparing ratings before and after the program, using self-assessment from the participants or ratings from the immediate manager. Based on the post data (application), we would expect this improvement to be significant. Let's assume a 20 percent improvement. Then 20 percent of $15,000, or $3,000, is the value added from this program. This participant is worth $3,000 more per year, although we are still only paying the $50,000 original salary. When this is compared to the cost per participant, which is about $2,700 per participant ($2,000 direct and $700 indirect), this yields a benefit cost ratio (BCR) of

$$BCR = \frac{\text{Benefits}}{\text{Costs}} = \frac{\$3,000}{\$2,700} = 1.11$$

And the return on investment (ROI) of

$$ROI = \frac{\text{Benefits-Cost}}{\text{Cost}} \times 100 = \frac{\$3,000 - \$2,700}{\$2,700} \times 100 = 11\%$$

For some executives, this is value for money. It shows that the competencies have improved, and that improvement adds value. For others, it doesn't show the impact of actually using these competencies, just the extent that the competencies are improved.

#5 - Cost-Effective Approach

Another way to consider value for money is to compare the cost of a particular program to the cost of similar programs. If the program delivered measurable impact, and if this impact is delivered with less cost than what would be expected in other programs, then this becomes a cost-effective approach.

We are always seeking a less expensive way to deliver a program. We may find a cheaper way to stop smoking, reduce infant mortality, increase personal income, secure jobs, improve patient outcomes, or prevent accidents. The challenge is to make sure that the impact is the same or greater with the less expensive option.

In a Washington, D.C.-based NGO, a comprehensive two-week leadership program for middle-level executives was implemented. The fully loaded cost for this top-notch program, including direct and indirect cost items, is estimated to be $27,000 per participant. The direct cost includes facilitation, facilities, materials, and travel/ lodging. Indirect costs are needs assessment and development costs (prorated), program coordination and administration, and participant salaries for the time away from work. This is expensive, but it's expected because of the expert facilitation, extensive travel, and two weeks off the job.

For comparison, we examined benchmarking data for similar programs. We consider this program to be a premium program with high-quality faculty and state-of-the art content. Although it's difficult to find an exact comparison, several resources are available that show the direct cost for this kind of leadership development on a per week basis. For example, a Harvard comparison program is $24,000 per participant for facilitation, materials, and lodging for two weeks. Travel cost is not included. For a similar program at Kellogg (Northwestern University), the two-week equivalent is $24,333. When air travel costs are added, the direct costs are about $30,000. When the indirect costs are added, the alternative cost is around $37,000 for these two examples. This means that this program was actually less expensive than similar counterparts. For some executives, this is value for money.

#6 - Cost of Not Implementing the Program

Many programs are necessary and must be implemented. For example, the police force must be trained, the pay for firefighters must be competitive to attract new recruits, the systems must be in place to ensure the safety of employees, and procedures need to be implemented to provide fair and unbiased workplaces. For nonprofits, diseases must be eliminated, poverty rates must be improved, infant mortality must be reduced, and education goals must be obtained. The basis of value for some programs comes from thinking about what would happen if the program was not implemented.

For example, executives invest in employee engagement so that employees are not disengaged. The image of employees not engaged in the work is unpleasant. Imagine what would happen if employees were not accountable for their work. Disengaged talent means low productivity, decreased work quality, missed deadlines, improper decisions, inadequate teamwork, and ineffective relationships. For some executives, the image of effective employees compared to ineffective employees represents value for money, knowing that the employees will be effective based on investing in an engagement program.

Organizations of all types invest heavily in cybersecurity because of the consequences of not investing in this critical issue. Sometimes, these organizations report on the success of cybersecurity by listing the investments in cybersecurity projects.

Of course, this approach to value for money ignores the outcomes. The problem being solved, or the cause being addressed, is enough justification to invest in it. Internally, it shows the executive commitment to the problem or opportunity but does reflect results. For example, Jack Welch, former CEO of General Electric, reported the company's commitment to quality in an annual report by detailing how much the company invested in Six Sigma quality programs. The Social Security Administration in the United States government boosts its success with information technology by listing the $1.6 billion IT budget.

A better approach is to define the impact measure and convert it to money, showing the costs when this happens (such as a cyberattack). Next, the change in this measure is estimated if we do nothing. Then the change or status is estimated with a proposed project implementation. This will require expert estimation, usually based on previous studies, experience, or benchmarking. The monetary benefits of this change are compared to the cost of the project implementation. This could be an ROI forecast, which is fully explored in Chapter 11.

Conclusion

So, there you have it, six ways to address the value for money issue. Multiple ways should be explored. Some methods are more credible than others. You should develop credibility to tackle all the approaches, except maybe number four, the Payoff of Improving Behaviors, which has limited use. This book will be a valuable resource for the other five approaches. Most of the book focuses on numbers one, two, and three, which are the most credible approaches. The key is to understand which way (or methods) are appropriate for key decision makers in your organization.

Barriers to Showing Value for Money

Several persistent barriers slow down the progress with efforts to show value for money. Some are real but can be minimized. Some are myths that can be overcome. Here are some of the most common.

We Don't Make Widgets

A familiar statement from governments, nonprofits, and NGOs is that "we are not a production team, we don't make widgets." This common expression, which sparked a book by the same name, implies that because we don't produce a tangible product, our success cannot be judged on the same type of criteria as a business that produces a product [4]. This is not necessarily true. Few would argue that the first three levels of value from any project or program (reaction, learning, and application) would exist in the public-sector setting. The widgets argument often stems from the fourth level (impact), suggesting that those impacts either do not exist, are not measured, or not very accurate if they are measured.

In reality, any work unit in a government or nonprofit setting will have the same four categories of classic hard data items: output, quality, cost, and time. While these measures are often associated with businesses, they equally apply to governments and nonprofits. For example, a work unit, which is a team with a team leader, or even an individual performing a function in the government, will have output. The output may be the number of forms approved, licenses issued, projects completed, calls taken, or responses provided. We all have output of our work, the things that we are doing.

Quality measures include mistakes, errors, waste, or rework which are available in any work unit. These impact measures exist, to some degree, in all functions. The third measure, time, is the time it takes to complete tasks or procedures, process forms, issue a license, and complete a response. If a new program can cause these times to be reduced, we save time. Time savings add value to the organization. Finally, there is the cost category. Because all work units operate under a budget with some type of accounting system, costs are available for performing any task, process, or procedure. That's an easy way to get to the cost savings from a new program.

Because There are No Profits, ROI is Not Possible

The issue here is converting data into money. In the public sector, the impact data that is often missing is sales, unless an agency is taking revenue for fees, permits, licenses, etc. Yes, the value added for sales would be profit. However, there are still monetary values associated with the other measures in the form of cost reduction. If we can produce more output through a particular program with the same resources involved, then we save the agency money. For example, if a participant normally approves five applications a day, but now with a new program can approve six, then the organization is actually getting one more approval per day with no additional resources. Therefore, the value added would be the cost of processing the application. If the workday cost is $160 to approve four applications, then it is costing $40 per application approval. Now that five are being approved, the added value, with an additional application, is $40. Essentially, we are saving $40 for the organization. That is *real money*.

If mistakes are made, the tasks, process, or procedure has to be repeated. If reworks are averaging 10 percent and, with a new program, that number can be reduced to five percent, the organization has saved the cost of half the time for the rework. The amount of time it takes to do the rework can be converted to money, and we have prevented half of the cost of reworks—this is cost avoidance.

The same logic holds true with time savings. If we can reduce the time to do something, time savings have occurred, which translates directly into money. Of course, the time saved must be used on other productive work. It is often not difficult to calculate the monetary values.

ROI is Just Not Appropriate for the Public Sector

Because the public sector is not a business and not motivated by profit, money is not the issue here. Subsequently, ROI should not be applied in this setting. This is not necessarily true. ROI can be a great tool to manage resources and make an organization more efficient in the use of those resources.

For example, consider a smoking cessation program targeted for people under the age of 35. The program is successful with 80 percent of the participants stopping smoking. If they sustain the smoking cessation for six months, they will usually stop smoking completely. The impact of having a person stop smoking is dramatic in terms of the healthcare costs avoided for those individuals. Fortunately, there is enough data to suggest that in any given healthcare system, regardless of who is paying for it, if a person stops smoking at age 35 or below, the cost savings from preventing cancer, heart problems, hospitalizations, doctor visits, emergency room visits, and surgeries—all tremendous medical expenses are impressive.

Given the money associated with this situation, we can see if the cost of the smoking cessation program is worth it from an ROI perspective. More than likely, it would be very positive unless the program is extremely expensive. ROI tells us if we are using our funds efficiently, because there may be another program or system that has a higher rate of success at the same cost, and the ROI would increase because there would be more people stopping smoking. Or, suppose there's another program that can have the same effectiveness, but can be implemented with less cost. This will have a greater ROI as it shows that the organization is more efficient at using funds.

ROI is a useful tool because it helps us think about the effectiveness of how things are working, which is the numerator (that's the monetary benefits provided). In the public sector, this is usually cost avoidance. It also shows the cost of doing it, and that's in the denominator, which is efficiency. The pressure is on governments and nonprofits to do more with less, while is addressing both sides of the equation, getting more accomplished, and yes, trying to do it with less cost, improves the ROI. When you tackle both, you are bound to have a dramatic improvement on the ROI. ROI can be a very effective tool. It just needs to be used selectively and for important projects where it makes sense.

We Don't Have the Resources

A typical comment is that "we don't have the resources to show value for money." This is very common—nonprofits, NGOs, and governments operate very lean. Businesses also operate lean. They have to operate this way to compete. The question is, "How much does this cost?" When you examine the time and resources needed, the ROI Methodology may not be that expensive.

You can actually have a very successful evaluation practice following the recommended (best practice) percentages evaluated at each level. This means that every program (100 percent) is evaluated at Level 0 input and at the reaction level. Almost all of them (90 percent) are measured at the learning level. It is important to make sure that the people involved know what they must do. At least 30 percent are measured in a follow-up evaluation to see if participants are doing what they are supposed to do to make a program successful. One-third of those, 10 percent, are pushed to the impact level so that we can sort out the effects of the influence of the program from other influences. And then, half of that 10 percent (5 percent) are pushed to the ROI level to make sure that it is an efficient use of the resources.

This profile of evaluation can be achieved for about 3 to 5 percent of the operating budget for these programs. It's helpful to examine the total operating budget and then take 4 percent of it (the middle of this range). This is best practice. You may not have these resources now, but you have to start somewhere. Connect an important program to impact in a credible way so that you get the attention of the sponsors or donors. Then take it to the ROI level, if possible. As you're making a presentation to the key stakeholders, make the case for allocating more funds to evaluation. Some donors may be willing to allocate more money into the evaluation because they appreciate these results.

Unfortunately, too much evaluation is conducted at the lower levels and is not appreciated so much by the donors. If the reaction is not where it needs to be, we need to correct it. If participants are not learning what to do to make the program successful, we need to correct it. If participants are not doing what they need to do to be successful, we need to correct it. Although this is critical and necessary, it doesn't get the sponsors excited. This is an operational issue that must be tackled. When we present impact from programs, we receive attention from the sponsors. If we present ROI, it receives even more attention. That might make the case for more investment in measurement and evaluation.

What we're suggesting is that you may not be able to move quickly to best practice if you're not there now. You have to migrate to best practice by evaluating one program at the higher levels first, use the results to get more funding, and then use the next evaluation to secure even more. We've seen organizations start with a low level of evaluation activity, but they are at best practice in three to five years because they migrate to it incrementally as they build support.

Another issue to consider when resources are low is to ask, "What are the consequences if you don't do it? If you don't do this, what happens?" Well, as you will see throughout this book, particularly this chapter and the first chapter, we probably won't have the appropriate funding. In the worst-case scenario, funding can disappear. It can be disastrous.

This is Too Complicated

We understand this issue as well. Some models are very detailed, complicated, and sometimes require highly sophisticated analysis and statistics. We need a model that uses a logical flow of data, a step-by-step sequence, and a systematic process where the math is simple, yet credible, and the time to use it is kept to a minimum.

Also, a model is needed that is not heavy in finance and accounting, particularly when the financial ROI is part of the process. The model presented in this book is a step-by-step methodology to move through the process to yield the outcomes. At each step of the process, several options are available to address this step. For example, when collecting data at Levels 1 and 2, many options are possible, so it is a matter of selecting the appropriate method. For collecting data at levels three and four, there are many options as well. Many options exist for isolating the effects of the program and converting data to money. The ROI Methodology operates like a drop-down menu. At each step a menu is available to choose from, and one approach will always work. It will be an exhaustive list of the possibilities. That makes it easy to follow and easy to use. In essence, it has to be user friendly, as evidenced by more than 5,000 organizations using it. It is rare for someone to say, "This is too complicated."

No One is Asking for this

Managers and professionals face so many priorities, tasks, and deadlines that have to be completed with so little. Why should you spend time on this when you are not asked to do it? It's a logical question.

Here's what happens if you don't focus on this issue and wait for a funder, sponsor, or client to suggest, "Show me the value for money," or you have a grant that is based on showing the value for money and key stakeholders are asking you to provide value for money. You have to do it now, because of the request.

Three things happen when this occurs. First, you are now on the agenda of the key stakeholder. That is not a good place to be. Second, you have a short time frame to show results. They want results quickly. This was evidenced in the opening story of this chapter. They are impatient; they need something quickly. And third, you are now defensive. You need to be on the offensive. You need to drive this process.

The irony is that the time to tackle this is when you are not required to do it. If you wait until you must respond, it's too late. It's like planning to mitigate risk; you do some things now to prevent the disaster later. You have to take the proactive approach, get started, and gain some support. You can experiment, build capability, and provide data to key stakeholders ahead of the request for these levels of results, ensuring that you are keeping the requestor away from your door.

Just remember, when it comes to delivering results from your program:

- hope is not a strategy
- luck is not a factor
- doing nothing is not an option

Our processes are changing. Our requirements are changing. The accountability needs are changing. Change is inevitable. Progress is optional.

> *"It's more effective to do something valuable than to hope a logo or name will say it for you." – Jason Cohen*

Final Thoughts

In a very broad way, this chapter addresses the concept of value for money. While there are six ways to do this, the most important and credible way is to show the actual financial ROI. The ROI calculation is the undisputable value for money, taken from the finance and accounting field, and is the basis for this book. It is appropriate for many public-sector programs and projects. There are other ways to show value for money which might suffice. Not every project should be subjected to ROI analysis. You need to consider the other methods and, if they are appropriate, you may want to utilize them.

The key is to do it. There are also some challenges we have to overcome. Six challenges were identified in this chapter. In reality, most of them are myths which can be addressed, minimized, or removed to make this work. The next chapter examines how current models are not quite living up to client expectations and needs today.

3

Needed: An Enhanced Logic Model

In 1989, Stephen R. Covey wrote the book, *The 7 Habits of Highly Effective People*®, which became one of the most important, influential, and best-selling books in history with more than 20 million copies sold [1]. This book is based on much research that defines the journey to effectiveness into seven easy-to-understand habits:

Habit 1: Be Proactive
Habit 2: Begin with the End in Mind
Habit 3: Put First Things First
Habit 4: Think Win/Win
Habit 5: Seek First to Understand, Then to Be Understood
Habit 6: Synergize
Habit 7: Sharpen the Saw

Covey built a business around the book to support the implementation of the seven habits. With the acquisition by Hyrum Smith's company, Franklin Quest, the company evolved into the FranklinCovey Company.

Although Covey expected widespread adoption of these habits, he was surprised that many school systems began adopting them and teaching the seven habits to schoolchildren. The process had been adopted for schools as illustrated by Muriel Summers, principal at A.B. Combs Elementary School, the first school to use the seven habits [2]. As Summers sat among business leaders, she could not help but think, "If children learned the seven habits at an early age, how different their lives might be and how different our world might be." The following is a synopsis of the seven habits in kids' language. See if you come to the same conclusion.

Habit 1: Be Proactive. I am a responsible person. I take initiative. I choose my actions, attitudes, and moods. I do not blame others for my mistakes. I can only be offended if I choose to be.

Habit 2: Begin with the End in Mind. I plan ahead and set goals. I do things that have meaning and make a difference. I am an important part of my classroom and contribute to my school's mission and vision and look for ways to be a good citizen.

Habit 3: Put First Things First. I spend my time on things that are most important. This means I say no to things I know I should not do. I set priorities, make a schedule, and follow my plan. I am disciplined and organized.

Habit 4: Think Win-Win. I balance courage for getting what I want with consideration for what others want. I make deposits in others' emotional bank accounts. When conflicts arise, I look for options that work for both sides.

Habit 5: Seek First to Understand, Then to Be Understood. I listen to other people's ideas and feelings. I try to see things from their viewpoints. I listen to others without interrupting. I am confident in voicing my ideas. I look people in the eyes when talking.

Habit 6: Synergize. I value other people's strengths and learn from them. I get along well with others, even people who are different than me. I work well in groups. I seek out other people's ideas to solve problems because I know that by teaming with others we can create better solutions than any one of us alone. I am humble.

Habit 7: Sharpen the Saw. I take care of my body by eating right, exercising, and getting sleep. I spend time with family and friends. I learn in lots of ways and lots of places, not just school. I take time to find meaningful ways to help others.

By 2008, about half a million schoolchildren were using the seven habits and school administrators were experiencing some important outcomes with student grades, behavior, and performance. These amazing results led to more adoptions.

At the same time, school systems faced tremendous budget strains and did not necessarily have extra money to spend on this program. Consequently, FranklinCovey decided to show the value for money to the school system. Ideally, the value should be translated into monetary benefits and compared to the cost of the program. In essence, they needed the ROI.

Several studies were conducted using the assistance of a major university. School systems, which had implemented the program, were compared to school systems that had not used the program. The systems were matched using the type of school systems, population demographics, number of students served, and other factors. The results were quite dramatic, revealing improvements in outcomes such as attendance, grades, test scores, reading levels, promotions to the next grade, student retention, incidents, counseling, and tardiness. Some of these were converted to money.

Other intangibles that could not credibly be converted to money were identified and reported. These results made the decision of a school superintendent much easier. If they invested in this program, they would be getting the money back and then some. What the FranklinCovey team did was to make the business case for using seven habits in schools by building in all the stakeholders, as shown in Figure 3.1.

The 7 Habits	What Parents, Teachers, and Businesses Want	
Habits 1 – 3 (Independence) Be Proactive Begin with the End in Mind Put First Things First	• Goal Setting • Planning • Time Management • Organization	• Initiative • Responsibility • Vision • Integrity
Habits 4 –6 (Interdependence) Think Win-Win Seek First to Understand, Then to be Understood Synergize	• Conflict Management • Listening/Empathy • Speaking Skills • Problem Solving • Teamwork	• Respect • Ethics/Manners • Honesty • Openness • Valuing Diversity
Habit 7 (The Whole Person) Sharpen the Saw (Care for Body, Heart, Mind, and Spirit)	• Physical Wellness • Social Skills • Mental Skills • Emotional Stability	• Contribution/Meaning • Desire to Learn • Fun

Figure 3.1 The 7 Habits in Schools.

It's a great way to see value and improve support for programs that, on the surface, appear to be very important but just don't have the monetary connections required to make the fiscal decision in today's economic climate.

As this situation underscores, there is a need to have an evaluation system that will serve the needs of top leaders in organizations and funders for the program. At the same time, it must have the ability to show the value of a particular project in ways that executives can understand and assist them in making the decision to continue to invest in the future. Most evaluation models don't seem to have the capacity to do this. This chapter explains the need for an enhanced evaluation system, taking it beyond the classic program evaluation models that exist.

A Review of Models

First, it's helpful to show the basis for many evaluation models and that's a logical framework. Often labeled logic model, this approach is a general representation of how change will occur as the program is designed, implemented, and delivers results.

Definition

According to Wikipedia, a logic model (also known as a logical framework, theory of change, or program matrix) is a tool used by funders, managers, and evaluators of programs to evaluate the effectiveness of a program. They can also be used during planning and implementation. Logic models are usually a graphical depiction of the logical relationships between the resources, activities, outputs and outcomes of a program. While there are many ways in which logic models can be presented, the underlying purpose of constructing a logic model is to assess the "if-then" (causal) relationships between the elements of the program.

In its simplest form, a logic model has four components, as shown in Figure 3.2.

Following the early development of the logic model in the 1970s by Carol Weiss, Joseph Wholey and others, many refinements and variations have been added to the basic concept. Many versions of logic models set out a series of outcomes/impacts, explaining in more detail the logic of how an intervention contributes to intended or observed

Input	Activities	Outputs	Outcomes/Impacts
What resources go into a program	What activities the program undertakes	What is produced through those activities	The changes or benefits that result from the program
e.g., money, staff, equipment	e.g., development of materials, training programs	e.g., number of booklets produced, workshops held, people trained	e.g., increase skills/knowledge/confidence, leading in longer-term to promotion, new job, etc.

Figure 3.2 The Components of a Logic Model.

results. This will often include distinguishing between short-term, medium-term, and long-term results, and between direct and indirect results [3].

Some logic models also include assumptions, which are beliefs the prospective grantees have about the program, the people involved, and the context and the way the prospective grantees think the program will work, and external factors, consisting of the environment in which the program exists, including a variety of external factors that interact with and influence the program action.

University Cooperative Extension Programs in the United States have developed a more elaborate logic model, called the Program Action Logic Model, which includes six steps:

- Input (what we invest)
- Outputs:
  - Activities (the actual tasks we do)
  - Participation (who we serve; customers and stakeholders)
  - Engagement (how those we serve engage with the activities)
- Outcomes/Impacts:
  - Short Term (learning: awareness, knowledge, skills, motivations)
  - Medium Term (action: behavior, practice, decisions, policies)
  - Long Term (consequences: social, economic, environmental etc.)

In front of Input, there is a description of a situation and priorities. These are the considerations that determine what Input will be needed.

Logic Model Elements

Program logic models display what an existing idea, new program, or focused change effort might contain from start to finish. This assumes that some type of analysis or assessment has been conducted to determine the need for the new program. The elements in a program logic model consist of a step-by-step sequence to reach the desired result. The level of detail increases so that the relationships shown by the model illustrate essential linkages needed to make a plan fully operational. The primary elements for a program logic model include resources, activities, outputs, outcomes, and impact. Figure 3.3 is a template of the elements for most program logic models [4].

Input or resources are essential for activities to occur. Human, financial, organizational, community, or systems resources, in any combination, are used to accomplish activities.

Activities are the specific actions that make up the program. They are the tools, processes, events, technology, and other devices that are a part of the program. Activities are synonymous with interventions deployed to secure the desired change or results.

Outputs are what specific activities will produce or create. They can include descriptions of types, levels, and audiences or targets delivered by the program. Outputs are often quantified and simply characterize the application of activities with selected audiences.

Outcomes are about changes, often in program participants or organizations, as a result of the program. They often include specific changes in awareness, knowledge, skill, and behavior. Outcomes are dependent on preceding resources, activities, and outputs. Sometimes outcomes are parsed by time increments into short, intermediate, and long term.

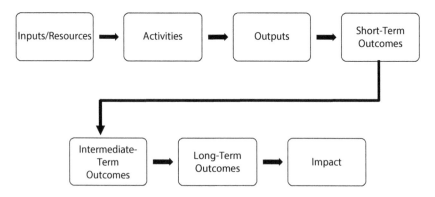

Figure 3.3 A Basic Program Logic Model.

Time spans for outcomes are relative and should be specified for the project described. However, short term is often one through three years, intermediate-term outcomes are four through six years. Long-term outcomes might be achieved in seven through ten years. The intervals specified for any given model would depend on the size and scope of the effort. Figure 3.4 shows an example of the classic logic model applied to a healthy living program [5].

Other Models

In addition to the Logic Model and its variations, many other models have been developed and used. The CIPP Evaluation Model is one of the most widely used evaluation approaches. The CIPP Model provides direction for assessing a program's Context, Input, Process, and Products. Unlike many other evaluation approaches, the CIPP model assesses not only an enterprise's outcomes, but also its environment, goals, plans, resources, and implementation. Its orientation is proactive in guiding needs assessments, goal setting, planning, implementation, and quality assurance, with an emphasis on continuing improvement. It is also retrospective in looking back on, summing up, and judging the accountability and value of completed programs or other enterprises [6].

Daniel L. Stufflebeam, Distinguished University Professor Emeritus at Western Michigan University (WMU), was the developer of the CIPP evaluation model, which has its beginnings in 1965. In a recent book,

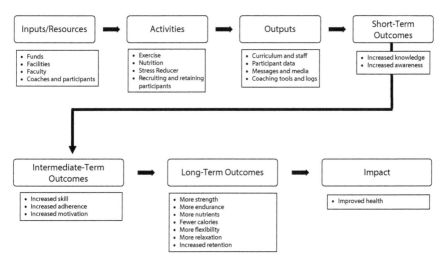

Figure 3.4 An Example of a Basic Program Logic Model.

Stufflebeam compared his model and other models to a set of criteria that he viewed as necessary to be labeled an evaluation model. First, he defined program evaluation as the systematic process of delineating, obtaining, reporting, and applying descriptive and judgmental information about a program's quality, cost-effectiveness, feasibility, safety, legality, sustainability, transferability, fairness, and importance. The result of an evaluation process is an evaluation as a product—that is, an evaluation report for intended uses by intended users.

Next, he set out the criteria to be a program evaluation model. In his view, an evaluation model should stipulate, define, and illustrate the following aspects:

- The types of evaluation purposes served.
- The general sequence of steps for conducting a sound evaluation.
- The approach's orientation to grounding evaluations in explicit values.
- The sources of evaluation questions to be addressed.
- Key foci for collecting data.
- The recommended extent and nature of stakeholder engagement.
- Main inquiry designs and data collection and analysis methods.
- The appropriate means and schedule for reporting evaluation findings.
- The model's underlying epistemology.
- Core qualifications for lead evaluators.

In his research, he suggested that only 10 models meet the criteria, in addition to his model:

- CIPP evaluation model (Stufflebeam, 1985) [7]
- Experimental and quasi-experimental design (Campbell & Stanley, 1963) [8]
- Deliberative democratic evaluation (House and Howe, 2000) [9]
- Discrepancy evaluation (Provus, 1969) [10]
- Educational connoisseurship and criticism (Eisner, 1983) [11]
- EPIC evaluation (Hammond, 1972) [12]
- Goal-free evaluation (Scriven, 1973) [13]

- Naturalistic evaluation (Guba, 1978) [14]
- Responsive evaluation (Stake, 1976) [15]
- The success case method (Brinkerhoff, 2003) [16]
- Utilization-focused evaluation (Patton, 2008) [17]

Later in this chapter, we will present additional criteria to evaluate models, taking into consideration the funding pressures, limited budgets, and trends in accountability.

Concerns about Current Models

These models fall short in several different areas. In the current economic climate with the need for impact and ROI analysis, most of these models don't step up to this challenge very well. This is not meant to be a criticism of any of the models, as they have served useful purposes. However, the economic climate where our programs are implemented has changed. When the founders of the largest foundation in the world (the Gates Foundation) devote their annual letter to ROI, things have changed. When one of the largest hospital chains in the world demands that the impact and ROI of chaplains be calculated, things have changed. When donors for a program to reduce infant mortality demand that the nongovernmental organization show the amount of improvement connected to the program, things have changed. Funding formulas for programs have been altered. Additionally, current expectations of the leaders of organizations have shifted. This means that we must have a system in place to evaluate our programs that serves many more purposes than most of the evaluation models presently address. Here are a dozen concerns about current models.

> *"Success is the sum of small efforts – repeated day in and day out."*
> *– Robert Collier*

Lack of Focus on Benefit-Cost Analysis

Although some models mention the possibility of showing the benefit-cost analysis, few actually include ROI as a possibility. At best, they offer a few comments about what goes into the calculation. Rarely will a model offer, in the model itself, a way to calculate the benefit-cost ratio (BCR) and the ROI, although the benefit-cost ratio is a term that has a steep history. Initially, it was developed by governments as they conducted benefit-cost analysis for government decisions. Historically, the earliest mention of the concept we find was when Great Britain used the benefit-cost analysis to fight the plague in the seventeenth century.

Return on investment (ROI) is a more of a business term, although the concept is actually used in governments. This concept was developed as a method for evaluating capital expenditures, which is the investment in buildings, equipment, and tools. We can trace the first use of ROI to the Dutch when they sent ships to what is now Indonesia to collect spices and bring them back to Europe to sell them. They would calculate the return on investment for the voyage, comparing the revenue from the spices while recognizing that some of the ships would be lost, a cost to them. With the revenue from the sales, they could calculate the profit and ROI on each voyage.

Return on investment subsequently worked its way into finance and accounting principles and into text. By the 1800s it was well-used in many accounting standards. In 1925, the *Harvard Business Review* suggested that ROI was now the dominant way to show results. In those days, though, the results were for capital expenditures.

As we fast-forward to today's economic environment, the capital expenditures are a minor part of an organization's expenses, usually comprising 25-30 percent of total expenditures. Noncapital investments represent the remaining 70-75 percent. Most program evaluations involve noncapital expenses. With this perspective, a company like Verizon, for example, would have only about 25-30 percent of its total expenditure in capital expenses. These include cell towers, stores, equipment, trucks, or any item that must be capitalized. Some technology expenses are capitalized. But Verizon's primary expenses would be with people (human resources), marketing, quality processes, and much of the technology. It's easy to see that noncapital expenditures account for the majority of expenses inside many organizations today.

Think about a United Nations agency like UN Women. Essentially, no capital expenditures are present except for the buildings, some of the technology used, and any vehicles connected to the agency. Perhaps 95 percent of the budget for the UN Women involves their programs, which all are noncapitalized. A program to implement microfinancing for women in Eastern Europe is a noncapital project. A program to reduce domestic violence in Kazakhstan is a noncapital expenditure. A model is needed that can evaluate noncapital expenditures up to the ROI level when needed, but most models don't include this. The opening story in this chapter, and also in Chapters 1 and 2, clearly show that things have changed. There is a need to show value beyond what is typically reported, and that pushes the evaluation to the ROI.

Lack of Emphasis on Attribution

A program may be implemented to improve impact measures such as infant mortality, maternal morbidity, incidences of malaria, HIV and AIDS, water quality, crime, and poverty rates. All are important measures that would be the focus of many projects and programs. However, when a program is implemented to tackle any of these measures, an important issue almost always surfaces. This involves the ability to show how much of the improvement is attributed to the program. This is sometimes called isolating the effects of the program, attribution, causation, or separating the factors that have caused the results. Whatever the label, the process needs to be part of a model, not just a process that *could* be considered, but actually *must* be considered when a program connects to impact. Without it, there is no credibility.

In the past, the United Nations system developed the habit of ignoring this issue in almost every program. Rarely would it pursue a process or method to sort out the effects of the program. A humorous video about the attribution issue was created, basically telling clients not to worry about attribution. They should be happy that they were making a difference. Obviously, this effort turned off their donors. Key donors wanted to know what difference they were making. The UN headquarters public relations team has clearly stated on many occasions that one of the concerns of the donors is how much effect the UN programs have on the impact measures they are driving. If this is not pursued and addressed, you lose credibility and can easily lose funding. The evaluation model must include this step.

Confusion on Outcomes and Impact

Sometimes, there is confusion about the differences between output, outcomes, and impact. Some program owners think of outputs as outcomes. With most of the logic models, an output could be that a training program is conducted, and another output could be that people are trained. Another output may be that a new procedure is put into place. In reality, the success of that training or procedure is the first two levels of outcomes, which are reaction and learning. Outcomes are usually presented as immediate (or short term), intermediate, and long term, and then there is impact. What might be more helpful is to have a value chain with a common set of definitions, such as reaction, learning, application, and impact. This may remove some of the confusion.

Little Focus on the Chain of Value of a Particular Program or Project

Most would agree there is a logical flow of value that comes from any project or program when it is successful. The reaction to the program is always important. Next is learning what's necessary to make the program successful—always an important issue. Then there are actions participants take; that's the application of what is learned. Lastly, there is a consequence of that application, which is the impact.

This combination of reaction, learning, application, and impact has been in existence for a long time. John Quincy Adams, who was president of the United States from 1825 to 1829, suggested that successful leaders inspire people (reaction), cause them to learn more (learning), do more (application), and become more (impact). In essence, this value chain is the basis for a logic model and a logical flow of data. The first level of outcome is reaction, and almost everyone has experienced a situation where a program fails because the users, the people who must make the program work, rejected it. They didn't see the need for it. They didn't think that it was helping them or the situation. The chain of value must be an important part of an evaluation and is necessary to understand this powerful first level of outcome. A measure of reaction is missing on some of the models.

The next emphasis must be placed on measuring learning to make sure that participants know what's necessary to make the program successful. For example, one of the United Nations developmental goals is for citizens in a particular country in a certain age group to be aware of HIV and AIDS. An awareness means that they must know about HIV and AIDS, which requires the evaluators for this program to focus on measuring their awareness of the issue—and this is learning. Measuring learning is an important part of any project, and it's always present because failure to know what to do and how to do it will result in failure of the program. Some models do not require a learning measure. The chain of value can be broken at this point, but most of the time the chain of value breaks at the next level, Application.

When participants, the users, do what you want them to do, the program is successful with application and implementation. Professional evaluators will quickly confirm that this is where projects usually go astray. Participants just don't do what you want them to do. Systems must be in place to ensure that application is supported, required, or reinforced. Resources must be allocated to this critical issue. It has to be a part of any evaluation model.

Next, there's the consequence of application, which is the impact of the program. The impact must not only be measured, but it must be sorted out to isolate the effects of the program from other influences as mentioned above. The impact needs to be precise and clear and, ideally, be defined at the beginning of the project or program. Unfortunately, many of the existing models do not focus on the chain of value that must exist and be in place for success.

Unclear Timing of Data Collection

Data collection involves methods, sources, and timing. The methods and sources are straightforward for a particular program. What is not clear is when to collect data, the timing. The time frame for data collection for short term, intermediate term, and long term described in the logic model definition earlier appear to be excessive. It may be more helpful to replace these three terms for outcomes with a five-level framework: reaction, learning, application, impact, and ROI.

Reaction and learning data are usually collected early in the program launch, although reaction can be captured at any point of the process, not just in the beginning. Learning what to do to make the program successful will affect reaction. Sometimes the desired reaction may not occur until the person has actually experienced the impact. For example, until citizens have actually seen that the use of malaria nets prevents incidences of malaria, citizens may not see the nets as helpful. When the reaction is appropriate, they may use the nets properly instead of discarding them, using them for fishing, or selling them on eBay.

The confusion often lies with when to measure at the application level. Application should occur quickly when a program participant learns concepts, procedures, tasks, and skills to use to make the program successful— it must be applied soon, or it will be forgotten. Rules must be in place to determine data collection timing at the application level for the given program with a rule that can be followed in any setting. Data collection should be as early as possible. If there are cases where subsequent data collections are needed, then the rules would show those time frames as well.

The timing of impact is even more of a mystery, particularly for long-term impact. Timing of impact measures should follow prescribed guidelines. Also, because no one wants to wait for the long-term impact, you may have to substitute surrogate measures, suggesting that you will know the connection to the impact. For example, healthcare professionals involved in diabetic education can show that when a set of behaviors are in place for the diabetic, the major impact of the disease is prevented. The impacts are hospitalizations, clinic costs, emergency room visits, surgeries, amputations, and even death, which have been converted into a monetary value based on previous studies. You don't have to wait for the long-term impact in many situations. The model must contain rules for data collection to help the evaluator make this important decision.

Needs Assessments versus Activities

The logic model process starts with input, the resources needed to make the program successful. The resources are usually people, time, and money. However, the program should start with a problem or an opportunity. The classic logic model assumes that a problem or opportunity has been identified and the activities are an attempt to pinpoint the details of the solution to address it. In many cases, the solution is predetermined by the requestor or donor. Some attempt may be needed to connect the problem or opportunity to business measures and focus on making sure that the right solution is being implemented to correct the problem once the solution is obvious. This could be labeled *needs assessment*, which involves clearly understanding the desired outcome and the right solution to drive that outcome. This must be accomplished quickly to connect to the desired impact. Then the activities focus on understanding what is needed to drive that impact. The process is not so clear in the classic logic model, and most of the other models rarely address alignment and needs assessment.

Lack of Focus on Results

Some researchers have suggested that the evaluation process should not influence the results. This assumption forces evaluators to function as auditors, essentially surprising the participants in the program to see how things are working, sometimes taking extreme measures not to influence the results. This thinking is faulty in today's environment. Even in the auditing situation, the fact that a program may be audited does influence the results because participants know they will ultimately be accountable. When an evaluation plan is shared with the group, there will be some expectation of what will be evaluated and that will influence the results.

In reality, you want to influence the results. Ideally, you need a system in place that will help the participants drive the desired results. For example, action planning is an important technique in some programs to collect the data for application and impact evaluation. In the planning process, the action plan begins with an impact measure that should improve. Then, the action plan indicates what the participant will be doing to reach that objective. For example, consider the action plan that is built into the counseling system in the opening story of Chapter 2. There, the action plan starts with the end in mind (resolving their issue) and includes the steps to take to achieve that goal. If the objective is to land a job, the impact is to become employed in the right job with the desired salary. The action steps define what this participant will do to secure that job. It serves as evaluation data because the steps that are taken clearly provide data on what participants are doing (application), and the impact is recorded on the plan itself, showing what is achieved as impact. Although it is a data collection method, it has a powerful effect on the outcome.

We have conducted studies about the power of having an action planning process compared to not having an action planning process. As you can imagine, action planning drives more success. Although it is perhaps designed to collect the data needed to see the value of the program, when this evaluation tool is used, it has a positive effect on application and impact. With this, we are sometimes asked by executives, "*It appears that your data collection process influences the results of the program?*" We always answer *yes* and ask them if they have a problem with that issue from their prospective. Their answer is usually *no*. The usual conclusion from the executive is, "*let's always put these kinds of processes in place.*" Let's not surprise participants with data collection. Instead, let's have them expecting the data collection with much detail about what success should look like when the data are collected. This has a huge impact on getting participants to take action at Level 3 where the chain of value often breaks.

This phenomenon is even more pronounced when you consider the power of having application and impact objectives for the program. Application objectives define what will be accomplished by the participant involved in the program. Impact objectives indicate why the program exists, the desired impact. These objectives should evolve from the activities in a classic logic model. They, in effect, cause more performance. By design, an objective defines success at each level. When the objectives are developed for reaction, learning, application, and impact, a clear path to success is provided, a path that influences results. This is *why* the objectives are in place. We have to remove the stigma that an evaluation system shouldn't influence results.

Inability to "Show the Money"

As the opening stories in the first three chapters illustrate, the client has expressed a need to see the monetary value of the program. While this is not needed in most programs, sometimes it is needed, particularly when funding is critical or hard to secure and when the efficient use of funds in an issue. The funder often is suggesting that, "If you can show me the money from this program, I can do my own ROI calculation because I know what I'm paying for it." Essentially, this is reflecting the need for ROI. Some evaluators think that this request is misplaced, distasteful, and unnecessary.

In the opening story of Chapter 1, you could easily say that it is a potentially distasteful situation when chaplains have to show the monetary value of what they do. In reality, they can and they are. In the healthcare system, where most of the chaplains in that story are situated, the chaplains have data that suggest they make a difference in patient outcomes (getting well), length of stay, patient safety, and readmissions. In the American healthcare system, all of these can be converted to money. When these impacts are converted to money, it's helpful for the funder who knows what it's costing them for the chaplains.

Additionally, the chaplains also suggest they are helping the staff and have influenced staff turnover. Hospital employees must cope with many difficult situations in the daily ground, and the chaplain provides needed comfort and reassurance. That makes a difference in their intent to stay with the hospital. Because of the chaplain's support, a portion of employee retention can be claimed, which can easily be converted to money.

Chaplains work with the patients and their families, and patient satisfaction is improved because the chaplain is there helping them to cope with injury or illness, explaining the situation, and providing reassurances. This comforting translates directly into increased patient satisfaction. In the American healthcare system, one factor for reimbursement of charges is now the patient satisfaction. Higher levels of patient satisfaction influence the reimbursement for some procedures. Patient satisfaction is easily converted to money.

This example illustrates that it is possible to show the monetary value for this role in a healthcare situation. This type of analysis may make the difference on whether or not chaplaincy can continue to exist in healthcare settings.

Some evaluators refuse to go down this path, and this may be destroying or killing programs. Capability to show the money needs to be part of the process. Distasteful as it may seem, it is the reality in many organizations—and the reality of some funding. Organizations, governments, NGOs, and nonprofits don't have unlimited budgets and must push some programs to this level of evaluation to understand how budgets are used efficiently.

In many situations, a measure cannot be converted to money, but is still an important measure, an intangible. For example, many of the UN programs are aimed at saving lives, from UN peacekeeping to the World Health Organization, UN Aids, and UN Environment—it's all about saving lives. Also, the existence of the Organization for the Prohibition of Chemical Weapons (OPCW) is based on the lives they have saved since the agency was created. OPCW was created by the UN, but it is not a UN agency. It had three goals: to stop the production of chemical weapons, to decrease and eliminate the stockpile of chemical weapons, and to prepare countries for a chemical attack. The value of this organization has been questioned by the countries that provide funding. It is possible to calculate the value. The OPCW can develop a credible estimate of the number of lives that have been saved because of their efforts. To show value for money, the value of a human life is needed. Should we place a monetary value on human lives? The quick answer is that it's possible, but should we?

There has been a tremendous amount of work in this area, particularly by insurance companies as they pay for death claims. For example, compensation paid to the families of the victims of the 9/11 terrorist attacks was based on the victims' occupations and where they were in their careers, accounting for income, age, career, and position. These were all factors that contributed to the worth of that individual at the time that life was taken. It becomes very distasteful when you consider third world countries and realize that the lives there may not be as valuable as the lives in highly developed countries. We have found values ranging from $300,000 to $9,000,000. While it's distasteful, it is also the reality. In the UN system, we usually leave the human life as an intangible in our studies. Obviously, it's a critical measure for those whose lives were saved or for the families of those who died. However, because of the emotion and difficulty in dealing with the issue, we rarely place a monetary value on it.

Other measures are difficult to measure and value, such as teamwork, image, reputation, stress, and family cohesiveness. Even items than can be measured, such as complaints, alliances, and partnerships, may be difficult to convert to monetary terms. When that's the case, the measure is intangible. A model is needed that clearly distinguishes impacts into two categories: the tangible, which can be converted to money; the intangible, that cannot be converted to money credibly with a reasonable amount of resources.

Not CEO- and CFO-Friendly

An evaluation system is usually created with certain stakeholders in mind. Most were created to make sure it is a valid and reliable process because researchers and academicians created most models. Having a model based on sound principles and foundations that can withstand the scrutiny of the academic and research community is essential. A model must be valid and reliable; otherwise, it's not effective.

Some models focus on the users, recognizing that they may not have advanced degrees. The users are the evaluators in the field who are implementing the evaluation system, who may not have any evaluation training at all. A model must be user-friendly and void of very complex processes. The use of complex statistical techniques should be the exception, not the rule. This is particularly important for evaluations in a society where we are moving toward simplicity. This requirement could be a concern if efforts to make it easy will decrease the validity. Some models are user-friendly and offer a reliable and valid process.

Still, there is another important group of stakeholders—the donors, sponsors, clients, and supporters who need to see impact data and ROI. Not enough attention has been placed on development of an evaluation model to satisfy the needs of donors and funders, particularly those who are at the top of an organization (e.g., CEO, top administrator, or managing director). These executives are very concerned about having data that they can understand and that they see as valuable to them and the organization. In the last two decades, the chief financial officer (CFO), the manager of finance, or the finance minister may be the one who needs to see the value.

For example, we evaluated the success of the eLearning investment at King Khalid University in Abha, Saudi Arabia, a very large government university with about 60,000 students. Tuition was provided free to citizens of Saudi Arabia, and they were paid a stipend for attending. As expected, this often creates some issues about the motivation to learn. Many students were there for the money and not necessarily for learning. At the same time, the university was switching much of its content into eLearning formats. When the motivation to learn is an issue, learning can rapidly deteriorate with eLearning unless some processes are put into place to make it work. With eLearning investment in the university continuing to grow, the minister of finance wanted to know the ROI of this investment. The financial section of the government is usually concerned about expenditures and the value received for the money.

Internally in an organization, the CFO is the driver of value for money these days. Even in government agencies, having a process that will meet their needs is very important. The process must be very systematic and connected to data that CFOs can appreciate and understand. The assumptions and standards for using the model must be very conservative, essentially taking the error out of the process with worst-case scenarios. If CFOs don't buy into the model, they won't believe the data that it delivers. Very few evaluation models and systems have specifically been designed with that audience in mind. Yet that audience, the top executives, chief financial officers, and donors are the groups that are demanding more accountability, as can be seen in the opening stories of the first three chapters of this book. Your model must address their needs.

Managing Resources for Evaluation

Obviously, there is much pressure on evaluators to keep their costs low. The cost of evaluation is increasing because of the cost of staff, time, and external resources. Consequently, evaluators are facing much scrutiny about the money being spent on evaluation. Evaluation models should help with this issue of controlling evaluation costs.

Two processes can be addressed in model design. First, the models should provide shortcuts that can be taken when resources are tight. What can be streamlined? What can be simplified or omitted? For example, we suggest that every evaluation system always require a process to isolate the effects of the program on the impact data. This is best achieved by using a classic, experimental-versus-control-group evaluation. Sometimes, mathematical modeling can be used. But if we absolutely can't afford that, do we take some shortcuts? Yes, is the appropriate answer. You can use expert estimation adjusted for error, which is proven to be effective and even a little more conservative than classic experimental versus control group analysis. This topic will be covered later in this book and is an excellent way to take a shortcut, if necessary. Although we always want to use the most credible process, if for some reason we cannot, we need some alternatives. Shortcuts should be possible and designed into the model.

The second way that costs can be controlled is by recognizing that not every program needs to be evaluated completely through the value chain. If the evaluation for each program was pushed all the way to the impact level, far too many resources would be consumed by the evaluation system. That is not appropriate or necessary. Criteria should be established for deciding where to stop the evaluation. Programs that are very expensive and strategic, with large audiences that attract interest with the top administrators and executives, need to be evaluated to impact and ROI. If the evaluation is conducted to ensure a program is in compliance with a rule or regulation, then you need to evaluate at the level for the definition of compliance. Sometimes that simply means that participants need to have knowledge, which is Level 2, Learning. Evaluation models must be smart about evaluation costs and be able to manage those resources to keep the costs low.

"Capital isn't scarce; vision is." – Sam Walton

Lack of Focus on Process Improvement

Our friends in the British government explained a dysfunctional approach: When a new program is approved by Parliament, a percentage of the budget is allocated to evaluation. The evaluators evaluate the program and send in a report, usually several years after a program is initiated, and the results show that it didn't work. At that point, no one really cares. The sponsors have moved on and other programs are being funded. This is a vicious cycle that affects several elements in the evaluation model, and one of those is failure to focus on results throughout the process.

Every evaluation model should have a process improvement focus, not just suggesting that changes be made when disappointing results are revealed, but a relentless focus on making improvements, even when results are satisfactory; the aim should be to look for better ways to do it. The chain of value suggests there are opportunities for making changes at each level of outcome. If participants do not have the proper reaction, the program should be adjusted to resolve the reaction issues or at least a plan should be in place to improve reaction later. If participants didn't learn how to make the program successful, then there is no need to continue until the learning issues have been resolved. If the program is not being implemented properly, changes are necessary to put it on track. This process forces changes and improvements at every level. At the end, if the results are there, adjustments are made to improve the results for the next group or program. If the results are not present, the pressure is there to show what can be done to make it work in the future.

This focus on process improvement is a way to overcome the greatest barrier to evaluation: fear of the outcome. When a program is evaluated, it is usually owned by someone (or a team). The owner has a fear the program may not deliver the desired value and the shortcomings will be exposed in the evaluation study. This accounts for the resistance to evaluation, particularly at the impact and ROI levels. With process improvement as the focus for the model, adjustments are made to ensure that results are delivered. Also, it is usually not the substance or content of the program that is causing the disappointing results, it's something not being done, supported, or available on the job, in the field, at the clinic, at home, etc. This essentially takes the program owner off the hook, to a certain extent, because it is not the program that's a problem. It's the support of the program that's the problem. When evaluation focuses on process improvement, it is not the individuals that we are evaluating, but the performance of the program. If the program is not delivering the value, then adjustments are made.

The Inability to Influence Investment

Evaluation should lead to program improvement, which optimizes the return on investment in the program. Optimization of the investment helps to influence the investment in the future. While this can be a confusing and even controversial issue, the challenge is to help the program owners, developers, implementers, and sponsors know the value, prove the value, and show the value so that they can continue to fund the program, if it's adding desired value. The opening stories from the first three chapters illustrate funding is the issue. Whether funding chaplains in healthcare, counseling for citizens at the food bank, or empowering students in the school system, making the case for funding is the issue.

An evaluation model needs the capability to help keep a successful program alive and improve or discontinue a program that is not adding value. If the evaluation kills a program that could have added value, we may have provided a disservice. Evaluation data needs to be used to improve programs, and when the improvement is realized, a better case for funding is made. As shown in Figure 3.5, measurement takes place in the evaluation phase and improvement will optimize the value of the program. With optimization of ROI, you can make a better case to increase the allocation of funding to programs. If you do that, you have a great evaluation model, one that really adds value, moving completely away from the classic concept of evaluator as an auditor. Incidentally, these days the auditing departments are using their results to make the system or process better. Some auditors have even calculated the impact and ROI of the auditing process by showing what happens when the recommendations are implemented.

Figure 3.5 Optimize Results.

How Does Your Current Model Stack Up?

As suggested in this chapter, most of the current models of measuring and evaluating programs fall short of providing the proper system for accountability, process improvement, and results generation. To meet today's requirements, 10 criteria are identified for an effective evaluation model. Figure 3.6 lists each issue and presents what is needed for improvement. It

Topic	Problem or Issue	What Is Needed	ROI Methodology
Focus of use	Audit focus; punitive slant; surprise nature	Process improvement focus	This is the number one use for the ROI Methodology
Standards	Few, if any, standards exist	Standards needed for consistency and credibility	Twelve standards accepted by users
Types of data	Only one or two data types	Need a balanced set of data	Six types of data representing quantitative, qualitative, financial, and non-financial data
Dynamic adjustments	Not dynamic; does not allow for adjustments early and often in the programcycle	A dynamic process with adjustments made early and often	Adjusts for improvement at four levels and at different timeframes
Connectivity	Not respectful of the chain of value that must exist to achieve a positive impact	Data collected at each stage of the value chain	Every stage has data collection and a method to isolate the program's contribution to impact
Approach	Activity based	Results based	Twelve steps are used to design for results
Conservative nature	Analysis not very conservative	A conservative approach is needed for buy in	Very conservative: CFO and CEO friendly
Simplicity	Not user-friendly; too complex	User friendly, simple steps	Twelve logical steps
Theoretical foundation	Not based on sound principles	Should be based on theoretical framework	Endorsed by hundreds of professors and researchers; grounded in research and practice
Acceptance	Not adopted by many organizations	Should be used by many	More than 5,000 organizations using the ROI Methodology

Figure 3.6 Problems and Opportunities with Current Measurement Systems.

also shows how the ROI Methodology, presented in this book, addresses all 10 of these areas.

Focus of Use

Sometimes evaluation looks like auditing. Usually during a surprise visit, someone checks to see whether the project is working as planned, and a report is generated (usually too late) to indicate that a problem exists. Evaluation of many capital expenditures, for example, is often implemented this way. The project is approved by the board, and after it is completed, a board-mandated follow-up report is produced by internal auditors and presented to the board. This report indicates what is working and not working, often at a point that is too late to make any changes.

Even in government, social sciences, and education, the evaluations are often structured in a similar way. When a program is implemented, an evaluation is conducted, and a detailed report is sent to appropriate authorities. Unfortunately, these reports reveal that many of the programs are not working, and it is too late to do anything about them. Even worse, the people who implemented the program are either no longer there or no longer care. When accountability issues are involved, the evaluation reports usually serve as punitive information to blame the usual suspects or serve as the basis for performance review of those involved.

Standards

Unfortunately, many of the approaches to evaluate projects and programs lack standards unless the project is a capital expenditure, in which case the evaluation process is covered by Generally Accepted Accounting Principles (GAAP). However, most programs are not capital expenditures. In these instances, standards must be employed to ensure consistent application and reliable results. Overall, the standards should provide consistency, conservatism, and cost savings as the project is implemented. Use of standards allows the results of one project to be compared to those of another and the project results to be perceived as credible.

Types of Data

The types of data that must be collected vary. Unfortunately, many programs focus on impact measures alone, showing job creation, patient outcomes, incidents of diseases, student debt load, crime rates, number of homeless people, cost savings, improved productivity, or improved citizen complaints. It is assumed that these measures will change if this program is implemented. More focus is needed on the measures with details on how the impact was achieved. The types of measures should also include intangibles, measures that cannot be converted to money credibly within a reasonable amount of time.

What is needed is a balanced set of data that contains financial and non-financial measures as well as qualitative and quantitative data. Multiple types of data not only show results of investing in projects and programs, but also help explain how the results evolved and how to improve them over time. To effectively capture the return on investment, six types of data are needed: reaction, learning, application, impact, ROI, and intangible benefits.

Dynamic Adjustments

As mentioned earlier, a comprehensive measurement system must allow opportunities to collect data throughout program implementation rather than waiting until it has been fully completed (perhaps only to find out it never worked from the beginning). Reaction and learning data must be captured early and often, if necessary. Application data must be captured when project participants are applying knowledge, skills, and information routinely.

All these data should be used to make adjustments in the program to ensure success, not just to report post-program outcomes at a point that is too late to make a difference. Impact data are collected after routine application has occurred and represent the consequences of implementation. These data should be connected to the program and must be monitored and reviewed in conjunction with the other levels of data. When the connection is made between impact and the project, a credible ROI is calculated.

Connectivity

For many measurement schemes, it is difficult to see the connection between a program and the results. It is often a mystery as to how much of the reported improvement is attributed to the program or even whether a connection exists. Data need to be collected throughout the process so that the chain of impact is validated. In addition, when the impact measure improves, a method is necessary to isolate the effects of the project on the data to validate the connection to the impact measure.

Approach

Too often, the measurement schemes are focused on activities. People are busy. They are involved. Activity is everywhere. However, activities sometimes are not connected to impact. Most programs must be based on achieving results at the impact and, sometimes, ROI level. Not only should the program track results, but also, the steps and processes along the way should focus on results. Driving improvement should be inherent to the measurement process.

By having a measurement process in place, the likelihood of positive results increases. A complete focus on results versus activity improves the chances that people will react positively, change their attitude, and apply necessary actions, which lead to a positive impact on immediate and long-term outcomes.

Conservative Nature

Many assumptions are made during the collection and analysis of data in program evaluation. If these assumptions are not conservative, then the numbers may be overstated and unbelievable, which decreases the likelihood of accuracy and buy in. The conservative approach removes much of the error and doubt. The worst-case scenario is presented. The results, including ROI, will be CFO, CEO, and executive director friendly.

Simplicity

Too often, measurement systems are complex and confusing for practical use, which leaves users skeptical and reluctant to embrace them. The process must be user-friendly, with simple, logical, and sequential steps. It must be void of sophisticated statistical analysis and complicated financial information, at least for most programs. The reality is that most program evaluations are conducted by individuals who are not professional program evaluators. They often lack statistical expertise. It must be user-friendly, especially for those who do not have statistical or financial backgrounds.

Theoretical Foundation

Sometimes measurement systems are not based on sound principles. They use catchy terms and trendy processes that make some researchers and professors skeptical. A measurement system must be based on sound principles and theoretical frameworks. Ideally, it must use accepted processes as it is implemented. The process should be supported by professors and researchers who have used the process with a goal of making the process better.

Acceptance

A measurement system must be used by practitioners in all types of organizations. Too often, the measurement scheme is presented as theoretical but lacks evidence of widespread use. There are more than 100 books on program evaluation with about 50 of them written by ROI Institute authors. Book sales do not translate into use, however. There are many workshops and courses on program evaluation. ROI Institute has trained more than 50,000 managers and professionals in its 25 years of existence. However, attending a workshop or college course does not translate into actual use. The challenge is to track actual use in a completed program evaluation. In 1995, ROI Institute achieved this through its ROI certification process. This process requires participants to complete a program evaluation at the impact and ROI levels, following ROI Institute standards. To date, more than 14,000 individuals have participated in the ROI certification process, with more than 6,000 completing the requirements to become a Certified ROI Professional (CRP).

The ROI Methodology, first described in publications in the 1970s and 1980s (with an entire book devoted to it in 1997), now enjoys more than 6,000 users. It is used in all types of projects and programs. In recent years it has been adopted for green projects, sustainability efforts, and innovation. Now, it is used extensively in governments, nonprofits, universities, and healthcare systems. The success of the ROI Methodology will be highlighted in detail throughout this book with all types of examples of applications. It is a comprehensive process that meets the important needs and challenges of those striving for successful program evaluation.

Requirements for the Value for Money: A Measurement Process

When these requirements are considered, the ROI Methodology developed by ROI Institute meets these requirements. For over two decades, program evaluation practitioners have experimented with the use of the ROI Methodology and have essentially performed a proof of concept for all types of professional fields, showing how the ROI is developed on a variety of programs, not only just in the USA but also in other countries. It is now, through this book, we bring this to the mainstream of professionals in the program evaluation area.

ROI Methodology

ROI Methodology measures the success of programs in all types of organizations: corporations, small businesses, service organizations, universities, cities, states, countries, nongovernmental organizations, nonprofits, universities, healthcare organizations, religious institutions, and associations. The process collects six types of data: reaction, learning, application, impact, ROI, and intangibles. Data are collected, analyzed, and reported using a systematic and logical model. Conservative standards generate results that are both CEO- and CFO-friendly.

The methodology was created and has been continuously improved by ROI Institute, a global center of excellence that focuses exclusively on this methodology. ROI Institute was founded the meet the need to evaluate the results of complex but "softer" noncapital programs. ROI Institute founders are the lead authors of this book.

During the last 25 years, the ROI Methodology has been applied at more than 6,000 client organizations across the globe, through client ROI projects and capability building sessions. ROI Institute executives have authored more than 50 books that explain how the methodology is best applied in a wide range of applications. More than 300 detailed case studies have been published, to show how the method is tailored to the unique needs of client groups.

As a program is implemented, the six types of data, five levels of outcomes plus intangibles are collected. The six types of data can be considered to be leading indicators (Reaction, Learning, and Application) and lagging indicators (Impact, ROI, and Intangible Benefits) as shown in Figure 3.7. For these measures, the focus of the analysis is to make the program matter to an important group. With the last three measures, the focus is on being credible with the analysis. Objectives for each

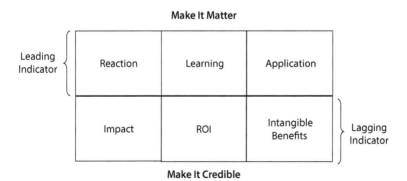

Figure 3.7 The Data from the ROI Methodology.

level are built into the design and planning phase of a project, and these measures are subsequently evaluated during the implementation and post-implementation.

Terminology: Projects, Solutions, Participants

In *The Value for Money*, the term *program* is used to describe a variety of processes that can be evaluated using the ROI Methodology. This is an important issue because readers may vary widely in their perspectives. Individuals involved in technology applications may use the terms *system* and *software* rather than *program*. In public policy, on the other hand, the word *program* is prominent. For a professional meetings and events planner, the word *program* may not be very pertinent, but in human resources, *program* fits quite well. Finding one term that fits all these situations is difficult. However, the term *program* is used in most examples in this book. Figure 3.8 lists these and other terms that may be used depending on the context.

Term	Example	Participant
System	A home-based telehealth system	Nurses
Initiative	A faith-based effort to reduce recidivism	Inmates
Policy	A new preschool policy for disadvantaged citizens	Students
Procedure	A new medical procedure for clinics	Healthcare professionals
Event	A healthy living event	Attendees
Project	A reengineering project for the plastics division	Team members
Meeting	U.S. Coast guard innovation conference	Delegates
Process	A new intake process for claims	Employees
People	Staff additions to the AIDS center	Team members
Tool	A new toolto select volunteers	Recruiters
Program	Leadership for senior executives	Senior executives

Figure 3.8 Terms and Applications.

The term participant is used to describe the person involved in the program, the person who should make it successful. Examples are provided in the figure. Sometimes there are multiple groups as participants.

Final Thoughts

This chapter makes the case for a new evaluation model, describing the different criteria that must be addressed in adopting a new system for program evaluation. Clearly, current models are not working. The funders of programs are restless, and the various supporters and stakeholders need to make sure that value is being delivered so that their participation in the process is at the optimal level. This chapter concluded with a brief introduction to the ROI Methodology, which meets the measurement needs for knowing, proving, and showing the value for money. The good news is that it has been used in program evaluation now for more than two decades, and this book brings it to the mainstream of program evaluation globally. The next chapter provides more detail on this methodology.

4

Introducing the
ROI Methodology

A group of hospitals in the Birmingham, Alabama, metro area were seeking an innovative approach to reduce bloodstream infections in the intensive care unit. Participating hospitals comprised a mix of religious-affiliated, government-owned (city, county, and state), university-affiliated, and private-sector organizations. These hospitals were concerned about the excessive number of central line blood infections that were occurring as a result of a central vascular catheter, inserted into a large vein in the chest, introducing infection.

As the group developed and implemented a new set of procedures for reducing the number of infections, they realized that the procedures represented a cultural shift in the way they operated. This comprehensive, unit-based safety program required participants to use checklists, gain knowledge, double-check, and speak up. For the new procedures to be successful, various levels of data were needed beyond the traditional monitoring of infections, length of stay, and costs associated with these infections. Successive sets of data were needed that would examine the team's reaction to the new procedures, the extent of learning of new processes and procedures, and correct application of new procedures and tools, all of which are aimed at the impact: infections, mortality rates, length of stay, and operating costs. This group envisioned sets of data that represented a chain of impact that must be present for the project to be effective. These sets represent four levels of outcome data (reaction, learning, application, and impact). A fifth level, financial ROI, is possible and is sometimes necessary to calculate in today's environment. Collecting data along these levels and using a method to isolate the effects of this program from other factors provides comprehensive data to show the impact of this program. Figure 4.1 shows the types of data from this study [1].

The richness of the ROI Methodology is inherent in the types of data monitored during the implementation of a particular program. These data are categorized by levels. The process for showing monetary value, including ROI, is a comprehensive, systematic methodology that includes defining the types of data, conducting an initial analysis, developing objectives, forecasting value (including ROI), using the ROI process model, and implementing and sustaining the process. The following sections briefly describe the approach necessary to achieve the level of accountability demanded in today's business climate.

Types of Data

An attempt to summarize what's needed in the innovation area brings into focus some very key issues that have been presented in the previous two chapters, as well as in this chapter. This must be considered from perspectives of principal funders of programs, as well as the need for the various stakeholders who are involved. Add to this the need to have a systematic, logical flow of data for an evaluation and you have the data set in Figure 4.2 with input into the process and the six categories of data arranged in a logical chain of value, moving from input through five levels of outcomes, including the financial ROI.

Input

In any program, there is input. This is usually the people who are involved, both in terms of number and the time they're involved in the activity, and the cost of the process. This is important because having the right

Project: The Comprehensive Unit Based Safety Program

Description: Infections in the bloodstream can be dangerous and hard to treat. According to the Centers for Disease Control and Prevention, almost 250,000 occur in U.S. hospitals each year, often in patients who have a central vascular catheter, a tube inserted into a large vein in the chest, which may be used to provide medication or fluids or check blood oxygen levels and other vital signs. The catheters are very important in treatment but inserting them correctly and keeping the entry site and dressings clean can be complicated.

The Comprehensive Unit Based Safety Program is focused on reducing central blood line infections in intensive care units. The hospital instituted a checklist system that sets up specific steps for doctors, nurses, and technicians to take when inserting and managing a central line. The checklists give nurses explicit permission to challenge their superiors—including doctors—if they don't follow the steps without fear of reprisal. They also require workers to assess each day whether a centralline catheter needs to remain in place or can be removed, which reduces the patient's risk of infection.

Levels	Objectives
Level 0—Input	• All doctors, nurses, and technicians (participants) in the intensive care units are involved.
Level 1—Reaction	All participants must see this program as: • Necessary • Important • Feasible • Practical.
Level 2—Learning	• All participants must demonstrate knowledge of the checklist and new procedures. • Participants must practice "speak up" conversations with colleagues and visitors.
Level 3—Application	• Checklist will be monitored. • The use of new procedures will be observed. • Extent of "speak up" conversations will be collected.
Level 4—Impact	• Central line bloodstream infections will be reduced by 50 percent in six months. • Mortality rates reduced by five percent. • Days in hospital reduced by two percent. • ICU costs reduced by three percent.
Level 5—ROI	• ROI objective is 25 percent.

Source: Data from Alabama Hospital Association/ROI Institute, Inc.

Figure 4.1 Example of Levels of Evaluation.

people involved is critical. Ideally, we want people involved who want to be involved in an engaged way. Therefore, the starting point for knowing, showing, and proving the value is having the right people involved at the right time with the right amount of time available and in the right program. Input is important, but doesn't speak to the outcomes, the results.

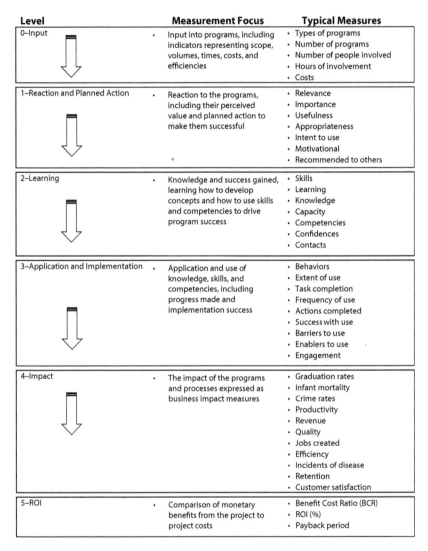

Level	Measurement Focus	Typical Measures
0–Input	• Input into programs, including indicators representing scope, volumes, times, costs, and efficiencies	• Types of programs • Number of programs • Number of people involved • Hours of involvement • Costs
1–Reaction and Planned Action	• Reaction to the programs, including their perceived value and planned action to make them successful	• Relevance • Importance • Usefulness • Appropriateness • Intent to use • Motivational • Recommended to others
2–Learning	• Knowledge and success gained, learning how to develop concepts and how to use skills and competencies to drive program success	• Skills • Learning • Knowledge • Capacity • Competencies • Confidences • Contacts
3–Application and Implementation	• Application and use of knowledge, skills, and competencies, including progress made and implementation success	• Behaviors • Extent of use • Task completion • Frequency of use • Actions completed • Success with use • Barriers to use • Enablers to use • Engagement
4–Impact	• The impact of the programs and processes expressed as business impact measures	• Graduation rates • Infant mortality • Crime rates • Productivity • Revenue • Quality • Jobs created • Efficiency • Incidents of disease • Retention • Customer satisfaction
5–ROI	• Comparison of monetary benefits from the project to project costs	• Benefit Cost Ratio (BCR) • ROI (%) • Payback period

Figure 4.2 Six Categories of Data.

Reaction and Planned Action

Reaction is often omitted from most current models of measurement under the assumption that people involved in a program are involved because they want to be. They see value in the program and they see it as important to their success as well as the success of the owner. But that may be a false assumption. The key is to collect data at this level, to make sure that the participants involved in the program see it as relevant to their situation, important to their individual success and to the success of others. Reaction data should also be useful, helpful, and appropriate—and should show intent to make the program successful because participants are motivated to do it. Perhaps they would even recommend others be involved as well.

Without this proper reaction, their efforts will be minimal at best. Some of the participants involved in a program may see it as a waste of time or money. Others would see these efforts as additional, unnecessary work. Still others may see the program as misguided and inappropriate. In these cases, the results may not materialize. Consequently, our first set of data is a very important first outcome level.

Learning

The next logical step is learning, and this is closely related to reaction. Reaction will be influenced by what participants in the program are learning about the process that they're involved in, the rules and the conditions under which they are operating, the tips to make the program successful, and how to overcome the barriers. The more they know, the more the resistance reduces and motivation increases.

It's all about learning new ways, new processes, and new situations through exploring, experimenting, and adjusting. Learning is critical, and we must measure it. Learning measurements ensure that the knowledge, skills, and competencies are there, with the confidence to make it work, and the contacts to make it successful. Learning measurement is necessary but is still a long way from the end game.

> *"I have spent more time learning from the things that didn't work than I have spent learning from the things that do work."*
> *– Thomas Edison*

Application and Implementation

For some stakeholders, the challenge of program success is at this level. Participants are doing something. They're trying new procedures, testing new concepts, completing tasks, exploring options, and identifying possibilities. The participants are mobilized, making progress, and taking action. This is helpful because at this level of outcome, resistance has been reduced to a certain extent and the inertia of getting people to do something has been overcome. It's also critical because programs must follow certain procedures. Application and implementation includes all processes and procedures necessary to make the program successful, such as tasks, actions, checklists, and policies. This is powerful, and it can only be accomplished when participants learn what to do to make the program successful.

Impact

The level is critical to donors and sponsors. The impact is the consequence of actions, and includes increased productivity, improved quality, or improved times. These impacts are in the system, and they define the organization. In governments, NGOs, and nonprofits, impacts include patient outcomes, jobs secured, students graduated, infant mortality rates, addictions, crime rates, and auto accidents. The impacts will make the difference. Not only do we have the tangible impacts that we've just described, but the intangible ones as well. These usually include customer satisfaction, image, stress, patient satisfaction, teamwork, collaboration, quality of life, and alliances. These impacts are important but maybe not easily converted to money, credibility.

Return on Investment

As mentioned earlier, the return on investment is needed in some programs, and this can be measured in three very common ways. One is the benefit-cost ratio, which is the monetary benefits from the program divided by the cost of the program. Benefit-cost analysis has been used for centuries and is meaningful to many executives, particularly those in nonprofits, governments, and NGOs.

Next, there's the ROI, expressed as a percentage, which is the net benefits divided by the cost times 100. The net benefits are the monetary benefits minus the project costs. This is a very common measure in businesses and often is even understood by consumers, as they clearly see their ROI for investing their money in a savings account in a financial institution. The ROI formula is derived from the finance and accounting field. ROI measures keep the CFO and the CEO happy. And it's the ultimate accountability. For most executives, it shows the efficient use of funds. Just getting the impact is one thing but seeing how this could be achieved with less cost is another. The higher your ROI, the more efficient the use of the funds. Finally, the payback period is another possibility, and this is a calculation of how long it takes to get the money back from this investment. This is also a financial measure.

"The ROI is a way to keep score." – Warren Buffett

So, there you have it. Six categories of data that are necessary, arranged in a logical flow so that one level or one category is a precondition for the others. This is a foundation that will be critical for the material in the book, but there's more.

The Initial Analysis

Our research suggests that the number-one reason for programs failing is lack of alignment with the business. The first opportunity to obtain business alignment is in the initial analysis. Several steps are taken to make sure the program is absolutely necessary. As shown in Figure 4.3, this is the beginning of the complete, sequential model representing the ROI Methodology. The first step in this analysis examines the potential payoff of the program. Is this a problem worth solving or an opportunity worth pursuing? Is the program worthy of implementation? For many situations, the answer is obvious: *Yes*, the program is worthy because of its critical nature, its relevance to the issue at hand, or its effectiveness in tackling a major problem or opportunity affecting the organization or community.

The next step is to ensure that the program is connected to one or more impact (business) measures. Defined are the measures that must improve with the overall success of the program. Sometimes the measure is obvious; other times, it is not.

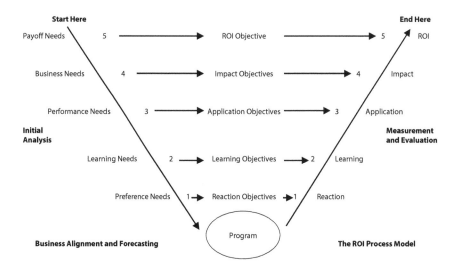

Figure 4.3 The ROI Methodology.

Next, the performance needs are examined, with the question: "What must we do to influence the business measures defined previously?" This step aligns the program with the business and may involve a series of analytical tools to solve the problem, analyze the cause of the problem, and ensure that the program is connected with business improvement in some way. This may appear to be quite complex, but in fact is a simple approach. A logical series of questions helps: What is keeping the business measure from being where it needs to be? If it is a problem, what is its cause? If it is an opportunity, what is hindering the measure from moving in the right direction? This step is critical because it provides the link to the program.

After performance needs have been determined, the learning needs are examined next by asking: What specific skills or knowledge need to change or improve so that performance can change? Every program involves a learning component, and this step defines what the participants or users must know and be able to do to make the program successful. The needed knowledge may be as simple as understanding a policy or be as complicated as learning many new competencies.

The final step is pinpointing the perceived value of the program. These are the preference needs. This is important to ensure that necessary knowledge will be acquired, and performance will solve the problem. Participants in the project should see it as important (to their success, health, family, or work; to customers, patients, or refugees; to the organization, community, or country), relevant (to the participant, organization, or situation), and necessary (to their work, for survival, or for growth). This level of analysis could also involve issues surrounding the scope, timing, structure, method, and budget for program implementation and delivery.

Collectively, these steps clearly define the issues that led to initiation of the project. When these preliminary steps are completed, the project can be positioned to achieve its intended results. The next two chapters focus on alignment and selecting the proper solution.

Understanding the need for a program is critical to positioning that project for success. Positioning a program requires the development of clear, specific objectives that are communicated to all stakeholders. Objectives should be developed for each level of need and should define success at each level, answering the question: "How will we know the need has been met?" If the criteria of success are not communicated early and often, process participants will go through the motions, with little change resulting. Developing detailed objectives with clear measures of success will position the project to achieve its ultimate objective.

Before a project or program is launched, forecasting the outcomes may be important to ensure that adjustments can be made, or alternative solutions can be investigated. This forecast can be simple, relying on the individuals closest to the situation, or it can be a more detailed analysis of the situation and expected outcome. Recently, forecasting has become a critical tool for program sponsors who need evidence that the program will be successful, before they are willing to invest in it. Because of its importance, forecasting is the sole focus of Chapter 16.

Using Design Thinking to Deliver and Measure Results

It is useful to think about using an innovation technique to deliver the value from a program or project and capture the data. A very popular concept in innovation is design thinking. This process rests on the assumption that when success is clearly defined, the entire team designs for that definition of success. If you want higher graduation rates, everyone works on that. If you want low costs, everyone is focused on that issue. If you want to reduce crime rates, the focus is there for every stakeholder. For most programs, success is achieved when the impact has occurred. This can mean low costs in a new product, higher graduation rates, or less crime.

With that success defined, the team works through a series of steps, using design thinking principles to reach the desired success. Although design thinking had its beginnings a few decades ago with the first book written in 1987, it really gained popularity with the book, *Change by Design,* by Tim Brown with IDEO [2]. A more recent book seemed to broaden the scope and the flexibility of the process, *Design Thinking for Strategic Innovation* [3]. Figure 4.4 lists some of the common design thinking principles, though they're not the same from one author to another. This figure lists 10 principles that seem to be universal, taking the first eight principles and placing them in the steps to implement a program. This creates a model to design for results, capture that data, and make the case for more investment [4]. This is fully described in Figure 4.5. For each of these steps, the design thinking principle used is highlighted. These steps form the structure for the ROI Methodology, which is an enhanced logic model.

> *"Every system is perfectly designed to achieve exactly the results it gets."* – W. Edward Deming

Basic Principles

1. A problem-solving approach to handle problems on a systems level
2. A mindset for curiosity and inquiry
3. A framework to balance needs and feasibility
4. A way to take on design challenges by applying empathy
5. A culture that fosters exploration and experimentation
6. A fixed process and a tool kit
7. A storytelling process to inspire senior executives
8. A new competitive logic of business strategy
9. A means to solve complex or wicked problems
10. A means to reduce risks

Mootee, Idris. (2013). Design Thinking for Strategic Innovation. Hoboken, NJ: Wiley.

Figure 4.4 Design Thinking.

The ROI Process Model

The challenge for many program leaders is to collect a variety of data along a chain of impact that shows the program's value. Figure 4.6 displays the sequential steps that lead to data categorized by the five levels of outcome data using the design thinking concepts. This figure shows the ROI Methodology, a step-by-step process beginning with the *why* and concluding with optimizing the results [5].

Plan the Evaluation

The first step of the ROI Methodology is business impact, connecting the program to important impact measures. *Start with Why* is Chapter 5. The next step is to select the proper solution to improve the impact measure. This is the program and is in Chapter 6, *Make it Feasible*. The third step involves the actions to define and plan for success. It involves defining success, setting objectives, and clarifying roles of the stakeholders to deliver success. This phase also involves several procedures, including understanding the purpose of the evaluation, confirming the feasibility of the planned approach, planning data collection and analysis, and outlining the details of the project. Chapter 7 covers *Expect Success*.

#1 - Start with Why: Align Programs with the Business

In this step, the design thinking principle is to use a problem-solving approach at the systems level. The first step is defining clearly why we're pursuing the program, and this is usually one or more impact measures,

1. Start with Why: Align Programs with the Business
- Alignment is the key
- Is it a problem or opportunity?
- Need specific business measure(s)

> Design Thinking Principle:
> A problem solving approach to handle problems on a systems level

2. Make it Feasible: Select the Right Solution
- What are we doing (or not doing) that's influencing the impact measure?
- How can we achieve this performance?

> Design Thinking Principle:
> A mindset for curiosity and inquiry

3. Expect Success: Design for Results
- Set objectives at multiple levels
- Define success
- Expand responsibilities

> Design Thinking Principle:
> A framework to balance needs and feasibility

4. Make it Matter: Design for Input, Reaction, and Learning
- Focus on the objectives
- Think about ROI
- Make it relevant
- Make it important
- Make it action-oriented

> Design Thinking Principle:
> A way to take on design challenges by applying empathy

5. Make it Stick: Design for Application and Impact
- Focus on objectives
- Ensure the application of the program
- Design application tools
- Collect data

> Design Thinking Principle:
> A culture that fosters exploration and experimentation

6. Make It Credible: Measure Results and Calculating ROI
- Isolating the effects of projects
- Converting data to money
- Tabulating costs
- Calculating ROI

> Design Thinking Principle:
> A fixed process and a tool kit

7. Tell the Story: Communicate Results to Key Stakeholders
- Define audience
- Identify why they need it
- Select method
- Move quickly
- Consider one-page summary

> Design Thinking Principle:
> A storytelling process to inspire senior executives

8. Optimize Results: Use Black Box Thinking to Increase Funding
- Measure
- Improve
- Fund

> Design Thinking Principle:
> A new competitive logic of business strategy

Taken from Phillips, Patti P. and Jack J. Phillips. (2017). *The Business Case for Learning: Using Design Thinking to Deliver Business Results and Increase the Investment in Talent Development.* West Chester, PA: HRDQ and ATD Press.

Figure 4.5 Designing for Results.

described earlier. For many proposed programs, the impact is clearly known. For the public sector, a homeless program is reducing the number of homeless, a jobs program is creating jobs, a drug awareness program is reducing incidents of drug addiction, and a recidivism program is reducing incidents of returning to prison. Inside an organization, a marketing program may be securing new clients, a quality program may be reducing rework or waste, and a safety program may be reducing lost time accidents.

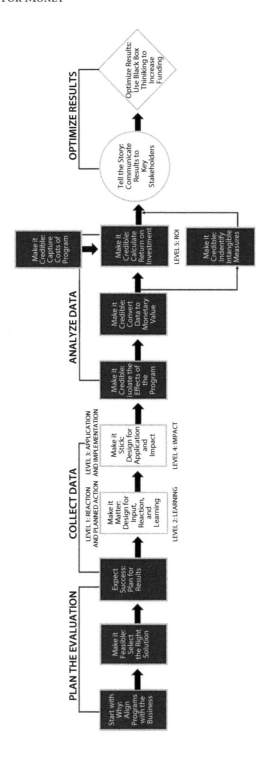

Figure 4.6 The ROI Methodology.

In some programs where new issues are tackled, the impact may not be clearly known, but the general categories of impact should certainly be identifiable. Essentially, this requires the program evaluator to ask the question: is it a problem we're trying to solve, or an opportunity we want to pursue? For example, the creators of Uber wanted a lower cost, more convenient, and efficient way to catch a ride from one place to another. The problem was that it was costing too much and taking too long for the ride. Taxis are inefficient and expensive. At the same time, they saw a great opportunity to build loyal customers, provide a great experience, and not only solve the problem of time and costs, but for comfort and experience. In this step, it's important to have as many specific measures identified as possible.

#2 - Make it Feasible: Select the Right Solution

In this step, the design thinking principle is a mindset for curiosity and inquiry. This means the way in which the program unfolds is identified. If you want to reduce domestic violence in Kazakhstan, what is the most feasible solution? Is legislation needed? Is a communication program needed? What is the right solution to get there? This defines what people will be experiencing and accomplishing as they are involved in the process. If it's tackling an existing process, is there a clear indication that what we're doing now is not working? Or, are we not doing now something that would make the impact measure improve? For example, if victims are not reporting incidents of domestic violence in Kazakhstan, what is needed to make that happen? The solution may be to create a law to make domestic violence illegal and require reporting incidents to the local police.

#3 - Expect Success: Design for Results

Four issues are addressed here. First, this step requires the success definition to be developed, particularly for the participants in the program, and this is usually at the impact level. The second issue is to make sure objectives are set for the program along the levels of outcomes mentioned in the previous data categories. The objectives at the application and impact level indicate what the individuals involved in the program will be doing to make the program successful and the impact that should be realized. The third issue is that this definition of success is provided to all the designers, developers, and other team members who are supporting the program. All of these stakeholders can clearly see what will be achieved and their role in making it successful. They will also design for the outcome. Lastly, the fourth issue is to complete the planning documents: the data collection plan, the ROI analysis plan, and the project plan.

"Limitations live only in our minds. But if we use our imaginations, our possibilities become limitless." – Jamie Paolinetti

Collect Data

Data collection is central to the ROI Methodology. Two steps are involved to verify success at various levels. Chapter 8, *Make it Matter*, measures success at Levels 0 (input), 1 (reaction), and 2 (learning). Chapter 9, *Make it Stick*, involves data collection to measure success at Levels 3 (application) and 4 (impact). Both hard data (representing output, quality, cost, and time) and soft data (including satisfaction, happiness, and image) are collected. Data are collected using a variety of methods, including:

- Surveys
- Questionnaires
- Tests
- Observations
- Interviews
- Focus groups
- Action plans
- Performance contracts
- Business performance monitoring

The important challenge in data collection is to select the method or methods appropriate for the setting and the specific program, within the time and budget constraints of the organization.

#4 - Make it Matter: Design for Input, Reaction, and Learning

In this step, the design thinking principle is a way to take on design challenges by applying empathy. Here, all members of the team are placing themselves in the position of the people who will use and support the program. In the Uber example, this requires the designers and developers working on the technology to think about the driver and how this technology can be used without being distracting and without any delays. Also, thinking about the customer, the customer experience must be designed from their perspective. They may be in a hurry, they may be at a location not easy to find, and they need to know not only an accurate description of when someone will be there, but where they are now and the progress they're making to pick them up. This step is focusing on making sure that the program will be relevant, important to the parties involved, and it's something that is action-oriented. It's something that they will do to make this work.

#5 - *Make it Stick: Design for Application and Impact*

The design thinking principle applied here is to create a culture that fosters exploration and experimentation. In this process, the designers and developers must do what's necessary to achieve success. They're following through on the plans, they're taking the steps, and there is action to achieve what needs to be accomplished to meet the end goal, the impact. They are exploring what works and does not work. This is essentially transferring what needs to be done into the environment where it is actually being done now; transferring it to the workplace, community, patient, or organization. This requires data collection to make sure the program is operating smoothly, and built-in tools are available to measure, drive, and influence the success at the application and impact levels.

Analyze Data

In this series of five steps with four chapters, the design thinking principle is using a fixed process and a toolkit, which are the steps in the ROI Methodology. These steps produce data that is important to all stakeholders, but particularly those who fund the program. These steps show the actual business results achieved with the program and the calculated financial ROI of this investment in the program.

#6 - *Make it Credible: Isolate the Effects of the Program*

An often-overlooked issue in evaluation is the process of isolating the effects of the program. In the next step, specific strategies are explored to determine the amount of outcome performance directly related to the project. This step is essential because many factors can influence performance data. The specific strategies of this step pinpoint the amount of improvement directly related to the program, resulting in increased accuracy and credibility of ROI calculations. The following techniques have been used by program evaluators to tackle this important issue:

- Control group analysis
- Trend line analysis
- Mathematical modeling
- Participant estimates
- Manager or significant other estimates
- Senior management estimates
- Experts' input
- Customer input

Collectively, these techniques provide a comprehensive set of tools to handle the important and critical issue of isolating the effects of the program. Chapter 10, *Make it Credible: Isolate the Effects of the Program*, is devoted to this important step in the ROI Methodology.

#7 - Make it Credible: Convert Data to Monetary Value

To calculate the return on investment impact data are converted to monetary values and compared with program costs. This requires a value be placed on each unit of impact data connected with the program. Many techniques are available to convert data to monetary values. The specific technique selected depends on the type of data and the situation. The techniques include:

- Use the value add of output data, as standard values
- Use the cost of quality as a standard value
- Convert time savings to wage and employee benefits (standard value)
- Calculate the value using an analysis of historical costs
- Use internal and external experts to provide value
- Search external databases for the value
- Use participant estimates
- Use manager estimates
- Locate soft measures mathematically linked to easy to value measures

This step in the ROI model is absolutely necessary to determine the monetary benefits of a program. The process is challenging, particularly with soft data, but can be methodically accomplished using one or more of these strategies. Because of its importance, this step in the ROI Methodology is described in detail in Chapter 11, *Make it Credible: Convert Data to Money*.

#8 - Make it Credible: Identify Intangible Benefits

In addition to tangible, monetary benefits, the intangible benefits—those not converted to money—are identified for most programs. Intangible benefits include items such as:

- Enhanced work-life balance
- Improved image
- Less stress
- Increased engagement
- Improved quality of life
- Increased brand awareness
- Improved health status
- Improved networking
- Enhanced patient satisfaction
- Improved service
- Fewer complaints
- Reduced conflict

During data analysis, every attempt is made to convert all data to monetary values. All hard data—such as output, quality, and time—are converted to monetary values. The conversion of soft data is also attempted for each data item. However, if the process used for conversion is too subjective or inaccurate, and the resulting values lose credibility in the process, then the data are listed as intangible benefits with the appropriate explanation. For some programs, intangible, nonmonetary benefits are extremely valuable, and often carry as much influence as the hard data items. Chapter 12, *Make it Credible: Identify Intangible Benefits*, is devoted to the intangible benefits.

#9 - Make it Credible: Capture Costs of Projects

An important part of the ROI equation is the denominator, the calculation of program costs. Tabulating the costs involves monitoring or developing all the related costs of the program targeted for the ROI calculation. Among the cost components to be included are:

- Initial analysis costs
- Cost to design and develop the program
- Cost of program materials
- Costs for the program team
- Cost of the facilities for the program
- Travel, lodging, and meal costs for the participants and team members
- Participants' salaries (including employee benefits)
- Facilitator costs, if appropriate
- Administrative and overhead costs, allocated in some convenient way
- Evaluation costs

The conservative approach is to include all these costs so the total is fully loaded. Chapter 13, *Make it Credible: Capture Costs of the Program and Calculate ROI*, includes this step in the ROI Methodology.

#10 - Make it Credible: Calculate the Return on Investment

The return on investment is calculated using the program benefits and costs. The benefits-costs ratio (BCR) is calculated as the program benefits divided by the program costs. In formula form:

$$BCR = \frac{\text{Program Benefits}}{\text{Program Costs}}$$

The return on investment is based on the net benefits divided by program costs. The net benefits are calculated as the program benefits minus the program costs. In formula form, the ROI becomes:

$$ROI(\%) = \frac{\text{Net Program Benefits}}{\text{Program Costs}} \times 100$$

This is the same basic formula used in evaluating other investments, in which the ROI is traditionally reported as earnings divided by investment. Chapter 13, *Make it Credible: Capture Costs of the Program and Calculate ROI*, provides more detail.

Optimize Results

The next category in the ROI Methodology is reporting and optimizing, with two critical steps that are often deficient in the degree of attention and planning required to ensure success. The reporting step involves developing appropriate information in impact studies and other brief reports. In most ROI studies, several audiences are interested in and need the results. Improvements are made in the program which lead to optimization. This section also includes the process of using the results to increase funding for the program in the future.

#11 - Tell the Story: Communicate Results to Key Stakeholders

In this step, the design thinking principle is the use of storytelling. Even with results in hand, the efforts are not finished. The results must be communicated to all the stakeholders as quickly as possible to let them know the success of the program. In case of a lack of success, the data will show what needs to improve to make it better. Storytelling will inspire senior executives and other key stakeholders. Audiences love stories, and now the story can be told with different levels of data, a total of six types. It makes a more powerful story when they can clearly see that the dramatic events, the interesting anecdotes, and the insightful comments are backed up with proof that this program has made a difference. Chapter 14, *Tell the Story: Communicate Results to Key Stakeholders*, is devoted to this critical step in the ROI process.

#12 - Optimize the Results: Use Black Box Thinking to Increase Funding

The design principle used is a new competitive logic of business strategy. The key concept is to make sure that programs are properly supported and funded. The next step is to use a concept of black box thinking to analyze the results and use them to increase funding. This can be accomplished when improvements are made, especially if there's a lack of improvement. Black box thinking focuses on serious process improvement when a failure is identified. Even with success, improvements are made to make it deliver even more value. Ultimately, the ROI is optimized, and this optimization leads to the allocation of more funds. This builds the case for more investment (instead of less investment) in this program because there is a positive return on the investment. This series of events are powerful: design for the needed results, capture data to tell a compelling story, use data to improve the program and optimize ROI, and then make the case for more funding. It's a novel way to think about the power of an innovation technique (design thinking) to show the value for money. Chapter 15, *Optimize Results: Use Black Box Thinking to Increase Funding*, focuses on this issue.

Operating Standards and Philosophy

To ensure consistency and replication of impact studies, operating standards must be applied as the process model is used to develop ROI studies. The results of the study must stand alone and must not vary with the individual who is conducting the study. The operating standards detail how steps and issues of the process will be handled. Figure 4.7 shows the Twelve Guiding Principles of the ROI Methodology that form the basis for its operating standards.

The guiding principles serve not only to consistently address each step, but also to provide a much-needed conservative approach to the analysis. A conservative approach may lower the actual ROI calculation, but it will build credibility and secure buy in and support from the target audience.

Implementing and Sustaining the Process

A variety of environmental issues and events will influence the successful implementation of the ROI process. These issues must be addressed early to ensure its success. Specific topics or actions include:
A policy statement concerning results-based programs and projects

- Procedures and guidelines for different elements and techniques of the evaluation process
- Formal meetings to develop staff skills with the ROI process

1. When conducting a higher-level evaluation, collect data at lower levels.
2. When planning a higher-level evaluation, the previous level of evaluation is not required to be comprehensive.
3. When collecting and analyzing data, use only the most credible sources.
4. When analyzing data, select the most conservative alternative for calculations.
5. Use at least one method to isolate the effects of a project.
6. If no improvement data are available for a population or from a specific source, assume that little or no improvement has occurred.
7. Adjust estimates of improvement for potential errors of estimation.
8. Avoid use of extreme data items and unsupported claims when calculating ROI.
9. Use only the first year of annual benefits in ROI analysis of short-term solutions.
10. Fully load all costs of a solution, project, or program when analyzing ROI.
11. Intangible measures are defined as measures that are purposely not converted to monetary values.
12. Communicate the results of the ROI Methodology to all key stakeholders.

Figure 4.7　Twelve Guiding Principles of ROI.

- Strategies to improve management commitment to and support for the ROI process
- Mechanisms to provide technical support for questionnaire design, data analysis, and evaluation strategy
- Specific techniques to place more attention on results

The ROI Methodology can fail or succeed based on these implementation issues.

The ROI Methodology should undergo periodic review by the organization. An annual review is recommended to determine the extent to which the process is adding value. This final element involves securing feedback from the process and determining how well it is understood and applied. Essentially, this review follows the process described in this book to determine the ROI of the ROI Methodology. Chapter 17 focuses on implementing and sustaining the use of ROI.

Benefits of This Approach

The methodology presented in this book has been used consistently and routinely by thousands of organizations worldwide over the past 25 years. In some fields and industries, it is more prominent than in others. Much has been learned about the success of this methodology, and the benefits it can bring to organizations.

Aligning with Business

The ROI Methodology ensures alignment with business impact, enforced in three steps. First, even before the program is initiated, the methodology ensures that alignment is achieved upfront, at the time the program is validated as the appropriate solution. Second, by requiring specific, clearly defined objectives at the impact level, the program focuses on the ultimate outcomes, in essence driving the business measure by its design, delivery, and implementation. Third, in the follow-up data, when the business measures may have changed or improved, a method is used to isolate the effects of the program on that data, consequently proving the connection to that business measure (i.e., showing the amount of improvement directly connected to the program and ensuring there is business alignment).

Validating the Value Proposition

Most programs are undertaken to deliver value. As described in the first three chapters, the definition of value may be unclear, or may not be what a program's various sponsors, organizers, and stakeholders desire. Consequently, shifts in value often occur. When the values are finalized, the program's value proposition is detailed. The ROI Methodology can forecast the value in advance; and if the value has been delivered, it verifies the value proposition agreed to by the appropriate parties. Chapter 16, *Forecast the ROI*, focuses on this issue.

Improving Processes

The ROI Methodology is a process improvement tool, by design and by practice. It collects data to evaluate how things are, or are not, working. When things are not where they should be—as when programs are not proceeding as effectively as expected—data are available to indicate what must be changed to make the program more effective. When things are working well, data are available to show what else could be done to make them better. As a program is conducted, the results are collected, and feedback is provided to the various stakeholders for specific actions for improvement. These changes drive the program to better results, which are then measured while the process continues. This continuous feedback cycle is critical to process improvement and is inherent in the ROI Methodology approach. In essence, the process uses design thinking principles to design for the results needed.

Enhancing the Image and Building Respect

Many functions, and even entire professions, are criticized for being unable to deliver what is expected. Consequently, their public image suffers. The ROI Methodology is one way to help build the respect a function or profession needs. The ROI Methodology can make a difference in any function, and not just those under scrutiny. Many executives have used ROI to show the value of a program, perhaps changing the perception of a program from one based on activity to one that credibly adds value. This methodology shows a connection to the bottom line, and shows the value delivered to stakeholders. It removes issues about value and a supposed lack of contribution to the organization. Consequently, this methodology is an important part of the process of changing the image of the organization, externally in the community, and building respect for various programs.

Improving Support

Securing support for programs and projects is critical, particularly with organizations. Many programs enjoy the support of the top-level executives who allocated the resources to make the programs viable. Unfortunately, some middle-level managers and administrators may not support certain programs because they do not see the value the programs deliver in terms these managers appreciate and understand. For nonprofits, support is needed from significant others who can have tremendous influence on participants. Having a methodology that shows how a program is connected to important business goals and objectives can change this support level. When middle managers and significant others understand that a program is helping them meet specific performance indicators, they will usually support the process, or will at least resist it less. In this way, the ROI Methodology can improve needed support.

This is more important when many individuals are involved in program activities. For example, as program implementation becomes a part of everyone's job, the support level needs to move from "we are involved in program implementation activities when we have time" to "program implementation is our top priority."

Justifying or Enhancing Budgets

Some organizations have used the ROI Methodology to protect current budgets or support proposed budgets. Because the methodology shows the impact or ROI expected or achieved with specific programs, the data can often be leveraged into budget requests. When a particular program is budgeted, the amount budgeted is often in direct proportion to the value that the program adds. If little or no credible data support the contribution, the budgets are often trimmed—or at least not enhanced. Bringing accountability to this level is one of the best ways to secure future funding.

Building Productive Partnerships

Almost every organization attempts to partner with partners and other key managers in the organization or community. Unfortunately, some managers may not want to be partners. They may not want to waste time and effort on a relationship that does not help them succeed. They want to partner only with groups and individuals who can add value and help them in meaningful ways. Showing the program results will enhance the likelihood of building these partnerships, with the results providing the initial impetus for making the partnerships work.

Final Thoughts

This chapter introduced the ROI Methodology that underlies the Value for Money approach. The chapter briefly presented the different elements and 12 steps in the ROI Methodology, and the standards necessary to understand how the ROI Methodology works in practice. The chapter concluded with the benefits of using this approach. It serves as a quick reference guide to the ROI Methodology and may be useful for clients, sponsors, or donors. The next eleven chapters provide more details on the 12 steps of the ROI Methodology. The next chapter takes a closer look at how to establish the needs for your program.

5

Start with Why: Align Programs with the Business

Much work has been done in the last decade to show the value of college education from the point of view of the consumer of the education and the funders of education. Showing the value of the education in impact and economic terms along with the quality of life are very helpful. Sometimes there is a need to show the value for money for a particular degree program, or to change the measurement system of success for degree programs.

Recently, we were on the campus of the University of California Berkeley teaching a group of administrators about the ROI Methodology, building expertise to become certified ROI professionals. During the week of the visit, the new ROI rankings from *Businessweek* magazine were released for MBA programs [1]. These rankings examined the outcomes of an MBA from the student perspective. The financial ROI is based on salary increases, comparing the salary before attending the MBA program, with five years of salary after the program. The cost includes tuition and the loss of income while attending the program. With monetary benefits and costs, the financial ROI is calculated. ROI can increase if the salaries are substantially higher for graduates, or the tuition is reduced, or not increased as much as some competition. UC-Berkeley was disappointed to see its ranking fall, not because salaries were lower for graduates, but because it had raised the tuition for the program. This is a good economic way for a potential MBA student to evaluate the degree program. A lower cost program may have a higher ROI.

Measurement systems on the success of universities are changing and Figure 5.1 shows the traditional ways of evaluating the success, and the emerging ways. The shift is from measuring input and the lower part of the value chain to pushing it to the higher levels of value. It's the outcome of the education that really makes a difference. Graduation rates are more important than enrollment. Placement rates are more important than grades. Student success is more important than the diversity of programs. The ROI of a degree program may be better than the additional investment in new buildings. A good experience for students is not necessarily as important as career satisfaction for the graduates. You get the picture.

Taking a page from cash-strapped parents, states increasingly are telling their public universities to prove they are worth the investment. Kentucky lawmakers in March 2017 approved a new formula that ties a significant portion of the state's roughly $1 billion in public higher-education funding to

Traditional (Usually Levels 0, 1, 2)	Emerging (Usually Levels 3, 4, 5)
Enrollment	Graduation Rates
Number of Courses Taken	Time to Graduate
Grades	Placement Rates
Diversity of Programs	Student Success
Quality of Faculty	Real Work Experiences
Investment in Facilities	ROI in Degree Programs
Student Activities	Student Debt Load
Student Satisfaction with Experience	Student Career Satisfaction
Reputation of University	Donations

Figure 5.1 Traditional and Emerging Ways of Evaluating Success.

student outcomes, like earning certificates and degrees. In 2017, Arkansas signed into law a funding model that, over a few years, will increase the pot of money and begin judging schools against their own baseline figures for keeping students on track toward on-time graduation [2].

At least 33 states now use performance-based funding, according to the National Conference of State Legislatures, where appropriations are based on outcomes that might include graduation rates, debt loads, or graduates in high-demand fields like engineering. Funds tied to such outcomes range from a few percent in Washington state to nearly the entire pool in Tennessee.

Historically, states have provided funds based on enrollment or building on the prior year's allotment—which some call the inertia model. Now, the focus is on getting students to graduate and land jobs, not just getting into school.

Universities are stepping up to the challenge. For example, in a recent brochure to donors, Georgia State University (GSU) touted outcome measures. GSU could have focused the information on enrollment (50,000 students, making it the largest university in Georgia), facilities (with its massive number of buildings in downtown Atlanta), or its reputation (#4 in innovation in the US, according to *U.S. News & World Report* [3]). Instead, it focused on:

- 22 percentage-point increase in graduation rates over 10 years
- $15 million saved when students graduate faster and avoid unnecessary classes
- 1,700 more graduates per year than just five years ago
- 7,200+ microgrants, averaging $900 awarded since 2012
- Increased scholarship awards by more than 50 percent
- With a $2.5 million grant, SunTrust Bank helps 19,000+ students budget and reduce debt through one-on-one counseling at the new Financial Management Center

Indeed, measurement systems are changing. Programs or projects to improve colleges and universities must now focus on outcome measures. They should begin with why…and that should be one or more of the outcomes at the impact level.

Impact Measures are Critical

Most programs do not connect directly to business measures. They often start at the suggestion of someone on the team or as a specific request from senior executives or requirements from a sponsor. Sometimes, the function team initiates programs they believe are necessary to make improvements. Who could resist programs that focus on:

- Providing support for abused women,
- Managing a global team,
- Keeping families together,
- Leading confidently,
- Improving female empowerment,
- Influencing others when you're not in charge,
- Communicating effectively in a digital workplace,
- Preventing infectious diseases,
- Gaining respect for police officers,
- Fostering employee engagement,
- Improving healthcare delivery, or
- Providing financial planning for low income families?

When the business need is unknown at the time a program is launched, it may be difficult to make that connection later in the process. "Begin with the end in mind" is an old adage popularized by Stephen R. Covey in his best-selling book, *The 7 Habits of Highly Effective People*®. "Start with why" is the advice from Simon Sinek in his best-selling book, *Start with Why*. In the context of programs and projects, the end is improvement in business measures. Clarifying these business measures up-front helps answer the question, "Why this particular program at this time?"

This chapter presents the first of the 12 steps to transform programs into a business-contributing process, defined in Figure 4.6. Step six in the figure has five parts, making it 12 steps in total. Whether you are in a business enterprise, government, NGO, nonprofit, or university, business needs exist and are often expressed in terms of output, quality, time, and costs. Defining business needs clearly and early avoids inefficiencies and problems that usually permeate the process and produce disappointing results. This chapter explains the five levels of needs assessments: (1) addressing payoff needs, (2) defining business needs, (3) analyzing performance needs, (4) determining learning needs, and (5) uncovering preference needs.

The Challenge

Based on the approximately 5,000 evaluation studies that ROI Institute has conducted or reviewed, the number-one cause of program failure is lack of business alignment. Program failure represents waste, and the principal culprit is lack of business alignment from the beginning.

As presented in Chapter 1, research continues to suggest that the top measure desired by executives, sponsors, and donors is impact. They want to see the connection of programs to important business measures. The second-most important measure is the financial ROI, comparing monetary benefits of a particular program to the cost of the program. Alignment between the program and the business must be explored when the proposed program exceeds thresholds of costs, importance, and strategic and operational implications. Four challenges must be addressed to make this step successful.

Begin with the End in Mind

Solutions to problems (or opportunities to improve) must begin with a clear focus on the outcome. The end result must be specifically defined in terms of business needs and business measures, so that the outcome—the actual improvement in the measures—and the ROI are clear. This provides the necessary focus on the problem through every step in the process. Beginning with the end in mind also involves pinpointing all the details to ensure proper planning and successful execution.

This is uncomfortable for some program implementers. For example, consider the organizers of leadership development programs, which often begin with leader behavior. They want to have new skills and competences in place. However, top executives want improved organizational performance, expressed as key performance indicators (KPI).

It's a Change

The process of connecting programs to a business need, including a specific business measure, represents a change that has evolved in recent years. Chapter 1 details this important change. Although it seems logical to start with "why," so many programs actually start with a solution first, followed by an effort to find the precise reason for the solution. Consequently, adjusting to focus on "why" first requires changing the way programs are initiated in organizations to ensure the connection exists prior to making an investment. Some people will resist the change, but it is necessary to ensure the delivery of business value. Chapter 17 details ways to overcome the resistance. It is difficult to have a business contribution without beginning with the business measure.

It Requires Discipline

Proper analysis requires discipline and determination. A structured, systematic process will enhance credibility and allow for consistent application. The process calls for focus and thoroughness, leaving little room for major shortcuts.

While the process described in this book is necessary, not every program should be subjected to the type of analysis presented in this chapter. Some business needs are obvious and require little analysis other than to develop the program. Additional analysis may often be needed to ensure that the program is the right solution or perhaps to fine-tune it for future application. The amount of analysis required often depends on the stakes involved.

Avoid Paralysis by Analysis

Whenever a needs analysis is proposed, many individuals respond with concern and, at times, resistance. Some worry about "paralysis by analysis," fearing that requests and directives may place them in a cycle of additional analyses. This represents a dilemma for many organizations, because analysis must occur to ensure that programs are appropriate. Unfortunately, analysis is often misplaced, misunderstood, and misrepresented, and individuals imagine the worst—complex problems, confusing models, and an endless array of data requiring complicated statistical techniques to ensure that all the bases are covered. In reality, analysis does not have to be so difficult. Simple techniques may uncover the cause of the problem or the need for a specific program.

> *"Too much knowledge and analysis can be paralysis."*
> *– Alejandro Gonzalez Iñárritu*

The Alignment Model

To understand alignment, it is helpful to review the model shown in Figure 5.2, and also presented in the previous chapter. This chapter and the next explore the left side of the model, beginning with payoff needs and

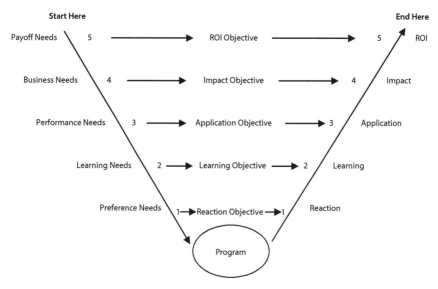

Figure 5.2 The Alignment Model.

progressing to preference needs. The objectives derived directly from these needs are defined, making a strong case for having multiple levels of objectives that correspond with specific needs. The right side of the model is essentially the measurement of success presented in Chapters 8 through 13.

Identifying payoff needs, those opportunities for the organization to add money, reduce costs, or do some greater good, begins with the following questions.

- Is this program worth doing?
- Is this a problem or issue worth addressing?
- Is this an opportunity worth pursuing?
- Is the program feasible?

Will this new program add enough value to offset its costs?

Payoff Needs

The answer is clear for programs that address significant problems or opportunities with potentially high rewards. The questions may be more challenging to answer for lower-profile programs or those for which the possible payoff is less apparent. Regardless of the situation, these questions present an initial opportunity to ensure a program is aligned with the needs of the organization. The analysis can be simple or comprehensive. A program's ultimate payoff will be in either profit or cost savings, as shown in Figure 5.3, though most will be in the cost-avoidance category.

Programs in businesses can improve sales, increase market share, introduce new products, open new markets, enhance customer service, or increase customer loyalty and will generate improvements in profit by increasing sales revenue. Other revenue-generating measures include increasing memberships, increasing donations, obtaining grants, and generating tuition from new and returning students—all of which, after taking out the administrative costs, leave a "profitable" benefit.

For a nonprofit, the "profit" increase is possible. For example, a fundraising project in a nonprofit will generate $400,000 in donations. The project will cost $80,000. What's the expected benefit-cost ratio? Let's assume that the value added from the donations going directly to the programs is 80 percent, or $320,000. The expected benefit-cost ratio is

$$BCR = \frac{\$320,000}{\$80,000} = 4:1$$

This suggests that every dollar spent on the fundraising project generates four dollars in benefits.

However, most programs will pay off with cost savings, which occur through cost reduction or cost avoidance. Examples of cost savings include programs that improve quality, prevent diseases, reduce cycle time, lower incarceration days, decrease crime rates, avoid hospital readmissions, and minimize delays. When the goal is solving a problem, monetary value is often based on cost reduction.

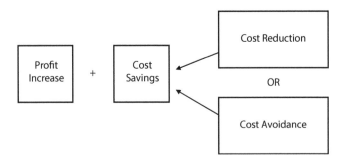

Figure 5.3 The Payoff Opportunity.

Cost-avoidance programs sometime aim at reducing risks, avoiding problems, or preventing unwanted events, such as the opioid epidemic. Some finance and accounting staff may view cost avoidance as an inappropriate measure for developing monetary benefits and calculating ROI. However, if the assumptions are correct, an avoided cost (for example, compliance fines) can be more rewarding than reducing an actual cost. Preventing a problem is more cost-effective than waiting for it to occur and then having to correct it.

Determining the potential payoff, the first step in the needs analysis process, is closely related to the next step, determining the business need, since the potential payoff is often based on one or more business needs. Determining the payoff is a function of two factors: the potential monetary value of improving an impact measure and the approximate program cost. Ascertaining these monetary values in detail usually yields a more credible forecast of a program's potential to add value. However, this step may be omitted in situations in which the issue (business need) must be resolved regardless of the cost or it is an obviously high-payoff activity. For example, if the problem involves a safety concern, or a regulatory compliance issue, or a competitive matter, then a detailed analysis may not be needed.

The extent of the detail may also hinge on securing program funding. If the potential funding source does not see the value of the program compared to the potential costs, more detail can provide a convincing case for funding.

Provide greater detail under the following circumstances:

- *When minimal support for the proposed program exists.* The payoff analysis can provide an estimated value of the improvement (or cost avoidance) and the potential contribution to business goals.
- *When the proposed program is anticipated to be very expensive.* Estimating the potential payoff is important before spending significant resources on a program.
- *When funding is needed for a program.* This is particularly true if the funding comes from external resources or there is serious competition for internal funding sources.
- *When a key sponsor wants more analysis before the program moves forward.* Although a sponsor may support it enthusiastically, more analysis may solidify his or her confidence in the proposed program and provide the needed information to secure final approval.

Knowledge of the potential payoff is not needed when most of the stakeholders agree that the payoff from the program will be high or if the problem in question must be resolved regardless of the cost.

Key Questions to Ask

Begin the analysis with several questions, such as the ones shown in Figure 5.4. The answers will help make the case for proceeding with or without analysis. They may also indicate there is no need for the program. Understanding the implications of moving forward (or not) can reveal the legitimacy of the proposed program.

The good news is that answers to these questions may be readily available for many potential programs. The need may have already been realized, and the consequences might be validated. For example, many organizations with an employee retention problem for a critical talent group have a standard value for the cost of employee turnover. This cost may come from existing data or from published studies. With this cost in hand, the impact of the problem is known. For a program designed to reduce recidivism (returning to prison), the cost of incarceration is known, so the impact of the problem can be quickly calculated. The proposed program's cost can be compared to the problem's cost to get a sense of added value. The cost of the program can usually be estimated, even if the specifics are not fully developed.

Obvious versus Not-So-Obvious Payoffs

The potential payoff is obvious for some programs but not-so-obvious for others. Figure 5.5 lists some opportunities with obvious payoffs. Each item

• Why is this an issue?	• Are there multiple solutions?
• What happens if we do nothing?	• Who will support the program?
• Is this issue critical?	• Who will not support the program?
• Is this issue linked to our strategy?	• How much will the solution(s) cost?
• Is it possible to correct it?	• How can we fund the program?
• Is it feasible to improve it?	• Are there some important intangible benefits involved?
• How much is it costing?	
• Who is paying for this?	• Is there a potential payoff (positive ROI)?
• Can we find a solution?	• Do we need to forecast outcomes, including ROI?

Figure 5.4 Some Key Questions to ask about the Proposed Program.

- The annual cost to the city for each homeless person is $52,000.

- The time to process a disability claim has increased 30 percent in two years.

- Sexual harassment complaints per 1,000 employees are the highest in the industry.

- The average cost of an opioid addict is $45,000.

- System downtime is double last year's performance.

- Excessive turnover of critical talent: 35 percent above benchmark data.

- The student debt load is $125,000 for each graduate.

- Very low market share in a market with few players.

- Inadequate customer service: 3.89 on a 10-point customer satisfaction scale.

- Safety record is among the worst in the industry.

- Hospital readmissions rate is 35 percent, seven times the national average.

- This year's out-of-compliance fines total $1.2 million, up 82 percent from last year.

- The unemployment rate for veterans is three times the total unemployment rate.

- Excessive product returns: 30 percent higher than previous year.

- Excessive absenteeism in call centers: 12.3 percent vs. 5.4 percent for industry.

- More than 35 percent of the population is below the poverty income level.

- Grievances from prison guards are up 38 percent from last year.

Figure 5.5 Obvious Payoff Opportunities.

is a serious problem that executives, donors, administrators, or officials want to address. For these situations, moving to the business needs level would be safe.

In other circumstances, the issues might be unclear, arising from intuition, political motives, biases, or perceptions of a problem. Figure 5.6 shows opportunities for which the payoff may not be as obvious. The not-so-obvious opportunities need clarification. Some requests are common, as executives and administrators suggest a different process to change a dysfunctional situation or to achieve vague or nonspecific goals. The opportunities listed are common requests that can deliver value, but only if they are focused and clearly defined at the start. Some of the more open-ended and vague opportunities can pay off tremendously. In our work at ROI Institute, we have seen most of these opportunities lead to valuable programs. Sometimes, overlooking a vague request may not be appropriate, because that request may have valuable consequences. The key is to define, approve, and focus on the desired business impact of the programs.

- Provide job opportunities for autistic young adults
- Implement a teambuilding project
- Provide counseling at the food bank
- Improve leadership competencies for all city managers
- Provide empowerment training for grade seven and eight students
- Establish a project management office
- Implement mindfulness sessions with team members
- Provide job training for unemployed workers
- Conduct healthy living sessions for the community
- Implement recycling in all communities
- Create a green organization
- Provide training on sexual harassment awareness for all associates
- Reduce the number of homeless in our city
- Offer family planning sessions for newlyweds
- Become a technology leader
- Implement lean thinking throughout the healthcare system
- Create a great place to work
- Provide legal assistance to refugees
- Implement career counseling for prison inmates
- Implement stress reduction sessions for new parents
- Create a wellness and fitness center
- Build capability for future growth
- Create an engaged workforce
- Conduct compliance sessions with all staff

Figure 5.6 Not-So-Obvious Payoff Opportunities.

Reasons for New Programs

From the value for money perspective, the main reasons that programs fail are:

- There is no connection to a business measure from the outset.
- There is not enough monetary value generated to cover the cost of the program.

A lack of initial business alignment brings into question the reasons for new program or project implementation. Figure 5.7 shows some of the main reasons organizations implement programs. Some of these appear to be legitimate reasons to move forward. If analysis supports a credible reason, then a program is probably needed. If a regulation requires it, then it must be implemented. Some reasons listed for a new program may appear to be necessary, but they are necessary only if the program is implemented efficiently. For example, if a program supports new policies and practices, new equipment, new procedures, new technology or existing processes, it appears to be a legitimate request, but only if support for implementation exists.

Other reasons for a new program can be suspect, and some are often misguided. For example, if other organizations have implemented a particular program, or if it is based on a fad, it is suspect from the beginning. These are the types of programs that often do not add adequate value and create concerns about chasing a particular trend or fad. Unfortunately, executives often pursue these programs in their never-ending desire to find the right solutions or to pursue any new idea [4].

The Costs of the Problem

Problems can be expensive and resolving them can have a tremendous impact. Determining the cost of the problem requires examining potential

- An analysis indicates a need exists.
- A regulation requires it.
- It appears to be a serious problem.
- Management or a community leader requests it.
- A donor wants the program.
- It is a change that is needed.
- Other organizations have implemented it.
- The topic is a fad.
- It supports new policies and practices.
- Staff members thought it was needed.
- It supports new equipment, procedures, or technology.
- It supports other processes.
- A trendy book has been written about it.

Figure 5.7 Reasons for Programs.

consequences and converting those consequences to monetary values. Figure 5.8 shows a list of potential problems. Some measures that define these problems can easily be converted to money. Others require data conversion techniques that are too costly or for which the results lack credibility. These measures remain as intangibles. For example, inventory shortages often result in the direct cost of the inventory as well as the cost of carrying the inventory. Time can easily be translated into money by calculating the fully loaded cost of the individual's time spent on unproductive tasks. Calculating time for completing a task or procedure involves measures that can be converted to money. Errors, mistakes, waste, delays, and bottlenecks can often be converted to money through their consequences. Productivity problems and inefficiencies, equipment damage, and equipment in use are other examples of easy conversions. Injuries, addictions, crime, pollution, poverty, and unemployment are very expensive and are well documented.

When examining costs, it is important to consider all the costs and their implications. For example, the full costs of accidents include not only the cost of lost workdays and medical expenses but also the effect on insurance premiums, the time required for investigations, damage to equipment, and the time of all employees who address the accident. The cost of a customer complaint includes the cost of the time in resolving the complaint as well as the value of the item or service that is adjusted because of it. The most important item in a complaint is the cost of lost future business and goodwill from both the complaining customer and potential customers who learn of the issue.

• Injuries	• Poverty
• Waste	• Unemployment
• Delays	• Incidents
• Addictions	• Excessive employee turnover
• Inventory shortages	• Employee withdrawal
• Wasted time	• Accidents
• Errors/mistakes	• Excessive staffing
• Productivity problems	• Employee dissatisfaction
• Inefficiencies	• Customer dissatisfaction
• Excessive direct costs	• Excessive conflicts
• Equipment damage	• Tarnished image
• Excessive crime	• Obesity
• Pollution	• Excessive stress

Figure 5.8 Potentially Costly Problems.

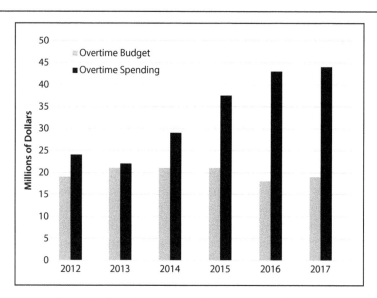

Figure 5.9 Baltimore's Allotted Overtime Budget For Police Officers Versus Actual Overtime Spending.

Case Study

Because of a shortage of police officers in Baltimore, the police force has been working an excessive amount of overtime. According to Figure 5.9, the difference in planned overtime and overtime spending for 2016 and 2017 is about $50 million—clearly a problem worth solving. Additionally, police officers are overworked, stressed out, and are missing out on family time. The solution is to hire more police officers, which is difficult in an environment where otherwise suitable candidates are not attracted to this type of work. If the solution costs less than $25 million per year, the ROI is positive (not to mention the improvements in work-life balance and stress) [5].

The Value of Opportunity

Just as it is possible to tabulate the cost of a problem in most situations, it is also possible to determine the value of an opportunity. Examples of opportunities include:

- Creating a positive mindset
- Implementing innovation and creativity programs
- Developing an inclusive workforce

- Implementing a wellness and fitness program
- Installing new technology and systems
- Upgrading the workforce
- Improving engagement

In these situations, a problem may not exist, but there is a tremendous opportunity to get ahead of the competition or prevent a problem in the future. Properly placing a value on this opportunity requires considering what may happen if the program is not pursued or taking into account the windfall that might be realized by seizing the opportunity. The monetary value is derived by following the different scenarios to convert specific business impact measures to money. The difficulty in this situation is ensuring a credible analysis. Forecasting the value of an opportunity relies on many assumptions, whereas calculating the value of a known outcome is often grounded in a more credible analysis.

To Forecast or Not to Forecast

Seeking and placing value on an opportunity leads to an important decision: to forecast or not to forecast business value and ROI. If the stakes are high, and support for the program is not in place, a detailed forecast may be the only way to gain support and funding. When the forecast is pursued, the rigor of the analysis becomes an issue. In some cases, an informal forecast is provided, given certain assumptions about alternative outcome scenarios. In others, a detailed forecast is needed that involves collecting data from a variety of experts, using previous studies from another program, or perhaps a more sophisticated analysis [6]. Chapter 16 also addresses the issue.

Case Study

Following a case study through the different levels of needs may be helpful. This section explores the analysis at Level 5, determining payoff needs. The following case study examines Southeast Corridor Bank (SCB), which operated branches in four states. (After expanding from a one-state operation to a multistate network through a strategic acquisition campaign, SCB was acquired by Regions Bank, one of the top 10 banks in the United States.) Like many fast-growing organizations, SCB faced merger and integration problems, including excessive employee turnover. SCB's annual employee turnover was 57 percent for branch staff, compared with an industry average of 26 percent. The first step in tackling the problem was answering these questions:

- Is this a problem worth solving?
- Is there a potential payoff to solving the problem?

To the senior vice president of human resources the answers were clear. After reviewing several published studies about the cost of turnover, including one from a financial institution, he concluded that the cost of employee turnover ranged between 110 percent to 225 percent of the average annual salary for the job group. At the current rate, employee turnover was costing the bank more than $6 million per year. Lowering the rate to the industry average would save the bank more than $3 million annually. Although the structure and cost of the program weren't known at this point, it became clear that this problem was worth solving. Unless the program appeared to be very expensive, solving the problem would have a tremendous impact. Senior executives did not need further analysis to decide to pursue resolution of the opportunities. The next step was to clarify the measures, or business need, discussed next.

Business Needs

Determining specific business needs is directly linked to developing the potential payoff. When determining the business needs, specific measures are pinpointed in an effort to clearly assess the business situation. The term "business" is used in governments, nonprofits, NGOs, and educational institutions, as well as in private-sector organizations. Programs and projects in all types of organizations can lead to monetary value add by improving productivity, quality, and efficiency and by saving time and reducing costs.

Determining the Opportunity

A business need is represented by a business measure. Any process, item, or perception can be measured, and this measurement is critical for this level of analysis. If the program focuses on solving a problem, something clearly established in the minds of program initiators, the measures are often obvious. If the program prevents a problem, the measures may also be obvious. If it takes advantage of a potential opportunity, the measures are usually still there. Otherwise, how will the opportunity be described? How will the value proposition be defined? The important point is that measures are in the system, ready to be captured for this level of analysis. The challenge is to identify the measures and to find them economically and swiftly.

Identifying the Business Measure—Hard Data

To help focus on the desired measures, a clarification between hard data and soft data is needed. Hard data are primary measures of improvement presented in rational, undisputed facts that exist somewhere in the organization's system. They are easy to measure and quantify and are relatively easy to convert to monetary values. The ultimate criteria for measuring the effectiveness of an organization rests on hard-data items—such as revenue, productivity, profitability, cost control, and quality assurance. Governments have output, quality, costs, and time. NGOs and nonprofits have many hard data items such as students placed, patient outcomes, crime rates, and water quality.

Hard data are objectively based and represent common and credible measures of an organization's performance. Four categories of hard data grouped by output, quality, cost, and time are shown in Figure 5.10.

Output

The visible hard-data results from a particular program or project involve improvements in the output of the work unit or entire organization. Every organization, regardless of type, must have basic measurements of output, such as the number of patients treated, students graduated, packages shipped, or forms processed. Since organizations routinely monitor these measures, it is easy to compare outputs before and after. When programs are anticipated to drive an output measure, estimates of output changes can usually be made by those who are knowledgeable about the situation.

Quality

Another category of hard data is quality. If quality is a major concern for the organization, processes are most likely in place to measure and monitor quality. Thanks in part to the rising popularity of quality-improvement processes (such as total-quality management, continuous quality improvement, and Six Sigma), organizations are now routinely pinpointing the correct quality measures—and, in many cases, placing a monetary value on them. For programs or projects designed to improve quality, the results can be documented using the standard cost of quality as a value. For healthcare programs, it's infections, patient outcomes, readmission, and patient safety.

Cost

Another important hard-data category is an improvement in cost. Many projects and programs are designed to lower, control, or eliminate the cost

OUTPUT	TIME
Citizens vaccinated	Length of stay
Graduation rate	Cycle time
Placement rate	Equipment downtime
Units produced	Overtime
Income increased	On-time shipments
Items assembled	Project time
Money collected	Processing time
Licenses issued	Supervisory time
New accounts generated	Time to proficiency
Forms processed	Time to graduate
Loans approved	Meeting schedules
Inventory turnover	Repair time
Criminals prosecuted	Time to replace
Inspections made	Work stoppages
Applications processed	Response time
Patients X-rayed	Late times
Students graduated	Lost time days
Permits issued	Wait time
Projects completed	
Jobs secured	**QUALITY**
Productivity	
Patients discharged	Readmissions
Criminals captured	Failure rates
Shipments processed	Dropout rates
	Scrap
COSTS	Waste
	Rejects
Budget variances	Error rates
Unit costs	Rework required
Costs by account	Complications
Variable costs	Shortages
Fixed costs	Product defects
Overhead cost	Deviations from standard
Operating costs	Product failures
Program cost savings	Inventory adjustments
Accident costs	Infections
Program costs	Incidents
Incarceration costs	Compliance discrepancies
Shelter costs	Agency fines
Treatment costs	Accidents
Participant costs	Crime rate
Cost per day	

Figure 5.10 Examples of Hard Data.

of a specific process or activity. Achieving these cost targets contributes immediately to the bottom line. Some organizations have an extreme focus on cost reduction. Consider Walmart, whose tagline is "Always low prices. Always." The entire organization focuses on lowering costs on all processes and products and passing the savings along to customers. When direct cost savings are used, no efforts are necessary to convert data to monetary value. There can be as many cost items as there are accounts in a cost accounting system. In addition, costs can be combined in any number of ways to develop the costs related to a particular program or project.

Time

Time, which is becoming a critical measure in organizations, is also a hard-data category. Some organizations gauge their performance almost exclusively by time. For example, consider FedEx, whose tagline is "The World on Time." When asked what business FedEx is in, the company's top executives usually say, "We engineer time." For FedEx, time is so critical that it defines success or failure. Time savings may mean a program is completed faster than originally planned, a product was introduced earlier, or the time to restore a network was reduced. These savings can translate into lower costs. In many organizations, time is an important measure, with projects and programs aimed directly at time savings.

Case Study

Sometimes, measures are interrelated, and it is not unusual for a particular learning program to focus on influencing several of them at once. For example, a government agency that processes visas for international visitors was experiencing a problem. The main issue was that it was taking too long to process the visas, and they were making too many mistakes, which required reprocessing. If the visa process could speed up, this would allow for more to be processed with the same number of people (increase in output). Thus, the cost per visa processed would actually be reduced when compared to the cost of the old way (cost reduction). Reprocessing a visa also takes time, and this was a known cost (quality). Thus, improving quality and reducing time would result in a reduction in costs per visa processed and the cost of reprocessing. This example also underscores the fact that hard data that are easy to quantify and convert to money exist in any type of organization, including governments or nonprofits.

Defining the Business Need—Soft Data

Hard data may lag behind changes and conditions in the organization by many months. Therefore, supplementing hard data with soft data—such as attitude, motivation, and satisfaction—may be useful. For example, customer dissatisfaction leads to lost customers. Employee dissatisfaction leads to employee turnover.

Often more difficult to collect and analyze, soft data frequently serve as proxies for or supplement hard data. Soft data are also more difficult to convert to monetary values and are often subjective. They are often seen as less credible as a performance measurement, but still important. Figure 5.11 shows common examples and types of soft data.

LEADERSHIP	CLIENT SERVICE
Teamwork	Client complaints
Collaboration	Client satisfaction
Networking	Client dissatisfaction
Communication	Client impressions
Alliances	Client loyalty
Decisiveness	Client retention
Caring	Client value
Compassion	Clients lost
WORK CLIMATE/SATISFACTION	**EMPLOYEE DEVELOPMENT/ ADVANCEMENT**
Grievances	Promotions
Discrimination charges	Capability
Employee complaints	Intellectual capital
Job satisfaction	Programs completed
Organization commitment	Transfers
Employee engagement	Performance appraisal ratings
Employee loyalty	Readiness
Intent to leave	Development assignments
Stress	
	IMAGE/REPUTATION
INITIATIVE/INNOVATION	
	Brand awareness
Creativity	Reputation
New Ideas	Impressions
Suggestions	Social responsibility
Trademarks	Environmental friendliness
Copyrights and patents	Social consciousness
Process improvements	Diversity/inclusiveness
Partnerships	External awards

Figure 5.11 Examples of Soft Data.

Leadership

Leadership is important to the success of work groups. Dysfunctional leadership can lead to an unproductive and ineffective work group, while effective leadership can boost the group's success in many ways. Some examples that may be difficult to measure or convert to monetary values are shown in the figure.

Work Climate/Satisfaction

When employees are dissatisfied or the work climate is unfavorable, several measures can show their discontent. Complaints and grievances are sometimes in the hard-data category because of their ease of conversion to money. However, most of these measures are considered soft-data items. Job satisfaction, organizational commitment, and employee engagement show how attitudes shape the organization. Stress is often a by-product of a fast-paced work climate. These issues are becoming increasingly important.

Client Service

Most projects and programs serve clients. Increased global competition fosters a greater need to serve and satisfy these clients. Consequently, more organizations are using client service measures to show the levels of satisfaction, loyalty, and retention.

Employee Development/Advancement

Employees are routinely developed, assigned new jobs, and promoted throughout organizations. Building capability, creating intellectual capital, and enhancing readiness are important processes. Many soft-data measures are available to indicate the consequences of those activities and processes.

Initiative/Innovation

Creativity and innovation are critical processes within successful organizations. A variety of measures can be developed to show the creative spirit of employees and the related outcomes—such as ideas, suggestions, copyrights, and patents. While the collective creative spirit of employees may be a soft-data item, the outcomes of creativity and innovation may be placed in the hard-data category. Still, many executives consider innovation measurements to be soft data.

Image/Reputation

Perhaps some of the softest measures are in the image category. Executives are attempting to increase brand awareness, particularly with sales and marketing programs or projects. Reputation is another key area, as more organizations seek to improve their standing as a good employer, a good citizen, and a good steward of investors' money. Image, social responsibility, environmental friendliness, and social consciousness are key outputs of a variety of programs and projects aimed at making the organization well rounded. Diversity and inclusion is important for organizations. Many programs are aimed at increasing the diversity of people, ideas, products, and programs. Finally, external awards are the outcomes of many activities and programs, often reflecting the external variation of an organization.

Using Tangible versus Intangible—A Better Approach

The critical issue with soft-data categories is the difficulty of converting them to monetary values. While some of the measures listed in Figure 5.11 could be converted to money, considering most of them as soft-data items is more realistic and practical. It is important to remember that the definition of an intangible measure (based on the standards of the ROI Methodology) is a measure that cannot be converted to money credibly or with minimum resources. If a soft-data measure can be converted to money, it becomes tangible.

To avoid debates over what should be considered soft or hard data, the terms *tangible* and *intangible* will be used most often in this book. This is the best approach to program evaluation, because the data classification is specific to the organizational setting. Each organization determines whether a measure is tangible or intangible. For example, in some organizations, a measure for customer satisfaction is easily available and costs little to obtain. Therefore, the measure is tangible, because it has been converted to money. However, in other organizations, customer satisfaction is not connected to money, and the measure is usually left as intangible because of the efforts needed to credibly convert data to money is too much for the particular project.

Finding Sources of Impact Data

The sources of impact data, whether hard or soft, are plentiful. They come from routine reporting systems in the organization or externally in governments or private databases or systems. In many situations, these items have led to the need for the program or project. Figure 5.12 shows a sample of

Local Records	Government Reports
Safety and Health Reports	Payroll Records
Quality Reports	Design Documents
Project Reports	Test Records
Compliance Reports	Marketing Reports
Annual Reports	Service Records
Benchmarking Reports	Human Capital Databases
Community Databases	Industry/Trade Association Records
Cost Statements	UN System
Scorecards	EDIC Database
Productivity Records	Financial Records

Figure 5.12 Sources of Data.

the vast array of possible documents, systems, databases, and reports that can be used to select the specific measure or measures to monitor throughout the program.

Some program planners and program team members believe organizational data sources are scarce because the data are not readily available to them within easy reach through database systems. With a little determination and searching, the data can usually be identified. In our experience, more than 80 percent of the measures that matter to a specific program or project have already been developed and are easily available in databases or systems. Rarely do new data collection systems or processes have to be developed.

Identifying All the Measures

When searching for the proper measures to connect to the program and pinpoint business needs, considering all the possible measures that could be influenced is helpful. Sometimes, collateral measures move in harmony with the program. For example, efforts to improve safety may also improve productivity and increase job satisfaction. Thinking about the adverse impact on certain measures may also help. For example, when cycle times are reduced, quality may suffer; or when sales increase, customer satisfaction may deteriorate. Finally, program team members must prepare for unintended consequences and capture them as other data items that might be connected to or influenced by the program.

What Happens if You Do Nothing?

When settling on the precise business measures for the program, several "what if" scenarios can be examined. If the organization does nothing, understanding the potential consequences may be beneficial. In these cases, asking the following questions may help in understanding the consequences of inaction:

- Will the situation deteriorate?
- Will operational problems surface?
- Will budgets be affected?
- Will we lose influence or support?
- Will we miss the opportunity?

Answers to these questions can help organizations settle on a precise set of measures with a hint of the extent to which the measures may change or improve. When examining the full context of the situation, other measures could be identified that may influence the program. This is a way to see the complete process and to pinpoint all the measures that may be connected to the project or program.

"Data beats emotions." – Sean Rad

Case Study

Let's return to SCB, where employee turnover was excessive. After determining that the cost of turnover was high, the bank found that at least $3 million could be saved annually if turnover was lowered to the industry average. Clearly defining the measure is important. In this case, the specific measure in question was voluntary turnover: the number of employees leaving voluntarily divided by the average number of employees, expressed as a percentage. Total turnover included voluntary and involuntary turnover. Analyzing avoidable turnover can be useful, but SCB did not have the means to determine which involuntary turnovers could have been avoided. Still another possibility is classifying turnovers as regrettable and nonregrettable. The difficulty with this measurement is that it is often a judgment call and may be based on a biased opinion. For example, if the manager of the departing employee labels the turnover as regrettable or nonregrettable, then a particular bias could enter the analysis.

Consequently, in the SCB case, voluntary turnover was used as the basis of the $3+ million payoff. Still, with any measure that improves, other measures should also improve, depending on the precise solution. For example, staffing levels, job satisfaction, customer service, sales revenue, and other items may change. These are detailed more specifically when the solution is determined, which occurs in the next few steps.

Final Thoughts

Starting with "why" is the first step in the ROI Methodology. The "why" of programs is the business need. This chapter illustrates the importance of connecting certain programs and projects to the business. At one extreme, some organizations do not pursue new programs unless there is a direct business connection. A more practical approach is to be selective, making the connection when the request seems to be expensive, critical to the organization, part of a strategy, or important to the management team. When this is done, it is important to explore two issues. The first issue is addressing the potential payoff needs, answering the fundamental two-part question: Is this a problem worth solving or an opportunity worth pursuing? In other words, is it worth it? The second issue is pinpointing one or more business measures already in the system that need to improve as a result of the program.

6

Make It Feasible: Select the Right Solution

"Right before our eyes, rapidly rising numbers of people are living—and dying—dying on our sidewalks, parks, and canyons. Something is deeply wrong. Dealing with homeless people is hard, dirty work, bereft of easy answers. Still, somebody has to do it. So far, we have outsourced our compassion to government, which mostly delegates the job to nonprofits, and they both are falling behind." These words appeared on the front page of the *San Diego Union-Tribune* in 2016. Since then, the problem has gotten much worse [1].

There isn't a major city in America that doesn't struggle with homelessness. It's also a major problem in other countries as well. Last year, about 550,000 people were believed to be homeless in the United States. The solution to homelessness is not, fundamentally, a resource issue; the United States spends billions to address the symptoms and results of homelessness. Nor is the solution undoing the safety net—shelters and specialized housing and advocacy organizations—already in place for the homeless. It's also not new "civility ordinances" or get-tough policing policies.

Any solution must be specific, requiring good data and focusing on housing first, the right kind of housing, with intensive wraparound case management. It also requires the will to push businesses and nongovernmental organizations (NGOs) to meet the need, move out of their comfort zone, and reprioritize money that is already being spent. Finally, it requires the creation of a dynamic system that can grow into the future, because homelessness is not preventable, though it is manageable.

One of the best examples of how a city tackled this problem and developed feasible solutions is the city of Houston, Texas, under the leadership of Annise Parker, who served as mayor from 2010 to 2016. What follows is based on her account of how the city found solutions to this persistent and serious problem [2].

While she was mayor, Houston led the nation in reducing homelessness between 2011 and 2015, the direct result of adopting a comprehensive regional plan that embraced best practices, while requiring an unprecedented level of collaboration between stakeholders. When this effort started, the homeless population was about 10,000, with roughly 2,500 chronically homeless. The first and most important step was understanding who they are and their needs.

The homeless were surveyed to find out who had physical, mental or addiction problems, who was a veteran, who had been in jail. Emergency room visits were tracked for the number and purpose of the visits. The homeless were asked how long they had been homeless, when they had last worked, and whether they had resources such as VA benefits or Social Security.

The next step was to pinpoint the cost of the homeless. Houston calculated a cost of $103 million in public resources annually (police, EMS, street/park cleanup, emergency room costs, etc.) on just the chronically homeless. Adding in the costs of shelters for the short-term homeless and the services—from meals to showers to case-managed apartments—provided by the nonprofits was staggering. With 2,500 chronically homeless at a cost per year of $41,200 for each homeless person, this was clearly a problem worth solving from a cost perspective. The city didn't attempt to calculate impacts on property values or lost business in areas of high concentration. These become the intangibles in the analysis.

Knowing who they were serving and the direct costs, the mayor convened significant stakeholders—government, providers and funders—and offered a plan. The hardest step was optimizing assets. They analyzed how much each service provider was spending, in what areas and from what source of funds. They also asked all housing providers their total number of beds managed, how long each remained vacant and their target population. This exercise confirmed what they already knew—many dedicated agencies were working in parallel, but not converging on the problem.

But when they compared the services available to the demographics of the homeless individuals, they saw something startling. The resources did not align. Successful agencies that had arisen over the years to serve specific populations had significant resources—dozens of vacant beds for example—while other agencies were routinely over capacity. They also realized that they were funding agencies broadly for the same services, but that their outcomes varied widely. These were agencies with high-profile boards, strong community brands and decades of service carrying out their missions in good faith. Unfortunately, those missions no longer served the broader needs of Houston.

The mayor set performance goals and shifted dollars to higher-performing organizations. For example, the focus was on outcomes and not input. She worked with the Houston City Council to pass unpopular ordinances that required coordination with the city for groups that fed or distributed resources to the homeless. The city created the Houston Center for Sobriety, which allowed it to divert thousands of those arrested every year for public intoxication away from jail and into a safe place to sober up and walk away without an arrest record.

But what made the difference, according to the mayor, was having business and philanthropic leaders step up and agree to align funding to the plan that was established. Because they had appropriate stakeholders at the table and started from a shared set of facts, agencies came together, whether willingly or grudgingly. Ultimately, the city, county, federal government, Houston Coalition for the Homeless, the private sector, philanthropic community, and nearly 70 local homeless service providers all worked together to implement a single, comprehensive plan.

The city had the responsibility to address homelessness as a moral, economic and quality of life imperative. They did this with the feasible solution to achieve the business need – reduce the number of homeless.

×

We have all been there. We implement a program requested by officials and the program generates excitement, and the team is committed to getting it done. Unfortunately, the follow-up data reveal that it didn't work, because it was the wrong solution. The program was suggested, recommended, or even required by someone without having the proper dialogue, assessment, or analysis. Even if there is a clear business need and the program at hand appears to be the right choice, without proper focus and analysis, your results can demonstrate a disconnect between need and solution. The mayor's approach to homelessness is a great example of how to select the right solution.

"Ideas are easy. Implementation is hard." – Guy Kawasaki

In the last chapter, we discussed the obvious and not-so-obvious payoff opportunities along with the importance of uncovering the business need that defines those problems and opportunities. Defining potential payoff and specific business measures that need to improve are the first steps in clarifying "why" an organization needs a specific program. The next challenge is selecting the proper solution. That's the focus of this chapter.

Solution selection is a serious issue. The wrong solution will waste resources and tarnish the image of the organization. Even if the senior executive requests a program, it is incumbent on the program implementation team to clarify that the solution is appropriate and position that program for success.

Performance Needs

With business needs in hand, the next step is determining how to improve the business measures. This step identifies the causes of problems or explores the various approaches to address an opportunity. For some program owners, this may require a new role and skills for the team.

Some program owners are moving from request taker to business contributor. They are resisting the temptation to say yes to every request for a new program. Rather than take the request and implement the program, team members must understand the problem with business impact measures and identify the solution that will meet the business needs.

In the past, an analyst might pinpoint needs that might translate into program implementation. This has evolved into a performance consulting role where the analyst delves deeper into the analysis looking for causes of problems or opportunities and uncovering solutions. The skill set for the performance consultant is different than that of a typical analyst [3]. It begins with the ability to have a productive dialogue with the requestor.

The Performance Dialogue

This sort of dialogue is one the requestor often prefers not to have. After all, this requestor is a sponsor, donor, or supporter, and they often believe that they are perfectly clear about the problem and its solution. Given that they think the requested program is the solution and that the organization has the power to address their need, it's hard to turn them down. If the requestor is asked too many questions, he or she may perceive the organization as an unwilling partner and take the request elsewhere. Here are a few tips to help open the conversation that will result in more appropriate and effective programs.

Examine the Data and Records

Sometimes, a request is connected to particular documents, such as government reports, health studies, or organizational records. It might be helpful to review the records and explore trends. Perhaps the cause is evident in the data. For example, in one organization, a senior executive requested a leadership program for managers to control talent retention. Exit interviews show that employees are leaving for higher pay, and if the data are credible, then a leadership development solution will not correct the problem. If employees are having too many accidents because the personal protective equipment is not adequate, a safety incentive solution is not the answer.

Initiate the Discussion

Pinning down the details of the request is necessary to drive real results. The alignment model, discussed in the previous chapter, Figure 5.2, is a perfect guide to initiating this conversation. On the left side of the alignment model are the different levels of needs assessment. In the ideal world, the requestor identifies the payoff and business needs and asks for help identifying the other levels of needs, which point to a solution. Reality, however, is different. The requestor begins with a requested program; a solution. The conversation may move up the left side of the model. In doing so, the performance consultant clarifies learning, performance, business, and payoff needs.

Case Study

A senior executive in a large nonprofit organization requests a team-building program for his team. The performance consultant asks, "What is occurring (or not occurring) in your team that led you to conclude you need team building?" This harmless question receives the following response. "They are working in silos, they don't communicate very well, they don't seem to want to help each other, they won't share information, and they see others make mistakes without helping them." These are critical behaviors that point toward a solution that

---

will embed new behaviors in the team. These are performance needs. But more information is needed if the program is to contribute to the business. It is helpful to validate the learning needs with another question, "Do they know how to work this way now?" The quick response was "no." This conclusion can be validated with a few interviews, if necessary.

Next, the performance consultant asks, "How is this affecting your key performance indicators (KPIs) or other important measures?" The response was, "We don't really have a problem with our KPIs. I just don't want this behavior, so please implement the program." The performance consultant explains the situation using the alignment model as a guide. "We can implement the program, but there are no business needs for it, except maybe an intangible of teamwork. Is that OK with you?" This question requires the executive to think about the request, and possibly decide not to pursue it.

Use Benchmarking from Similar Solutions

Perhaps there are similar programs with business outcomes that can help you assess the situation when speaking with the requestor. If the requestor suggests a well-documented program but has no clear idea of the outcomes he or she seeks in terms of business impact, refer to measures in a case study. For example, a financial planning program for families in the Philippines is aimed at the families of spouses working in other countries who send money home to the Philippines. The impacts are to increase the savings rate, improve the return on savings investment, diversify the savings portfolio, and to start a new business. Case studies and benchmarking data are excellent tools that show how other programs have tackled this problem and to keep a conversation going.

Use Evaluation as the Hook

If the discussion is going nowhere on the left side of the alignment model, maybe it's time to move to the right side. This leads to a simple question, "What levels of evaluation do you expect to achieve as a result of the program?" Then take the requestor through the different measures that can be captured at each of the five levels. The typical requestor would like to see the impact. Some may be intrigued with the concept of ROI. If they indicate interest in these two levels, remind them that you don't see business needs. Provide examples of business needs. Have them elaborate on the business measures that matter to them and how this requested program could influence these impact measures. In this situation, the focus of the conversation is more on evaluation and less on analysis. The potential evaluation is a hook to have more analysis or discussion.

Involve Others

If the request is coming from the senior executive, top administrator, or high-profile donor, more than likely there are other individuals who understand the issues in more detail. Engaging them in the conversation may lead to some interesting discussions regarding the cause of the problem and potential solutions, including the one requested. Sometimes, the individuals who are closest to the work being done will suggest something that's completely different than those who observe a situation at a distance. The day-to-day context is an advantage.

Discuss Disasters in Other Places

Sometimes it is helpful to bring out examples where programs went astray in other organizations or even within the same organization. Disasters happen. Implementing programs for the wrong reasons and failing to deliver results is not an isolated concept. It may be helpful to discuss the suggested program's previous failings, if they are known, and what it would take to avoid these failings in the future.

For example, the IT function in a large U.S. government agency introduced several projects to automate processes that were very labor intensive. The impact is cost reduction through staff reduction. With the automated procedures, less staff are needed. However, the agency was unwilling to eliminate the jobs. With almost no attrition, there were no job opportunities available for reassignments. Thus, the project yielded a very negative ROI, reflecting unfavorably on the IT staff.

When discussing disasters, it is sometimes important to assess the risks and consequences of pursuing a program that may not be the right solution. Have the requestor consider the time, resources, and costs associated with implementation. That information may be enough for the requestor to allow more analysis and discussion or to consider alternatives.

Use Analysis Techniques

Another approach to assessing performance needs is to use one or more of the many analytical techniques as listed in Figure 6.1. These analytical

• Brainstorming	• Focus groups
• Problem analysis	• Probing interviews
• Cause-and-effect diagram	• Job satisfaction surveys
• Force-field analysis	• Engagement surveys
• Mind mapping	• Exit interviews
• Affinity diagrams	• Exit surveys
• Simulations	• Nominal group technique
• Diagnostic instruments	• Statistical process control

Figure 6.1 Diagnostic Tools.

techniques often use tools from problem solving, quality assurance, and performance improvement to search for these causes. Searching for multiple solutions is important since impact measures are often inhibited for several reasons. However, multiple solutions must be considered in terms of implementation—deciding whether to explore them in total or tackle them in priority order. Detail of these techniques is contained in many references [4]. One such technique, the nominal group technique, is explored in the SCB Case Study, presented later.

Keep it Sensible

Considering the resources needed to examine records, research databases, and observe situations and individuals is important. Analysis takes time. Performance needs can vary considerably and may include ineffective behavior, inadequate systems, disconnected process flow, improper procedures, unsupportive culture, insufficient technology, and unsupportive environment

Uncovering those needs through either conversation or using the analytical techniques listed in Figure 6.1 may seem like a daunting task. It can be, especially when considering the number of factors that could be causing business measures to perform at the current level. The risk of overanalyzing the situation is great. Take a sensible approach to assessing the performance gaps that need closing. Consider the value of improving the targeted business measures and balance the analysis investment with the benefits of solving the problem.

For example, if the opioid epidemic is increasing and the number of deaths is increasing 30 percent per year, and the cost of an opioid death is $40,000, not to mention the loss of a mother, father, or child, you would quickly analyze the issue and find a solution. In another example, if the business need is to increase sales in a culture where salespeople have not fully engaged in conversation with customers, it isn't necessary to have a deep analysis to know that piloting a simple, off-the-shelf interactive selling skills program might be a good idea. Always bear in mind, when thinking about the level of investment in analysis, that there is a difference between statistical significance and practical significance. Sometimes, a cause-and-effect relationship is based on a practical, logical, and sensible approach.

Case Study

At the SCB, employee turnover was a serious problem, costing more than $6 million per year. The bank determined that it could save at least $3 million annually by reducing turnover, which would place it in line with the industry average. The specific measure was voluntary turnover. To uncover the actual need at Level 3, the cause of the problem had to be determined. When the cause was known, a solution could be developed.

The nominal group technique was selected as the analysis method, because it allowed unbiased input to be collected efficiently and accurately across the organization. A focus group was planned, with 12 employees from each region, for a total of six groups representing all the regions. This approach provided approximately a 10 percent sample, which was considered sufficient to pinpoint the problem.

Focus group participants who represented areas in which turnover was highest described why their colleagues were leaving, not why they would leave (the branch network). Data were collected from individuals in a carefully structured format—during two-hour meetings at each location, using third-party facilitators—and were integrated and weighted so that the most important reasons were clearly identified. This process had the advantages of low cost and high reliability as well as a low degree of bias. Only two days of external facilitator time were needed to collect and summarize the data for review.

The nominal group technique unfolded in 10 steps:

1. The process steps were briefly described. A statement of confidentiality was presented. The importance of the participants' input was underscored so that they understood what they must do and the consequences for the bank.

2. Participants were asked to make a list of specific reasons why they felt their colleagues had left the bank and why others might leave. It was stressed that the question dealt with the actions or potential actions of employees other than themselves, although the program team realized that participants' comments would probably reflect their own views. Indications of why participants would leave is exactly what the team was striving to acquire.

3. In a round-robin format, each person revealed one reason for turnover, which was recorded on flip-chart paper. At this point, no attempt was made to integrate the issues, just to record the data in writing. The lists were placed on the walls, so that as many as 60 items were listed and visible when this step was complete.

4. The next step was to consolidate and integrate the list. Some of the integration was easy, because the items contained the same words and meanings. In other cases, ensuring that the meanings for the causes were the same before items were consolidated was important. When this process was complete, the list contained approximately 30 different reasons for turnover.

5. Participants were asked to review all the items, carefully select those they considered to be the top 10 causes, and list them individually on index cards. Participants were told not to concern themselves about which cause was number one. (In this process, participants may become convinced that their original list was not complete or accurate or may identify other reasons for turnover.)

6. Participants then ranked their top 10 items by importance, with the first item as the most important.

7. In a round-robin format, each individual revealed his or her number-one item, and 10 points were recorded on the flip-chart paper next to the item. Next, the number-two reason was identified, and nine points were recorded. This process continued until all reasons had been revealed and points recorded.

8. The numbers next to each item were totaled. The item with the most points was the leading cause of turnover, and the one with the second-highest number of points was the second most important cause of turnover. This

continued until the top 15 causes had been captured based on the weighted average of causes of turnover from that group.

9. This process was completed for all six regional groups. Trends began to emerge quickly from one group to another.

10. The actual raw scores were then combined to integrate the results of the six regional focus groups.

The 15 items with the highest scores were the top 15 reasons for turnover across all the branches and clerical groups. Here are the 10 most important reasons given for turnover in the bank branches:

1. Lack of opportunity for advancement
2. Lack of opportunity to learn new skills and gain new product knowledge
3. Pay level not adequate
4. Not enough responsibility and empowerment
5. Lack of recognition and appreciation of work
6. Lack of teamwork in the branch
7. Lack of preparation for customer service problems
8. Unfair and unsupportive supervisor
9. Too much stress at peak times
10. Not enough flexibility in work schedules

Branch turnover was the most critical issue, involving the highest turnover rates and the largest number of employees. The focus group results provided a clear pattern of specific performance needs that, if addressed, could reduce branch turnover. Recognizing that not all the causes of turnover could be addressed immediately, the bank's management set out to work on the top five reasons while it considered a variety of options.

They sought a single solution that would influence many or all of them. A skill-based pay system appeared to address the top five reasons for turnover. The program was designed to expand the scope of the jobs, offer increases in pay for acquiring skills, and provide a clear path for advancement and improvement. Jobs were redesigned from narrowly focused teller duties to an expanded job description with a new title: the tellers all became a banking representative I, II, or III. A branch employee would be considered a banking representative I level if he or she could perform one or two simple tasks, such as processing deposits and cashing checks.

As an employee at the banking representative I level took on additional responsibilities and performed different functions, he or she would be eligible for a promotion to banking representative II. If the representative could perform all the basic functions of the branch, including processing simple consumer loan applications, a promotion to banking representative III was appropriate. Training opportunities were available to help employees develop the requisite job-related skills, and structured on-the-job training was provided through the branch managers, assistant managers, and supervisors. Self-study information and e-learning programs were also available. The concept of performing multiple tasks was intended to broaden responsibilities and empower employees to perform a variety of tasks that would provide excellent customer service. Pay increases recognized skill acquisition, demonstrated accomplishment, and increased responsibility.

Although the skill-based system had some definite benefits from the employees' perspective, the bank also benefited. Not only was turnover expected to decline, actual staffing levels were expected to be reduced in larger branches. In theory, if all employees in a branch could perform all the duties, fewer employees would be needed. Prior to this time, minimum staffing levels were required in certain critical jobs, and those employees were not always available for other duties.

Additionally, the team anticipated improved customer service. For example, in the typical bank branch, long lines for special functions—such as opening a checking account, closing out a certificate of deposit, or making a consumer loan application—were not unusual, but routine activities, such as paying bills and receiving deposits, often required little or no waiting. The new approach would prevent customers from having to wait in long lines for specialized services. With each employee performing all the tasks, shorter waiting lines would not only be feasible but expected.

To support this new arrangement, the marketing department referred to the concept in its publicity about products and services. Included with checking account statements was a promotional piece labeled "In our branches, there are no tellers." This document described the new process and stated that all the branch employees could perform all branch functions, and consequently, the bank could provide faster service.

Learning Needs

Performance needs uncovered in the previous step often require a learning component to ensure all stakeholders know what they need to do and how to do it if the needed change in performance is to be delivered. In some cases, learning itself becomes the principal solution, as in competency development, major technology changes, capability development, and system installations. For other programs, learning is a minor part of the solution and often involves simply understanding the process, procedure, or policy. For example, when implementing a new ethics policy, the learning component requires understanding how the policy works and the participants' role in it. In another example, for a new drug addiction program to be successful, participants (and others) must know how it works and what they must do to make it successful. In short, a learning solution is not always needed, but all solutions have a learning component.

A variety of approaches are available to measure specific learning needs. Because multiple tasks and multiple jobs are frequently involved in any program, each should be addressed separately. Sometimes, the least useful way to find out what skills and knowledge are needed is to ask the participants involved in the program. They may not be sure of what is needed or may not know enough to provide adequate input.

Subject-Matter Experts (SMEs)

One of the most important approaches to determine learning needs is to ask the individuals who understand the requirements to make the proposed program successful. They can best determine what skills and knowledge are necessary to address the performance issues defined above. Then it may be appropriate to discover how much of the knowledge and skills already exist. Ideally, subject matter experts are in two categories. One group knows the content of the program and the other knows the context of the situation and place where it will be applied.

Job and Task Analysis

A job and task analysis is effective when a new job, procedure, or process is created, or an existing process changes significantly. As procedures are redesigned and tasks are identified, this technique offers a systematic way of detailing the steps and relevant tasks. A task analysis determines specific knowledge, skills, tools, and conditions necessary to perform a particular task or procedure. The task analysis collects information about the scope, responsibilities, and steps related to the procedure.

Performing a job and task analysis not only helps the individuals who will use the program develop a clear picture of their responsibilities but will also indicate what is expected of them. It may involve identifying high performers, preparing a task analysis questionnaire, or developing other materials as necessary to collect information. During the task analysis, responsibilities are defined, tasks are detailed, and specific learning requirements are identified.

Observations

Current practices and procedures may have to be observed to understand the situation as the program is implemented. This often indicates the level of capability as well as the correct procedures. Observations can be used to examine workflow and interpersonal interactions, including those between leaders and team members. Sometimes, the observer is unknown to those being observed (placed in the environment specifically to watch the current processes). At other times, the observer is someone previously in the work environment but now in a different role. Another possibility is that the observer is invisible to those being observed. Examples of the latter include retail mystery shoppers, electronic observation, or individuals who have joined a group temporarily but have been there long enough to be considered part of the team. The advantages of observation as a data collection tool are described in Chapter 8. Here, it is merely important to remember that observation can be a tool used to uncover what individuals need to know or do as a program is changed.

Demonstrations

In some situations, having employees demonstrate their abilities to perform a certain task, process, or procedure is important. The demonstration can be as simple as a skill practice or a role play or as complex as an extensive mechanical or electronic simulation. The issue is to use this as a way of determining whether employees know how to perform a particular process. From that, specific learning needs can evolve.

Tests

Testing as a needs assessment process is not as common as other methods, but it can be very useful. Employees are tested to find out what they know about a particular situation. This information helps guide learning issues.

For example, in one healthcare organization, management was concerned that employees were not aware of the company's sexual harassment policy or what actions constituted sexual harassment. In the early stages of the program analysis, the target audience for the program, a group of supervisors and managers, were given a 20-item test about their knowledge of the sexual harassment policy (10 items) and knowledge about sexual harassment actions (10 items). The test scores revealed where insufficient knowledge existed and formed the basis of a program to reduce the number of sexual harassment complaints.

Management Assessment

When implementing programs in organizations where there is an existing manager or team leader, input from the management team may be used to assess the current situation and the knowledge and skills required by the new situation. This input can be collected through surveys, interviews, or focus groups. It can be a rich source of information about what the users of the program will need to know to make it a success if it is implemented.

Where the learning component is minor, learning needs are simple. However, determining the specific learning needs can be very time-consuming for major programs for which new procedures, technologies, and processes are developed. As in the previous step, it is important not to spend excessive time analyzing at this early stage in the process but to collect as much data as possible with minimum resources.

Case Study

Now, we return to SCB, where an employee turnover reduction program was proposed to save the bank at least $3 million annually. At the Level 2 needs assessment, learning needs fell into two categories. First, for each learning program designed to build the skills of employees to be promoted, both skill acquisition and knowledge increase needs were identified. These learning measurements were self-assessment, testing, demonstrations, and others, and were connected to each specific program.

The second learning need was for employees to understand how the new program worked. As the program was introduced in meetings with all employees, a simple measurement of learning was necessary to capture the employees' understanding of the following issues:

- How the program works
- What employees must do to be successful in the program

> - How promotion decisions are made
> - The timing of various aspects of the program
>
> These major learning needs were identified and were connected specifically with the solution being implemented.

Preference Needs

The final level of needs analysis is based on preferences, which drive the program requirements. Essentially, individuals prefer certain processes, schedules, venues, or activities for the structure of the program or project. These preferences define how the particular program should be implemented. If the program is a solution to a problem, this step defines how the solution will be implemented and how participants should perceive its value. If the program addresses an opportunity, this step outlines how participants should see value in the program.

Key Issues

Figure 6.2 shows the typical preference needs from the participant's perspective. These represent statements that define the parameters of the program in terms of value, necessity, and convenience. Implementation is based on the input of several key stakeholders. For example, participants involved in the program (those who must make it work) may have a particular preference, but their preference could exceed the available resources, time, and budget. The immediate manager's input may help minimize the

This solution should be:

Relevant to my work	Easy to use
Relevant to the community	Convenient for me
Important to my success	New to me
Important to the program	A good investment of funds
Valuable to me	Implemented without disruption of work
Valuable to society	Seamless with our systems
Action oriented	Something that I will recommend to others
Necessary for our solution	Something I will use

Figure 6.2 Typical Preference Needs.

amount of disruption and maximize resources. Those who support or own the program often place preferences around the program in terms of urgency and importance. Because this is a Level 1 need, the program structure and solution will directly relate to the reaction objectives and to the initial reaction to the program.

Case Study

As the skill-based pay program at SCB rolled out and a solution was developed, the preference needs were defined, and these involved several issues. The program was to be rolled out as soon as possible, so that its effects could lead to lower employee turnover. All the training programs had to be in place and made available to employees. The amount of time employees needed to spend away from their jobs to attend training was an issue, and the managers had some control over when the resulting promotions would occur. This process should not take too long; otherwise, it would disappoint employees who were eager to be trained and promoted. At the same time, the staffing and workload issues had to be balanced so that the appropriate amount of time was devoted to training and skill building. More specifically, when the program was announced, the desired employee reaction was defined. Program leaders wanted employees to view the program as challenging, motivational, rewarding, fair, and a good investment in their futures. These needs easily translated into the solution design as well as the detailed objectives of the reaction.

Matching Solutions to Needs

Sometimes, the most difficult part of the process is to match the best solution or solutions to the needs or causes of the problem. This task is as much an art as it is a science. Several principles should be followed to ensure that the solution addresses all the needs or causes.

Some Solutions are Obvious

Some causes point directly to a solution. If employees need more flexibility in scheduling their work hours, flexible scheduling is the obvious solution. If employees need the flexibility to work at home, telecommuting is an appropriate solution. If houses without smoke detectors are three times more likely to have serious fire damage, then installing smoke detectors is a way to reduce house fire damage. Although design issues are important, the solutions may become obvious in some situations.

Solutions Can Come in Different Sizes

Solutions come with a full range of possibilities and represent a broad scope of investment needs and levels of complexity. For example, if employees have expressed a need for more tuition assistance, the solution could range from identifying a limited program only for certain technical areas to the implementation of an expensive, liberal, open program completely funded by the organization. It is helpful to understand what would be considered an acceptable solution versus not addressing the issue at all.

Some Solutions Take a Long Time

Although some issues respond to a short-term fix, such as compliance, others take a long time to rectify. For example, eliminating poverty will take a long time with many solutions. However, this would have to start with one program. This concept must be recognized early, and while it may take a long time to eliminate poverty, we must see progress along the way.

> *"If you look really closely, most overnight successes took a long time."*
> *– Steve Jobs*

Solutions Should be Tackled with the Highest Priority Items First

This principle seems obvious, but it requires further discussion. If everything is a top priority, then nothing is a top priority. Those issues causing most of the problem demand the most attention and perhaps even the most investment. This is difficult because there are so many problems and opportunities to explore.

Designing a solution following these principles will identify the appropriate mix of solutions. The results of these steps are easily presented as a matrix diagram, described next.

The Matrix Diagram

A matrix diagram is one way to organize a large amount of information. It can be used to arrange the information so that elements are logically connected and presented in a graphic form. A matrix diagram also shows the importance of each connecting point in a relationship and presents the relationships that exist among these variables. The matrix diagram can be "L" shaped, with one row across the top and one column down the side of the page, or it can be "T" shaped, in which two columns containing two types of data are compared with a third. As an alternative, words can be used in place of a dot to indicate the relative priority, strength, or importance of a particular cause, solution, or job group. Matrix diagrams provide an excellent way of summarizing information about a problem's cause and relating it to job groups, regions, or other breakdowns. In addition, as shown in Figure 6.3, this can also be used to relate cause to solutions.

In Figure 6.3, a T-shaped matrix diagram presents a plan to reduce turnover in four job groups. The job groups with the most turnover in this banking organization are listed at the top of the matrix. Six causes of turnover are identified along the middle of the diagram, with each matched to a job group. Listed at the bottom are the solutions that are matched to the particular causes. For example, "Implement Pay for Skills" is aimed primarily at the branch teller group and focuses on both the concern about inadequate pay and the lack of career advancement.

	Inadequate Pay	Inadequate Supervision	Lack of Job Autonomy	Job Stress	Career Advancement	Ineffective Communication
Teller	•	•			•	•
Customer Service Representative		•		•		•
Branch Managers			•			•
Loan Officers		•				•
Job Groups ⟨Causes / Solutions⟩						
Adjust Base Pay	•					
Revise Incentives	•					
Train Immediate Manager		•				
Revise Job Responsibilities			•			
Increase Staffing				•		
Implement Pay for Skills	•				•	
Improve Communication						•

Figure 6.3 Matrix Diagram: A Plan to Reduce Turnover.

Selecting Solutions for Maximum Payoff

The next step is to make sure that the focus is only on those solutions with maximum payoff. Two major issues can affect that payoff: the cost of the solution and the monetary benefit from the implementation. To achieve maximum payoff, costs should be considered. The lower the cost, the greater the potential payoff. (ROI will be covered in detail in several chapters.) From the benefits side, the greater the benefits, the greater the potential payoff with ROI. Several issues must be considered.

Short-Term versus Long-Term Costs

Some solutions, such as changing management, will be expensive to implement on a short-term basis. The initial cost of this solution might be prohibitive. Other solutions, such as communication training for police officers, may have little up-front cost but a tremendous long-term payoff that may exceed the costs. Major change programs are usually long-term and require careful consideration before implementing. The short-term versus long-term cost implication must always be considered and is fully explored in later chapters.

Consider Forecasting ROI

A forecast can be developed showing the expected monetary benefits compared to the projected cost of the solution. A forecast could have been developed for the homeless project in the opening story but wasn't necessary. It was an obvious payoff need. If the need and potential solutions are not so obvious, an ROI forecast may help with the decision-making process. An ROI forecasting wasn't pursued for the SCB case, but could have been developed. An entire chapter is devoted to ROI forecasting. The solutions with the highest forecasted ROI value may become the best prospects for speedy implementation.

Time Needed for Implementation

Some solutions are implemented quickly, while others take a long time. This may mean that long-term solutions should be implemented in conjunction with short-term fixes. In other words, the organization should recognize that both quick fixes and long-term changes are necessary. This approach shows participants and others that the organization is taking steps now and also building for the future, which results in enhanced commitment and loyalty.

Avoid Mismatches

The impact of a mismatched problem and solution can be significant. For example, having to discontinue an employee benefit plan can affect job satisfaction. Mismatches can cause three major problems:

1. Funds are wasted, because money is spent on a solution that did not correct the problem. Additional funds may not be allocated.
2. Inappropriate solutions can have a negative impact for the organization, participants, and the community. The participants have been required to participate in a solution that has no value for them.
3. When time, effort, and money are spent on a mismatched solution, an opportunity to implement the correct solution has been missed. The problem is still there, and it might be getting worse.

The message: Avoid mismatches at all costs!

Verifying the Match

After identifying possible solutions, you should verify the match between the need and the solution. It is often helpful to return to the source of input (focus groups, employees, etc.) to affirm that the solution meets the need. This approach is not applicable for every solution, because original inputs may be biased. However, their input may provide insight into progress made or indicate whether a solution is on target or off base. When input was obtained from interviews or focus groups, it may be easier to return to these groups to check whether a solution is addressing the cause of the problem. The important point is to find a way to discover whether a mismatch exists.

The initial implementation of the solution provides an opportunity to obtain feedback to ensure that the solution is a fit. Early feedback can prompt adjustments that need to be made or, in worst-case scenarios, suggest abandonment of the solution altogether. Seeking feedback represents another opportunity to involve a group of experts. In addition, communicate early results quickly, letting the target group know that a solution has been implemented.

Tackling Multiple Solutions

Should you tackle a problem with more than one solution at a time? To a certain extent, the answer depends on the relative priority of the causes. Clearly, too many solutions undertaken at the same time can reduce the potential effectiveness of each one and result in confusion and potential waste.

It is essential to examine the top priorities to determine which solutions are feasible, the time needed for implementation, and the level of others' involvement. These factors may mean taking on three or four (five, at the most) solutions. Avoid the quick fix, especially if the issue calls for a longer-term solution. Many problems are not solved through quick fixes and tend to be issues that have evolved over time (either internally or externally). Poverty, illiteracy, diseases, lack of clean water, and addictions are long-term problems. As a result, they will take time to correct.

Consider the level of involvement and support needed for the solution. Participants are involved in the solution, requiring time away from other tasks. The level of support from managers (or significant others) is also important. They need to be on board with solutions and their implementation. How much they can (or are willing to) support is significant.

Finally, available resources play a key role in whether multiple solutions can be implemented. For most organizations, the costs of the solutions can be substantial, and taking on too many solutions may drain available resources. The result may even have an impact on the earnings of the organization, potentially creating another serious problem.

Final Thoughts

This chapter focuses on step two in the ROI Methodology, "Make it Feasible." The objective of making it feasible is to ensure that you have the right solution. This chapter builds on the previous chapter, where business alignment begins with answering the question "Why?" Making it feasible can help the program owners move from request takers to business contributors. It can lead the team toward the right solution for the business need. This chapter provides steps and processes to fully understand the problem or opportunity, making sure the solution is feasible and appropriate. This is a critical role in program planning, implementation, and evaluation and will require serious attention. You must be on the right path to deliver value. This path includes clearly defined business needs and proper solutions to resolve them. The next chapter focuses on expecting success.

7

Expect Success: Design for Results

A new president was selected to lead Global Finance Organization (GFO), an NGO created to make loans and provide funding to developing countries. This new president was doing what new presidents typically do, reviewing the budgets of different departments. One particular item caught his attention, which was an executive coaching program involving 400 managers and 75 external coaches, representing a sizeable budget. This prompted a discussion with the talent development team about the value of this coaching.

Although the new president was supportive, he asked, "I would like to see the ROI of this program. Do you have that?"

The team indicated that they had not evaluated this program at that level, but perhaps they could, if necessary.

The president added, "We need to do this for expenditures this large and for programs that are designed to help our managerial and executive teams."

This request prompted an evaluation of the coaching process with the goal to track the business value and the financial ROI of this program. To accomplish this task, GFO engaged a consulting firm that focused on ROI studies.

In the initial meeting with GFO, the consultant asked about the nature and scope of the program: "Are there any business objectives for this coaching program specifically detailing the business need for this coaching process?"

The team responded, "No, there were actually no objectives for the program, just agenda items created by the coach and some very broad goals."

The consultant replied, "When launching this program, was there a mention in the description about the business connection of the program in any way?"

"No," said the talent development team.

"Was there any discussion with the participants about the business value?" asked the consultant.

Again, the answer was "No."

"Was there any correspondence or discussion with the coaches to push the engagement to the business level?"

"No," replied the talent representative. "The focus is on behavior. Some of the coaches were for career transitions, some were there to address difficult people issues, and a few were focused on business performance."

"Good," said the consultant. "What percent focused on the business performance?"

"Well, it's really a small number," replied the team member.

"Were there any discussions with the coaches about the specific business measures on which the managers were to focus?" inquired the consultant.

"Not really; it was left open."

The consultant summarized, "Well, there's a good chance that this program has not delivered business value—at least in terms of business measures that can be monitored and converted to money, like productivity, quality of work, timeliness of the projects, or specific cost reductions. This may result in a negative ROI. Quite frankly, I have to ask, do you really want to see the ROI for this program?"

The team member responded, "We have to. The new president has requested it."

The consultant replied, "The danger is that the program was not designed for the business connection, and yet we are evaluating it at the business impact and ROI levels."

"We realize this," responded the team member. "But I think our new president would be okay if we demonstrate the current value and make the changes necessary to improve its value contribution in the future."

The consultant added, "We could recommend the changes now to make it more successful. You would begin the coaching assignment with a business measure if you want to measure at that level. You would adjust the coaching engagement around actions and behaviors that will influence that business measure, using the processes in the coaching program. The improvement in this business measure becomes an impact objective. In addition, you would create objectives at the application, learning, and reaction levels to clearly focus on both the participant and the coach. You would build in data collection to make it easy for the participant to track action items and the subsequent changes in the business measure. In essence, the program would begin with clear business measures in mind, and the focus throughout the coaching process is on these business measures. You can make those changes now and moving forward to show the value of the next few groups of individuals coming through the program."

The team member replied, "Well, we understand that, but we think we need to follow through and show the value. If it is negative, as we expect it to be, your study can be the basis for our recommendation going forward."

The consultant agreed and began the process of evaluating the program. As expected, there were no tangible measures connected to the program, although there were some very important intangibles, such as collaboration, teamwork, career satisfaction, and engagement. These measures were reported as intangibles, because it was difficult to convert them to money within this organization credibly. As a result of this, it was decided not to push the evaluation to ROI, but to stop with the impact expressed as intangibles. This would be used to discuss how a positive ROI could be delivered.

The good news was that the program was seen as a valuable process to participants. It was reported that the program was helpful with career issues and guiding managers through important challenges. There seemed to be some business connection, but nothing specific tied to key performance indicators. This data should provide an opportunity to improve the program going forward, if the purpose of the program is to drive business. The consultant agreed to present the data to the top executives and discuss the opportunities for business value with a few changes in the process. The president reviewed the study and agreed to have the meeting to present the results to executive groups "in the near future." Meanwhile, he asked that the coaching programs be placed "on pause."

Unfortunately, that meeting never occurred, and the team never had a chance to improve the coaching process. The program is still on pause.

———————————— × ————————————

This case study reveals that programs should start with a clear definition of success . . . "Why are we doing this?" The "why" should be one or more business measures, if the program should drive business value. With this definition, everyone involved should expect this level of success and take steps to deliver it. SMART objectives are needed at four levels (reaction, learning, application, and impact) and the stakeholders use these objectives to design and deliver the highest levels (impact).

"The best way to predict the future is to create it." – Peter Drucker

The Power of Expectations

Perhaps Peter Drucker had a better way of expecting success—you need to create it. You must not only expect success from programs, but also create success by designing for results. The two previous steps ensure programs are aligned with the business, and you have the right solution to get there. Now let's focus on how to design for business results.

Too often, organizations implement programs without clearly defining the expectations of each stakeholder group at the appropriate level of success. Without clear expectations, participants may not know what they must do to make it successful. It is difficult for them to step up to responsibility when they do not understand that responsibility. Clear expectations take the mystery out of someone's role in implementing a program and the reasons for doing so.

The initial analysis of the need for the program is the foundation for building expectations. From that analysis, specific objectives are set at multiple levels, detailing how participants should react to the program, what they will learn, how they should use it, and what the impact on their work and the organization will be. This chapter shows how to set expectations, develop objectives, and ensure that stakeholders are doing their part to meet the objectives. But first, here's a coaching example to illustrate the power of creating expectations of results. This is a contrasting view of the GFO coaching project, the opening story of this chapter.

Case Study

Nations Hotel, a well-respected global hotel chain, has survived and thrived in a highly competitive industry. To be one of the leaders in this field requires the executive team to constantly focus on client satisfaction, operational efficiency, revenue growth, and talent retention.

To achieve these ambitious annual goals, the talent development team makes available a number of learning processes. Formal programs are available that focus on process improvement. Leadership and management development programs are offered to help drive improvement. A variety of technology and productivity tools are also accessible. And, finally, a successful coaching process, "Coaching for Business Impact," is available. This coaching process, designed by a prestigious external coaching firm, focuses on business improvement [1].

As part of the process, individuals who are involved in this coaching focus on measures under their responsibility in the areas that represent challenges. Specific business measures are the beginning point of this process, and objectives for the program are developed at four different levels (reaction, learning, application, and impact). Participating in the coaching process is voluntary. With almost 200 of the 500 eligible managers wanting to participate, the top executive team suggested that the talent development group show the business value of this program.

The talent development group agreed and worked with the coaching provider to make sure that the program was focused on business needs. Objectives were developed, and data-collection tools were built into the program. The first 25 participants who signed up for the program were considered to be the sample to measure the actual ROI. Effort was made to ensure that this initial group was representative of the entire group of candidates for the program (performance rating, tenure, job roles, etc.).

The coaching engagement process was altered slightly to ensure that each participant focused on at least three business measures that should be improved as a result. An action planning module was added to support a built-in data-collection process that began with the end in mind (a business measure) and also to show the action steps that would be taken to improve those measures with the support, advisement, and collaboration of the coach. Three action plans were developed as part of the process. Objectives for all five levels, including ROI, are listed in Figure 7.1.

With this in mind, the project began, and the rest, as they say, is history. The project generated a positive ROI of 221 percent.

This true story reinforces the importance of setting expectations for success early. The participants (executives) knew that success was necessary and possible all the way to the business value. Objectives were set to push the program through the different levels all the way to the impact and financial ROI levels. The coaches connected the engagement to business impact. The designers built tools into the process to facilitate completing the actions and document the business impact, showing the success at the end. Essentially, the program was designed to drive success. The coaches expected business success, the participants were willing to deliver business success, designers and developers designed for business results, and the executives expected success. There was no mystery about what this program should achieve.

Level 1. Reaction Objectives

After participating in this coaching program, the managers being coached will:

1. Perceive coaching to be relevant to the job
2. Perceive coaching to be important to their performance
3. Perceive coaching to be value added in terms of time and funds invested
4. Rate the coach as effective
5. Recommend this program to other managers and executives

Level 2. Learning Objectives

After completing this coaching program, the managers being coached should improve their skills for each of the following:

1. Uncovering personal strengths and weaknesses
2. Translating feedback into action plans
3. Involving team members in projects and goals
4. Communicating effectively
5. Collaborating with colleagues
6. Improving personal effectiveness
7. Enhancing leadership skills

Level 3. Application Objectives Six months after completing this coaching program, managers being coached should:

1. Complete the action plan for application and impact
2. Adjust the plan as needed for changes in the environment

Level 3. Application Objectives (continued)

3. Show improvements on the following items:
   a. Uncovering personal strengths and weaknesses
   b. Translating feedback into action plans
   c. Involving team members in projects and goals
   d. Communicating effectively
   e. Collaborating with colleagues
   f. Improving personal effectiveness
   g. Enhancing leadership skills
4. Identify barriers and enablers to success.

Level 4. Impact Objectives

After completing this coaching program, managers being coached should improve at least three specific measures in the following areas:

1. Sales growth
2. Productivity/operational efficiency
3. Direct cost reduction
4. Retention of key staff members
5. Customer satisfaction

Level 5. ROI Objective

The ROI value should be at least 25 percent.

Figure 7.1 Objectives of Coaching for Business Impact.

Keep it Sensible

This case study can create anxiety among some practitioners. The typical worry might be "Do we need all these levels of objectives for every program?" The short answer is "no." You have to take a sensible approach. From its beginning, this program was designed to drive the business impact level. Even the name, "Coaching for Business Impact," implies that it should affect business impact. Because executives wanted to see the financial ROI, this shifted the focus from behavior change, the typical target for coaching, to business results and on to ROI. With the focus on impact and ROI, the engagement now is "What specific measures need to change, and what should I do differently with my team to change them?"

But not every program should be positioned this way. This level of analysis is reserved for those programs that are important, strategic, expensive, and involve a lot of people. Some would argue that a business focus is needed, even if success is not measured at the higher levels. That may be true, but a sensible approach that includes tackling one program at a time will increase the chances of success and long-term value of programs.

Defining the Success of Programs

Reflect on "What is your business?" While it is important for the organization to clearly articulate and understand its "business," it is also helpful to understand the business of the programs and projects implemented. What one sentence description represents the current definition of success of all your programs? This is a critical issue, because it can vary significantly.

Figure 7.2 shows six possible descriptions of success for the programs [2]. Complete the following exercise to bring into focus the current description of programs and, perhaps, how it should change in the future.

Your Choice	Value Description	Rank	Measure Now	Donor/ Sponsor Rank	Percent Measured Now	Best Practice
	"Serve the largest number of people with the least amount of disruption and cost."					100%
	"Participants are engaged, enjoy the programs, and see their experience as valuable."					100%
	"Participants are learning the content, information,and skills to make this program successful."					90%
	"Participants take action, use the content, and make important changes."					30%
	"Participants are driving important impact measures and having an impact in their work, community, or organization."					10%
	"Participants and the organization have a positive return on the investment of their time and the resources for this program."					5%

The Possible Measures

Figure 7.2 What's Your Business?

- As a first step, read each value description and select the one (only one) that is the most important to you right now. Place a check to the left of that description.
- Next, rank each of these statements in terms of importance to measuring the success of your programs. Place a number one for the item that you would consider your most important and continue numbering until the least important measure is ranked sixth (6).
- In the next column, check the statements that define the categories you are measuring now. For example, if you are counting the number of people, time in the program, and the costs, check the first item. Check all that apply.
- In the next column, indicate how your sponsors or donors would rank these data items in terms of what is valuable to them from one to six, with one being the most valuable and six the least valuable.
- In the next column, indicate the percentage of programs measured annually now at each of the levels.
- The best practice profile is in the last column, representing the percentages of programs evaluated at each level for each year. Usually, the current versus best practice comparison reveals gaps that serve as opportunities to pursue.

The six statements represent the input (Level 0) and five levels of outcomes: 1) reaction, 2) learning, 3) application, 4) impact, and 5) ROI. The typical conclusion from this exercise is that the program implementation team needs to change their definition of success. From the exercise, most teams reveal that their definition hovers around Level 0, 1, or 2.

The goal is to change the definition of success to focus on outcomes at Level 3 or Level 4 and occasionally Level 5. For example, the success of a chaplaincy program in a healthcare system might be described as improvement in patient outcomes and patient satisfaction, which are measured in the system. This would be Level 4.

By defining success at these higher levels, commitment to achieving that level of success increases. Expectations are greater for program owners as well as donors, executives, and administrators, who want to see impact for programs, and maybe the ROI for some programs. However, the dilemma is that commitment and achievement are not the same. If the commitment is to drive business impact, then it is important to achieve business impact.

When the program achieves this, donors will perceive the program as a true business contributor. They will recognize the program as an investment, not a cost.

Definitions of success at the business impact and ROI levels drive the process described in this book. The definition will appear in field handbooks, policy guides, opening statements, and maybe even in the name of the program.

Designing for Results at Each Level

It is helpful to think of design on the basis of the levels presented in Chapter 4. The levels of success define the chain of impact that must occur as the participants react, learn, apply, and have an impact. But it all starts with Level 0 (input). Figure 7.3 summarizes the topics around which designing for results should occur. These issues are explored in more detail in the next two chapters.

> *"A wise man will make more opportunities than he finds."*
> *– Francis Bacon*

Level 0, Input

Success begins with involving the right people in the program at the right time with the right amount of content at the lowest possible cost to achieve the desired results. Too often, programs miss the mark with the target audience and the timing, sometimes with too much content, the wrong

Level	Design Issues
0 Input	Who, what, where, when, how long, costs
1 Reaction	Important, necessary, relevant, intent to use
2 Learning	Action oriented, relevant, easy, engaging, motivating, confidence-inspiring
3 Application	Ease of use, frequency of use, success with use, inhibitors, enablers
4 Impact	Specific measures, alignment, line of sight, access, connectivity
5 ROI	Efficiency, effectiveness

Figure 7.3 Designing for Results.

participants, the wrong time, or too much cost. Design begins with thinking about the key inputs shown in Figure 7.3.

Level 1, Reaction

Determining the desired reaction is important. The principal target for reaction is the participants. Will they see the program as important, relevant, easy, and something they intend to use? Clarifying these issues helps design the location, flow, content, examples, activities, communications, and all the other elements that motivate the participant to use the program and have an impact.

Level 2, Learning

At the heart of any process is learning to use it. The key to designing for learning is that it must matter to the individual and to the organization. The content must be action oriented, relevant, easy, engaging, and motivating. Participants must leave the program with the confidence and determination to use it. This drives many design activities.

Level 3, Application

Simply learning the content doesn't ensure that participants will apply it. Many design opportunities are available to ease the application of content. Participants should know when they should use it, how often they should use it, and how to identify success. Design should limit the various inhibitors and enhance the enablers that support application. While these issues will be covered later, the point is that they must be designed into the process to achieve the results.

Level 4, Impact

Ideally, the desired impact of a program should be clearly known in the beginning with specific measures, which is the focus of Chapter 5. The solution must be the right one to deliver that impact, as illustrated in Chapter 6. Participants must see the business alignment and have a direct line of sight from what they are doing to those impact measures. They should have access to the impact data and know their connection to that data. Because of the importance of impact, several design issues will influence the impact requirement.

Case Study

A successful organizer of a conference for sustainability wanted to ensure that the individuals who attended actually used what they took away. If participants attend the conference but never really change anything or do anything differently, then the conference provider is essentially in the entertainment business and not necessarily making a professional difference. As a design change, the organizers required the conference speakers to provide application objectives, clearly defining how attendees would use what they learn in their work, school, community, or life. Additionally, speakers had to provide impact objectives, illustrating the impact of their session, as attendees used what they learned and had a consequence with their actions. Moving from learning objectives to application and impact objectives had an important effect. It made the speakers more focused on content use, with more job aids, application activities, and tools for application. It also eliminated some potential speakers who focused on "fluff" and entertainment, with little potential for use.

Level 5, ROI

Even if the ROI is not calculated, it is helpful to think about ROI from a design perspective. ROI has two key components. The first is the impact outcome, which is converted to monetary benefits. Impact focuses on the effectiveness of the program. The second component is the cost of doing it; that's the efficiency. In the design phase, the focus is on achieving greater impact and keeping the costs low. Together, these concepts will keep the ROI on track.

Use Empathy

All the stakeholders, content, and resources focus on enabling the participant to have success at the application and impact levels. This requires the stakeholders to know the viewpoint and situation of the participants. They must have empathy for participants, so they can clearly put themselves in the participant's role. They must be aware of the participant's challenges and opportunities as well as their frustrations, difficulties, and stresses. The design team must constantly put themselves in the participant's shoes. In addition to a subject-matter expert (SME) for the program content, an expert on the participant's role is needed, and this SME will be responsible for bringing in that perspective.

It is also necessary to empathize with the participants' manager or significant other. In nonprofits, the significant other is usually a family member. In an organization, the significant other is the participant's manager. These individuals often have to make sacrifices while the participant is involved in the program. With the stresses, strains, and struggles of their situation, they must know that the program is delivering enough value to overcome this inconvenience. Someone on the design team must understand the significant other's connection to the program, their resistance to becoming involved, and the challenges they face. These individuals are human, they are not perfect, and the design team has to put themselves in that role.

> *"The essence of being human is that one does not seek perfection." –*
> *George Orwell*

Developing Objectives at Multiple Levels

To cover all the outcome levels, objectives must be set for receiving a positive reaction from stakeholders, ensuring participants have learned what's required, completing what's expected of them, improving impact measures, and achieving the minimum ROI. Objectives are powerful, because they provide direction, focus, and guidance.

An important part of this step of delivering results is to set objectives, especially at the application and impact levels. It is the higher level of objectives that positions programs to achieve business results. Setting higher levels of objectives keeps business alignment on track during the program. However, to have impact, objectives at the reaction, learning, and application levels must be set. When performing an ROI calculation, an objective at the ROI level must be set. Figure 7.4 summarizes these levels. Ideally, these objectives should be specific, measurable, achievable, relevant, and time-based (SMART). The precision is important.

Case Study

The importance of setting objectives at the higher level was underscored by a publication from the Association of Talent Development (ATD). A few years ago, we were asked by ATD to write a book about developing objectives, pushing the objectives to the application, impact, and ROI levels, and providing tips on how to write these objectives and how to use them in the work environment. We wrote the book, and ATD selected the title. We were surprised at the title, but we clearly embraced it.

The title was, *Beyond Learning Objectives: Develop Measurable Objectives That Link to the Bottom Line.* [3] What ATD wanted to do was to remind the profession that they are quite good at developing learning objectives, thanks to people like Robert Mager and Benjamin Bloom, who provide great advice on how to write learning objectives [4, 5]. But it is now time to push those objectives to the higher levels so that we can achieve and maintain the proper business focus for programs.

Reaction Objectives

For any program to be successful, various stakeholders must react favorably, or at least not negatively. Ideally, the stakeholders and especially the participants should be satisfied with the program, because the best solutions offer win-win outcomes for all. Reaction objectives are necessary to maintain proper focus. Unfortunately, many programs do not have specific objectives at this level, although data-collection mechanisms are in place to measure the feedback almost every time. These objectives are missing because the designers and developers assume a particular reaction, but it's best to drive that reaction with specific objectives. Figure 7.5 presents typical reaction objectives.

Levels of Objectives	Focus of Objectives
Level 1, Reaction	Defines specific measures of reaction to the program as it is revealed and communicated to the stakeholders
Level 2, Learning	Defines specific measures of knowledge, information, contacts, and skills as the participants and other stakeholders learn how to make the program successful
Level 3, Application	Defines specific measures of actions that define success with application and implementation of the program
Level 4, Impact	Defines the specific impact measures that will change or improve as a consequence of the program's implementation
Level 5, ROI	Defines the minimum return on investment from the program, comparing program costs with monetary benefits from the program

Figure 7.4 Multiple Levels of Objectives.

At the end of the program, participants should rate each of the following
statements at least a 4 out of 5 on a 5-point scale:

- The program is relevant to my (our) situation.
- The facilitators/organizers were effective.
- The program is valuable to this mission, cause, or organization.
- The program is important to my (our) success.
- The program is motivational for me (us).
- The program is practical.
- The program contained new information.
- The program represented an excellent use of my time.
- I will recommend the program to others.
- I will use the concepts and materials from this program.

Figure 7.5 Typical Reaction Objectives.

Learning Objectives

Every program will involve learning. In some cases, the learning component is significant, such as major skill-building solutions, large change
projects, and comprehensive technology implementations. To ensure that
the various stakeholders have learned what's required in order to make the
program successful, learning objectives are developed.

Learning objectives are critical, because they communicate expected outcomes from the learning and define the desired competence or the required
performance to make the program successful. Learning objectives should
clearly indicate what participants must learn—sometimes with precision.
The best learning objectives describe behaviors that are observable, measurable, and necessary for success with the program. They are often outcome based, clearly worded, and specific. They lay out what the particular
stakeholder must know and do to implement the program successfully.
Learning objectives can have three components:

- Performance—what the participant or stakeholder will be
  able to do to make the program successful
- Conditions under which the participant or stakeholder will
  perform the various tasks and processes
- Criteria—the degree or level of proficiency necessary to perform a new task, process, or procedure that is part of the
  program

Figure 7.6 shows typical learning objectives.

After completing the program, participants will be able to:

- Name the three pillars of the new AIDS strategy in three minutes.
- Identify the four conditions for a microfinance loan.
- Complete the leadership simulation in 15 minutes.
- Identify the six features of the new ethics policy.
- List five benefits of healthy living.
- Demonstrate the use of each software routine in the standard time.
- Use problem-solving skills, given a specific problem statement.
- Determine whether they are eligible for the early retirement program.
- List seven out of 10 harmful effects of pollution.
- Score 75 or better in 10 minutes on the new-product quiz on the first try.
- Demonstrate all five customer-interaction skills with a success rating of four out of five.
- Explain the five benefits of diversity in a work group in five minutes.
- Document suggestions for award consideration.
- Secure an accreditable job in 30 days.
- Score at least nine out of 10 on a sexual harassment policy quiz.
- Identify five new technology trends presented at the conference.

Figure 7.6 Typical Learning Objectives.

Application Objectives

Program implementation should be guided by application objectives clearly defining what is expected and to what level of performance, reflecting the action desired from the program. They also should involve particular milestones, indicating specifically when steps or phases of the process are completed. Application objectives are critical, because they describe the expected outcomes in the intermediate area between learning what is necessary to make the program successful and the actual impact that will be achieved because of it. Application objectives describe how participants should perform, the process steps that should be taken, or technology that should be used as the program is implemented. The emphasis of application objectives is on tasks, action or activity.

The best application objectives identify behaviors or action steps in a process that can easily be observed or measured. They specify what the various stakeholders will change or have changed as a result of the program. As with learning objectives, application objectives may have three components: performance, condition, and criteria.

Figure 7.7 shows typical application objectives and key questions asked at this level. Application objectives have been included in projects to some degree, but they have not been as specific as they could be or need to be. To be effective, they must clearly define the environment where the program is successfully implemented.

Typical Questions for Application Objectives

- What new or improved knowledge will be applied?
- What is the extent of skills used?
- What specific new tasks will be performed?
- What new steps will be implemented?
- What new procedures will be implemented or changed?
- What new guidelines will be implemented?
- Which meetings need to be held?
- Which tasks, steps, or procedures will be discontinued?

Typical Application Objectives

When the program is implemented:

- Within one month, participants will be involved in five job interviews.
- In 15 days, participants will apply for a microfinance loan.
- Ninety-five percent of high-potential employees will complete the steps of their individual development plans within two years.
- At least 50 percent of participants will join a hiking/walking group in 20 days.
- At least 99.1 percent of software users will be following the correct sequences after three weeks of use.
- Diabetic patients will implement three of the four critical behaviors in 30 days.
- Within one year, 10 percent of participants will submit documented suggestions for saving costs.
- Participants will routinely use problem-solving skills when faced with a quality problem.
- Participants will take steps to engage team members each day.
- Sexual harassment activity will cease within one month after the zero-tolerance policy is implemented.
- Thirty percent of citizens will start recycling household waste.
- Eighty percent of employees will use one or more of the three cost-containment features of the healthcare plan in the next six months.
- Fifty percent of conference attendees will follow up with at least one contact from the conference within 60 days.
- By November, pharmaceutical sales reps will communicate adverse effects of a specific prescription drug to all physicians in their territories.
- Customer service representatives will use all five interaction skills with at least half the customers within the next month.
- The average 360-degree leadership assessment score will improve from 3.4 to 4.1 on a 5-point scale in 90 days.

Figure 7.7 Typical Application Objectives.

Impact Objectives

Most programs should have impact objectives, even in governments, non-profits, and NGOs. Business impact objectives are expressed in terms of the key business measures that should be improved as the application objectives are achieved. Impact objectives are critical to measuring business performance, even in governments and nonprofits. They place emphasis on achieving impact results that key stakeholders expect and demand. Finally, they ensure business alignment throughout the program.

The best impact objectives contain data that are easily collected and well known to the client group. They are results based, clearly worded, and specify what the stakeholders have ultimately accomplished as a result of the program.

The four major categories of hard-data impact objectives are output, quality, cost, and time; the major categories of soft-data impact objectives are client service, leadership, and image. Typical measures that frame the objectives are presented in Chapter 5, and Figure 7.8 shows examples of impact objectives.

After program completion, the following conditions should be met:

- The infant mortality rate will reduce by 10 percent per year for five years.
- The health status index should improve by five percent during the next calendar year.
- The student debt load should be reduced by 30 percent in three years.
- After nine months, grievances should be reduced from 12 per month to no more than two per month in six months at the VA center.
- Incidents of malaria should reduce by 17 percent in one year.
- Turnover of high-potential employees should be reduced to 10 percent in nine months.
- Complaints of abusive force by police should reduce by 10 percent in six months.
- The average number of new accounts should increase from 300 to 350 per month in six months.
- Unplanned absenteeism of call center associates should decrease by 30 percent within the next calendar year.
- At least 50 microfinance loans will be approved in quarter one.
- At least 90 percent of microfinance loans will be paid back on schedule.
- A 20 percent reduction in overtime should be realized for front-office managers in the third quarter of this year.
- Citizen complaints should be reduced from an average of three per day to an average of one per day.
- Process time for work visas will be reduced by 30 percent in two months.
- By the end of the year, the average number of product defects should decrease from 214 per month to 150 per month.
- Operating expenses should decrease by 10 percent in the fourth quarter.
- There should be a 10 percent increase in brand awareness among physicians during the next two years.
- Product returns per month should decline by 15 percent in six months.

Figure 7.8 Typical Impact Objectives.

Return on Investment (ROI) Objectives

A fifth level for program objectives is the ROI which defines the minimum payoff from the program and compares its cost with the monetary benefits from the program. The traditional financial ROI is this comparison expressed as a percentage when the fractional values are multiplied by 100. In formula form, the ROI is:

$$ROI(\%) = \frac{\text{Net Program Benefits}}{\text{Program Costs}} \times 100$$

Net benefits are program benefits minus costs. This formula is essentially the same as the ROI for capital investments. For example, when an organization builds a new building, the ROI is developed by dividing annual earnings by the investment. The annual earnings are comparable to net benefits (annual benefits minus the cost). The investment is comparable to fully loaded program costs, which represent the investment in the program.

A program ROI of 50 percent means that for every dollar invested, that dollar is recovered, and an additional 50 cents is returned. An ROI of 150 percent indicates that after the invested dollar is recovered, $1.50 is returned.

Case Study

Public and private sector groups have been concerned about absenteeism and have developed a variety of programs to tackle the issue. A city bus system was experiencing excessive unplanned absenteeism. Two solutions were implemented, a No-Fault disciplinary system and a new selection tool that would prevent habitual offenders from being employed. The ROI objective was 25 percent; this is the minimum acceptable percentage. The results of the program were impressive. Absenteeism was reduced from 8.7 percent to 4.8 percent with most of it connected to the program. This yielded an annual value of $662,000 when converted to money. The fully loaded costs for both programs were just $67,400. Thus, the ROI was:

$$ROI(\%) = \frac{\$662,000 - \$67,400}{\$67,400} \times 100 = 882\%$$

For each dollar invested, the bus system received \$8.82 in return after the dollar had been recovered [6].

Using the ROI formula essentially places program investments on a level playing field with capital investments by using the same formula and similar concepts. The ROI calculation is easily understood by key management and financial executives, who regularly use it with other investments.

Specific objectives for ROI should be developed before an evaluation study is undertaken. While no generally accepted standards exist, four strategies have been used to establish a minimum acceptable ROI objective for a program. The first approach is to set the ROI using the same values used to invest in capital expenditures, such as equipment, facilities, and new companies. For North America, Europe, and most of the Asia-Pacific area (including Australia and New Zealand), the cost of capital is quite low, and the ROI objective is usually in the 10 to 15 percent range.

A second strategy is to use an ROI minimum that represents a higher standard. This target value is above the percentage required for other types of investments. The rationale is that the ROI process for programs is still relatively new and often involves subjective input, including estimations. For most areas in North America, Europe, and the Asia-Pacific area, this value is usually set at 20–30 percent.

A third strategy is to set the ROI value at a break-even point. A 0 percent ROI represents break-even, where the benefits equal the costs. The rationale for this approach is an eagerness to recapture the cost of the program and a realization that additional benefits from the program have come through the intangible measures (those that are not converted to monetary values). This is the ROI objective recommended for many public-sector organizations, with the philosophy that they are not attempting to make a positive return from a particular program.

Finally, a fourth strategy is to let the client or program sponsor set the minimum acceptable ROI value. In this scenario, the individual who initiates, approves, sponsors, funds, or supports the program establishes the acceptable ROI. Almost every program has a major sponsor or donor, and that person may be willing to offer the acceptable value. This links the expectations of financial return directly to the minimum expectations of the individual sponsoring the program.

The Power of Objectives

Objectives are powerful. In addition to creating expectations, they provide direction, focus, and guidance to all stakeholders. They also create interest, commitment, satisfaction, and excitement, making them a necessity, not a luxury. While the power of objectives at the reaction and learning levels may be evident, objectives at higher levels are more powerful and require additional explanation.

Application/Impact Objectives Drive Programs

Objectives at application and impact levels are sometimes omitted from programs. Ironically, these objectives are the most powerful, as they focus on success with application and the corresponding outcomes. More specifically, they fuel a program or project by providing:

- Focus and meaning to the program
- Direction to the stakeholders
- Definitions of success

Application/Impact Objectives Enhance Design and Development

Sending vague objectives to a program designer or developer is a risk not worth taking. Designers are creative, using their imaginations to build program content. Without clear and specific direction, they will insert their own assumptions regarding the ultimate use of the program (application) and the impact.

Application/Impact Objectives Improve Facilitation

Objectives are the first information reviewed prior to facilitating a meeting, program, launch, or learning session, and they define the facilitator's approach in teaching the project or program. They provide guidance to the facilitator for how to present, what to present, and the context in which to present. More specifically, these higher levels of objectives provide facilitators with the information to:

- Show the end result and provide the focus to achieve it.
- Focus the discussions on application and impact.

- Ensure that the participants have the capability to reach the impact.
- Enable participants to succeed with the program.

Application/Impact Objectives Help Participants Understand What Is Expected

Participants need clear direction as to why they are involved in the program and what they are expected to do. Essentially, the role of a participant changes at higher levels of objectives. Participants are always expected to attend programs, become involved and engaged in programs, and learn what to do to make the program successful. By communicating application and impact objectives, participants will realize there is an expectation for them to apply what they learn and reap results, which is the impact.

Again, application and impact objectives remove the mystery from the program and the roles within it.

Impact Objectives Excite Sponsors and Donors

The sponsors and donors who actually fund the program often request data that shows how well the program achieved its goal. Impact measures resonate with executives and program sponsors. It is no secret that executives do not get excited about reaction and learning objectives. Rather, their interest lies in what participants do with what they learn and the ultimate impact it delivers. Impact objectives grab the attention of executives, as they:

- Connect the program to the business results
- Connect the program to key performance indicators
- Show the business value

Application/Impact Objectives Simplify Evaluation

These high-level objectives pave the way for evaluation by providing the focus and details needed for the evaluator to collect and analyze results. From an accountability perspective, the primary reason to have higher levels of objectives is that they:

- Identify data to be selected
- Define specific measures reflected in the data
- Suggest the appropriate data-collection method

- Suggest the source of data
- Suggest the timing of data collection, and
- Suggest responsibilities to collect data

All Levels of Objectives Inform the Stakeholders

Collectively, all levels of evaluation help stakeholders clearly and specifically understand the program. All stakeholders need to know not only why the program is being developed but also about participant reaction, what the participants have learned, what actions they will take, and, ultimately, what they will accomplish with impact and, maybe, ROI.

Defining Roles and Responsibilities

There are many stakeholders involved in programs, and they all have a role in delivering results and in creating the expectations for success. Figure 7.9

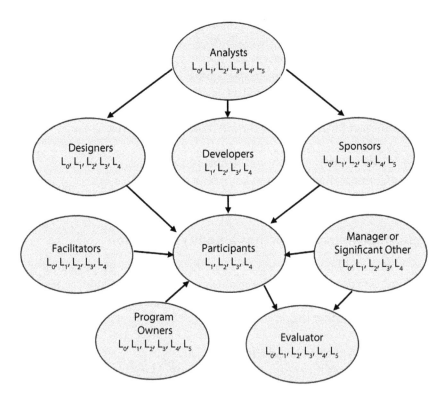

Figure 7.9 The Objectives Needed for Important Stakeholders.

shows the different stakeholders, and under each stakeholder listing is a set of numbers. These numbers represent the objectives they need to drive their work and the success of the program.

Analysts

The role of the analyst (sometimes referred to as performance consultant) is to align the program to the business needs in the beginning by selecting the proper solution. Part of this process, as explained in Chapters 5 and 6, is to develop the objectives. The objectives, ranging from Level 0 (input) to outcomes at Level 1 (reaction) to Level 5 (ROI), essentially create the expectations from the program, clearly defining minimum expectations at each level. ROI objectives are usually developed when an ROI evaluation is planned. These objectives are approved by the requestor (or key sponsor), SMEs, and the program owners, confirming that it is possible to achieve the objectives with this program and audience within the time frame. The objectives are created in a principal document using the SMART format (Specific, Measurable, Achievable, Relevant, and Time-Based).

Designer

The designer role focuses on creating the solution in a way that will maximize results. Having Level 3 and 4 objectives provides clear guidance for the designer so that they can ensure that the right audience is there in a convenient time and place, the proper reaction is realized, the skills and knowledge are acquired easily, the application is feasible, and, finally, that the desired impact is achievable.

Developer

In concert with the designer, the developer actually acquires or writes the content based on the skills and knowledge needed to make the program successful. The content is driven by multiple levels of objectives (Level 1–4) and the need to develop materials that will clearly help the participants successfully achieve those objectives at each level. The flow and sequencing of the content is arranged to ensure there is proper learning. At Level 3, job aids, application tools, templates, and action plans are developed as a way for participants to clearly see the expectation of use. Examples, cases, and scenarios show the participants why they are there, with typical impact data from impact objectives.

Program Owner

Sometimes labeled program manager or program administrator, the program owner is the person who owns the program and communicates information about it to all stakeholders. Armed with objectives at Levels 0 to 5, program owners prepare communication, correspondence, and materials that are all focused on the desired results, particularly at Level 3 and Level 4. Program owners can be very influential, creating the expectation of results. They remind the participants that the program is not successful unless the content of what they are learning is actually used and that there is a corresponding impact.

Facilitator

The facilitator's role is to explain, encourage, and validate expectations, because they have Level 1–4 objectives. In the past, facilitators operated from Level 2 objectives to teach the skills and knowledge and measure improvements in the session, to ensure that participants have learned the content. Most are very comfortable with that role because they have control over learning. But that must change when the program has Level 3 and 4 objectives. The facilitator may resist these higher levels of the objectives because of the perceived lack of control. While facilitators cannot control what happens with the participant, they can influence it. Facilitators can discuss application, explain how the content should be used, and provide tips and advice based on their experience with the use of the content. They can provide documents to help plan for application. They can discuss the importance of impact and the typical impacts from these types of programs. They are now teaching to Level 3 and 4, pushing the discussion beyond learning to include application and impact.

Participants

While the other stakeholder groups are there to expect and support success, the participants must deliver the results. If they don't, this program has been a waste of time. Participants need expectations clearly defined, with objectives at Levels 1 to 4. Level 1 objectives show the expected reaction as participants shape their perception of the program. Level 2 objectives clearly show them what they must learn, how they demonstrate the learning, how long it should take, and what they must do to make the program successful. Level 3 objectives clearly define what participants should be doing with what they have learned, how they should use it, how often they should use it, and the success they should have with it. Those important issues can otherwise be a mystery. Level 4 objectives address the impact. Participants should not complete a program and be left wondering "Why are we here?" Level 4 objectives describe the impact the program will have and whether that impact represents an improvement in a measure or maintaining a good record.

Sponsor or Donor

The sponsor is the individual or group who wants this program. They have supported, requested, or funded it. They are very interested, and they are powerful and influential. Sponsors will have objectives at all levels provided to them, including Level 5 if the project will be evaluated at the ROI level. Sponsors often drive these expectations and analysis. Impact and ROI objectives will be developed in the discussions with the sponsor during the initial analysis phase. They have expectations and communicate them in correspondence, discussions, and kick-off sessions.

Managers of Participants/Significant Others

The significant others are perhaps the most influential group when it comes to ensuring that participants are using what they have learned and that there is a corresponding impact. In a nonprofit, the significant other may be a family member. In an organization, the significant other is the participant's manager. They must be involved in the process of creating an expectation before the program and following up afterwards to make sure that expectation is met. Special activities are necessary (and will be described later in Chapter 9) to ensure the transfer of learning actually takes place and the material is applied.

Evaluator

Whether full-time or part-time, the evaluator will collect data along each of the four levels. They will need the four levels of objectives, and if the program is set for an ROI evaluation, the evaluators will also need data for the ROI calculation. The evaluator positions evaluation as process improvement for the program and provides participants and their managers with data to see the value of this program.

Other Stakeholders

Other stakeholders may be appropriate within a particular system. If so, the important point is to define the other stakeholders and communicate

Level 1 to 4 objectives as they are developed, so these people can clearly see where the program is going and their role in its success. At this point, they can help create the expectations from their perspective.

We realize that there are many defined roles and stakeholders. For large organizations, these are clearly defined in job titles and full-time responsibilities. In others, particularly in smaller organizations, many of these roles are accomplished by one individual. Even if one person has four different roles in the process, when they are in those roles, they have to think about the issues that are described in this section. Let's keep a sensible approach. We are not suggesting to add staff, only clarification of the roles established. The power of these objectives to make a difference in those roles will drive the needed business success.

Planning the Evaluation

A final part of expecting success is evaluation planning. This phase involves several procedures, including understanding the purpose of the evaluation, confirming the feasibility of the planned approach, planning data collection and analysis, and outlining the project schedule.

Evaluation Purpose

Evaluations are conducted for a variety of reasons:

- To improve the quality of programs and their outcomes
- To determine whether a program has accomplished its objectives
- To identify strengths and weaknesses in the process
- To enable the cost-benefit analysis
- To assist in the development of programs in the future
- To determine whether the program was the appropriate solution
- To establish priorities for program funding

The purposes of the evaluation should be considered before developing the planning document because the purposes will often determine the scope of the evaluation, the types of instruments used, and the type of data collected. As with any project, understanding the purpose of the evaluation will give it focus, and will help gain support from others.

Feasibility of Outcome Evaluations

Another important planning consideration is determining the levels at which the program will be evaluated. Some evaluations will stop at Level 3, where the data will determine the extent to which participants are using what they have learned. Others will be evaluated through Level 4, where the consequences of application are monitored, and measures linked directly to the program are monitored. If the ROI calculation is needed, the evaluation will proceed to Level 5. To reach this level of measurement, two additional steps are required: the Level 4 impact data must be converted to monetary values, and the costs of the program must be captured so that the ROI can be developed. Evaluation at Level 5 is intended for projects that are expensive, high profile, and linked directly to business needs.

Three simple planning documents are developed next: the Data Collection Plan, the ROI Analysis Plan, and the Project Plan. These documents should be completed during evaluation planning, and before the evaluation phase is implemented. Appropriate up-front attention will save time later, when data are actually collected [7].

Data Collection Plan

Figure 7.10 shows a sample Data Collection Plan for a project undertaken to show the value of a chaplaincy program in a healthcare organization.

This document provides a place to capture the major elements and issues regarding data collection. Broad objectives are appropriate for planning. Specific, detailed objectives are developed later, before the program is designed. Entries in the Measures column define the specific measure for each objective; entries in the Method/Instruments column describe the technique used to collect the data; in the Sources column, the source of the data is identified; the Timing column indicates when the data are collected; and the Responsibilities column identifies who will collect the data. The information needed to complete this plan is found in this chapter (for objectives and measures, see Chapters 8 and 9 for the rest of the plan).

ROI Analysis Plan

Figure 7.11 shows a completed ROI Analysis Plan for the same chaplaincy program. This planning document captures information on key items that are necessary to develop the actual ROI calculation. In the first column,

Figure 7.10 Data Collection Plan.

The purpose of this evaluation is to measure the impact and ROI of a chaplaincy program.

Program/Project: *Value of chaplaincy*   Responsibility: Date:

Level	Broad Program Objective(s)	Measures	Data Collection Method/Instruments	Data Sources	Timing	Responsibilities
1	REACTION Patients will rate the following reactions: • The chaplain was important to my care • My chaplain was helpful • The support from my chaplain was relevant to my needs • I will follow the advice of my chaplain • I realize the importance of spiritual care • I would recommend this chaplain to others	4 out of 5 on a 5-point scale	Questionnaire	Patients	2 to 4 months from start of program (some items collected one month after start of workshop)	Support staff
2	LEARNING Because of my chaplain, I am able to: • Identify opportunities to improve my health • Address challenges and setbacks • Have trust and confidence in my caregivers • Set clear expectations • Manage conflicts and differences • Receive feedback and support • Provide recognition to care staff	3 out of 4 on a 4-point scale	Questionnaire	Patients	After five visits with chaplain	Support staff

3	APPLICATION/ IMPLEMENTATION Patients will: • Use the chaplain • Identify opportunities to improve my health • Address challenges and setbacks • Have trust and confidence with caregivers • Set clear expectations • Manage conflicts and differences • Receive feedback and support • Provide recognition to care staff	• Checklist • 4 out of 5 on a 5-point scale	Questionnaire	Patients Staff	• End of hospital stay • Four months after the start of the program	Support team
4	BUSINESS IMPACT Improvements in at least two of the following measures: • Length of stay • Patient outcomes • Readmissions • Staff turnover • Patient satisfaction	All are measured in the system	• Performance monitoring • Questionnaire	Hospital records Patient	• End of hospital stay • One month after hospital stay	Support team
5	ROI 15%	Comments:				

Figure 7.11 ROI Analysis Plan.

Purpose of this evaluation: to measure the impact and ROI of a Chaplaincy program.

Program/Project: _Value of chaplaincy_   Responsibility: Date:

Data Items (Usually level 4)	Methods for Isolating the Effects of the Program/Process	Methods of Converting Data to Monetary Values	Cost Categories	Intangible Benefits	Communication Targets for Final Report	Other Influences/Issues During Application	Comments
Patient outcomes	Patient and expert estimates	Standard values or expert input	• Initial analysis and assessment • Development of chaplaincy program • Implementation and application • Salaries and benefits for support staff • Salaries and benefits for chaplains' time • Program materials, if applicable • Travel, lodging, and meals, if applicable • Use of facilities, if applicable • Administrative support and overhead • Evaluation and reporting	• Staff engagement • Stress • Image • Reputation • Brand • Chaplain engagement	• Top administrators • Management team • Chaplaincy leaders • Patients • Chaplains • Prospective chaplains • Professional chaplaincy groups		
Length of stay	Expert estimates	Standard values or expert input					
Readmissions	Patient estimates	Standard values or expert input					
Staff turnover	Staff estimates	Standard values or expert input					
Patient satisfaction	Patients and expert estimates	Standard values or expert input					

significant data items are listed. Although these are usually Level 4 impact data from the data collection plan. These items will be used in the ROI analysis and calculation.

The method employed to isolate the project's effects is listed next to each data item in the second column. The method of converting data to monetary values is included in the third column for those impact measures that will be converted to money. The cost categories that will be captured for the project are outlined in the next column. Normally, the cost categories will be consistent from one project to another. The intangible benefits expected from the program are outlined in the fifth column. This list is generated from discussions about the program with sponsors and subject-matter experts. Communication targets are outlined in the sixth column. Finally, other issues or events that might influence program implementation and its outputs are highlighted in the last column. Typical items include the capability of participants, the degree of access to data sources, and unique data analysis issues.

The ROI Analysis Plan, when combined with the Data Collection Plan, provides detailed information for calculating the ROI, while explaining how the evaluation will develop from beginning to end. The information needed to complete this plan is found in chapters 10 through 14.

Project Plan

The final plan developed for the evaluation planning phase is a Project Plan, as shown in Figure 7.12. The Project Plan consists of a project description, including brief details of project implementation. It also shows the timeline of the project, from the planning through final communication of the results. This plan becomes an operational tool to keep the project on track.

	F	M	A	M	J	J
Decision to conduct ROI study	▓					
Evaluation planning complete	▓					
Data collection instrument designed	▓					
Data collection instrument is pilot tested		▓				
Data collected		▓	▓			
Data tabulation preliminary summary			▓	▓		
Analysis conducted				▓		
Report is written and finalized					▓	
Results communicated					▓	
Improvements initiated						▓

Figure 7.12 Project Plan.

Collectively, these three planning documents provide the direction necessary for the Impact/ROI study. Most of the decisions regarding the process are made as these planning tools are developed. Thereby, the remainder of the project becomes a methodical, systematic process of implementing the plans. This is a crucial step in the ROI Methodology, where valuable time allocated to planning will save precious time later.

Final Thoughts

This chapter shows what must change to design for success in four categories. First, the definition of success for programs must change. The new definition pushes success beyond having a great reaction and acquiring the knowledge and skills, all the way to actually applying the learning in the proper situation and having an impact.

Second, expectations must be created with objectives at each level of outcome. The objectives are SMART statements that define success. Ideally, they are needed for reaction, learning, application, and impact. If the ROI is pursued in a program, then an ROI objective is needed as well. The objectives at Level 3 and 4 are powerful, as they connect learning to the bottom line for all the stakeholders. We recommend developing these higher-level objectives for new programs. Although it may take a little more time, it provides much more focus for the program and helps to ensure that business results are delivered.

Third, it is necessary to recognize that designing for business results involves design thinking at each level (0, 1, 2, 3, 4, and 5). Specific actions designed to achieve the desired outcomes must be taken at each level. Stakeholders use the objectives at the multiple levels for designing for the definitions of success, which is usually at the impact level. They support, reinforce, and enable participants to achieve this level of success.

Fourth, detailed evaluation planning is necessary for data collection, ROI analysis, and project scheduling. This step, Expect Success, is one of the most powerful parts of the results-based methodology. The next chapter focuses on the actions to make it matter.

8

Make It Matter: Design for Input, Reaction, and Learning

When the Nobel Prize-winning physicist Richard Feynman was still working on his graduate degree at Princeton, he was asked to oversee a group of engineers who were tasked, without much context, to perform an endless series of tedious calculations. The math wasn't especially difficult for an engineer, but the work was very slow and full of errors. Growing more frustrated with the team's performance, Feynman made a critical discovery that would dramatically alter the course of events. He realized the problem wasn't the math but that the engineers were totally disengaged. So, he convinced his superiors to let the engineers in on what he already knew—why they were performing the calculations, and why they were sweating their tails off in the New Mexico desert—specifically, in Los Alamos, New Mexico [1].

It was at that time that Feynman's boss, Robert Oppenheimer, pierced the veil of secrecy that had surrounded the work and let the engineers in on the enormity of what they were doing. They weren't simply doing routine math for some inconsequential lab exercise. They were performing calculations that would enable them to complete the race to build the atomic bomb before the Germans did.

Their work would win the war.

The workplace, the work, and the workers' performance completely transformed when the task was imbued with meaning. From that point forward, Feynman reported that the scientists worked ten times faster than before, with fewer mistakes, and with fierce commitment.

Meaning matters. Obviously, not every workplace has as meaningful a backdrop as global conflict. However, when meaning-rich experiences are facilitated, and the resultant energy is channeled toward work that truly matters, engagement and productivity will know no limits—and that's something needed more than ever.

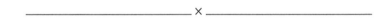

"Make it matter" is a critical concept for program input (who's involved), reaction (how participants perceive it), and learning (what participants will learn). This chapter will show how to make it matter and communicate that to the individuals who will achieve success.

In the early stages, the program must be considered to be meaningful, memorable, and motivational—it must matter to the participants. The design issues involve a variety of ways to communicate expectations, decide whom to involve and where to involve them, define the value of the program from participants' perspectives, and design the learning to deliver the results needed.

Designing for results throughout the cycle of delivering results ensures that the focus is on results at every phase of the program and that the tools, templates, and processes are in place to ensure achievement of those results.

Communicating with Results in Mind

A chain of communication begins when initiating and designing a program. These communications describe the expectations of those involved in the program. The principal audience is the participants, who will make the program successful. The participants' managers, who are expecting results in return for the participants' involvement in the project, are also a target for information. In nonprofits, instead of the participants' managers, it's usually the significant other—a friend or family member who provides support, encouragement, and reinforcement. At least four areas of communication are important.

"Words are all we have." – Samuel Beckett

Announcements

The initial communication for the program—whether an announcement, online blurb, email, text message, or blog—should include expectations of results. No longer should the focus be on describing the program in terms of its content or learning objectives. The focus is now on what participants will accomplish with a program and the impact that it will deliver, clearly articulated. "What's in it for me or my organization?" is more important than "what you will learn." This clearly captures the results-based philosophy of a program.

For example, in the counseling program at the food bank described in the opening story of Chapter 2, the focus and discussion of the program is on resolving the "presenting issue," such as securing a job, getting a spouse out of jail, etc. The focus is not on how to do it (although that's necessary)—the focus is on the impact.

Brochures

If the program is ongoing or involves a significant number of participants, brochures may be appropriate. Brochures are typical for most programs and are often cleverly written from a marketing perspective, are engaging, and attractive. An added feature should be a description of the results that will be or have been achieved from the program, detailing specific outcomes at the application level (what individuals will accomplish) and the impact level (the consequence of application). For major executive education, for example, a typical brochure would describe the beautiful location, outstanding facilitators, effective learning environment, and the wonderful facility. Results-focused brochures describe what participants will do and achieve as a result of the program. This additional content can be powerful and make a tremendous difference to the business results of the program.

Case Study

The Indian School of Business (ISB), based in Hyderabad, India, was developed through formal partnerships with the Kellogg School of Management (Northwestern University) and the Wharton School of Business (University of Pennsylvania). ISB has been a very successful university for developing managers and leaders, and an important part of this is the executive education that is offered to the business community.

In an effort to distinguish itself from other business schools, the executive education division rebranded executive education as delivering results. The executive education team (faculty and coordinators) developed the capability to measure the success of their programs all the way to impact and ROI. Many of the ISB team members became ROI certified as they evaluated major executive education programs. With these evaluations in hand, they now have data that show what participants learn, what they accomplish on the job, and the impact that it has in their organizations, and yes, the actual ROI.

To attract new participants, program information was redesigned for some programs to focus on what individuals have been able to do and accomplish on the job (Level 3) and the impact it has had in their respective work (Level 4). Some of the information include a brief reference to the ROI study, indicating that a positive ROI has been achieved, with participants using the content at work.

Correspondence

Correspondence with participants before they become fully engaged with their program is critical. Memos, emails, and instructions should outline the results described in the announcements and brochures and focus on what individuals should expect when they participate in the program. Preparation for participating in the program, if appropriate, should focus on results, which gives purpose not only to the program, but also to the actual pre-work activities. Sometimes, participants are asked to bring specific examples, case studies, problems, measures, or challenges. Communications should be consistent with the results-based philosophy, underscore the expectations and requirements, and explain what must be achieved and accomplished. Also, the request to provide feedback and document results is explained to participants, emphasizing how they will benefit from responding.

Workbooks and Participant Guides

Workbooks and guides are designed with higher levels of objectives in mind. Application and impact objectives influence the design of exercises and activities, as they emphasize results. Application tools are spaced throughout the workbook to encourage and facilitate action. Impact measures, and the context around them, appear in problems, case studies, learning checks, and skill practices.

Changing the Role of Participants

There is no one more important to achieving business success than the program participant. The participant is the person who is learning the skills and knowledge that will be used to drive business performance. It is this person's availability, readiness, and motivation to achieve success that makes the difference. Sometimes, this begins with changing the role of this person, more clearly defining the expectations, and expanding expectations beyond traditional requirements.

The Necessity

Most programs and projects fail because the individuals involved did not do what they were supposed to do. While there are many barriers to achieving success, including those in the workplace, perhaps the most critical barrier is that the person involved didn't want it, didn't have time, or didn't see any reason to do what was necessary to achieve success. While they normally blame others, the participant may actually be the problem. The efforts of the participant must change. This requires clearer definition and documentation of their role and an explanation of the impact if they use the program properly.

For example, in a developing country, if a person wants to prevent malaria or AIDS, there are a set of prescribed actions, procedures, and behaviors that must be in place. But first, the participants must see the need to do it (reaction) and know what to do (learning). Then, their actions are detailed and the subsequent impact is explained.

Defining Roles

The first issue is to define the role of the participant, clearly outlining expectations. For formal programs, participants should always understand their specific roles. Participants should:

1. Be prepared to take advantage of the opportunity to learn how to make the program successful, seeking value in any type of project or program.
2. Attend (or log on), be on time, engage fully, and be productive.
3. Seek the positives in the program and focus on how the content can be implemented.

4. Meet or exceed the learning objectives, fully understanding what is expected.
5. Share experiences and expectations freely, recognizing that others are learning from them.
6. Plan to apply what is learned in their setting.
7. Remove, minimize, or work around barriers to application and impact.
8. Apply what they learned in their situation, making adjustments and changes as necessary to be successful.
9. Follow through with application to achieve the impact from the program.
10. Provide data that shows success, and the barriers and enablers to success, when requested.

These expectations establish the participants' role as fully engaged actors in the program's success with a focus on results. The participants' role is to seek impact improvement through application of knowledge and skills gained in the program. Additionally, and more importantly, the role requires participants to provide data. It is only through participants' efforts and subsequent information that others will recognize their success.

Documenting the Roles

The participants' role should be clearly documented in several places. During formal learning sessions conducted to the program, the name tent lists roles and responsibilities so that they are visible throughout the learning sessions. In other cases, the role is presented as a handout, outlining what is expected of the participant all the way through to impact results. Sometimes, it is included in the program material or participants' guide, usually as the first page. It is also placed in program descriptions. The role can be included as an attachment to the registration documents as participants begin involvement in the program. It is often included in application documents as a reminder. Finally, some learning centers place the roles in each conference room, so they are clearly visible. The key issue in documenting roles is to display them permanently and prominently so that they are easily seen and followed.

Creating Expectations

Defining the participants' role creates the expectations of them. The challenge is to advise participants of these expectations and to avoid any surprises throughout the process. Participants resist surprises involving expectations, application tools, or action plans. Also, when a questionnaire, interview, or focus group is scheduled on a post-program basis, participants often resent these add-on activities. It is better to position any necessary actions or data collection as a built-in part of the process and not an add-on activity.

Identifying Impact Measures Before Participating in the Program

For some projects, the participants will define the specific business measures that they need to improve. For example, in leadership development programs involving cross-functional areas, participants are often asked to identify the business measures that matter to them, but only if those measures can be changed by working with their team using the competencies of the program. Although this approach may seem dysfunctional, it represents the ultimate customization for the participant, creating a learning experience that is valuable to them. The implementation of Lean programs, for example, requires participants to identify specific business measures that they want to improve by making a process more efficient or effective. Leadership development should be the same way.

In another example, a program to integrate refugees into the United States has several impact measures as possibilities, such as: establish financial support needs, secure a job, find a shelter, resolve a health issue, learn a new language, or resolve a legal issue. These are presenting issues that are identified at the beginning of the process. In still another example, a healthy living program can have multiple impacts. The participants define the desired impact at the beginning of the program.

All types of programs offer this opportunity. This creates an expectation, and it often receives a pleasant reaction from participants, because they now know they can focus on a measure that matters to them.

Case Study

To make the first-level management team clearly understand the importance of safety and the improvements that need to be made, the CEO of an iron and steel manufacturing company made an opening statement to the participants as they embarked on a new safety program. Citing the impact objectives for the program, the speech was conducted live and recorded on video when the CEO could not make a live appearance in the future. This part of the opening speech positions the expectations for business connections. Here's the message:

Thank you for taking the time to participate in this important program. I am confident that this is the right time and the right place to achieve some major safety improvements. Although we have a safety record that is among the best in the industry, there is still room for much improvement. We cannot accept any lost-time injuries, let alone a fatality in our workplace. This is unacceptable for top executives, and I'm sure it's unacceptable to you.

We have many business measures that you will review in this particular program. The focus of the program is to improve as many of these as possible. The measures are ranked in the order of the seriousness in terms of pain and suffering for employees and also cost and disruption to the workplace. We expect you to make significant improvements in these measures.

During the program, you will learn a variety of techniques and processes to achieve success with these measures. We want you to select the measures that need to improve in your area. You have our support to make change in the workplace a reality. Here are the overall impact objectives for this program:

Measure	Reduction
Fatalities	50%
Lost-time injuries	12%
Accident severity rate	12%
OSHA-reportable injuries	13%
OSHA fines	18%
First aid treatments	23%
Near misses	16%
Property damage	29%
Downtime due to accidents	18%

You can do even better than these amazing expectations. I have confidence in you. You have my full support. You have the full support of our safety and health team. And you have the full support of your operating executives, managers, and supervisors. If you have a problem or issue that needs resolving, and you are having difficulty, contact my office and I will take care of it.

> *The improvement in these measures is on your shoulders. Only you can do this. We cannot do it at a distance, and our safety and health team cannot do it alone. The actions you take with your employees will make the difference.*
>
> *Good luck. We look forward to celebrating success with you.*
>
> When this speech was delivered to participants, all doubt regarding expectations was removed. The message was clear: they must learn new approaches and tools that they will use or implement, and ultimately, success must be achieved at the business level.

Involving Managers or Significant Others

In addition to creating expectations directed at participants, it is important to involve their immediate managers or significant other. Participants may be asked to meet with the manager to ensure that the manager has input into their involvement in the program. Sometimes, this includes an agreement about what must improve or change as a result of the program. One of the most powerful actions that can be taken is having the managers set goals with participants prior to the program.

For nonprofits and NGOs, the significant other replaces the role of immediate manager. For example, in an AIDS prevention program, the tribal leader (a significant other) served as a supporter, reinforcer, and trusted advisor to ensure that the actions needed to prevent AIDS were implemented.

As well as the immediate manager involvement, having other executives create expectations can be powerful. In most organizations, the top leaders are often highly respected, and their requirements or expectations are influential. Most executives are willing to communicate these expectations.

Think ROI

We have seen it too often: an inexpensive solution fails to deliver results, or an expensive solution exceeds expectations. This issue brings a focus to both parts of the ROI equation, monetary benefits from learning and the cost of the learning. The challenge is to address both sides. It could be that the lowest-cost solution does not produce the best ROI results or that the highest-cost solution delivers the best ROI results.

"Price is what you pay. Value is what you get." – Warren Buffett

ROI Review

While most programs should not be evaluated at the ROI level, the ROI concept is a good way to think about the value of any type of effort. All of us are faced with purchasing decisions from time to time, and we often purchase an item, service, or product based on the perceived ROI. Do we receive enough benefits from the purchase to justify its cost? Ideally, we want more benefits than cost. When this occurs, we have a positive ROI, representing a good purchase decision. This concept permeates everything we do, as well as this book. Essentially, the question constantly examined in this book is "How do we increase the ROI from our program?"

To understand this, it is helpful to review the ROI calculation again. The net monetary benefit is the program monetary benefits minus the costs. Net implies how much is "earned" from this project, and the cost is the full cost of the project, including both direct and indirect costs. ROI equals net monetary benefits divided by costs, multiplied by 100. In formula form, the ROI is:

$$ROI(\%) = \frac{\text{Net Program Benefits}}{\text{Program Costs}} \times 100$$

The unique thing about this calculation is that it aligns with the ROI calculation in finance and accounting books. In a finance book, ROI equals earnings (how much is earned from the project) divided by investment (how much the project costs), multiplied by 100 (so that it is presented as a percentage).

Case Study

IAMGOLD, a gold mining company based in Toronto, conducted an ROI study on a leadership program involving almost 1,000 first-level managers [2]. The purpose of the program was to improve employee engagement, set and achieve goals with employees, and produce results for the company. Each first-level manager identified two specific business measures important to their team. These measures would be improved using the leadership program. This should drive more monetary benefits. Because the program was very expensive, the chief operating officer asked for the ROI evaluation. The program produced monetary benefits for a specific sample of first-level managers, $9,915,532 with a cost of $2,226,660, resulting in the ROI calculation below:

$$ROI(\%) = \frac{\$9,915,532 - \$2,226,660}{\$2,226,660} = 3.45 \times 100 = 345\%$$

For every dollar invested, the program recovered the dollar, plus another $3.45.

Actions to Take

To maximize ROI, these actions are possible:

1. Increase the monetary benefits so that a given program produces more results at the business level.
2. Lower the costs of the program when all the costs are included.
3. Address both the numerator and the denominator by improving monetary benefits and lowering the costs.

This chapter explores program evaluation in three levels of measurement: Levels 0 (input), 1 (reaction), and 2 (learning). It describes specific actions resulting from these data to increase monetary benefits, lower the program costs, or both.

Design Input for Results

Although input is usually classified as volume (how many people are involved), costs (direct and indirect costs of the program), and time (the time that they are involved), there are many variations and breakdowns within these measures, with the most important ones covered here.

Target Audience

The target audience is important for delivering impact and ROI. It is important to select the right participants for a program. In some cases, it is immediately clear. Aspiring female entrepreneurs need to be involved in a microfinance program. Refugees are involved in a refugee integration program, and convicted felons are involved in a recidivism program. However, some audiences are not so clear. For example, a stress management program is relevant to a wide variety of audiences. A creativity program has many audiences. A disease prevention program has many audiences.

General target audience categories need to be defined. The key is to clearly communicate this information to potential participants, the managers of those participants, and to significant others. Participants should be in a position to benefit most from the program. If the wrong audience is chosen, problems will occur. When a participant does not have an opportunity to use the content of the program, this represents a loss for the program; to be exact, it is a negative 100 percent ROI for that participant. There will be no monetary benefits, yet there will be costs. The wrong audience lowers benefits and raises costs, and this has a dramatic impact on the ROI of the program.

Case Study

In our work with Caltex, a large oil company located in Indonesia on the island of Sumatra, we experienced an interesting dilemma. When a new learning program was developed for a particular work unit, the leader of the work unit made the decision of who should attend, which is quite normal. However, the criteria for that selection were not so normal. The people who attended were selected based on seniority in the unit. The most experienced individuals took the training first. If there were many senior people, they would all take the training. In many situations, they ran out of budget, and some didn't get to attend. You guessed it; those who didn't get to attend were less senior and were often the people who needed it most.

The Need

Although this seems obvious, it is still a persistent problem for some programs. Do participants really need the program? While the program may be designed for a particular audience, and the people in this audience need this program, some individuals may not need it, and some may need only parts of it.

This can be difficult to sort out from a process perspective. Perhaps the best way to tackle this is to determine who needs the program in advance, using an assessment or interview. For example, a program in the

Philippines involved family members who have spouses or children who work abroad. The program provides financial planning aimed at increasing the savings and the return on the investment in those savings. To be eligible for this program, which is funded by the Central Bank, families had to meet certain income and financial status requirements, obtained in a pre-assessment.

Fortunately, this practice is changing. More and more organizations are having potential participants demonstrate that they need the program. If they are involved in the program when they don't need it, it adds to the costs with little or no extra benefits, and it minimizes the ROI.

Case Study

In another example with a US military civilian workforce, we discovered that the people sent to a learning program were chosen based on their availability. While this seems like a rational way to think about learning, a deeper analysis revealed it was the people who could be easily spared. It was often a person in a role requiring basic skills, or an extra person in the unit, who could be available for these types of assignments. The problem was that a very high percentage of people attending were not in the position to actually use the skills. The manager of the unit believed they were in compliance with the request to send people to training by simply sending anyone. In reality, they were not sending the right person, thereby wasting money.

Timing and Duration

Timing of participation is another important opportunity that can have an effect on both the program benefits and costs. Timing refers to when participants should be involved in a program, relative to their need for it. Problems develop when a participant needs the program and they haven't participated in the program yet or they participated in the program too early to be successful.

This is a challenge when developing new team leaders. In some organizations, a development program for new managers is offered infrequently because of convenience, scheduling logistics, or number of candidates. They may offer only one program each year for all new managers promoted in the last year. Sometimes, new managers have floundered while waiting for the program or developed bad habits that needed to change. This challenge can often be handled with the help of technology, coaches, and mentors. The important point is to realize that placing employees into a new role without training can be inefficient and ineffective, lowering the ROI.

Duration can be a tricky issue with regard to the effectiveness (benefits) and efficiency (costs). The duration refers to the amount of time devoted to the program. If the duration is too short, the participant may not be successful with the program. This lowers the impact, ultimately lowering the monetary benefits and reducing effectiveness and the ROI. If the duration is too long, it adds to the cost of the program, increasing the denominator and reducing the ROI. Duration should be set from the perspective of maximizing the ROI.

Motivation

Motivation is important, because it spans what participants do before program participation (input), how participants see value in the program (reaction), and the program content (learning). Sometimes, participants are not motivated to participate in the program. If they are unmotivated, the odds of them delivering impact are very low. Without motivation, there will be no positive ROI. So what causes participants to be motivated? While there are many factors, here are a few keys to motivation:

1. Build on anticipated impact.
2. Expect success from participants.
3. Select the right content for the target audience.
4. Use an appealing context.
5. Have the participants perform multistep tasks.
6. Provide intrinsic feedback.
7. Delay judgment [3].

Readiness

Readiness means that participants are fully prepared for the program, have been informed of the expectations, have completed all the necessary prerequisites, and are in a role to complete the program. If they are not ready, the impact will be diminished. When that occurs, the monetary benefits (effectiveness) will be minimized. If they are ready, the likelihood of success is enhanced.

Conclusion

As this brief description has emphasized, many types of input issues can have a dramatic effect on either the effectiveness or efficiency of the program. Input must be properly managed throughout the process, and this involves a variety of different individuals performing system checks to make it work. Figure 8.1 shows a checklist of the items that can influence the success of the fully prepared participants with the right mindset at the right time.

Design Reaction for Results

Gram Vikas, which literally means "village development," is a successful nongovernmental organization (NGO) that works with rural communities in India and Africa. Gram Vikas partners with rural communities to address their critical needs of education, health, safe drinking water, sanitation, livelihoods, and alternative energy in a manner that is sustainable, socially inclusive, gender equitable, and empowering [4].

Founded by Joe Madiath, this NGO has a reputation for being innovative with their solutions. In a recent interview, the founder reflected on the need for a proper reaction to innovation.

This program must be:	Parameter
• Conducted with at least 100 participants per month.	Volume/Staffing
• Implemented as a pilot project only.	Scope
• For individuals testing positive for AIDS HIV virus.	Audience/Coverage
• Completed by September 1.	Timing
• Completed in less than three months.	Duration
• Less than $1,000 in cost per participant.	Budget/Efficiency
• Cover all microfinancing options.	Content
• Implemented to support new revenue for the university.	Origin
• Implemented with blended learning.	Delivery
• Conducted in each West African country.	Location
• Implemented without disruption of family activities.	Disruption
• Using virtual reality.	Technology
• Implemented with no more than 50 percent outsourcing.	Outsourcing

Figure 8.1 Examples of Input.

> I think with most of the innovations, because I took the initiative, I had an advantage. I happen to be the boss. The boss can innovate and fail. So, there was the feeling, 'OK, let Joe do it. Then if it fails, it would be he who fails.' But it's very, very difficult initially to cut through the resistance in the organization. For example, the first idea for a gravity flow. I asked my colleagues and the engineers to implement it. But they were not convinced, and they would not do it. They said: You are wasting the organization's money, which is a big challenge. So, I said: OK, if it does not work, I will pay for the entire thing, and I will slowly pay it back to the organization. At least on the moral ground, you cannot now refuse to work with me [5].

The proper reaction to a project or program is critical to its success. As this story illustrates, the founder of this NGO went to extreme measures to develop the desired reaction.

Reaction, the first level of outcome measurement, is often the most measured level of outcome. Yet, it is the least desired outcome measure of the sponsors of the program. So, does it have value? The short answer is "yes." It holds much value, because it is the first indicator of success or failure. When collecting data at this level, the potential for program success comes to light immediately. Potential roadblocks are identified. An adverse reaction is a good indicator that participants will not be applied.

While having the right reaction is critical, it often gets less attention from executives, administrators, and donors. Let's review some of the key issues of measuring at this level.

Topics to Measure

Figure 8.2 shows potential topics that could be measured to capture reaction. It is helpful to divide the topics into experience and content. The experience is what makes participants feel good about the program, and this includes service, comfort, surroundings, communications, facilities, and the

• Useful	• Leading edge	• Intent to use*
• Necessary*	• Enjoyable	• Good use of funds
• Appropriate	• Timely	• Information
• Motivational	• Easy/difficult	• Facilities
• Rewarding	• Engaging	• Facilitator
• Practical	• Relevant*	• Recommend to others*
• Valuable	• Important to success*	• Overall evaluation

*Usually correlates with application

Figure 8.2 Topics for Reaction.

coordinator. While experience makes people feel good about the program, unless the experience is horrible, it will have limited effect on the outcomes.

Content is more important than experience. We suggest about 80 percent of the questions on a feedback survey be content related and only 20 percent experience related. It's the content and the use of the content that will drive the necessary impact. The focus should be on content questions such as relevance to your situation, importance to your success, and intent for use. Experience is important, but only as much as it influences the relevance and usefulness of the content. Even then, if the experience is not going so well, adjustments can be made on the fly.

Content questions are important to the organization. Some measures are more meaningful than others because of their predictive capability. The items with an asterisk on Figure 8.2 are those that have a significant correlation with application. This means that on a classic 5-point scale, a 4 on reaction should correspond to a 4 on extent of use, where 1 is not at all likely to use and 5 is very significant use.

Case Study

The difference in experience and content is easily visualized with an interesting example. A very large global NGO was considering a common leadership program for all of its different agencies. Previously, each agency had its own leadership program, and they decided to replace it with one program so that they would have leaders operating as one in a particular country. The assignment was given to the Staff Development Center, and the project was placed for bid with a request for proposal (RFP). The proposal included only the competencies that they wanted to develop. The RFP required the program to be developed in detail, with a participants' guide, auxiliary handouts and materials, and a facilitator's guide. It would be taught twice by the developers and then handed off to the agency.

The bids were received, and the school of business for a European university got the project and proceeded to develop the program. After the program was implemented, the director of staff development for the NGO, Fernando, wanted to collect feedback directly from the participants. At the end of the five-day program, Fernando asked the faculty to leave the meeting room. He wanted to collect data on four predictive measures. But first, he asked the participants a straightforward question, "What did you like about this program?"

One person responded by saying, "We love this facility for this program." (It was conducted in a completely refurbished and redecorated facility that had been donated to the agency by a large Italian bank.) "This was a beautiful place to conduct this program, and we appreciate having it here."

Fernando continued, "So what else did you like?"

Another participant said, "We loved the food you provided. Italy is in the slow-food movement, and we sampled the regional cuisines during this program. Thanks for providing this."

Fernando continued, "What else did you like?"

Another person said, "We really appreciated the cocktail hours at the end of each day. It provided us an opportunity to network and get to know each other much better. So, thank you for offering them."

"So, what else?" Fernando asked with a little frustration.

Another participant said, "We appreciate the opportunity to have all the recreation, ranging from golf to tennis, right here at the facility. Thank you for allowing us to do that and for having everything readily available."

Now Fernando was a little concerned. What he just heard would be four reactions about the experience. He needed to hear more about the content, so he turned directly to the questions. He started with relevance, "So, is this program relevant to our context?"

The first person replied, "Not necessarily; it is interesting, but the examples are from the business school. After all, that's their background, and it just doesn't seem to fit our situation." Others echoed this same sentiment. Now Fernando felt disappointed and concerned. He had nothing yet that would connect to impact later. He moved on to the question that he thought was the most important, the intent to use.

He asked, "Do you intend to use this in your agency?"

With some hesitation, someone said, "Well, probably not, because it doesn't fit so well with our needs. But they are interesting concepts." No one said that they would probably use it. Some participants said they would think about it, but no one was firm in their commitment.

So Fernando did something that most would not do in his role. He actually discontinued the program and went back to the drawing board. He knew that if the program was not perceived as relevant, and the participants did not intend to use the content, the program would fail. He had to go back to the head of the NGO and ask for more money, which was an unpleasant task. This left his reputation a little tarnished with the top executives. In the next funding discussion, the donors added the requirement that this program must deliver a posi-tive impact. Otherwise, the invoice should not be paid.

Fernando assembled a group of experts to work on the new version. Each person was knowledgeable about the process in this book. They quickly focused on the reason for the failure. No objectives were in the RFP. Having objectives at all four levels would have made the differ-ence. In fact, just having reaction objectives for relevance and intent to use would have made the difference. Armed with the two objec-tives, the designer, developer, and facilitators would spring into action and make the content relevant (with actual examples) and intent to use would be high (with action plans and job aids). Reaction objec-tives based on content are powerful. Add learning, application, and impact objectives, and the program is now very focused on application and impact outcomes. The next implementation was very successful, exceeding objectives at these levels.

Measuring Reaction

Reaction is usually measured on a 4-, 5-, 7-, or 10-point scale. The chal-lenge is to keep it simple, limit the number of questions, and use forced-choice questions with space for comments.

Most organizations use technology to measure reaction, and that's important. Technology allows for easy data collection, analysis, and report-ing. The downside is that it adds costs, but its value is in time savings and convenience. We recommend 100 percent measurement at this level, so this can be a massive amount of data for a larger organization. The key is to make the data easy to collect and easy to use.

One issue to consider when measuring reaction is timing of data collec-tion. The measurement could occur before the program, during the pro-gram, after the program, or all three. This is an interesting issue, because reactions often change. Even before they come to the program, participants can provide a reaction to the issue of concept, and this initial reaction may be very interesting and useful. Typically, data collection at this level occurs at the end of the formal learning session when the learning has influenced the reaction. Learning is designed to influence reaction so that participants can see it as relevant, important to their success, and easy to use after they have experienced it. But, sometimes, the desired reaction won't be fully developed until application and impact, several weeks or months after the program. At times, this time frame is necessary to capture the desired reaction.

> **Case Study**
>
> In one large government agency in the United States, a new method for processing disability claims was implemented with the use of technology. Participants were involved in the program to introduce the change, but they did not see a need for this change. They liked their old way better and didn't see value in this new process. Even after learning how to use the new system, they felt the same way. But the designers and developers expected this reaction and they knew that eventually the participants would see the value. The program leader repeatedly pointed out that, in two weeks, participants should realize this new process was the best way. If not, the program leader indicated that the new system would be discontinued. On a follow-up survey, the participants all loved it and would not go back to their previous method. They didn't have the desired reaction until they tried it and experienced the time savings, the convenience, and the client's satisfaction with the process.

Using Reaction Data

The reaction data must be used. The data indicate what is working, and what is not working which should lead to action. On a typical scale, upper and lower numbers serve as markers for action. For example, if you are using a five-point scale, you may want to know what causes reaction to go beyond four and what causes it to drop below three.

A variety of reasons exist for scores to be more or less than the target. The actions needing change may include adjusting objectives, redesigning content, modifying the pre-work, shifting the expectations, or counseling the facilitator or program coordinator. The changes may involve several stakeholder groups, including analysts, designers, developers, facilitators, program owners, or coordinators. The important point is to monitor the critical data reflecting reaction measures that link to application data.

Forecasting ROI at this Level

Occasionally, it may be important to have participants forecast improvement in business impact measures, including the financial ROI. This process requires participants to consider how they will apply the concepts from the program and achieve the impact benefits. A supplemental form in addition to the standard feedback questionnaire provides space for participants to list planned actions and potential impacts. Participants explain their estimates of impact measurement and the monetary values, if possible. This activity should be reserved for those participants who can understand the connection between the program and its impact. In addition to collecting planned actions and a forecast impact, participants estimate monetary value, describe their basis for arriving at these numbers, and provide the confidence in their estimate on a scale of zero to 100 percent (where zero is no confidence and 100 percent is certainty). Figure 8.3 illustrates a version of this supplemental form. Chapter 16 has a case study to show how this works with an actual example.

Design Learning for Results

Every program involves learning and some will include the acquisition of serious knowledge and skills. A part of designing for results is to make sure that the program is designed for proper learning. As the program is designed for participants to learn the content, the focus ultimately shifts to the business results. Several areas need attention.

Planned improvements

1. Please indicate the specific actions you will take as a result of this program (please be specific).
   a. _____
   b. _____
   c. _____

2. Which specific impact measure(s) will improve? _____

3. How much will it improve in one year? _____

4. (Optional) As a result of your actions and subsequent changes in impact, please estimate (in monetary values) the benefit to you, your community, or your organization over a period of one year._____

   a. What is the basis of this estimate?_____

   b. What confidence, expressed as a percentage, can you put in your estimate? (0%=No Confidence; 100%=Certainty) _____%

Figure 8.3 Forecasting ROI with Reaction.

The Learning Style

Sometimes, it is helpful to understand the learning style of the participants for particular age groups. For example, programs that support Millennials and Generation Z can (and should) incorporate technology. Boomers, and most Generation X, on the other hand, as a group prefer face-to-face participative approaches (older groups often need visual or participative approaches). Taking inventory of learning styles can help ensure that the project or program is suitable for participants.

Sequencing and Time

Sequencing the materials, from easy to hard, or for the natural flow of the learning, is helpful. Advanced material should be placed near the end. Small quantities of information should be presented sequentially, keeping a balance so not too much content is offered, but making sure there is enough to keep the individuals challenged.

The materials for learning should come at the right time for the participant; ideally, this is just before they need to use it. If content is presented too early, it will be forgotten; if it is too late, they will have already learned another way to do it.

Activities

All activities should focus on situations that define the application of what participants are learning, the consequences of their learning, or both. Breakout sessions, working groups, individual projects, and any other assignments should focus on the actions that participants will be taking on the job to achieve business success.

Data Collection for Input, Reaction, and Learning

The methods of data collection for all levels are comprehensive, including surveys, questionnaires, interviews, focus groups, tests, simulation, observation, action plans, performance contracts, and monitoring business performance data from the system and records. Here we will examine the typical data collection methods for input, reaction, and learning.

Questionnaires and Surveys

Questionnaires, the most common data collection method, come in all sizes, ranging from short surveys to detailed instruments. They can be used to obtain subjective data about participant reaction and learning, as well as to document data for use in a projected impact. With this versatility and popularity, it is important for questionnaires and surveys to be designed properly to satisfy both purposes.

Five basic types of questions or statements are available. Depending on the purpose of the evaluation, the questionnaire may contain any or all of the following types of questions:

1. Open-ended question – Has an unlimited answer. The question is followed by ample blank space for the response.
2. Checklist – A list of items. A participant is asked to check those that apply to the situation.
3. Range of responses – Has alternate responses, a yes/no, or other possibilities. This type of question can also include a range of responses from Disagree to Agree, or varying degrees such as a five or seven-point scale.
4. Multiple-choice question – Has several choices, and the participant is asked to select the most appropriate.
5. Ranking scales – Requires the participant to rank a list of items.

Questionnaire design is a simple and logical process. An improperly designed or worded questionnaire will not collect the desired data, and is confusing, frustrating, and potentially embarrassing. The following steps will help ensure that a valid, reliable, and effective instrument is developed [7].

- *Determine the information needed* – The first step of any instrument design is to itemize the topics, issues, and success factors for the project. Questions are developed later. It may be helpful to develop this information in outline form so that related questions can be grouped together.
- *Select the type(s) of questions* – Determine whether open-ended questions, checklists, ranges, multiple-choice questions, or a ranking scale is most appropriate for the purpose of the questions. Take into consideration the planned data analysis and variety of data to be collected.
- *Develop the questions, keeping them simple* – The next step is to develop the questions based on the types of questions planned and the information needed. The questions should be simple and straightforward enough to avoid confusion

or leading the participant to a desired response. Unfamiliar terms or expressions should be avoided.

- *Test the questions* – After the questions are developed, they should be tested for understanding. Ideally, the questions should be tested on a small sample of participants in the project. If this is not feasible, the questions should be tested on employees at approximately the same job level as the participants. Collect as much input and criticism as possible and revise the questions as necessary.
- *Prepare a data summary* – A data summary sheet should be developed so data can be tabulated quickly for summary and interpretation. This step will help ensure that the data can be analyzed quickly and presented in a meaningful way.

Measuring with Tests

Testing is important for measuring learning in program evaluations. Baseline and post-program comparisons using tests are common. An improvement in test scores shows the change in skill, knowledge, or capability of the participant attributed to the program. While questionnaires and surveys can be used in testing for learning, other techniques are available. For more information on test design, see other references [8].

Measuring with Simulation

Another technique for measuring learning is simulation. This method involves the construction and application of a procedure or task that simulates application situations in the program. Participants try out their performance in the simulated activity, and have it evaluated based on how well the task is accomplished. Simulations are typically used during the program learning sessions.

A typical approach uses a simulated task as part of an evaluation. For example, in a program for healthcare assistants in a developing country, participants must perform the proper sequence of tasks in a minimum amount of time. To become certified in the process, participants are observed in a simulation where they perform all the necessary steps on a checklist. After they have demonstrated that they possess the skills necessary for the safe performance of this assignment, they are certified by the designated evaluator. This task simulation serves as the evaluation.

Role-playing, sometimes referred to as skill practice, may be helpful to gauge learning soft skills. Participants practice a newly learned skill and are observed by other individuals. Participants are given their assigned role with specific instructions, which sometimes include an ultimate course of action. The participants then practice the skill with other individuals to accomplish the desired objectives. This scenario is intended to simulate the real setting to the greatest extent possible.

For example, a nonprofit offers a program for parents of newborn babies. The program is aimed at reducing stress. During the program, participants (the parents) are placed in several role-play situations to practice stress reduction techniques. The difficulty sometimes arises when other participants involved in the skill practice make the practice unrealistic by not reacting in the same way that individuals would in an actual situation. To help overcome this obstacle, trained role players (nonparticipants trained for the role) may be used in all roles except that of the participant. This can possibly provide a more objective evaluation.

Case studies are another simulation process and are often a part of many programs, particularly for well-documented programs. Case studies rely on documented real situations to illustrate the desired success. Case studies should be selected based on relevance to, and suitability with, the program. Application issues and success measures should be scattered throughout the case study. The case study focuses on results and recommendations for changes. This reminds the audience of the impact that should be driven by the program.

For example, when implementing a recycling program in a city, case studies are distributed and discussed, illustrating how a recycling program should be developed, launched, funded, and implemented to deliver success in terms of impact on the environment and relevance to the city.

Case studies can range from one page to 25 pages, depending on the details needed. Case studies are used in formal sessions in the early stages of the program. Case studies are read and discussed by participants. Sometimes, they are presented by participants. The evaluation of learning can be self assessment, peer assessment, or facilitator assessment. Sometimes a simple text can assess learning.

Timing of Data Collection

The timing of data collection revolves around particular events connected with the program. Any particular topic, event, or activity is an appropriate time to collect data, beginning with pre-program data collection and progressing to end-of-program collection.

Early, Detailed Feedback

As discussed previously, the detailed feedback gathered during the early stages of implementation is critical. For the most part, this feedback may validate the decision to go forward with the program and ensures that alignment exists. Noting problems in this early feedback means that adjustments can be made early on in the program. In practice, however, this early feedback is often not taken with a comprehensive approach; waiting until significant parts of the program have been implemented, when feedback may be more meaningful. However, early feedback can help spot problems and save tremendous amounts of time when adjustments are made.

Pre-Program

Sometimes, collecting pre-assessment data is helpful to know who should be participating in a particular program. In addition to determining eligibility (Level 0), pre-program assessments are a way to gauge the current attitudes toward the program (Level 1). Also, pre-assessments may also involve learning assessments that can be used to understand the degree to what participants currently know about a particular issue (Level 2).

Collecting at Periodic Intervals

Sometimes, collecting data during programs that occur over multiple days is important. For example, if a program has a long duration, then waiting until the impact is achieved to collect feedback data may be inappropriate. By then, participants may not be able to judge some of the issues, events, and processes that occurred earlier. Consequently, data may need to be collected during the program. Several approaches may be taken to do this. First, capturing routine feedback may be appropriate. Under this scenario, feedback is taken at periodic intervals about the content, including the flow, degree of involvement, and other important issues surrounding the program.

Another approach is to collect data immediately after each milestone, giving the participants the opportunity to judge key issues and steps about that particular module while it is fresh in their minds.

Still another approach is to evaluate different events separately. For example, if an interviewing session is connected to a youth employment program, the session may need to be evaluated separately. Perhaps participants are involved in a separate networking event and are given an opportunity to provide quick feedback the next day. Even with daily or event-based feedback, capturing the end-of-program data is still important to reflect the entire program experience.

For Long Programs with Multiple Parts

Some programs have multiple parts spread over a long time period. In these cases, each individual part should be evaluated for reaction data. For example, in a program to show the impact of a master's degree program inside a government agency, reaction data were collected at several different times [9]. During the introduction of the program, reaction data were collected from the participants following a meeting. At the end of each program course, reaction data were collected concerning that particular course. At the end of each semester, reaction data were collected regarding the progress on the program. The important issue here is that multiple data collection points will be needed for these kinds of programs.

Final Thoughts

This chapter addresses effectiveness and efficiencies of programs through a design approach. "Make it matter" covered designing for success at the first three levels: input, reaction, and learning. Data are collected at these levels with a focus on examining each measure or potential measure and making adjustments for improvements. Each adjustment will add monetary benefits, lower costs, or both. An important part of the process is to design for maximum ROI by increasing impact, which is converted to monetary benefits, or by reducing the cost of the programs. This is how to maximize the impact, even in the early stages of implementation and data collection. The chapter also focuses on what to measure for input, reaction, and learning, as well as how to collect data at these levels.

9

Make It Stick: Design for Application and Impact

If you're concerned about monitoring your exercise with the goal of becoming more fit and losing a few extra pounds, then the odds are that you're aware of Fitbit. Whether it's a device that clips to your pocket or is worn on your wrist, Fitbit monitors steps, hours of sleep, and more. The company behind it has been a phenomenal success. Since its beginning in 2008, Fitbit has sold more than 63 million devices, and the stock peaked at $48 a share shortly after it went public in 2015. As of 2017, it was just over $5. Quarterly sales at the beginning of 2017 were 40 percent lower than the previous period a year ago. Meanwhile, in July 2017, Jawbone, maker of the UP-wristband fitness tracker who at one time started UP fresh with venture capital funding and $3 billion evaluation, is liquidating its assets [1].

Does this mean that this is a fad that is going away, like so many others? Perhaps not. One thing is for certain: the Fitbit has more competition than before. Some of the competition is promising all types of measurement tracking, including monitoring blood sugar for diabetes without piercing the skin. The situation with Fitbit might need a little more explanation.

Of Fitbit's over 50 million registered users, less than half, 23.2 million, remain active. It seems the first generation of fitness trackers has largely run its course. Three major issues appear to have caused the decline of Fitbit. First, they are a victim of their own success. Tracking is now popular, and smartphones and smartwatches have all the functionality of the fitness tracker. Second, the devices have been notoriously inaccurate. For example, a recent study published in *The Journal of Personalized Medicine* found that seven popular fitness trackers all significantly miscalculated the number of calories that participants burned [2]. The third issue concerns the success of the fitness tracker to actually cause weight reduction. Most experts would agree that if a person needs to lose weight, there's a combination of fitness and diet involved. Perhaps Fitbit has done enough to study how that could be more closely related. Consider this study.

No Magic Bullet – In a 2016 study published in *JAMA*, 470 overweight participants were put on an exercise plan as well as a low-calorie diet. They were divided into two groups: One self-reported their diet and exercise, while the second was given fitness trackers to measure their activity. After two years, the group that had been given the fitness trackers lost, on average, around five fewer pounds than the group without the devices (7.7 pounds vs. 13).

For John Jakicic, a professor of health and physical activity at the University of Pittsburgh and the study's lead author, the results were surprising. He's currently working on new research exploring why fitness-tracking data doesn't necessarily translate to health results. (His personal hunch is that the device spat out lots of data without providing the support and context to incur a response.)

If you have a device and it works for you, "by all means, keep using it," says Jakicic. But "let's not make this too complicated." Weight loss is about moving more and eating less [3].

The problem may be focusing users' efforts on one important measure (exercise), causing them to ignore the other (diet). This is classic in many systems. Focusing on productivity sometimes has an adverse effect on quality. Focusing on quality can have an adverse effect on productivity. A focus on the cost of sales can have an effect on customer satisfaction.

We were working with a group of healthy living professionals in Canada, and one of the projects undertaken was the effect of Fitbits distributed to a group of citizens. The study would track the weight loss of the group and try to monetize the weight loss for the healthcare system, which is largely funded by the government, and to calculate the ROI. The question became: Is the money spent on buying the Fitbits and providing them to citizens worth it in the healthcare system in the long run? Incidentally, weight loss translates into future cost savings in the system. The study team sought the support of Fitbit—in terms of donations of the devices, advice, and previous studies. According to the researchers, when they contacted the Fitbit company, there was not much interest in assisting with this kind of study.

The major problem here is a failure to have a good measurement system with proper alignment to show the value of a new innovation, not only initially, but consistently. When the accuracy of the device itself is a problem and there's a lack of evidence available to users about how it connects directly to weight loss, then its value is questionable. This may be the reason that less than half of the registered users are still active. While no one knows for sure, we suggest that a balanced measurement system with ample studies of the success of the Fitbit in terms of weight loss, keeping the focus on diet as an important part of the process, could have shown more convincing data that this device does make a difference when used properly. This might have made a difference in sales and stock performance.

Most programs breakdown at Level 3, application. When application is not there, impact does not materialize, and the program fails to be successful. Unfortunately, there are many barriers to success, most notably a lack of support from the direct manager or significant other. At the same time, there are many enablers to success, most notably the support of the manager or significant other. Unfortunately, barriers and enablers are not addressed in a systematic way in many programs, certainly not before program implementation. The challenge is to address these at the beginning, during, and after the program.

For too long, program designers, developers, and facilitators have not fully adjusted to their role in driving application and impact. They have typically worked to create an engaging program that interests and excites participants, but that role has changed. Designers and developers can make a difference as to whether participants use the program material and the extent to which it has an impact in their lives, work, and community. They must step up to their responsibilities and drive application and impact.

Making it stick is an important step in the ROI Methodology. This chapter offers tips for program designers, developers, facilitators, owners, coordinators, and others to design for success at the application and impact levels.

Data Collection for Application and Impact

Before tackling strategies for making it stick, it's helpful to review data collection methods that measure success for application and impact. Data collection is necessary throughout the program cycle, both for reaction and learning data during the program and to confirm the effectiveness of the program via application and impact data in the follow-up. This chapter explores data collection methods, principles, and timing, with emphasis on application and impact, where the issue of "making it stick" is a concern. Data collection also reveals areas where the program isn't working and opportunities for improvement.

Questionnaires and Surveys

As briefly discussed in the previous chapter, the questionnaire is the most common method of data collection. Ranging from short reaction forms to detailed follow-up tools, questionnaires are used to obtain subjective information about participant action and objective data to measure business results and ROI analysis. With its versatility and popularity, the questionnaire is the dominant method for capturing all levels of data (reaction, learning, application, and business impact). Surveys are a specific type of questionnaire that capture attitudes, beliefs, and opinions. The principles of survey construction and design are similar to questionnaire design [4].

The areas of feedback used on questionnaires depend on the purpose of the evaluation. Some forms are simple, while others are detailed and require considerable time to complete. When a comprehensive evaluation is planned, and impact and ROI are being measured, a comprehensive list of questions is necessary. This feedback can be useful in making adjustments to a program and documenting performance after the program. Typical examples for application and impact are included in Figure 9.1.

Improving the Response Rate for Questionnaires and Surveys

Given the wide range of potential issues to explore in a follow-up questionnaire or survey, asking all of the potential questions can reduce the response rate considerably. The questionnaire becomes too long. The challenge, therefore, is to approach questionnaire and survey design and administration for maximum response rate. This is a critical issue when the questionnaire is a key data collection activity, and much of the evaluation hinges on the questionnaire results.

• Use of materials, guides, and technology	• Monetary impact of improvements
• Actions taken by participants	• Improvements linked to the program
• Procedures followed	• Confidence level of data supplied
• Application of knowledge and skills	• Linkage with output measures
• Frequency of use of knowledge and skills	• Barriers to implementation
• Success with use of knowledge and skills	• Enablers to implementation
• Change in behavior	• Support for implementation
• Improvements and accomplishments	• Recommendations

Figure 9.1 Questionnaire Topics for Application and Impact.

The following actions can be taken to increase response rate. Although the term questionnaire is used, the same rules apply to surveys.

- *Provide advance communication* – If appropriate and feasible, project participants and other stakeholders should receive advance communications about the questionnaire or survey. This minimizes some of the resistance to the process, provides an opportunity to explain in more detail the circumstances surrounding the evaluation, and positions the evaluation as an integral part of the program rather than an add-on activity that someone initiated three months after the program is completed.
- *Communicate the purpose* – Stakeholders should understand the reason for the questionnaire, including who or what initiated this specific evaluation. They should know if the evaluation is part of a systematic process or a special request for this program only.
- *Explain who will see the data* – It is important for respondents to know who will see the data and the results of the questionnaire. If the questionnaire is anonymous, it should clearly be communicated to participants what steps will be taken to ensure anonymity. If senior executives or administrators will see the combined results of the study, the respondent should know that.
- *Describe the data integration process* – The respondents should understand how the questionnaire results will be combined with other data, if available. Often the questionnaire is only one of the data collection methods utilized. Participants should know how the data are weighted and integrated into the entire Impact/ROI study, as well as interim results.

- *Keep the questionnaire/survey as simple as possible* – A simple questionnaire does not always provide the full scope of data necessary for a comprehensive analysis. However, the simplified approach should always be kept in mind when questions are developed, and the total scope of the questionnaire is finalized. Every effort should be made to keep it as simple and brief as possible.

- *Simplify the response process* – To the extent possible, it should be easy to respond to the questionnaire. If paper-based, a self-addressed stamped envelope should be included. Perhaps email could be used for responses, if it is easier. In still other situations, a web-based survey may be easier.

- *Utilize local management support* – Management involvement at the local level is critical to response-rate success. Managers can distribute the questionnaires themselves, make reference to the questionnaire in staff meetings, follow up to see if questionnaires have been completed, and generally show support for completing the questionnaire. This direct managerial support will prompt many participants to respond with usable data.

- *Let the participants know they are part of the sample* – For large projects, a sampling process may be utilized. When that is the case, participants should know they are part of a carefully selected sample and that their input will be used to make decisions regarding a much larger target audience. This action often appeals to a sense of responsibility for participants to provide usable, accurate data for the questionnaire.

- *Consider incentives* – A variety of incentives can be offered, and they usually are found in three categories. First, an incentive is provided in exchange for the completed questionnaire. For example, if participants return the questionnaire personally or through the mail, they will receive a small gift, such as a T-shirt or mug. If identity is an issue, a neutral third party can provide the incentive. In the second category, the incentive is provided to make participants feel guilty about not responding. Examples are money clipped to the questionnaire or a coupon enclosed in the envelope. Participants are asked to "Take the money, buy a cup of coffee, and fill out the questionnaire." A third group of incentives is designed to obtain a quick response. This approach is based on the assumption that a quick response will ensure a greater response rate. If some individual delays completing the questionnaire, the odds of completing it diminish considerably. The initial group of participants may receive a more expensive gift, or they may be part of a drawing for an incentive. For example, in one project, the first 25 returned questionnaires were placed in a drawing for a $400 gift certificate. The next 25 were added to the first 25 in the next drawing. The longer a participant waits, the lower the odds of winning.

- *Have an executive sign the introductory letter* – Participants are always interested in who sent the letter with the questionnaire. For maximum effectiveness, a senior executive who is responsible for a major area where the participants work should sign the letter. Employees may be more willing to respond to a senior executive than to a member of the outside team.

- *Use follow-up reminders* – A follow-up reminder should be sent a week after the questionnaire is received, and another sent two weeks later. Depending on the questionnaire and the situation, these times can be adjusted. In some situations, a third follow-up is recommended. Sometimes the follow-up is sent in a different media. For example, a questionnaire may be sent through regular mail, whereas the first follow-up reminder is from the immediate manager or significant other, and a second follow-up is sent via email.

- *Send a copy of the results to the participants* – Even if it is an abbreviated report, participants should see the results of the questionnaire. More important, participants should understand that they will receive a copy of the impact study when they are asked to provide the data. This promise will often increase the response rate, as some individuals want to see the results of the entire group along with their particular input.

- *Estimate the length of time to complete the questionnaire* – Respondents often have a concern about the time it may take to complete the questionnaire. A very lengthy questionnaire may quickly discourage the participants and cause it to be discarded. Sometimes lengthy questionnaires can be completed quickly because they contain forced-choice questions or statements that make it easy to respond. However, the number of pages may put off the respondent. Therefore, it is helpful to indicate the estimated length of time needed to complete the questionnaire, perhaps in the letter itself or at least noted in the communications. This provides extra information so that respondents can decide if they are willing to invest the required amount of time in the process. A word of caution: the amount of time must be realistic. Purposely underestimating it can do more harm than good.

- *Explain the timing of the planned steps* – Sometimes the respondents want to learn more about the process, such as when they can see the results. It is recommended that a timeline of the different phases be presented, showing when the data will be analyzed, when the data will be presented to different groups, and when the results will be returned to the participants in a summary report. This provides some assurance that the process is well organized and professional, and that the length of time to receive a data summary will not be too long. Another word of caution: The timetable must be followed to maintain the confidence and trust of the individuals.
- *Make it appear professional* – While it should not be an issue in most organizations, unfortunately, there are too many cases in which a questionnaire is not developed properly, does not appear professional, or is not easy to follow and understand. The participants must gain respect for the process and for the organization. To do this, a sense of professionalism must be integrated throughout data collection, particularly in the appearance and accuracy of the materials. Sloppy questionnaires will usually elicit sloppy responses, or no response at all.
- *Explain the questionnaire during the program meetings* – Sometimes it is helpful to explain to the participants and other key stakeholders that they will be required or asked to provide certain types of data. When this is feasible, questionnaires should be reviewed question by question so that the participants understand the purpose, the issues, and how to respond. This will take only 10–15 minutes but can increase the response rate, enhance the quality and quantity of data, and clarify any confusion that may exist on key issues.
- *Collect data anonymously, if necessary* – Participants are more likely to provide frank and candid feedback if their

names are not on the questionnaire, particularly when the project is going astray or is off target. When this is the case, every effort should be made to protect the anonymous input, and explanations should be provided as to how the data are analyzed, while minimizing the demographic makeup of respondents so that the individuals cannot be identified in the analysis.

Collectively, these items help boost response rates of follow-up questionnaires. Using all of these strategies can result in a 70–90 percent response rate, even with lengthy questionnaires that might take 30 minutes to complete.

Interviews

Another helpful data collection method is the interview. The program evaluation team or a third party usually conducts the interview, which can collect data not available in databases or data that may be difficult to obtain through questionnaires or observations. Interviews may also uncover success stories that can be useful in communicating evaluation results. Participants may be reluctant to describe their results in a questionnaire but may be willing to volunteer the information to a skillful interviewer who uses probing techniques. The interview is particularly useful when collecting application or performance data. However, one major disadvantage is that it is time-consuming, because it is one-on-one data collection and requires interviewer preparation to ensure the process is consistent.

Interviews are categorized into two basic types: structured and unstructured. A structured interview is much like a questionnaire. The interviewer asks specific questions that allow the participant little room to deviate from the menu of expected responses. The structured interview offers several advantages over the questionnaire, however. For example, an interview can ensure that the questions are answered, and that the interviewer understands the responses supplied by the participant. The unstructured interview has built-in flexibility to allow the interviewer to probe for additional information. This type of interview uses a small number of core questions that can lead to information that is more detailed as important data are uncovered. At Levels 3 and 4, the interviewer must be skilled in interviewing a variety of individuals and using the probing process to uncover barriers and enablers and to explore success stories. Interview design and steps are similar to those of the questionnaire.

Focus Groups

Much like interviews, focus groups are helpful when in-depth feedback is needed. A focus group involves a small group discussion conducted by an experienced facilitator, who solicits qualitative feedback on a planned topic. Group members are all invited to provide their thoughts because individual input builds on group input.

Focus groups have several advantages over questionnaires, surveys, or interviews. The basic premise of using focus groups is that when quality perspectives are subjective, several individual perspectives are better than one. The group process, where group members stimulate ideas in others, is an effective method for generating qualitative data. Focus groups are less expensive than individual interviews and can be quickly planned and conducted. They should be small (eight to 12 individuals) and should consist of a representative sample of the target population. Focus group facilitators should have expertise in conducting focus groups with a wide range of individuals. The flexibility of this data collection method makes it possible to explore organizational matters before the intervention as well as to collect unexpected outcomes or application after the program. Barriers to implementation can also be explored through focus groups, while examples and real concerns can be collected from those involved in the intervention.

Focus groups are particularly helpful when there is a need for qualitative information about the success of a program. For example, focus groups can be used to:

- Gauge the overall effectiveness of program application.
- Identify the barriers and enablers to a successful implementation.
- Isolate the impact of the program from other influences.

Focus groups are helpful when evaluation information is needed but cannot be collected adequately with questionnaires, interviews, or quantitative methods. However, for a complete evaluation, focus group information should be combined with data from other instruments.

Observations

Another potentially useful data collection method is observation. The observer may be a member of the program evaluation team, an immediate manager, a significant other, a member of a peer group, or an external third party. The most common observer, and probably the most practical, is the immediate manager or significant other.

To be effective, observations need to be systematic and well developed, minimizing the observer's influence and subjectivity. Observers should be carefully selected, fully prepared, and knowledgeable about how to interpret, score (if relevant), and report what they see.

This method is helpful for collecting data on programs, where a precise set of actions or skills are expected as part of program application. For example, observation is used to provide 360-degree feedback to evaluate the application of leadership development. Behavior changes are solicited from direct reports, colleagues, internal customers, immediate managers, and even self-input. This is considered a delayed report method of observation. This feedback process can be the actual program, or it could be used before participating in another development initiative.

For observation to be successful, it must be invisible or unnoticeable. Invisible means that the person under observation is not aware that it is taking place. For instance, Starbucks uses secret shoppers to observe their employees. A secret shopper goes to one of the stores and takes note of how long orders take to process, the demeanor of the server, whether the store and bathrooms are clean, and whether the server is familiar with new drink offerings. The observation continues immediately following the visit, when the secret shopper checks the temperature of the drink order. This observation activity is invisible to the server. Unnoticeable observations are situations in which the person under observation may know that it is taking place but doesn't notice it, because it occurs over a longer period of time or at random times. Examples of unnoticeable observations include listening in on customer service calls ("this call may be monitored for quality assurance purposes") or a 360-degree feedback process.

Action Plans

For many programs, impact data are readily available. However, data won't always be easily accessible to the program evaluator. Sometimes, data are maintained by the participant, in the community, or in a work unit and may not be accessible to anyone outside that area. Tracking down those data may be too expensive, very time-consuming, or impossible. In these cases, the use of action plans and performance agreements may be helpful for capturing data.

While action plans traditionally have captured application and implementation data, this method can also be a useful way to collect impact data. For impact data, the action plan is more focused and often deemed more credible than a questionnaire. This can be a powerful process that drives tremendous results, and it is appropriate for programs where there is a need to document improvement.

The basic design principles involved in developing and administering action plans keep the focus on both application and impact data. The following steps are recommended when an action plan is developed and implemented to capture business impact data and to convert that data to monetary values. The adjustments needed to convert action plans to performance agreements are described at the end of the section.

Set Goals and Targets

As shown in Figure 9.2, an action plan can be developed with a direct focus on business impact data. This is from a program in a government rail system in Europe. The program is designed to reduce passenger complaints for the service on the train. The plan has an overall objective, which is usually the primary objective of the program. In some cases, an organization may have more than one objective, which requires additional action plans. In addition to the objective, the improvement measure is defined, along with the current and target levels of performance and a timeframe to achieve the target. This information requires the individual to anticipate the application of skills and set goals for specific performances that can be realized.

The action plan is completed during the program, often with input and assistance program team. The practitioner approves the plan, indicating that the action steps meet the SMART requirements. Each plan can be developed in a 20- to 30-minute timeframe, and a plan often begins with action steps related to the intervention. These action steps are Level 3 activities that detail the application and implementation of program. They build support for and are linked to business impact measures.

Define the Unit of Measure

The next step is to define the actual unit of measure. In some cases, more than one measure may be used and will subsequently be contained in additional action plans. The unit of measure is necessary to break the process into the simplest steps in order to determine the ultimate value. The unit may be output data, such as one unit produced. In terms of quality, the unit can be one reject, one error, one rework, or in this case, one passenger complaint. Time-based units are usually measured in minutes, hours, days, or weeks, such as one hour of process time. Other units are

Figure 9.2 Sample Action Plan.

Name: Cynthia Pathmoor Facilitator signature _____ Follow-up date: ___Nov 30___ Objective: ___Reduce passenger complaints by at least 25%___

Evaluation period ___May___ to ___November___ Improvement measure: ___Passenger complaints___

Current performance ___21 per month___ Target performance ___15 per month___

Action steps		Analysis
1. Review reasons for complaints, sort out items under our control	May 30	A. What is the unit of measure? 1 passenger complaint
2. Change protocol with customers based on step 1	June 10	B. What is the value (cost) of one unit? €600
3. Have team sharing session each week to focus on complaints	June 11	C. How did you arrive at this value? Provided by the Services Dept.
4. Provide team feedback when necessary for members who need help	June 15	D. How much did the measure change during the evaluation period? (monthly value) 8 per month
5. When a team member prevents a complaint, establish a complaint prevention award	June 20	E. List the other factors that have influenced this change Service Delivery Process Enhancement, Customer First Campaign
6. Celebrate monthly successes	July 1	F. What percent of this change was actually caused by this program? 30 %
7. Have three-month review and adjust as necessary	Aug 15	G. What level of confidence do you place on the above information? (100%=Certainty and 0%=no confidence) 80 %
Intangible Benefits:		H. **Monetary value** (B x D x F x G x 12)
Customer satisfaction; customer engagement		

Comments: Program helped us focus on providing good service

specific to their particular type of data, such as one grievance, one day of incarceration, one incident of malaria, one absence, or one new job. Here, simplicity rules the day; we are breaking down impact data into the simplest terms possible.

Place a Monetary Value on Each Improvement

During the program, participants are asked to locate, calculate, or estimate the monetary value for each improvement outlined in the plan. The unit value is determined using a variety of methods, such as standard values, expert input, external databases, or estimates.

The process used to arrive at the value is described in the instructions for the action plan. When the actual improvement occurs, these values will be used to capture the annual monetary benefits of the plan. The program owner must be prepared to discuss values and reasonable methods in the session. The preferred method of determining value is to use standard values or expert input. In this case, the participant used expert input from the services department. However, in the worst-case scenario, those participating in the program are asked to estimate the value. When estimates are necessary, it is important to collect the basis of their calculations, so space for this information should be provided. The methods of converting data to money are described in more detail in Chapter 11.

Implement the Action Plan

Ideally, the action plan is implemented after the program. Action plan steps are followed (Level 3), and subsequent business impact improvements are achieved and documented (Level 4). At the end of the specified follow-up period—usually two, three, four, or six months—group members indicate the specific improvements they've made. This determines the actual amount of change that has been observed, measured, and recorded. The values are typically expressed as a daily, weekly, or monthly amount. In most cases, only the changes are recorded, because those amounts are needed to calculate the monetary values linked to the program. In other cases, before and after data may be recorded, which allows the evaluator to calculate the differences.

Isolate the Effects of the Program

Although the action plan is initiated because of the program, the actual improvements reported on the action plan may have been influenced by other factors. The program usually shares the credit for the improvement gained. For example, an action plan to implement leader competencies for department managers could only be given partial credit for a business improvement, because other variables in the work unit may have influenced the impact measures.

There are several ways to isolate the effects of a program, but participant estimation is often used in the action planning process. In this method, participants are asked to estimate the percentage of the improvement that is directly related to the talent development program. It's beneficial to precede this question with a request to identify all the other factors that may have influenced the results. This allows participants to think through the possible relationships before allocating a portion to program. Additional detail on methods to isolate the effects of talent development programs is presented in Chapter 10.

Provide a Confidence Level for Estimates

Identifying the amount of improvement directly related to the program is not a precise process—it is an estimate of the allocation. As a result, an error adjustment is made. Participants are asked to indicate their levels of confidence in their estimates using a scale of 0 to 100 percent—0 percent means no confidence, and 100 percent means absolute certainty. The confidence estimate is multiplied and serves as an error discount factor, reducing the allocation by the amount of the error in the allocation.

Collect Action Plans

A high response rate is essential, so several steps may be necessary to ensure that the action plans are completed and returned. Participants usually see the importance of the process and develop their plans during the program. Some organizations use follow-up reminders by email. Others call participants to check on their progress. Still others offer assistance in developing the final plan. These steps may require additional resources, which need to be weighed against the importance of having data that is more precise. Specific ways to improve response rates were discussed earlier in this chapter.

Summarize the Data and Calculate the ROI

If developed properly, each action plan will have annualized monetary values that are associated with improvements. Additionally, each individual will indicate the percentage of the improvement that is directly related to the program. Finally, group members provide a confidence estimate, expressed as a percentage to reflect their uncertainty with the estimates and the subjective nature of the data they provided.

This process may not appear to be accurate because it involves estimates; however, several adjustments during the analysis make it credible and more accountable than other research-focused methods, such as experimental versus control groups and mathematic modeling. More information on the credibility of estimates is presented in Chapter 10.

These adjustments reflect the guiding principles of the ROI Methodology and are outlined below.

1. For those group members who do not provide data, the assumption is that they had no improvement to report. This is a very conservative approach.
2. Each value is checked for realism, usability, and feasibility. Extreme values are discarded from the analysis.
3. Because improvement is annualized, the assumption is that a short-term talent development program had no improvement after the first year. Some programs are longer term and will have multiple years of value.
4. The improvement is adjusted by the percentage that is directly related to the program using multiplication. This isolates the effects of the program.
5. The improvement from step 4 is then adjusted using the confidence estimate, multiplying it by the confidence percentage. For example:
   - As shown in Figure 9.2, the program reduced passenger complaints from 21 per month to 13 per month, for a change of 8 per month. The cost of a service complaint is estimated to be an average of €600. This cost is provided by the service department and would be accepted by executives
   - The annual amount of improvement is $8 \times 12 = 96$ complaints.
   - The participant estimates that 30 percent of the improvement is caused by the program. This is $96 \times 30\% = 29$.
   - The participant indicates 80 percent confidence, reflecting a 20 percent error possibility ($100-80 = 20$). To reduce the estimated amount of improvement by 20 percent, it is multiplied by 80 percent. This is $29 \times 80\% = 23$. With an 80 percent confidence factor, the participant is suggesting that the value could be in the range of 23 to 35 (20 percent

less, to 20 percent more). To be conservative, the lower number, 23, is used. This is guiding principle number 4.

- The annual monetary value is $23 \times €600 = €13,800$.

6. The monetary values determined in these steps are totaled for all measures and participants to arrive at the final program benefit for all participants. Since these values are already annualized, the total of these benefits becomes the annual benefits for the program. This value is placed in the numerator of the formula to calculate the ROI.

Performance Contract

Perhaps the most powerful tool is the performance contract, which is much like an action plan. This is essentially a contract for performance improvement between the participant in the program and his or her immediate manager or significant other. Before a program is conducted, the participant meets with the manager or significant other and they agree on the specific measures that should be improved and the amount of improvement. This contract can be enhanced if a third party enters the arrangement (this would normally be the facilitator for the program or a program coordinator for other types of projects).

Performance contracts are powerful, as these individuals are now making a contract for performance change that will be achieved through the use of content, information, and materials from the program, and they have the added bonus of support from the immediate manager (or significant other) and the facilitator/program manager. When programs are implemented using a performance contract, they deliver very significant changes in the business measure.

The design of the performance contract is similar to the action plan. Figure 9.3 shows a performance contract for a participant involved in a weight-loss program, including a combination of formal nutrition classes, exercise, and support from a significant other. The goal is to lose weight. The significant other approves the contract, along with the participant and the facilitator of the program. Because this is in a Canadian province health system, the healthcare costs avoided by reducing weight has been developed and is $400 per pound lost. The improvement is 71 pounds, but only 90 percent of the improvement is caused by this program, resulting in $71 \times 90\% = 63.9$ pounds. Because this is an estimate, this amount is adjusted by the error of the estimate. Thus, the 63.9 is multiplied by 80 percent to yield $63.9 \times 80\% = 51.1$. The monetary value is $51.1 \times \$400 = \$20,440$.

Figure 9.3 Example of a Performance Contract.

Performance contract

Name: _____ Significant Other: _____ Facilitator: _____

Objective: Reduce weight by 20%

Evaluation Period: January to September

Improvement Measure: Individual weight

Current Performance: 250 lbs.　　Target Performance: 187.5 lbs.

Action Steps		Analysis
1. Set weekly goals.	31 January	A. What is the unit of measure? 1 lbs. of weight
2. Start exercise program.	2 February	B. What is the value (cost) of one unit? $400.00
3. Start nutrition classes.	5 February	C. How did you arrive at this value? Industry standard
4. Review data – look for trends and patterns.	Routinely	D. How much did the measure change during the evaluation period? 71 lbs.
5. Schedule celebrations.	15 February	E. What other factors could have contributed to this improvement? Support from family members
6. Complete nutrition classes.	20 February	F. What percent of this change was actually caused by this program? 90%
7. Follow up with significant other, discuss improvement, and plan other action.	Routinely	G. What level of confidence do you place on the above information? (100% = certainty and 0% = no confidence) 80%
8. Monitor Improvement and make adjustments when appropriate.	15 March	
Intangible benefits: More energy, less stress		Comments: Excellent, challenging program

Monitoring Business Performance Data

Data are available in every organization to measure business performance. Monitoring performance data enables management to measure performance in terms of output, quality, costs, time, engagement, and customer satisfaction. If they are important to an organization, they are collected, reported, and analyzed internally. They are also available in government, community, and private databases. When determining the source of data in the program evaluation, the first consideration should be any existing databases and reports. In most organizations, performance data suitable for measuring improvement from a program are available. If not, additional recordkeeping systems will have to be developed for measurement and analysis. Surfacing at this point is the question of economics. Is it economical to develop the recordkeeping systems necessary to evaluate a project? If the costs are greater than the expected return for the entire project, then it is pointless to develop those systems.

> *"You can have data without information, but you cannot have information without data." – Daniel Keys Moran*

Existing Measures

Existing performance measures should be researched to identify those related to the proposed objectives of the project. In many situations, it is the performance of these measures that has created the need for the project in the first place. Frequently, an organization will have several performance measures related to the same item. For example, the efficiency of a production unit can be measured in multiple ways, some of which are listed below:

- Number of units produced per hour
- Number of on-schedule production units
- Percentage utilization of the equipment
- Percentage equipment downtime
- Labor cost per unit of production
- Overtime required per unit of production
- Total unit cost

Each of these, in its own way, measures the efficiency of the production unit. All related measures should be reviewed to determine those most relevant to the program.

Similar measurement systems exist for nonprofits, NGOs, and governments. For example, consider the profile of measure for the homeless population:

- Total number of homeless
- Number of chronic homeless
- Number of homeless veterans
- Duration of homelessness
- Time since last job
- Health status of homeless
- Income of homeless (if any)

Each measure provides information about the status of the homeless.

Occasionally, existing performance measures are integrated with other data, and it may be difficult to keep them isolated from unrelated data. In this situation, all existing related measures should be extracted and retabulated to identify those most appropriate for comparison in the evaluation. At times, conversion factors may be necessary. For example, the average number of new sales orders per month may be presented regularly in the performance measures for the sales department. In addition, the sales costs per sales representative are also presented. However, in the evaluation of a consulting project, the average cost per new sale is needed. The average number of new sales orders and the sales cost per sales representative are required to develop the data necessary for comparison.

Case Study

WorkLife Partnership began proving the merits of their approach to economic vitality in Colorado with their Sustainable Workforce Model starting in 2010. This organization, paired with WorkLab Innovations (a network that is replicating the model nationally), has always focused on the ROI of their projects and programs.

"We have always had to explain the potential return on investment," said Liddy Romero, founder and executive director of WorkLife Partnership. "We have had to be impact driven from the very beginning, and ROI is one way in which we do that."

Key business measures—such as productivity, retention, and engagement—are expanded on to show how programs offered by WorkLife Partnership are making a difference in the lives and careers of their clients. These are the frontline workers who may struggle with finding and affording quality childcare, living space, and even food.

WorkLife Partnership's Upskill Services assist clients with working toward career advancement through competency-based coaching and help with planning career pathways for the businesses they serve.

In 2017, 58 percent of WorkLife Partnership clients reported positive change within their current circumstances, more than $10,000 in scholarships through collaborative agencies were awarded to clients, and $19,000 were invested in local childcare providers.

WorkLife Partnership is a supreme example of linking key business measures to the betterment of life and community.

Developing New Measures

In some cases, data are not available for the information needed to measure the effectiveness of a program. The organization must develop new recordkeeping systems, if economically feasible. In one organization, for example, a turnover problem with new professional staff prompted a program to fix the problem. To help ensure success of the program, several measures were planned, including early turnover defined as the percentage of employees who left the company in the first three months of employment. Initially this measure was not available. When the program was implemented, the organization began collecting early turnover figures for comparison.

In this situation, several questions should be addressed:

- Who will develop the measurement system?
- Who will record and monitor the data?
- Where will it be recorded?
- Will new forms or documentation be needed?

These questions will usually involve multiple departments. The administration department, operations, or the information technology unit may be instrumental in helping determine whether new measures are needed and, if so, how they will be developed.

Selecting the Appropriate Method for Each Level

This chapter presented several methods to capture data. Collectively, these methods represent a wide range of opportunities for collecting data in a variety of situations. Eight specific issues should be considered when deciding which method is appropriate for a situation or evaluation level.

Type of Data

One of the most important issues to consider when selecting the method is the type of data to be collected. Some methods are more appropriate for Level 4, for example, while others are best for Level 3, 2, or 1. Figure 9.4 shows the most appropriate methods of data collection for each of the four levels. For example, follow-up surveys, observations, interviews, and focus groups are best suited for Level 3 data, sometimes exclusively. Performance monitoring, action planning, and questionnaires can readily capture Level 4 data.

Participants' Time for Data Input

Another important factor in selecting the data collection method is the amount of time participants must spend with data collection and evaluation systems. Time requirements should always be minimized, and the method should be positioned so that it is a value-added activity (i.e., the participants understand that this activity is something valuable, so they will not resist). This requirement often means that sampling is used to keep the total participant time to a minimum. Some methods, such as performance

		Lev	el	
Method	1	2	3	4
• Surveys	✓	✓	✓	
• Questionnaires	✓	✓	✓	✓
• Observation		✓	✓	
• Interviews	✓	✓	✓	
• Focus Groups		✓	✓	
• Tests		✓		
• Simulations		✓		
• Action Planning			✓	✓
• Performance Contracting			✓	✓
• Performance Monitoring			✓	✓

Figure 9.4 Collecting Application and Impact Data.

monitoring, require no participant time, while others, such as interviews and focus groups, require a significant investment in time.

Manager (or Significant Other) Time for Data Input

The time that a participant's direct manager (or significant other) must allocate to data collection is another important issue in the method selection. This time requirement should always be minimized. Some methods, such as performance contracting, may require much involvement from the supervisor, before and after the intervention. Other methods, such as questionnaires administered directly to participants, may not require any supervisor time.

Cost of Method

Cost is always a consideration when selecting the method. Some data collection methods are more expensive than others. For example, interviews and observations are very expensive. Surveys, questionnaires, and performance monitoring are usually inexpensive.

Disruption of Normal Work Activities

Another key issue in selecting the appropriate method—and perhaps the one that generates the most concern among managers and administrators—is the amount of disruption the data collection will create. Routine work processes should be disrupted as little as possible. Some data collection techniques, such as performance monitoring, require very little time and distraction from normal activities. Questionnaires generally do not disrupt the work environment, and can often be completed in only a few minutes, or even after normal work hours. On the other extreme, some items such as observations and interviews may be too disruptive to the work unit.

Accuracy of Method

The accuracy of the technique is another factor to consider when selecting the method. Some data collection methods are more accurate than others. For example, performance monitoring is usually very accurate, whereas questionnaires can be distorted and unreliable. If actual on-the-job behavior must be captured, observation is clearly one of the most accurate methods.

Utility of an Additional Method

Because there are many different methods to collect data, it is tempting to use too many data collection methods. Multiple data collection methods add to the time and costs of the evaluation and may result in little additional value. Utility refers to the added value of the use of an additional data collection method. As more than one method is used, this question should always be addressed: Does the value obtained from the additional data warrant the extra time and expense of the method? If the answer is no, the additional method should not be implemented.

Cultural Bias for Data Collection Method

The culture or philosophy of the organization can dictate which data collection methods are used. For example, some organizations are accustomed to using questionnaires and find the process fits in well with their culture. Some organizations will not use observation because their culture does not support the potential invasion of privacy often associated with it.

Timing of Data Collection

One of the advantages of the ROI Methodology is that it provides very specific guidelines of when to collect data for application and impact. This is often a mystery in many evaluations and sometimes causes evaluators to wait too long to collect the data or collecting it too soon. If it is collected too late, participants may not be able to make the connections between this particular program and its application and impact. If it is collected too soon, it will have to be collected again. Here are a few basic guidelines.

Collecting Application Data

The issue for application is identifying the time needed for participants to be routinely using what they are supposed to be using or doing what they should be doing. Sometimes, the required action is just a one-time process, such as completing a conflict of interest questionnaire. At other times, the action needed might be systematic behaviors or procedures that must be followed, such as the behaviors of a diabetic patient to manage the effects of diabetes through the proper control of insulin.

First, the definition for success for application is documented, usually from application objectives (e.g., the routine use of information, skills, knowledge, contacts, etc.). Next subject-matter experts (SMEs) are identified, and at least two types are needed. The first SME knows the content of the programs and what participants are expected to do. The second SME knows that participants' situation; where they are located, their stressors, their environment, and the barriers that will naturally exist while trying to make this project successful.

Lastly, when these two SMEs are identified, they are asked to indicate how long it will take a participant to be successful with application, considering two issues. The first is the complexity of what a participant is being asked to do; the second is the opportunity to do it. If it is a simple process that individuals will do every day, then it is just a matter of days until they are routinely using the process. However, if it is a very complex task, it will take longer. If there is an opportunity to use a task only once a month, it is going to take longer to become successful. Those two factors – complexity and opportunity for use – are the factors for determining the timing of Level 3 data collection.

In some situations, this is immediate. For example, if the new action includes using an automated procedure to process a disability claim and the automation is the subject of the evaluation, the timing of the routine use of the new procedure is needed. If it is a fairly simple process that is being used many times each day, the routine profile of success can occur within the first week or two. Some research suggests that it takes 21 days for a new habit to be developed and internalized. This is a rule that several best-selling authors have adopted. For example, Stephen Covey in his book The 7 Habits of Highly Effective People and Will Bowen, author of A Complaint Free World, suggest that it takes 21 days to internalize a new habit [5, 6].

In another example, such as a youth unemployment program, it could take a large amount of time to be routine and systematic. The participant in the program may have to repeat the interviewing, searching, and relationship building process a number of times before this becomes routine, probably two to three months.

The good news about this level of evaluation is that Level 3 should occur quickly. If this level (application) does not occur soon, then the participant will not know how to do it or will forget it quickly. Learning retention is an important issue.

Collecting Impact Data

Impact is a consequence of the application. This is the data that is in the records in the system, such as crime rates, health status, productivity, mistakes, errors, infections, and readmissions. These are the "why" for implementing the program. The timing to capture impact is the length of time between the routine use of the process and the impact. Sometimes, this length of time is short, and other times it is much longer.

For example, when using new technology to process disability claims, described above, the impact is that claims are processed more quickly (time), with fewer mistakes (quality), and with less cost. That impact will occur quickly, most likely within about two to three weeks after routine use is in place. However, for youth unemployment, it may take several months to find a job that fits the career interests and income level of a participant.

The same two subject-matter experts (who know the content of the program and the context of the situation) would indicate how long it should take for the impact to occur. Sometimes, the ultimate impact may take much longer to manifest. For example, the impact of a diabetes education program should be preventing the serious adverse health outcomes from diabetes, such as hospitalization, surgeries, emergency room visits, and even amputations or death. Those consequences can be prevented, but it is generally a long time before that impact occurs. However, there are surrogate measures that can often be used. For example, having certain behaviors in place might correlate with these adverse outcomes, suggesting, "Doing this will save the healthcare system this much money." Most long-term impact outcomes have early indicators, predictors, or surrogate measures. This allows you to evaluate a program that has long-term impact early in the process. Adjustments can then be made at that time, instead of waiting for the long-term impact that may not be seen for five or 10 years.

Built-In Application Tools

Building application and data collection tools into the program is perhaps one of the most important areas where designing for results works extremely well. This is particularly helpful for programs where data collection can easily be a part of the program. Ranging from simple action plans to significant job aids, these tools come in a variety of types and designs. Action plans were discussed earlier, and their success depends on having them built into the process. Figure 9.5 shows the steps that are followed to ensure that the action plan is incorporated into the process and becomes an integral part of achieving business success.

Before	• Communicate the action plan requirement early.
	• Require one or more impact measures to be identified by participants.
During	• Describe the action planning process.
	• Allow time to develop the plan.
	• Teach the action planning process.
	• Have the facilitator/organizer approve the action plan.
	• With some assistance, require participants to assign a monetary value for each proposed improvement.
	• If possible, require action plans to be presented to the group.
	• Explain the follow-up mechanism.
After	• Require participants to provide improvement data.
	• Ask participants to isolate the effects of the program.
	• Ask participants to provide a level of confidence for estimates.
	• Collect action plans at the pre-determined follow up time.
	• Summarize the data and calculate the ROI (optional).
	• Report results to sponsor and participants.
	• Use results to drive improvement.

Figure 9.5 Sequence of Activities for Action Planning.

Improvement Plans and Guides

Sometimes, the phrase "action plan" is not appropriate; some organizations have used it to refer to many other projects and programs, creating an unsavory impression. When this is the case, other terms can be used. Some prefer the concept of improvement plans, recognizing that a business measure has been identified and improvement is needed. The improvement may involve the entire team or just an individual. There are many types of simple and effective designs for the process to work well. Also, the term "application guide" can be used and can include a completed example as well as what is expected from the participant and tips and techniques to make it work.

Application Tools/Templates

Moving beyond action and improvement plans brings a variety of application tools, such as simple forms, technology support to enhance an application, and guides to track and monitor impact improvement. All types of templates and tools can be used to keep the process on track, provide data for those who need it, and remind a participant of where he or she is going.

Job Aids

Job aids represent a variety of designs that help an individual achieve success with application and impact. A job aid illustrates the proper way of sequencing tasks and processes and reminds the individual what must be achieved, with the ultimate aim of improving a business measure. Perhaps the simplest example is the job aid used at a major restaurant chain to show what must go into a particular dish ordered by a customer. The individuals preparing the food use the job aid, which was part of a training program. The job aid demonstrates how the process flows, using various photographs, arrows, charts, and diagrams. It is easily positioned at the station where the food is prepared and serves as a quick reference guide. When used properly, the job aid drives important business measures: minimizing the time to fill the order (time savings), allowing the restaurant to serve more customers (productivity), and ensuring consistency with each meal while reducing the likelihood of a mistake (quality).

Case Study

Booz Allen Hamilton identified priority areas of business growth in the near and long term. To meet these growth targets, the firm needed a pool of affordable technical talent to meet current and future demand. The firm's Tech Tank program focuses on high-performing staff in a targeted functional area within a market team. Two market teams participated in the initial pilot program (100 learners). Based on the success of the pilot, the program is being scaled for company-wide implementation.

Tech Tank is a 9- to 12-month skills enhancement program designed to rapidly build an affordable pool of in-demand technical talent. This cohort-based program is designed to be scalable and repeatable. This allows for multiple cohorts to run at the same time, and each cohort can focus on very different targeted roles and skills.

The Tech Tank selection method is a highly competitive, five-step process. After eligibility criteria have been met, a cohort selection committee reviews the results of all staff that have completed the pre-test and assessments and determines the final participants. Selected staff members receive an offer to participate in the form of a program commitment letter that must be signed by the participant and endorsed by his or her leadership. Those who do not pass the technical pre-test are given information on how to develop the skills required and invited to apply to a future cohort.

There are six components to the Tech Tank program:

1. *Core Curriculum:* Participants receive training in industry-recognized skills to accelerate the learning curve and

enable them to support multiple complex client environments. They participate in classroom training, self-paced
training, experiential labs, interactive workshops, and
gamified social learning. The selection and development of
curriculum was done in partnership with business leaders.

2. *Events:* Participants attend in-person events throughout
the program. These are designed to measure progress
and to help participants discuss challenges, network
with colleagues/leaders within the functional area, and
engage in technically focused activities that apply content from the core curriculum.

3. *Assignments:* Participants engage in internally built
competitions and activities (e.g., "hack-a-thons," "pitch-
jams") using gamification and social learning. Points are
allocated to all assignments, allowing learners to earn
points as they compete with other participants, and
results are displayed on a badging leaderboard. These
practical applications are reviewed, and the content reinforced through one-on-one mentoring from SMEs.

4. *Engagement Plan:* Following the completion of the core
curriculum training and in coordination with their leadership, participants engage in a series of billable assignments or other projects that allow them to practice and
further develop the critical skills and competencies
gained throughout the program.

5. *Electives:* Technical and consulting courses are offered
for participants to take on their own time to increase
the breadth and depth of their skills beyond the core
curriculum.

6. *Mentoring:* Participants are matched with mentors to
foster functional development by identifying available experts and aiding staff to engage in activities that
focus on learning and growing functional skills that
can be directly applied to their work. In many cases,
the same business leaders who led the assignments and
helped develop the core curriculum serve as mentors to
participants.

The program has been very successful, based in large part on the six
components that were designed to deliver results [6].

"If you are not willing to risk the usual, you will have to settle for the ordinary." – Jim Rohn

Involving the Participants' Manager or Significant Other

A final area of design involves creating a role for the participants' managers. For nonprofits and NGOs, this may be the significant other. As mentioned earlier, this is a very powerful group, and having specific items, activities, tools, and templates for them can make a tremendous difference in business results.

The Most Influential Group

Research consistently shows that participants' managers (or significant others) are the most influential element, apart from their own motivation, desire, and determination, in helping participants achieve application and impact objectives. No other group can influence participants' use of the program. Figure 9.6 shows how the program is transferred to the workplace, organization, community, or present situation by using three important groups of stakeholders involved in this success: the participants, the participants' significant others, and the facilitator. The facilitator may be

		Timeframe		
		Before	During	After
Manager/ Significant Other		1	2	3
Participant	Roles	4	5	6
Facilitator/ Organizer		7	8	9

Figure 9.6 Translating the Program into Action.

the project organizer. Three timeframes are possible: prior to the program, during the program, and after the program.

This matrix creates nine possible blocks of activities to translate what is learned from a particular program into action. The transfer involves the behaviors, steps, and actions that must be taken by the participant (application) that will improve the impact measures. For example, the participant can be involved in pre-project activities to set specific goals that he or she wants to achieve before the program is implemented (block number 4). During the program, the participant will plan specific actions to improve an impact measure (block number 5). After the program is conducted, the participant will apply the material, achieve the impact improvement, and report it to interested stakeholders (block number 6).

In another example, the manager or significant other can meet with the participant and set a goal before attending the program (block number 1). During the implementation, the significant other observes part of the program or provides input for the content. In some cases, the manager may teach part of it (block number 2). After the program is conducted, the significant other follows up to make sure that the program is operating properly and the impact has been achieved (block number 3). The process continues until activities are identified for every block.

Research on this matrix shows that the most powerful blocks for achieving the transfer are one and three. Unfortunately, managers and significant others do not always see it that way. They underestimate their influence. They must be reminded of their influence and provided with tools to ensure that the learning from the program is used and drives the business results. This is one of the most powerful areas to explore for improving business results [7].

Pre-Program Activities

At the very least, significant others should set expectations for participants involved in any type of program. It only takes a matter of minutes, and the results can be powerful. Pre-program activities can range from the formal process of a performance contract, described earlier, to an informal two-minute discussion that takes place just before the program. A full array of activities should be provided that take very little time. Even a script could be helpful. The important point is that these managers must be reminded, encouraged, or even required to do this.

During the Program Activities

Sometimes, it is important for the manager or significant other to have input into the design and development of the program. Possible activities include having managers (or at least someone representing the manager group) help to design the content of the program. For example, a specific interest group, spouses of alcoholics, provided input into the design of a program at alcoholics anonymous. They could also review the content and serve as subject matter experts to approve it. Significant others could be involved in the program, teach sections of the process, provide one-on-one coaching for participants needing help with specific parts, or just observe the program (or a portion of it). They could serve on an advisory committee for the program or review the success of others in the program. The key is to connect the manager to the design and content of the program. Their involvement will help focus the program on business results, which they will find extremely important.

Post-Program Activities

The most basic action a significant other can take is to follow up to ensure the content of the program is being used properly. Suggesting, encouraging, or even requiring application and impact can be very powerful. Significant others should be available to provide assistance and support as needed to make the program successful. Just being available as a sounding board or to run interference to ease the application may be enough. Although it is not necessary, post-project activities can take place on a more formal basis, where the managers actively participate in follow-up evaluations. They may sign off on results, review a questionnaire, follow up on action plans, collect data, or help to present the results. In each case, they make a difference.

Reinforcement Tools

In some situations, a workshop is offered to teach significant others how to reinforce and guide the behaviors needed to achieve a desired level of performance in business measures. Reinforcement workshops are very brief, usually ranging from two hours to half a day, but can be extremely valuable. Some formal programs come with reinforcement or support workshops. In addition to the workshops, a variety of tools can be created and sent to significant others. These tools include checklists, scripts, key questions, resources, and contacts needed to keep the focus on results.

Sometimes, they volunteer for a role where they are asked to be available to assist the participants with a formal coaching process. In this scenario, significant others are provided with details about coaching, how to make it work, and what is required of them. In programs that are more formal, they will actually receive some coaching training. It is extremely powerful when a participant's significant other serves as a coach to accomplish impact results.

Case Study

One of the most successful computer companies in the world, a global company employing more than 100,000 people worldwide, implemented a career development program [8]. This program was a pilot performance improvement strategy in a dynamic manufacturing environment. Strategic goals for solution implementation included: enhanced operational capacity and bench strength; enhanced work climate for engaging employees; and increased labor efficiency. Components of this initiative included: an action learning workshop with performance objectives aligned to business needs; self-assessments and manager assessments of pilot participants' critical skills; and a development discussion action plan to assist participants in applying critical skills toward execution of operational performance priorities. Evaluation results showed a positive link between participants' applied knowledge/skills and desired business results.

Given the important role of managers in reinforcing this initiative and providing constructive, timely feedback, a transfer strategy was developed as part of the evaluation plan. Figure 9.7 shows the transfer strategy matrix used in this effort. This "before, during, after" implementation approach was rolled out in initial briefings about the project, had strong senior management support, and was instrumental in holding managers accountable for supporting employees' performance objectives throughout all phases of solution implementation. In communicating the vision for a results-based effort, the transfer strategy was instrumental in dispelling the notion of evaluation as an "add-on" activity that occurs at the end of a program. Defining specific responsibilities of stakeholders was a critical success factor. It also established a foundation of shared ownership for solution results.

Figure 9.7 Transfer Strategy Matrix for Career Development Initiative.

Planning → Implementation → Evaluation

Role	Before (Planning)	During (Implementation)	After (Evaluation)
Steering Committee	• Help define performance, business objectives • Participate in assessing skill gaps • Determine pilot selection criteria • Co-facilitate "kick-off" sessions or briefings • Require attendance at scheduled briefings	• Attend, co-facilitate select implementation sessions • Communicate importance of learning, performance, and business objectives • Assist in collecting, analyzing, converting data • Ensure managers fulfill coaching/advising roles	• Participate in reviewing evaluation plan • Reinforce follow-up and application of action plans • Recognize individuals for successful completion • Assist in removing barriers to application • Provide incentives • Determine viability of enterprise-wide roll-out of program
Managers, Supervisors	• Support HRD in defining performance objectives • Attend briefing sessions prior to implementation • Reinforce trainee participation • Complete pre-work assessments	• Remove barriers to employees' attendance • Provide coverage for individuals in training • Attend sessions as available • Directly discuss development discussion action plan • Ask employees about workshop progress	• Reinforce follow-up and application of development discussion action plans • Assist in removing barriers to application • Conduct development discussion meetings • Serve as mentor, coach, resource • Work with HRD around development options • Monitor performance progress
Human Resource Development (HRD)	• Align objectives with identified needs (organization, process, performer) • Customize curriculum to meet desired objectives • Incorporate benchmarked transfer strategies into course design • Design data collection instruments, evaluation plan(s) • Conduct briefings with pilot groups	• Communicate importance of learning, performance, and business objectives • Assess trainees for reaction, learning, and skill/knowledge transfer • Facilitate pre-work • Teach the development discussion and action planning process • Implement evaluation plan/tools; collect, analyze, report results data	• Continue implementing evaluation plan • Conduct action planning sessions • Facilitate 60-day follow-up sessions • Report results to key stakeholders • Use results for continuous improvement • Determine viability of enterprise-wide roll-out of program
Participants	• Assist HRD in job/task analysis • Attend briefing sessions • Complete pre-assessment survey and pre-work	• Attend full program • Complete self-assessment inventories • Demonstrate active participation in skill practices • Complete development discussion action plan	• Apply critical skills on the job • Seek support from supervisor in implementing development plan practices • Complete development discussion action plan

(Adapted from Broad and Newstrom)

Final Thoughts

"Make it Stick," step three in the ROI Methodology, focuses on what is necessary to achieve business results from a design perspective—at Levels 3 and 4 (application and impact). Tools, templates, and job aids are important to ensure that a participant is fully involved and delivers results, making it stick on the job. Participants explore the use of the learning from the program and increase their ability to implement the tools and techniques. This approach provides the readiness, motivation, commitment, and tools needed to help achieve the business impact. The next chapter begins the first of several steps to "Make it Credible," isolating the effects of the program on the impact data.

10

Make It Credible: Isolate the Effects of the Program

In the early 1990s, the crime rate in the United States had been rising relentlessly. Death by gunfire, intentional and otherwise, had become commonplace, as had carjacking, crack dealing, robbery, and rape. Violent crime had become a gruesome, constant companion. And things were about to get even worse, according to all the experts.

The cause was the so-called superpredator: a scrawny, big-city teenager with a cheap gun in his hand and nothing in his heart. Thousands just like him were out there, a generation of killers preparing to send the country into total chaos.

In 1995, criminologist James Alan Fox wrote a report for the US attorney general grimly detailing the forthcoming spike in murders by teenagers. Fox proposed optimistic and pessimistic scenarios. In the optimistic scenario, he predicted the rate of teen homicides would rise another 15 percent over the next decade; in the pessimistic scenario, it would more than double.

Other criminologists, as well as political scientists and similarly informed forecasters, laid out the same horrible picture, as did President Clinton.

Then, instead of going up and up and up, crime began to fall and fall and fall. The reversal was startling in several respects, with every category of crime falling in every part of the country. It was persistent, with incremental decreases seen year after year. And it was entirely unanticipated – especially by the "experts," who had predicted the very opposite.

The magnitude of the reversal was also astounding. The teenage murder rate fell more than 50 percent over five years. By 2000, the overall murder rate in the United States had dropped to its lowest level in 35 years, as had the rate of just about every other category of crime, from assault to car theft. Even though the experts had failed to anticipate the crime drop, they now hurried to explain it. Most of their theories sounded perfectly logical. It was the roaring 1990s economy, they said, that helped turn back crime. It was the proliferation of gun control laws, they said. It was the result of the innovative policing strategies put in place in New York City, where the number of murders would fall from 2,245 in 1990 to 596 in 2003.

These theories were not only logical; they were also encouraging, for they attributed the crime drop to specific recent human initiatives. If it was gun control, clever police strategies, and better-paying jobs that was quelling crime, then the power to stop criminals had been within our reach all along. And it would continue to be.

These theories were accepted seemingly without question. They became the conventional wisdom. There was only one problem: they were not true.

Another factor, it seemed, had greatly contributed to the massive crime drop of the 1990s. It had begun to take shape more than 20 years earlier and involved a young woman in Dallas. Norma McCorvey dramatically altered the course of criminal history without intending to. All she had wanted was an abortion. She was a poor, uneducated, unskilled, alcoholic, drug-using 21-year-old woman who had already given up two children for adoption; and now, in 1970, she found herself pregnant again. But in Texas, as in all but few states at that time, abortion was illegal. McCorvey's cause was taken up by people far more powerful than she. They made her the lead plaintiff in a class action lawsuit seeking to legalize abortion. The defendant was Henry Wade, the Dallas County district attorney. The case ultimately made it to the US Supreme Court, by which time McCorvey's name had been changed to Jane Roe to shield her identity. On January 22, 1973, the court ruled in favor of Ms. Roe, thereby legalizing abortion throughout the country. By this time, of course, it was far too late for Ms. McCorvey/Roe to have her abortion; she had given birth and put the child up for adoption.

So how did Roe v. Wade help trigger, a generation later, the greatest crime drop in recorded history? Decades of studies have shown that a child born into an adverse family environment is far more likely than other children to become a criminal. And the millions of women most likely to obtain abortions in the wake of Roe v. Wade—poor, unmarried, teenage mothers for whom illegal abortions had been too expensive or too hard to get—were common models of adversity. They were the very women whose children, if born, would have been much more likely to become criminals. But because of Roe v. Wade, these children weren't being born. This powerful ruling would have a drastic, delayed effect: in the years when these children, had they been born, would have entered their criminal primes, the rate of crime began to plummet.

It wasn't gun control or a strong economy or new police strategies that blunted the American crime wave. It was another factor, among these and other factors, that the pool of potential criminals had dramatically shrunk. Now, as the crime experts spun their new theories on the reversal to the media, how many times did they cite legalized abortion as a cause? Zero.

This example of the importance of isolating the effects of a program is a situation described in Steven D. Levitt and Stephen J. Dubner's best-selling book *Freakonomics* [1].

The *Freakonomics* authors provide much detail explaining how they attempted to isolate the effects of the various influences on the crime rate reduction. Their arguments, analysis, and data are credible; however, as you might expect, their conclusion is not without its share of critics. Some found the analysis to be distasteful and perhaps racist. However, these economists were merely trying to report the data in the most credible way while attempting to isolate the effects of many complicated factors interacting in this situation to improve a particular measure.

Reporting improvement in impact measures is an important step in program evaluation that leads to the money. Invariably, however, the question comes up (as it should): How much of this improvement was the result of the program? Unfortunately, the answer is rarely provided with any degree of accuracy and confidence. Although the change in an impact measure may in fact be linked to the program, other factors unrelated to the program may have contributed to the improvement as well. If this issue is not addressed, the results reported will lack credibility.

In this chapter we explore useful techniques for isolating the effects of a program. This is something referred to as attribution pinpointing—the amount of improvement that is linked to the program. These techniques have been used in some of the most successful organizations as they attempt to measure the ROI from all types of projects and programs.

The Importance of Pinpointing the Contribution

In almost every program, multiple factors influence the impact measures targeted by the program. Determining the effect of the program on the impact is imperative. Without a step to isolate the effects of the program from other influences, the program's success cannot be validated. Moreover, the effects of the program may be overstated if the change in the business impact measure is attributed entirely to the program. If this issue is ignored, the impact study may be considered invalid and inconclusive. This places pressure on evaluators and program leaders to demonstrate the effects of their programs on business improvement, when compared to other possible factors.

Reality

Routinely isolating the effects of programs on impact measures has led to four important conclusions. First, other influences are almost always present; multiple factors generate business results. The rest of the world does not stand still while a program is being implemented. Other processes and programs are also implemented to improve the same outcome metrics targeted by the program.

Second, if the program effects are not isolated, no business link can be established. There is no proof that the program actually influenced the measures. The evidence will show only that the program might have made a difference. Results have improved, but other factors may have influenced the data.

Third, the other factors and influences have their own protective owners. These owners will insist that it was their processes that made the difference. Some of them will suggest that the results are due entirely to their efforts. They may present a compelling case to supporters and sponsors, stressing their achievements.

Fourth, isolating the effects of the program on impact data is an achievable task. It can be accomplished in all situations with a reasonable degree of accuracy. Although challenging for complex programs in particular, the process will not always be easy, especially when strong-willed owners of other processes are involved. Fortunately, a variety of approaches are available to facilitate the procedure in every case.

Myths

The myths surrounding the isolation of program effects create confusion and frustration with the process. Some researchers, professionals, and evaluators go so far as to suggest that such isolation is not necessary. Here are the most common myths:

1. *Our program is complementary to other processes; therefore, we should not attempt to isolate the effects of the program.* A program often complements other factors driving the same measure, all of which together drive results. If the sponsor of a program needs to understand its relative contribution, the isolation process is the only way to do it. If accomplished properly, it will reveal how the complementary factors interact to drive improvements.

2. *Other program leaders do not address this issue.* Some program leaders do not grapple with the isolation problem because they pledge to make a convincing case that all of the improvement is directly related to their own processes. Others ignore the issue because they have a fear that their program doesn't deliver the results expected. Still others ignore the issue because they don't know how to isolate the effects.

3. *If we cannot use a research-based control group design or mathematical modeling, we should not attempt this procedure.* Although an experimental research design using randomly assigned control and experimental groups is the most reliable approach to identifying causes and effects, it is not possible in most situations. Consequently, other methods must be used to isolate the effects of a program. The challenge is to find a method that is effective and whose results are reproducible, even if it is not as credible as the group comparison method.

4. *The stakeholders will understand the link to business impact measures; therefore, we do not need to attempt to isolate the effects of the program.* Unfortunately, stakeholders try to understand only what is presented to them. The absence of information and a clear connection makes it difficult for them to understand the proportion of impact linked to the program, particularly when others are claiming full credit for the improvement.

5. *Estimates of improvement provide no value.* It may be necessary to tackle the isolation or attribution process using estimates from those who understand the process best, the most credible source. Although this should be used only as a last

alternative, it can provide value and credibility, particularly when the estimates have been taken from the most credible source, collected in a nonthreatening and unbiased way, and adjusted for error of the estimate to reduce subjectivity.

6. *Ignore the issue; maybe the others won't think about it.* Sponsors and supporters are becoming more sophisticated on this topic, and they are aware of the presence of multiple influences. If no attempt is made to isolate the effects of the program, the audience will assume that the other factors have had a major effect, and perhaps the only effect. A program's credibility can deteriorate quickly.

These myths underscore the importance of addressing this step. The emphasis on isolation is not meant to suggest that a program is implemented independently and exclusively of other processes. Obviously, all functions and teams should be working to produce the desired results. However, when funding is parceled out among different functions or organizations with different owners, there is always a struggle to show, and often to pinpoint, the connection between their activities and the results. If you do not undertake this process, others will – leaving your program with reduced budgets, resources, support, and respect.

> *"If you cannot show your direct contribution to the business, you have no credibility." – Jeff Bezos*

Preliminary Issues

The cause-and-effect relationship between a program and performance can be confusing and appear difficult to prove, but it can be demonstrated with an acceptable degree of accuracy. The challenge is to develop one or more specific techniques to isolate the effects of the program early in the process, usually as part of an evaluation plan conducted before the program begins. Upfront attention ensures that appropriate techniques will be used with minimal cost and time commitments. Two important issues should be considered before getting started.

Review Chain of Impact

Before presentation of isolation methods, it is helpful to reexamine the chain of impact implicit in the different levels of evaluation. Measurable results from a program should be derived from the application of the program (Level 3 data). Successful application of the program should stem from program participants learning to do something different and necessary to implement the program (Level 2 data). Successful learning will usually occur when participants react favorably to the program's content, purpose, and objectives (Level 1 data). The proper reaction will only be realized if the right people are involved in the program at the right time (Level 0 data). Without this preliminary evidence, isolating the effects of a program is difficult.

To be sure, if the wrong people are involved or if there is an adverse reaction, no learning, or no application, it cannot be concluded that any impact improvements were caused by the program. From a practical standpoint, this requires data collection at four levels for an ROI calculation (Guiding Principle 1 in Figure 4.7). Although this requirement is a prerequisite to isolating the effects of a program, it does not establish a direct connection, nor does it pinpoint the extent of the improvement caused by the program. It does show, however, that without improvements at previous levels, making a connection between the ultimate outcome and the program is difficult or impossible.

Identify Other Factors

As a first step in isolating a program's impact, all key factors that may have contributed to the impact improvement should be identified. This step communicates to interested parties that other factors may have influenced the results, underscoring that the program is not the sole source of improvement. Consequently, the credit for improvement is shared among several possible variables and sources—an approach that is likely to garner the respect of the client. Several potential sources are available for identifying major influencing variables:

- Program sponsor
- Participants in the program
- The immediate managers of participants (or significant others)
- Subject matter experts
- Technical advisors
- Experts on external issues
- Directors and leaders

The importance of identifying all of the factors is underscored by an example. The Royal Bank of Canada had a sophisticated system for identifying the reasons customers make product purchase decisions. At the point of sale, the purchaser records the reasons for the sale; was it the price, the product design, the advertising, or the referral from a satisfied customer? This system, owned by the marketing department, is designed to isolate the factors underlying the success of various marketing programs. However, it omits factors outside marketing. In essence, it assumes that 100 percent of the improvement in product sales can be attributed to a marketing influence. It ignores the effect of the economy, competition, information technology, reward systems, learning and development, job design, and other factors that could have had an important influence. Thus, competing factions within that organization had to address changing the system so that other factors are considered in the analysis.

Taking the time to focus on outside variables that may have influenced performance adds accuracy and credibility to the process. Program team leaders should go beyond this initial step and use one or more of the following techniques to isolate the impact of the program.

Quantitative and Research Isolation Methods

Just as there are multiple methods available for collecting data at different levels, a variety of methods are also available to isolate the effects of a program. It is recommended that multiple methods be considered and pursued to tackle this important issue.

> *"If we knew what it was we were doing, it would not be called research, would it?"* – Albert Einstein

---

Case Study

National Crushed Stone (NCS) is one of the leading firms in the crushed stone industry, with more than 300 locations in many geographic areas. The crushed stone industry is very competitive; profit margins are narrow and cost control is everything. Companies in this industry are constantly seeking ways to control costs to gain a competitive advantage in the marketplace.

There were some concerns that the costs at NCS were not as low as they could be, although they were among the lowest in the industry. Some costs were fixed and not under the control of the stone quarry team. However, many costs could be controlled. The executives wanted

---

an innovative approach to control costs, perhaps using a behavioral approach.

Based on engagement studies in the literature, the assumption was that if employees were really engaged in quarry operations, taking a very strong interest in maintaining and caring for the equipment, working smarter, and operating efficiently, the costs could be lower, perhaps even significantly so.

The talent development team suggested a simple employee engagement survey and proposed that if employees became more engaged, they would take more interest in their jobs, try to be more efficient, take better care of equipment, take better care of the facility, and even make suggestions for improvement. However, the company culture wasn't very open to employees accepting more responsibility, making recommendations, and being more involved in making decisions. In order to implement this plan, NCS would have to change its culture. To help augment change, the quarry superintendents assumed the role of plant managers with the additional expectation of having a more involved and engaged workforce. However, this does not happen just by decree, discussion, meeting, memo, or policy—it comes from changing the mindset of the organization while adjusting job descriptions and encouraging employees to open up and be engaged.

In early discussions, it was suggested that a portion of the cost savings be shared with the employees using the motivational effect of rewards. Using a concept called gainsharing, the decision was made to share half the gains in cost reductions with employees, providing a bonus for exploring options to lower costs.

The new system was planned for implementation in six locations that represented typical NCS plants. The complete process, which would comprise of several stages, was developed during a two-month period using an external consultant and the part-time assistance of two internal staff members.

Specific cost measures and other impacts (Level 4) would be monitored at each plant before and after the program, and these data would be compared with a group of similar plants. This control group arrangement involved identifying six other crushed stone plants to compare with the six plants destined for implementation. The selection was based on plants with similar operating costs, production volume, age of plant, market served, and employee retention rate.

This approach should ensure that the results achieved were directly related to the new system. The actual cost of the system would be compared with the monetary value of the benefits to develop an actual ROI (Level 5). To be conservative, one year of monetary benefits would be obtained and compared with the fully loaded costs of the program [2].

Experimental Design

Perhaps the most accurate approach for isolating the impact of a program is an experimental design with control groups. This approach involves the use of an experimental group that implements the program and a control group that does not. The two groups should be as similar in composition as possible and, if feasible, participants for each group should be randomly assigned. When this is achievable, and the groups are subjected to the same environmental influences, any difference in performance between the two groups can be attributed to the program.

As illustrated in Figure 10.1, the control group and experimental group do not necessarily require pre-program measurements. Measurements can be taken during the program and after the program has been implemented, with the difference in performance between the two groups indicating the amount of improvement that is directly related to the program.

One caution should be observed. In business and government settings, the use of control groups may create the impression that the program leaders are reproducing a laboratory setting, which can cause concerns for some executives and administrators. To avoid this perception, some organizations use the term *pilot group*, using participants as the experimental group. A similarly constituted nonparticipant comparison group is selected but does not receive any communication about the program. The terms *pilot* and *comparison group* are a little less threatening to some executives and leaders than experimental group and control group. This is not an issue with nonprofits and universities.

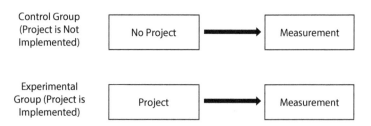

Figure 10.1 Use of Control Groups.

The control group approach involves several actions to apply it in practice. The first task is the selection of the groups. From a theoretical perspective, having identical control and experimental groups is next to impossible. Dozens of factors can affect performance, some individual and others contextual. On a practical basis, it is best to select the two to five variables that will have the greatest influence on performance. Essentially, this involves the 80/20 rule or the Pareto principle. The 80/20 rule is aimed at selecting the 20 percent of factors that might account for 80 percent of the difference. The Pareto principle requires working from the most important factor down to cover perhaps four or five issues that capture the vast majority of the factors having influence.

Another task is to make sure that the control group process is suited for the situation. For some types of programs, withholding the program from one particular group while implementing it with another may not be appropriate. This is particularly true where critical solutions are needed immediately; leaders are typically not willing to withhold a solution from one area to see how it works in another. This limitation keeps control group analyses from being implemented in many instances. However, in practice, many opportunities arise for a natural control group to develop even in situations where a solution is implemented throughout an organization. If it takes several months for the solution to be implemented system-wide, enough time may be available for a parallel comparison between the initial group(s) and the last group(s) for implementation. In these cases, ensuring that the groups are matched as closely as possible is critical. Naturally occurring control groups can often be identified for major enterprise-wide program implementations. The challenge is to address this possibility early enough to influence the implementation schedule to ensure that similar groups are used in the comparison.

Another task is to prevent contamination, which can develop when participants involved in the program group (experimental group) communicate with people in the control group. Sometimes, the reverse situation occurs, where members of the control group model the behavior or actions of the experimental group. In either case, the experiment becomes contaminated as the influence of the program is carried over to the control group. This hazard can be minimized by ensuring that the control and program groups are at different locations, on different shifts, or occupy different floors of the same building. When this is not possible, it should be explained to both groups that one group will be involved in the program now, and the other will be involved at a later date. Appealing to participants' sense of responsibility and asking them not to share information with others may help prevent contamination.

The duration of the experiment must be managed. The longer a control versus experimental group comparison operates, the greater the likelihood that other influences will affect the results; more variables will enter into the situation, possibly contaminating the results. However, enough time must pass to allow a clear pattern to emerge distinguishing the two groups. Thus, the timing of control group comparisons must strike a delicate balance between waiting long enough for impact differences to show, but not so long that the results become contaminated.

Another task is to make sure that the different groups function under the same environmental influences. If another new factor entered one group and not the other, the group differences cannot be attributed solely to the program. This is usually the case when groups are at different locations. Sometimes the selection of the groups can prevent this problem from occurring. Another tactic is to use more groups than necessary and discard those groups that show some environmental differences.

Because the use of control groups is an effective approach for isolating impact, it should be considered when a major ROI impact study is planned. In these situations, isolating the program impact with a high level of accuracy is essential, and the primary advantage of the control group process is accuracy.

Figure 10.2 shows an experimental and control group comparison for a program to reduce assaults on employees by mental patients in a psychiatric hospital. The program involved the intervention of a chaplain into a "situation." Both groups were experiencing about 40 assaults on employees

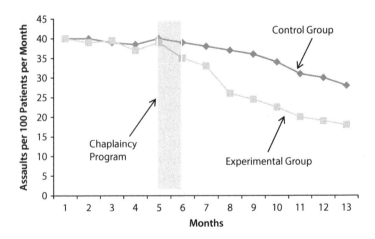

Figure 10.2 Experimental versus Control Group Comparison for Employee Assault Reduction Program.

per 100 patients per month, too much for these two nursing units. An assault reduction program involving chaplains was implemented with the experimental group. The control group was not involved in the program. The criteria used to select the two groups included current performance on staffing levels, type of care, and length of stay. The control group experienced a reduction from 40 to 30. The experimental group moved from 40 to 18. The improvement, connected to the assault reduction program, is 12 (18 assaults versus 30) assaults per month.

Trend Line Analysis

Another useful technique for approximating the impact of a program is trend line analysis. In this approach, a trend line is drawn to project the future, using previous performance as a base. When the program is fully implemented, actual performance is compared with the trend line projection. Any improvement in performance beyond what the trend line predicted can be reasonably attributed to program implementation, if certain conditions are met. Even though this process is not a precise one, it can provide a credible analysis of the program's impact.

Figure 10.3 shows a trend line analysis from a state transportation authority. The vertical axis reflects the rate of disabling injury. The horizontal axis represents time in months. Data reflect conditions before and after the safe operations practice (SOP) program was implemented in July. As shown in the figure, an upward trend for the data existed prior to

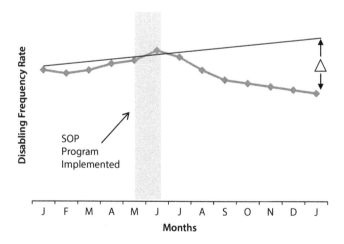

Figure 10.3 Trend Line Analysis for Disabling Frequency Rate.

program implementation. However, the program apparently had an effect on the disabling frequency rate (DFR) as the trend line is much greater than the actual. Program leaders may have been tempted to measure the improvement by comparing the six-month average for the DFR prior to the program to the one-year average after the program. However, this approach understates the improvement because the measure in question is moving in the wrong direction and the SOP turns the DFR in the right direction.

A more accurate comparison is actual value after the program impact has occurred (the last month or two) versus the trend line value for the same period. Using this measure increases the accuracy and credibility of the process in terms of isolating the program's impact.

A West Asian country, formerly a Soviet republic, implemented a domestic violence program. In this particular country, domestic violence was considered illegal in a very loosely defined law that was rarely enforced. In an effort to reduce domestic violence, and perhaps eliminate it altogether, a comprehensive domestic violence law was implemented to make it an enforceable crime and require reporting it to authorities. Because many of the victims of domestic violence are reluctant to report actual cases for fear of retaliation, the number of cases reported often underrepresent the actual problem. However, counselors, legal experts, and law enforcement personnel felt that the actual number was about twice the reported number. Figure 10.4 shows the trends of the domestic violence. The bottom curve shows the reported cases of domestic

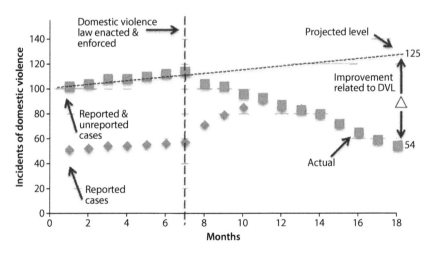

Figure 10.4 Trend Line Analysis for the Domestic Violence Law (DVL).

violence. The top line shows the reported and unreported totaled, using the estimate provided from the experts. The cases were increasing on a slightly upward movement and the trend that had begun before the new law was enacted was projected. Eleven months after the law was passed, there were a total of projected cases reported at 125 (reported and unreported). However, the actual was at 54. Before the law was enacted the slightly upward trend had to do with an increase in population and it was still increasing during the post period making it appropriate for the trending. Also, there were no other new factors besides the new comprehensive domestic legislation that decreased the incidences of domestic violence. The amount attributed to the domestic violence program is $125 - 54 = 71$.

To use this technique, two conditions must be met:

- It can be assumed that the trend that developed prior to the program would have continued if the program had not been implemented to alter it. In other words, had the program not been implemented, this trend would have continued on the same path. The process owner(s) should be able to provide input to confirm this assumption. If the assumption does not hold, trend line analysis cannot be used. If the assumption is a valid one, the second condition is considered.
- No other new variables or influences entered the process during the program implementation and evaluation period. The key word here is new; the understanding is that the trend has been established from the influences already in place, and no additional influences have entered the process beyond the program. If this is not the case, another method will have to be used. Otherwise, the trend line analysis presents a reasonable estimate of the impact of this program.

For this technique to be used, pre-program data must be available, and the data should show a reasonable degree of stability. If the variance of the data is high, the stability of the trend line will be an issue. If the stability cannot be assessed from a direct plot of the data, more detailed statistical analyses can be used to determine whether the data are stable enough to allow a reliable projection. The trend line can be projected directly from historical data using a simple formula that is available in many calculators and software packages, such as Microsoft Excel™.

A primary disadvantage of the trend line approach is that it is not always possible to use it. This approach assumes that the events that influenced the performance variable prior to program implementation are still in place, except for the effects of the implementation (i.e., the trends established prior to the program will continue in the same relative direction). Also, it assumes that no new influences entered the situation during the course of the program, which may not be the case.

The primary advantage of this approach is that it is simple and inexpensive. If historical data are available, a trend line can quickly be drawn and the differences estimated. Although not exact, it does provide a quick general assessment of program impact.

Mathematical Modeling

A more analytical approach to trend line analysis is the use of mathematical modeling to predict a change in performance variables. This approach represents a mathematical interpretation of the trend line analysis when other variables enter the situation at the time of implementation. A mathematical model has been developed to link the other variables to the measure in question, the impact measure. With this approach, the impact measure targeted by the program is forecast based on the influence of variables that have changed during the implementation or evaluation period for the program. The actual value of the measure is compared with the forecast value, and the difference reflects the contribution of the program.

An example will help illustrate the effect of the forecasting with the model. One healthcare organization was focusing on decreasing length of stay (LOS). In June, a new program involved changing several procedures that made the diagnosis, treatment, and healing process faster, with various ways to recognize improvement quickly and make decisions and adjustments accordingly. All of these procedures were aimed at reducing the average length of stay. Figure 10.5 shows that the length of stay prior to the change in medical procedures and the actual data shows a significant downward improvement in the 10 months since the program was implemented. However, two important changes occurred about the same time as the new program was implemented. A major provider issued a maximum length of stay that they would reimburse for specific illnesses. This influence has a tendency to cause organizations to focus more intensely on getting patients discharged as quickly as possible. At the same time, the severity of the influx of patients had slightly decreased. The types of illnesses dramatically affect the length of stay. The analysts in the business process improvement

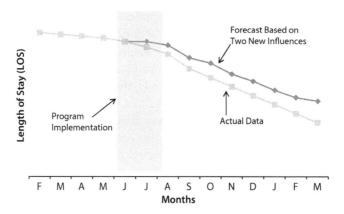

Figure 10.5 Mathematical Modeling Example.

department developed a forecast showing the effects of the provider reimbursement process and the change in the illnesses of the patients upon admission. They were able to develop a multiple variable analysis to forecast the LOS, as shown in the figure. The data from June show the difference in the forecasted value and the actual value. That difference represents the impact of the new medical procedures, because they were not included in the forecasted value.

A major disadvantage emerges when several variables enter the process. The complexity multiplies, and the use of sophisticated statistical packages designed for multiple variable analyses is necessary. Even with this assistance, however, a good fit of the data to the model may not be possible.

The good news is that some healthcare organizations have developed mathematical relationships for output variables as a function of one or more input items, making forecasting possible. The use of analytics has entered the healthcare industry, bringing a variety of tools for complex analysis [3].

Calculating the Impact of Other Factors

It is sometimes possible, although not appropriate in all cases, to calculate the impact of factors (other than the program) that account for part of the improvement and then credit the program with the remaining part. That is, the program assumes credit for improvement that cannot be attributed to other factors.

Although this process may not be applicable to all situations, it can sometimes be a helpful tool. One clinic changed a scheduling process for the MRI department. The new process was designed to implement more efficient scheduling of patients so the profit from the MRI technology could be maximized. The data were tracked before the new scheduling process was implemented and then compared to a post period. However, near the same time, new MRI equipment was installed, and the manufacturer indicated that MRIs administered from this equipment would increase 20 percent over the previous equipment, based on their analysis of several studies. When the study was completed, 35 percent more patients were processed through MRIs. With 20 percent being attributed to the new equipment, the remaining percentage (15 percent) was attributed to the new scheduling process.

This method is appropriate when the other factors can be easily identified, and the appropriate relationships are in place to calculate their impact on the improvement. In many cases, the impact of other factors is not mathematically linked to the impact of the program, limiting this approach's applicability. However, the results can be reliable if the procedure used to isolate the impact of other factors is sound.

Qualitative Isolation Methods

In real world applications, the quantitative approaches of research design and modeling will not always work. In our experience, about one-third (or more) of studies must use other approaches.

A common approach of isolating the effects of a program is to use qualitative analysis involving estimates from a group of expert individuals. Although this is potentially the weakest method, it is credible in many situations, and can greatly enhance the credibility of the analysis if adequate precautions are taken to make it more credible. The beginning point in using this method is to ensure that the estimates are provided by the most credible source, which is often the participant—not a higher-level administrator or executive removed from the process. The individual who provides this information must understand the different factors driving the impact and, particularly, the influence of the program on the impact.

Essentially, there are four categories of potential input for these estimates. The participants directly involved in the program are the first source considered. Managers (or significant others) are another possible source. The customers we serve can sometimes provide credible estimates in particular situations, and internal or external experts may provide insight into causes for improvement. These sources are described in more detail next.

Participants' Estimate of Impact

An easily implemented method of isolating the impact of a program is to obtain information directly from participants during program implementation. The usefulness of this approach rests on the assumption that participants are capable of determining or estimating how much of the impact improvement is related to the program implementation. Because their actions have led to the improvement, participants may provide accurate data. Although an estimate, the value they supply is likely to carry considerable weight with management because they know that the participants are at the center of the change or improvement. The estimate is obtained by defining the improvement, and then asking participants the series of questions in Figure 10.6.

Participants who do not provide answers to the questions in Figure 10.6 are excluded from the analysis. Erroneous, incomplete, and extreme information should also be discarded before the analysis. To obtain a conservative estimate, the confidence percentage can be factored into each of the values. The confidence percentage is a reflection of the error in the estimate. Thus, an 80 percent confidence equates to a potential error range of plus or minus 20 percent. Guiding Principle #4 (Figure 4.7) suggests that we should be conservative in the analysis and use the lowest number (minus 20 percent). To reduce a number by 20 percent, we should multiply it by 80 percent. With this approach, the estimate is multiplied by the confidence to be at the lower side of the range. For example, a participant

---

1. What is the link between these factors and the improvement?

2. What other factors have contributed to this improvement in performance?

3. What percentage of this improvement can be attributed to the implementation of this project?

4. How much confidence do you have in this estimate, expressed as a percentage? (0% = no confidence, 100% = complete confidence)

5. What other individuals or groups could provide a reliable estimate of this percentage to determine the amount of improvement contributed by this project?

Figure 10.6 Questions for Participant Estimation.

allocates 60 percent of the improvement to the program and has a confidence in the estimate of 80 percent. The confidence percentage is multiplied by the estimate to produce a usable program value of 48 percent. This adjusted percentage is then multiplied by the actual amount of the improvement (post-program minus pre-program value) to isolate the portion attributed to the program. For example, if errors declined 10 per week, 4.8 of the reduced errors would be attributed to the program (10 × 4.8%). The adjusted improvement is now ready for conversion to monetary value and, ultimately, use in the ROI calculation.

In the United Nations, one of the Development Results Goals for Zimbabwe is the increased economic empowerment of women, especially of those who are most excluded. One program supporting this goal works to allow women to access microfinance loans. Working with the Women Development Savings and Credit Union (WDSCU), the application outcome is to increase the accessibility of affordable microfinance loans to rural women. After this program was implemented, more women applied for loans and loans were approved for an additional 420 women. At the same time, there were several other factors that increased the amount of loans. One factor was the changing attitudes of microfinance institutions, as they realized these types of loans were not necessarily high-risk and may have a better repayment history than other types of loans. In addition, there was one other agency working on the same issues, pressuring microfinance institutions to make loans available to women. Finally, the government was also applying some pressure on institutions operating within the country to make loans available. In essence, all four factors have led to improving access to loans and the additional 420 loan approvals.

The program director assembled a group of microfinance lenders who were deemed experts in understanding the effect of all four factors in obtaining access to the loans. A neutral facilitator assisted a group of 10 lenders in sorting out the cause and effect of each factor, following these steps:

- Describe the task.
- Explain why the information was needed and how it would be used.
- Ask lenders to identify any other factors that may have contributed to the increase in access.
- Have lenders discuss the link between each factor and the specific measure.
- Provide lenders with any additional information needed to estimate the contribution of each factor.

Microfinance Loans for Women (420 Loans)

Contributing Factors	Average Impact on Results	Average Confidence Level
UN Program	39%	81%
Changing Attitudes of MF Institutions	11%	77%
Competing Program (NGO)	33%	60%
Pressure from Government	12%	72%
Other	5%	85%
	100%	

Figure 10.7 Participant Estimates for Microfinance Loans.

- Obtain the actual estimate of the contribution of each factor. The total had to be 100 percent.
- Obtain the confidence level from each lender for the estimate for each factor (100% = certainty; 0% = no confidence).

The results from this group are averaged and shown in Figure 10.7. The amount attributed to the UN program was determined by multiplying the percentage for the program factor times the confidence percentage. This, in effect, shows the impact of the program. In this case, the number is 420 × 39% × 81% = 132.7.

Although the reported contribution is an estimate, this approach offers considerable accuracy and credibility. Five adjustments are effectively applied to the participant estimate to produce a conservative value:

1. Participants who do not provide usable data are assumed to have observed no improvements.
2. Extreme data values and incomplete, unrealistic, or unsupported claims are omitted from the analysis, although they may be included in the "other benefits" category.
3. For short-term programs, it is assumed that no benefits are realized from the program after the first year of full implementation. For long-term programs, several years may pass after program implementation before benefits are realized.
4. The amount of improvement is adjusted by the portion directly related to the program, expressed as a percentage.

5. The improvement value is multiplied by the confidence, expressed as a percentage, to reduce the amount of the improvement in order to reflect the potential error.

Steps to Measure Attribution Using Estimates

If you find that a measure/indicator has improved, and you want to know how much your program influenced the improvement, use these steps:

a. Identify the sources of data who know best about the improvement and what may have caused it (most credible source/s).
b. Decide on the most appropriate data collection method (self-administered questionnaire, action plan, interview, focus group, etc.)
c. Ask:
1. Given the amount of improvement in this measure, what are the factors that you believe have contributed to the improvement (you can leave this question open or provide a list of potential factors based on what you know, then let the source add to the list).
2. Think through or discuss the linkage of each factor to the impact.
3. As a percentage, how much of the improvement is due to _____ program?
4. On a scale of 0% to 100%, how confident are you that your estimate is accurate (100% = certainty, 0% = no confidence)?
5. Analyze your data (Figure 10.8):

A	B	C	D
Start with fact ___ measure improved	Estimate contribution of the program	Error adjustment (confidence estimate)	Adjusted contribution (AxBxC)
Improvement	___%	___%	Your program's value contribution

Figure 10.8

As an enhancement of this method, the level of management above the participants may be asked to review and concur with each participant's estimate.

When using participants' estimates to measure impact, several assumptions are made:

- The program encompasses a variety of different activities, practices, and tasks, all focused on improving the performance of one or more business measures.
- One or more business measures were identified before the program and have been monitored since the implementation process. Data monitoring has revealed an improvement in the business measure.
- There is a need to associate the program with a specific amount of performance improvement and determine the monetary impact of the improvement. This information forms the basis for calculating the actual ROI.

Given these assumptions, the participants can specify the results linked to the program and provide data necessary to develop the ROI. This can be accomplished using a focus group, an interview, action plan, or a questionnaire.

Manager's Estimate of Impact

In lieu of, or in addition to, participant estimates, the participants' manager (or significant other) may be asked to provide input concerning the program's role in improving performance. In some settings, the managers may be more familiar with the other factors influencing performance, and therefore may be better equipped to provide estimates of impact. The questions to ask managers, after identifying the improvement ascribed to the program, are similar to those asked of the participants.

Managers' estimates should be analyzed in the same manner as the participant estimates, and they may also be adjusted by the confidence percentage. When participants' and managers' estimates have both been collected, the decision of which estimate to use becomes an issue. If there is a compelling reason to believe that one estimate is more credible than the other, then that estimate should be used. This is Guiding Principle #3. Then the most conservative approach is to use the lowest value and include an appropriate explanation. This is Guiding Principle #4.

In some cases, upper management may provide an estimate of the percentage of improvement attributable to a program. After considering other factors that could contribute to the improvement—such as technology, procedures, and process changes—they apply a subjective factor to represent the portion of the results that should be attributed to the program. Despite its subjective nature, this input by upper management is usually accepted by the individuals who provide or approve funding for the program. Sometimes, their comfort level with the processes used is the most important consideration.

Customer Estimates of Program Impact

An approach that is useful in some narrowly focused program situations is to solicit input on the impact of a program directly from customers who are served with the program. Customers are asked why they chose a particular product or service or are asked to explain how their reaction to the product or service has been influenced by individuals or systems involved in the program. This technique often focuses directly on what the program is designed to improve.

Routine customer surveys provide an excellent opportunity to collect input directly from customers regarding their reactions to new or improved products, services, processes, or procedures. Pre- and post-program data can pinpoint the improvements spurred by a new program.

Internal or External Expert Estimates

External or internal experts can sometimes estimate the portion of results that can be attributed to a program. With this technique, experts must be carefully selected based on their knowledge of the process, program, and situation. For example, an expert in quality might be able to provide estimates of how much change in a quality measure can be attributed to a quality program and how much can be attributed to other factors.

This approach has its drawbacks, however. It can yield inaccurate data unless the program and the setting in which the estimate is made are quite similar to the program with which the expert is familiar. Also, this approach may lack credibility if the estimates come from external sources and do not involve those close to the process.

This process has the advantage that its reliability is often a reflection of the reputation of the expert or independent consultant. It is a quick and easy form of input from a reputable expert or consultant. Sometimes top management has more confidence in such external experts than in its own staff.

Estimate Credibility: The Wisdom of Crowds

The following story is an example of the large amount of research showing the power of input from average individuals, taken from James Surowiecki's best-selling book, *The Wisdom of Crowds*. Other experiments are available in YouTube videos, found under "wisdom of crowds."

Case Study

One day in the fall of 1906, British scientist Francis Galton left his home in the town of Plymouth and headed for a country fair. Galton was 85 years old and was beginning to feel his age, but he was still brimming with the curiosity that had won him renown—and notoriety—for his work on statistics and the science of heredity. On that particular day, Galton's curiosity turned to livestock.

Galton's destination was the annual West of England Fat Stock and Poultry Exhibition, a regional fair where the local farmers and towns-people gathered to appraise the quality of each other's cattle, sheep, chickens, horses, and pigs. Wandering through rows of stalls examining workhorses and prize hogs may seem like a strange way for a scientist to spend an afternoon, but there was certain logic to it. Galton was a man obsessed with two things: the measurement of physical and mental qualities, and breeding. And what, after all, is a livestock show but a large showcase for the effects of good and bad breeding?

Breeding mattered to Galton because he believed that only a very few people had the characteristics necessary to keep societies healthy. He had devoted much of his career to measuring those characteristics, in fact, in an effort to prove that the vast majority of people did not possess them. His experiments left him with little confidence in the intelligence of the average person, "the stupidity and wrong-headedness of many men and women being so great as to be scarcely credible." Galton believed, "Only if power and control stayed in the hands of the select, well-bred few, could a society remain healthy and strong."

As he walked through the exhibition that day, Galton came across a weight judging competition. A fat ox had been selected and put on display, and many people were lining up to place wagers on what the weight of the ox would be after it was slaughtered and dressed. For sixpence, an individual could buy a stamped and numbered ticket and fill in his or her name, occupation, address, and estimate. The best guesses would earn prizes.

Eight hundred people tried their luck. They were a diverse lot. Many of them were butchers and farmers, who were presumably expert at judging the weight of livestock, but there were also quite a few people who had no insider knowledge of cattle. "Many non-experts competed," Galton wrote later in the scientific journal, *Nature*. "The average competitor was probably as well fitted for making a just estimate of the dressed weight of the ox, as an average voter is of judging the merits of most political issues on which he votes."

Galton was interested in figuring out what the "average voter" was capable of because he wanted to prove that the average voter was capable of very little. So, he turned the competition into an impromptu experiment. When the contest was over and the prizes had been awarded, Galton borrowed the tickets from the organizers, and ran a series of statistical tests on them. Galton arranged the guesses (totaling 787–13 were discarded because they were illegible) in order from highest to lowest and plotted them to see if they would form a bell curve. Then, among other things, he added up all of the contestants' estimates and calculated the mean. That number represented, you could say, the collective wisdom of the Plymouth crowd. If the crowd were viewed as a single person, that would be the person's guess as to the ox's weight.

Galton had no doubt that the average guess of the group would be way off the mark. After all, mix a few very smart people with some mediocre people and a lot of dumb people, and it seems likely that you would end up with a dumb answer. But Galton was wrong. The crowd had guessed that the slaughtered and dressed ox would weigh 1,197 pounds. In fact, after it was slaughtered and dressed, the ox weighed 1,198 pounds. In other words, the crowd's judgment was essentially perfect. The "experts" were not even close. Perhaps breeding didn't mean so much after all. Galton wrote later: "The result seems more creditable to the trustworthiness of a democratic judgment than it might have been expected." That was something of an understatement.

What Francis Galton stumbled on that day in Plymouth was a simple but powerful truth: under the right circumstances, groups are remarkably intelligent, and are often smarter than the smartest people in them. Groups do not need to be dominated by exceptionally intelligent people in order to be smart. Even if most of the people within a group are not especially informed or rational, collectively they can reach a wise decision [4].

Select the Method

With all of these methods available to isolate the impact of a program, selecting the most appropriate ones for a specific program can be difficult. Some methods are simple and inexpensive; others are time-consuming and costly. When choosing among them, the following factors should be considered:

- Feasibility of the method
- Accuracy associated with the method
- Credibility of the method with the target audience
- Specific cost (time) to implement the method
- Amount of disruption in normal work activities resulting from the method's implementation
- Participant, staff, and management time required for the method

The use of multiple methods should be considered since two methods are usually better than one. When multiple methods are used, the most credible method should be used for ROI calculation. If they are all credible, the most conservative one should be used in the calculation (this is the method that lowers the ROI). The reason is that a conservative approach builds acceptance. The target audience should always be provided with an explanation of the process and the subjective factors involved.

Multiple methods allow an organization to experiment with different strategies and build confidence in the use of a particular technique. For example, if management is concerned about the accuracy of participants' estimates, the combination of a control group arrangement and participant estimates could be useful for checking the accuracy of the estimation process.

It is not unusual for the ROI of a program to be extremely large. Even when a portion of the improvement is allocated to other factors, the magnitude can still be impressive in many situations. The audience should understand that even though every effort has been made to isolate the program's impact, it might be subject to error. It represents the best estimate of the impact given the constraints, conditions, and resources available. Chances are that it is more accurate than other types of analysis regularly used in other functions within the organization.

> *"Accuracy is the twin brother of honesty; inaccuracy, of dishonesty."*
> *– Nathaniel Hawthorne*

Final Thoughts

Isolating the effects of a program is an important step in answering the question of how much of the improvement in an impact measure was caused by the program. The methods presented in this chapter are the most effective approaches available to answer this question and are used by some of the most progressive organizations. Eight approaches were presented, four quantitative and four qualitative. Too often results are reported and linked to a program with no attempt to isolate the portion of the outcome associated with the program. This leads to an outcome with no credibility. When program owners are committed to meeting their responsibility to obtain results, the need for isolation must be addressed early in the process for all major programs. Without it, they lose support, commitment, respect, and...funding. When you complete this important step, you must convert the data to monetary values, detailed in the next chapter.

11

Make It Credible: Convert Data to Monetary Value

Networking is an important benefit from many programs, and the monetary value of networking is an elusive figure. One of Canada's largest banks decided to tackle this issue. This large banking system is on a path to be a major global organization with acquired banks in different countries and expanded divisions within the bank serving a global market.

Recently, the bank conducted a global leaders' meeting at its headquarters in Toronto where the heads of the banking units and banks around the world discussed a variety of strategy and leadership topics. The talent development team saw this as an opportunity to enhance networking. Top executives had always thought that these operating executives could benefit by working together, perhaps sharing some of the same clients and expanding specialized services to other countries. Some bank units offer services that could be purchased by other parts of the bank. With the urging of top executives, the team decided to track the success of the networking and develop the actual monetary value for networking.

The bank used innovative technology where the name tags of individuals could electronically track networking. The devices tracked which participants met other participants, how long they met, and how many times they met. Participants were asked to keep their name badges with them at all times with this message, "We want to try an experiment to see how much networking actually occurs and the value of that networking. This is not a performance issue. It's just an attempt to understand the value of networking." The bank engaged the services of external consultants to measure the monetary value of the networking.

More than 50 participants were involved in the meeting. Armed with the data that showed the networking profile, the external firm conducted interviews with each participant one month after the meeting to indicate what had actually happened with the networking, explore what had occurred since the meeting, and how it connected to the business.

Another follow up was set three months after the meeting with the specific goal of tracking the successes from the networking. A few had very little networking experience with no value. Some exchanged clients or obtained a client from another executive. For example, the headquarters of a client company may be in one country and the participants in another country used the headquarters connection to sell local financial services. A few were able to use the services of other divisions. Some were able to provide referrals. Each of these actions and consequences were detailed with as much specifics as possible to understand what happened and what was anticipated to happen in the future.

The participants attempted to place a monetary value on the outcome anticipating a profit (or cost savings) that would be generated from the contact. In some cases, a new client was secured, and they knew the value of a new client, based on the average tenure of a client and the average annual profit made with that particular product line. In interviews with 52 executives, 21 were able to provide specific data, and seven had very impressive results.

Part of the process included the question "How much of this improvement is actually caused by the networking?" There is a chance that the outcome could have happened through normal channels. In some cases, there was a possibility that the improvement could have happened without networking, as some were thinking about those particular clients. The networking helped. So, they gave a percentage of the improvement to the meeting. A final question asked for the confidence of the allocation to the program using a percent from 0 percent (no confidence) to 100 percent (certainty). This analysis of the data followed the procedures in Chapter 10 (*Make it Credible: Isolate the Effects of the Program*).

When all the money was tallied, divided by all 52 participants, an average value of the networking was $4,265 per person. Although the total amount was impressive, it wasn't enough to cover the total cost of the conference, but that wasn't the principal reason for the conference. This value gave executives some comfort that networking activities can add business value.

This case study illustrates an important trend as executives and administrators attempt to convert hard-to-value measures to money. The monetary value is a way for executives to understand the importance of measures typically not converted to money. This can be an eye-opening exercise.

To show the real money, the improvement in impact measures that is attributable to the program (after the effects of the program have been isolated) must be converted to monetary values, which are then compared with program costs to calculate ROI. This represents the ultimate level in the five-level evaluation framework presented in Chapter 4. In this chapter we will explain how business and organization leaders develop the monetary values used in the ROI calculation.

The Importance of Monetary Value

The need to convert data to monetary amounts is not always clearly understood by program leaders. A program can be successful just by providing impact data and the amount of change directly attributable to the program. For example, an improvement in health status, job growth, market share, or crime could represent a significant improvement linked directly to a new program. For some, this may suffice. However, more sponsors require the actual monetary value, and more program leaders are taking this extra step of converting data to monetary values.

> *"Making money is art and working is art and good business is the best art." – Andy Warhol*

Value Equals Money

For some sponsors, the most important value is money. As described in Chapter 4, there are many different types of value. Monetary value is becoming one of the primary criteria of success, as the economic benefits of programs are pursued. Executives, sponsors, clients, administrators, and other leaders are particularly concerned with the allocation of funds and want to see evidence of the contribution of a program in terms of monetary value. Any other outcome for these key stakeholders would be unsatisfactory. For example, in the counseling at the food bank in the opening story for Chapter 2, the provincial government asked for the ROI on the counseling program, fully explaining what it meant.

Money Makes Impact More Impressive

For some programs, the impact is more impressive when stated in terms of monetary value. Consider for example, the impact of a major program to improve the creativity of an organization's employees, and thereby enhance the innovation of the organization. This program involved literally all employees and had an impact on all parts of the organization. Across all departments, functions, units, and divisions, employees were being more creative, suggesting new ideas, taking on new challenges, driving new products—in short, helping the organization in a wide variety of ways. The best way to understand the value of this program is to convert the individual efforts and their consequences to monetary values. Totaling the monetary values of all the innovations would provide a sense of the value of the program.

Consider the impact of a leadership program directed at all of the middle managers in an organization. At the beginning of the program, the managers were asked to select at least two key performance indicators that should change or improve for them to meet their specific goals. The measures must be under the control of their team and can be changed using the leadership competencies with the team. For a group of 50 managers, 100 different measures could be influenced and reported as improvements. It's difficult to appreciate the value of these improvements. Converting them to monetary values allowed the improvements to be expressed in the same terms, expressed as total monetary benefits.

Monetary value is necessary to determine ROI. As described in earlier chapters, monetary benefits are needed to compare against costs in order to develop the benefits/costs ratio, the ROI (as a percentage), and the payback period.

Converting to Monetary Values is Similar to Budgeting

The monetary benefits resulting from a program is a natural extension of the budget. Professionals and administrators are typically required to have budgets and are expected to develop budgets for programs with an acceptable degree of accuracy. They are also comfortable with handling costs. When it comes to monetary benefits, however, many are not comfortable, even though some of the same techniques used in developing budgets are used to determine benefits. Most of the benefits of the program will take the form of cost savings or cost reductions, and this can make identification of the costs or value easier for some programs.

Monetary Value is Vital to Organizational Operations

With global competitiveness and the drive to improve the efficiency of operations, awareness of the costs related to particular processes and activities is essential. In the 1990s this emphasis gave rise to activity-based costing (ABC) and activity-based management. ABC is not a replacement for traditional, general ledger accounting. Rather, it is a translator or medium between cost accumulations, or the specific expenditure account balances in the general ledger, and the end users who must apply cost data in decision making. In typical cost statements, the actual cost of a process or problem is not readily discernible. ABC converts inert cost data to relevant, actionable information. ABC has become increasingly useful for identifying improvement opportunities, and measuring the benefits realized from performance initiatives on an after-the-fact basis [1]. Over 80 percent of the ROI studies conducted show programs benefiting the organization through cost savings (cost reductions or cost avoidance). Consequently, understanding the cost of a problem and the payoff of the corresponding solution is essential to proper management of the organization.

Monetary Values Are Necessary to Understand Problems and Cost Data

In any business, costs are essential to understanding the magnitude of a problem. Consider, for example, when Mayor Annise Parker of Houston, Texas, calculated the cost of chronic homelessness, it got everyone's attention. The cost for 2,500 chronically homeless people was $103 million in public resources annually; this includes cost of police, EMS, street/park cleanup, and the court system. The per person cost per year of $41,200 was clearly a problem worth solving from a cost perspective. The city didn't attempt to calculate impacts on property values, lost business in areas of high concentration, or the cost to nonprofits for meals, showers, and case-managed apartments [2]. A variety of estimates and expert input may be necessary to supplement costs to arrive at a credible value. The good news is that organizations have developed a number of standard values for identifying undesirable costs. For example, Walmart has calculated the cost of one truck sitting idle at a store for one minute, waiting to be unloaded.

When this cost is multiplied by the hundreds of deliveries per store and the result then multiplied by 5,000 stores, the cost becomes huge.

Key Steps in Converting Data to Money

Converting data to monetary values involves five steps for each data item:

1. *Focus on a unit of measure.* First, a unit of measure must be defined. For output data, the unit of measure is something produced or completed (e.g., one student graduated), or service provided (e.g., one package shipped). Time measures could include the time to complete a program, time to process a form, or response time; and the unit here is usually expressed in terms of minutes, hours, or days. Quality is another common measure, with a unit defined as one error, reject, defect, or reworked item. Soft data measures vary, with a unit of improvement expressed in terms of complaints or incidents. Specific examples of units of measure are:
   - One incident
   - One homicide
   - One student placed
   - One patient discharged
   - One hour of system downtime
   - One day of incarceration
   - One incident of AIDS
   - One sexual assault
   - One microfinance loan approved
   - One accident
   - One new job
   - One voluntary turnover
   - One infant death
   - One citizen complaint about police
   - One medication error
   - One infection
2. *Determine the value of each unit.* Now comes the important part: placing a value (V) on the unit identified in the first step. For most common and important measures, the process is relatively easy. Most organizations maintain records or reports that can pinpoint the cost of one unit. Soft data are more difficult to convert to money. For example, the

monetary value of one citizen complaint about police will be more difficult to determine. The techniques described in this chapter provide an array of approaches for making this conversion. When more than one value is available, the most credible value is generally used in the calculation. If the credibility is the same, the lowest value is used.

3. *Calculate the change in performance data.* The change in output data is calculated after the effects of the program have been isolated from other influences. This change (Δ) is the performance improvement that is directly attributable to the program, represented as the Level 4 impact measure. The value may represent the performance improvement for an individual, a team, a group of participants, or several groups of participants.

4. *Determine the annual amount of change.* The Δ value is annualized to develop a value for the total change in the performance data for one year (ΔP). Using annual figures is a standard approach for organizations seeking to capture the benefits of a particular program, even though the benefits may not remain constant throughout the year. For a short-term solution, first-year benefits are used even when the program produces benefits beyond one year. This approach is considered conservative. More will be discussed about this later.

5. *Calculate the annual value of the improvement.* The total value of improvement is calculated by multiplying the annual performance change (ΔP) by the unit value (V) for the complete group in question. For example, if one group of participants is involved in the program being evaluated, the total value will include the total improvement for all participants providing data in the group. This value for annual program benefits is then compared with the costs of the program to calculate the BCR, ROI, or payback period.

An example from a customer service program at a trucking company describes the five-step process of converting data to monetary values. This program was developed and implemented to address customer complaints as the company was experiencing an excessive number of complaints caused by inadequate or improper deliveries. The number of complaints was selected as an output measure. Figure 11.1 shows the steps in assigning a monetary value to the data, resulting in a total program impact of $228,000.

Setting: Customer complaints for a trucking company.

Step 1: Define the unit of measure.

The unit is defined as one customer complaint based on delivery service.

Step 2: Determine the value (V) of each unit.

According to internal experts (*i.e.,* the customer care staff), the cost of an average complaint in this category was estimated at $1,500, when time and direct costs are considered
(V = $1,500).

Step 3: Calculate the change (Δ) in performance data.

Six months after the project was completed, total complaints per month had declined by 25. Sixty-five percent of the reductions were related to the project, as determined by the frontline customer service staff ("Isolating project impact"), with an average confidence of 78 percent. Use the six-month value of 25 x 65% x 78% = 12.7 per month.

Step 4: Determine an annual amount for the change (ΔP).

The monetary amount is multiplied by 12 to yield an annual improvement value of 12.7 x 12 = 152
ΔP = 152

Step 5: Calculate the annual value of the improvement.

Annual value = $\Delta P \times V$
    = 152 x $1,500
    = $228,000

Figure 11.1 Converting Customer Complaint Data to Monetary Values.

Standard Monetary Values

A standard value is a monetary value assigned to a unit of measurement that is accepted by key stakeholders, including the sponsors and donors. Standard values have been developed because these are often the measures that matter to the organization and community. They often reflect problems, and their conversion to monetary values show their impact on the operational and financial well-being of the organization or the community.

For the last two decades, quality initiatives have typically focused only on the cost of quality, placing a value on mistakes, or the payoff from avoiding these mistakes. This assigned value— the standard cost of quality—is one of the critical outgrowths of the quality management movement. Additionally, a variety of process improvement programs— such as reengineering, reinventing the corporation, transformation, and continuous process improvement—have included a component in which the cost of a particular measure is determined. Also, the development of a variety of cost control, cost containment, and cost management systems, such as activity-based costing (ABC), have forced organizations, communities, and governments to place costs on activities and, in some cases, relate those costs directly to the revenues or profits of the organization.

The following discussion describes how measures of output, quality, and time are being converted to standard values.

Converting Output Data to Money

When a program results in a change in output, the value of the increased output can usually be determined from the organization's accounting or operating records. For organizations operating on a profit basis, this value is typically the marginal profit contribution of an additional unit of production or service provided. An example is a team within a major appliance manufacturing firm that was able to boost the production of small refrigerators after a comprehensive work cell redesign program; the unit of improvement is the profit margin associated with one refrigerator.

For organizations that are performance driven rather than profit driven, this value is usually reflected in the savings realized when an additional unit of output is realized for the same input. For example, in the visa processing section of a government office, one additional visa application may be processed at no additional cost; an increase in output translates into a cost savings equal to the unit cost of processing a visa application.

Most organizations have standard values readily available for performance monitoring and goal setting. Managers often use marginal cost statements and sensitivity analyses to pinpoint values associated with changes in output. If the data are not available, the program team must initiate or coordinate the development of appropriate values.

One of the more important measures of output is productivity, particularly in a competitive organization. Today, most organizations competing in the global economy do an excellent job of monitoring productivity and placing a value on it.

The benefit of converting output data to money using standard values is that these calculations are already available for the most important data items. Perhaps no area has as much experience with standard values as the sales and marketing area. Figure 11.2 shows a sampling of the sales and marketing measures that are routinely calculated and reported as standard values [4].

Metric	Definition	Conversion Notes
Sales	The sale of the product or service recorded in a variety of different ways: by product, by time period, by customer	The data must be converted to monetary value by applying the profit margin for a particular sales category.
Profit Margin (%)	Price-cost Cost for the product, customer, and time period	Factored to convert sales to monetary value add to the organization
Unit Margin	Unit price less unit cost	Shows the value of incremental sales
Channel Margin	Channel profits as a percentage of channel selling price	Used to show the value of sales through a particular marketing channel
Retention Rate	The ratio of customers retained to the number of customers at risk of leaving	The value is the saving of the money necessary to acquire a replacement customer
Churn Rate	Ratio of customers leaving to the number who are at risk of leaving	The value is the saving of the money necessary to acquire a new customer
Customer Profit	The difference between the revenues earned from and the cost associated with the customer relationship during the specified period	The monetary value added is the profit obtained from customers, which all goes toward the bottom line
Customer Value Lifetime	The present value of the future cash flows attributed to the customer relationship	Bottom line; as customer value increases, it adds directly to the profits; as a customer is added, the incremental value is the customer lifetime average
Cannibalization Rate	The percentage of new product sales taken from existing product lines	This is to be minimized, as it represents an adverse effect on existing product, with the value added being the loss of profits due to the sales loss
Workload	Hours required to service clients and prospects	This includes the salaries, commissions, and benefits from the time the sales staff spend on the workloads
Inventories	The total amount of product or brand available for sale in a particular channel	Since inventories are valued at the cost of carrying the inventory, costs involve space, handling, and the time value of money; insufficient inventory is the cost of expediting the new inventory or the loss of sales because of the inventory outage
Market Share	Sales revenue as a percentage of total market sales	Actual sales are converted to money through the profit margins, is a measure of competitiveness
Loyalty	The length of time the customer stays with the organization, the willingness to pay a premium, and the willingness to search	Calculated as the additional profit from the sale or the profit on the premium

Figure 11.2 Examples of Standard Values from Sales and Marketing [5].

Case Study

For organizations conducting studies on programs designed to increase the number of college graduates, the monetary value of a college degree is needed. Instead of calculating the value or searching the Internet for it, most have visited their most trusted source and located or tweaked the value. Executives, sponsors, administrators, and donors have accepted the value and refer to it as a "standard." That source is usually the U.S. Census Bureau.

There are many benefits that stem from college education, most of which justify the expenses incurred in the process of obtaining a degree.

Despite the fact that wages of high school and college graduates often do not vary significantly until years of work experience is acquired, as a general rule college graduates earn more money during their working lives than people with high school diplomas. According to statistical data from the U.S. Census Bureau people with bachelor's degrees earn nearly 2 million USD, associate's degrees nearly 1.5 million USD, and high school diplomas nearly 1.2 million USD in the course of their careers.

While obtaining a college degree can be expensive, college graduates earn more money during their lives than those who drop out of college. In sheer monetary terms, a college graduate with a bachelor's degree is expected to earn twice as much as a college dropout. This translates into about 1.6 million USD more in lifetime earnings than workers with a high school diploma. In the long run attending college should be viewed as an investment that pays off later in life and contributes to a higher living standard.

The substantial increase in salary is just one of the good reasons to consider acquiring a college degree. Most students currently enrolled in college and universities attend public institutions as these schools do not cost as much as private or ivy-league schools. Attending public college and universities usually comes to around 8,000 USD annually, and that includes tuition, books, and living expenses. Students who attend community colleges in general end up paying around 1,300 USD for tuition annually.

Research in recent years has proven a direct correlation between college education and morality. It has been demonstrated that mothers with a college degree are more likely to spend time with their children, teaching them social values and behavior that turns them into citizens who participate actively in and contribute to their community.

This goes on to show that the advantages of a college degree are not limited to financial gain only. College graduates have significantly lower rates of unemployment and poverty than high school graduates, and are generally healthier and more adaptable.

Overall, society benefits from higher education. Some of these benefits include higher tax receipts, increased public awareness about important social issues, and lower unemployment, teenage pregnancy, and birth rates. Educated parents in turn are far more likely to raise children who go on and obtain a college degree as well [3].

Calculating the Cost of Inadequate Quality

Quality and the cost of quality are important issues in all types of organizations. Because many programs are designed to increase quality, the program team may have to place a value on the improvement of certain quality measures. For some quality measures, the task is easy. For example, if quality is measured in terms of the defect rate, the value of the improvement is the cost to repair or replace the product. The most obvious cost of poor quality is the amount of scrap or waste generated by mistakes. Defective products, spoiled raw materials, and discarded paperwork are all the result of poor quality. Scrap and waste translate directly into a monetary value. In a production environment, for example, the cost of a defective product is the total cost incurred up to the point at which the mistake is identified, minus the salvage value. In the service environment, the cost of a defective service is the cost incurred up to the point at which the deficiency is identified, plus the cost to correct the problem, plus the cost to make the customer happy, plus the loss of customer loyalty.

In the public sector, quality measures are reflected in crime rates, diseases, poverty, injuries, homelessness, recidivism, student dropouts, and pollution. These are "mistakes" that should not have happened, and many programs are implemented to reduce or prevent them.

Employee mistakes and errors can be expensive. The costliest form of rework occurs when a product or service is delivered to a customer and must be returned for repair or correction. The cost of rework includes both labor and direct costs. In some organizations, rework costs can constitute as much as 35 percent of operating expenses.

Quality costs can be grouped into six major categories [6]:

1. Internal failure represents costs associated with problems detected prior to product shipment or service delivery. Typically, such costs are reworking and retesting.
2. Penalty costs are fines or penalties incurred as a result of unacceptable quality.
3. External failure refers to problems detected after product shipment or service delivery. Typical items here are technical support, complaint investigation, remedial upgrades, and fixes.
4. Appraisal costs are the expenses involved in determining the condition of a particular product or service. Typical costs

involve testing and related activities, such as product quality audits.

5. Prevention costs involve efforts undertaken to avoid unacceptable products or service quality. These efforts include service quality administration, inspections, process studies, and improvements.

6. Customer dissatisfaction is perhaps the costliest element of inadequate quality. In some cases, serious mistakes result in lost business. Customer dissatisfaction is difficult to quantify and arriving at a monetary value may be impossible using direct methods. The judgment and expertise of sales, marketing, or quality managers are usually the best resources to draw upon in measuring the impact of dissatisfaction. More and more quality experts are measuring customer and client dissatisfaction with the use of market surveys.

Quality is not just a measure that occurs within an organization. Consider the costs that a homeless person incurs upon city programs, law enforcement, public services, etc. This is a quality issue because something failed or broke down with that individual. Being homeless costs the city for justice and law enforcement, healthcare, sanitation, and parks and recreation. As mentioned in Chapter 6, in the city of Houston, the cost per homeless person is $41,200.

As with output data, the good news is that a tremendous number of quality measures have been converted to standard values. Some of these measures are:

- Readmissions into a hospital
- Incidents
- Sexual assaults
- Homicides
- Property thefts
- Rework
- Processing errors
- Student dropouts
- Accidents
- Addictions
- Grievances
- System downtime
- Incarcerations
- Delays
- Compliance discrepancies
- Student loan defaults
- Citizen complaints
- And many others…

Case Study

Burglary, murder, identity theft—all crimes have costs for victims and society. The Department of Justice reported that federal, state, and local governments spent more than $280 billion in 2012 on criminal justice, including police protection, the court system, and prisons.

However, there are many other costs that researchers and evaluators consider when estimating the total cost of crime in the United States. These can include tangible costs like replacing damaged property and intangible costs like victims' pain and suffering [7].

For a police force, evaluating programs to reduce crime will need a standard value for major crimes. To calculate the values would require too much time and effort. Searching the Internet for a value during a study may produce a value that may not be credible or accepted by key stakeholders. Instead, the evaluation team needs to locate a credible source (the most credible source) and review it for accuracy, credibility, and lack of bias. For some, it's the RAND Corporation.

The RAND Corporation is a research organization that develops solutions to public policy challenges to help make communities throughout the world safer and more secure, healthier and more prosperous. RAND is nonprofit, nonpartisan, and committed to the public interest.

Existing high-quality research on the costs of crime and the effectiveness of police demonstrates that public investment in police can generate substantial social returns. A RAND study from the Center on Quality Policing, *Hidden in Plain Sight: What Cost-of-Crime Research Can Tell Us About Investing in Police*, shows how this research can be used to better understand the returns on investments in police [8].

As shown in Figure 11.3, this study produced values for the cost of crime when considering all the tangibles costs.

Although these costs can be debated, the key is to secure an accepted value as a standard value in advance of conducting a particular study.

Crime Type	Cost per Crime
Murder	$8,649,216
Rape	$217,866
Robbery	$67,277
Aggravated Assault	$87,238
Burglary	$13,096
Larceny	$2,139
Motor Vehicle Theft	$9,079

Figure 11.3 The Cost of Crime

Converting Employee Time Savings Using Compensation

Saving time is a common outcome for programs. In a team environment, a program may enable the team to complete tasks in less time or with fewer people. A major program could lead to a reduction of the need for additional staff. On an individual basis, a program may be designed to help staff and volunteers save time in performing daily tasks. The value of the time saved is an important measure and determining a monetary value for it is relatively easy.

The most obvious time savings stem from reduced labor costs for performing a given amount of work. The monetary savings are found by multiplying the hours saved by the labor cost per hour. For example, a time-saving program in one organization, participants saved an estimated average of 74 minutes per day, worth $31.25 per day or $7,500 per year, based on the average salary plus benefits for a typical participant.

The average wage, with a percentage added for employee benefits, will suffice for most calculations. However, employee time may be worth more. For example, additional costs for maintaining an employee (office space, furniture, telephones, utilities, computers, administrative support, and other overhead expenses) could be included in calculating the average labor cost. Thus, the wage rate used in the calculation can escalate quickly. In a large-scale employee reduction effort, calculating the costs of additional employees may be more appropriate for showing the value. However, for most programs, the conservative approach of using salary plus employee benefits is recommended.

Beyond reducing the labor cost per hour, time savings can produce benefits such as improved service, avoidance of penalties for late programs, and serve more people. These values can be estimated using other methods discussed in this chapter.

A word of caution is needed concerning time savings. Savings are realized only when the amount of time saved translates into a cost reduction or a profit contribution. Even if a program produces savings in time, monetary value is not realized unless the participant puts the time saved to productive use. Having participants estimate the percentage of time saved that is devoted to productive work is helpful, if it is followed up with a request for examples of how the extra time was used. Ideally, a team-based program eliminates several hours of work each day, the actual savings will be based on the corresponding reduction in staff or the need for new staff. Therefore, an important preliminary step in figuring time savings is determining whether the expected savings will be genuine.

Case Study

A major healthcare system pursued lean healthcare in a very aggressive way, using workshops for managers and specialists in hospitals and clinics. The lean process teaches participants how to improve a particular process or procedure. The goal was to make hospitals more efficient and effective. Participants in the program were taught how to find short-cuts, simplified approaches, and alternative ways to perform a particular procedure, process or task. When completed, a time savings was found. In theory, when 10 minutes are saved on a procedure that is performed by hundreds of people each day, the time savings would be significant. Participants in the programs usually set a goal to achieve a certain amount of monetary savings as the time is converted to money using the hourly compensation for the total hours saved. When the target is achieved, participants could receive a green or black belt designation, suggesting that they have mastered the lean processes.

Because the lean budget was growing considerably, the chief financial officer (CFO) questioned the value of these programs. In response, the program coordinator solicited studies directly from the consultants providing the lean training. They selected some of their best studies, presented the monetary benefits, and compared it to the cost of the consultants to calculate the ROI. The numbers were quite high, reaching several thousand percent. These select case studies were presented to the CFO to address his concerns. Unfortunately, the CFO questioned the credibility of the data. For example, the time savings reported was dramatic in several of the hospitals. Yet, the payroll costs and overtime remained largely unchanged. The high numbers were difficult to accept, and it appeared that some of the assumptions that were made were not very critical.

The CFO forwarded the studies to ROI Institute to check the accuracy of the calculations and assumptions. While several assumptions led to the high ROI, one stood out as particularly significant. The time saved, although small and incremental for a given procedure, added up to be quite large. The assumption was that the time saved would be used on other productive work, such as seeing additional patients, implementing a new system, or performing other important tasks. Unfortunately, that was generally not the case. Another assumption that stood out is that the time saved was annualized and extrapolated over a five-year period—far too long for the analysis to be credible. The fully loaded cost of the program was not included; only the cost of the consultants, omitting the other major costs, covered in a later chapter. Lastly, it was assumed that all of the improvement was directly connected to this program. Sometimes these efficiencies are gained because of a need to become more efficient and the staff may pursue them on their own, not necessarily because of a program.

When adjustments were made on the existing studies to make them more credible, the large percentages went away. Still, they resulted in a respectable ROI. Sadly, because of the exaggerated assumptions made earlier, the CFO lost confidence in the consultants and rejected the program's request for additional funding. He felt that the results had been grossly exaggerated in order to secure a larger budget.

Finding Standard Values

Standard values are available for all types of data. Virtually every organization will develop standard values that are monitored for that area. Typical functions in a major organization where standard values are tracked include:

- Administration
- Operations
- Finance and accounting
- Engineering
- IT
- Sales and marketing
- Customer service and support
- Quality
- Procurement
- Logistics
- Compliance
- Research and development
- HR/Talent

Thanks to enterprise-wide systems software, standard values are commonly integrated and made available for access by a variety of people. In some cases, access may need to be addressed to ensure that the data can be obtained by those who require them.

When Standard Values are Not Available

When standard values are not available, several alternative strategies for converting data to monetary values are available. Some are appropriate for a specific type of data or data category, while others may be used with virtually any type of data. The challenge is to select the strategy that best suits the situation.

Using Historical Costs from Records

Historical records often indicate the value of a measure, and the cost (or value) of a unit of improvement. This strategy relies on identifying the appropriate records and tabulating the proper cost components for the item in question. Essentially, we calculate the value.

For example, a large construction firm initiated a program to improve safety. The program improved several safety-related performance measures, ranging from amounts spent in response to government fines to total workers' compensation costs. From the company's records for one year of data, the average cost for each safety measure was determined. This value included the direct costs of medical payments, insurance payments and premiums, investigation services, and lost-time payments to employees, as well as payments for legal expenses, fines, and other direct services. The amount of time used to investigate, resolve, and correct the issues was also factored in. This time involved not only the health and safety staff, but other personnel as well. Additionally, the costs of lost productivity, disruption of services, morale, and dissatisfaction were estimated to obtain a full cost. The corresponding costs for each item were then developed.

This example suggests the challenges inherent in maintaining systems and databases to enable the value for a particular data item to be identified. It also raises several concerns about using historical costs as a technique to convert data to money.

Time

Sorting through databases, cost statements, financial records, and activity reports takes a tremendous amount of time, and time that may not be available for the program. It is important to keep this part of the process in perspective. Converting data to monetary values is only one step in the ROI Methodology. Time needs to be conserved.

Availability

In some cases, data are not available to show all of the costs for a particular item. In addition to the direct costs associated with a measure, an equal number of indirect or invisible costs may be present that cannot be obtained easily.

Access

Compounding the problems of time and availability is access. Monetary values may be needed from a system or record set that is under someone else's control. In a typical implementation, the program leader may not have full access to cost data. Cost data are more sensitive than other types of data, and are often protected for a number of reasons, including competitive advantage. Therefore, access can be difficult and sometimes is even prohibited unless an absolute need-to-know can be demonstrated.

Accuracy

Finally, the need for accuracy in this analysis should not be overlooked. A measure provided in current records may appear to be based on accurate data, but this may be an illusion. When data are calculated, estimations are involved, access to certain systems is denied, and different assumptions are made (all of which can be compounded by different definitions of systems, data, and measures). Because of these limitations, the calculated values should be viewed as suspect unless means are available to ensure that they are accurate.

Calculating monetary value using historical data should be done with caution, and only when the sponsor has approved the use of additional time, effort, and money to develop a monetary value from the current records and reports. Otherwise, an alternative method is preferred.

A case study helps illustrate the detail that is needed in the time that is required to calculate a credible value. The metro bus system of a large city in the United States was experiencing significant unplanned absenteeism, which resulted in not only a huge operating cost, but also had a negative impact on customer satisfaction as many of the bus routes were experiencing delays. This system had more than a thousand buses with 2,900 drivers, and unplanned absenteeism had reached 8.7 percent. The system addressed the problem by creating a pool of substitute drivers. This pool grew steadily to the point that it reached 231 substitute drivers. These drivers reported to work with the expectation that other drivers would not show and that they would be dispatched to cover those particular routes.

While this helped avoid serious bus delays, it incurred a tremendous cost. The bus system contracted with an external firm to calculate the cost of absenteeism. This resulted in a detailed analysis of how the drivers were used, including how many were not utilized and the days that the absences actually exceeded the numbers of the pool. When all of the costs were calculated, the value was reported and was staggering. It took several weeks of work for the consulting firm but yielded a value that was helpful for the organization. Using this value, they then calculated the cost per absence and divided it by the average wage rate, which pegged the cost of absenteeism to the average pay rate. This gave them a benchmarking figure they could use in the future. Incidentally, because of this huge cost, two solutions were presented to control and drastically reduce unplanned absenteeism [9].

This story highlights the errors involved in calculating the actual cost of a specific measure. It is being tackled in organizations because of necessity. However, it should not be undertaken as part of an ROI study. In this particular calculation, the ROI study on the impact of the two solutions was a separate project, removed from the calculations on the cost of absenteeism. This underscores the cost of calculating the monetary value credibly.

Using Input from Experts

When it is necessary to convert data items for which historical cost data are not available, input from experts on the process might be a consideration. Internal experts can provide the cost (or value) of one unit of improvement in a measure. Individuals with knowledge of the situation and the confidence of management must be willing to provide estimates, as well as the assumptions behind the estimates. Internal experts may be found in the department in which the data originated—compliance, marketing, operations, logistics, support, or any number of other functions. Most experts have their own methodologies for developing these values. When their input is required, it is important to explain the full scope of what is needed, and to provide as many specifics as possible.

If internal experts have a strong bias regarding the measure, or the measures are not available, external experts are sought. External experts should be selected based on their experience with the unit of measure. Fortunately, many experts are available who work directly with important measures in healthcare, environment, economic development, justice, social services, and community development. They are often willing to provide estimates of the cost (or value) of these intangibles.

External experts—including consultants, professionals, or suppliers in a particular area—can also be found in obvious places. For example, the costs of accidents can be estimated by the workers' compensation carrier, or the cost of a grievance may be estimated by the labor attorney defending the organization in grievance transactions. The process of locating an external expert is similar to the external database search, described later.

The credibility of the expert, whether internal or external, is a critical issue if the monetary value placed on a measure is to be reliable. Foremost among the factors behind an expert's credibility is the individual's experience with the process or measure at hand. Ideally, he or she should work with this measure routinely. Also, the person must be unbiased. Experts should be neutral in connection with the measure's value and should have no personal or professional interest in it.

Additionally, the credentials of external experts—published works, degrees, and other honors or awards—are important in validating their expertise. Many of these people are tapped often, and their track records can and should be checked. If their estimate has been validated in more detailed studies and was found to be consistent, this can serve as a confirmation of their qualifications in providing such data.

Experts are available for all kinds of situations. For example, in green and sustainability projects, consultants can quickly tell you how much energy consumption and monetary savings are connected to different devices, systems, and equipment in a house. They can show how changing certain equipment or installing new devices can lead to direct money savings. These energy cost savings are standard values that are accepted in the industry and are known by the consulting organization.

Using Values from External Databases

For some measures, the use of cost (or value) estimates based on the work and research of others may be appropriate. This technique makes use of external databases that contain studies and research program focusing on the cost of data items. Fortunately, many databases include cost studies of data items related to programs, and most are accessible on the Internet. Data are available on the costs or value of illnesses, diseases, addictions, crimes, incarcerations, jobs, labor stoppage, accidents, and even customer satisfaction.

The difficulty lies in finding a database with studies or research germane to the particular program. Ideally, the data should originate from a similar setting in the same industry, but that is not always possible. Sometimes, data on industries or organizations in general are sufficient, with adjustments possibly required to suit the program at hand.

In the opening story in Chapter 2, Sarah Robertson found databases for the cost of incarceration and the cost of an addiction to the healthcare system in the province. In the opening story of Chapter 3, the researchers found the monetary value for improving reading levels among students. Figure 11.4 shows an example of data collected from an external database on the cost of employee turnover.

Job Type/Category	Turnover Cost Ranges as a Percent of Annual Wage/Salary
Entry Level - Hourly, Non Skilled (e.g. Fast Food Worker)	30 - 50%
Service/Production Workers - Hourly (e.g. Courier)	40 - 70%
Skilled Hourly (e.g. Machinist)	75 - 100%
Clerical/Administrative (e.g. Scheduler)	50 - 80%
Professional (e.g. Sales Representative, Nurse, Accountant)	75 - 125%
Technical (e.g. Computer Technician)	100 - 150%
Engineers (e.g. Chemical Engineer)	200 - 300%
Specialists (e.g. Computer Software Designer)	200 - 400%
Supervisors/Team Leaders (e.g. Section Supervisor)	100 - 150%
Middle Managers (e.g. Department M anager)	125 - 200%

Notes
1. Percentages are rounded to reflect the general range of costs from studies.
2. Costs are fully loaded to include all of the costs of replacing an employee and bringing him/her to the level of productivity and efficiency of the former employee. The turnover included in studies is usually unexpected and unwanted. The following costs categories are usually included:

- Customer dissatisfaction
- Employment cost
- Exit cost of previous employee
- Loss of expertise/knowledge
- Lost productivity
- Orientation cost
- Recruiting cost
- Supervisor's time for turnover
- Temporary replacement costs
- Training cost
- Quality problems
- Wages and salaries while training

3. Turnover costs are usually calculated when excessive turnover is an issue, and turnover costs are high. The actual cost of turnover for a specific job in an organization may vary considerably. The above ranges are intended to reflect what has been generally reported in the literature when turnover costs are analyzed.

Sources of Data
The sources of data for these studies follow two general categories:
1. Industry and trade magazines have reported the cost of turnover for a specific job within an industry.
2. Publications in general management (academic and practitioner), human resources management, human resources development training, and performance improvement often reflect ROI cost studies because of the importance of turnover to senior managers and human resources managers.

All of this comes from ERIC, which is the Education Resources Information Center – an online digital library of education research and information. ERIC is sponsored by the Institute of Education Sciences U.S. Department of Education. ERIC provides ready access to education literature to support the use of educational research and information to improve practice in learning, teaching, educational decision-making, and research.

Figure 11.4 Example of Using External Databases – Employee Turnover.

Linking with Other Measures

When standard values, records, experts, and external studies are not available, a feasible alternative might be to find a relationship between the measure in question and some other measure that can be easily converted to a monetary value. This involves identifying existing relationships that show a strong correlation between one measure and another with a standard value.

A classic relationship is the correlation between job satisfaction and employee turnover. Suppose that in a program designed to improve job satisfaction, a value is needed to reflect changes in the job satisfaction index. A predetermined relationship showing the correlation between increases in job satisfaction and reductions in turnover can directly link the two measures. Using standard data or external studies, the cost of turnover can easily be determined as described earlier. Therefore, a change in job satisfaction can be immediately converted to a monetary value, or at least an approximate value. The conversion is not always exact because of the potential for error and other factors, but the estimate is sufficient for converting the data to monetary values.

In some situations, a chain of relationships may establish a connection between two or more variables. A measure that may be difficult to convert to a monetary value is linked to other measures that, in turn, are linked to measures to which values can be assigned. Ultimately, these measures are traced to a monetary value typically based on profits. Figure 11.5 shows the model used by a major retail store [5]. The model connects job attitudes (collected directly from the employees) to customer service, which is directly related to revenue growth. The rectangles in the figure represent survey information, and the ovals represent hard data. The shaded measurements are collected and distributed in the form of store performance indicators.

As the model shows, a 5-point improvement in employee attitudes leads to a 1.3-point improvement in customer satisfaction. This, in turn, drives a 0.5 percentage point increase in revenue growth. If employee attitudes at a local store improved by 5 points, and the previous rate of revenue growth were 5 percent, the new rate of revenue growth would then be 5.5 percent.

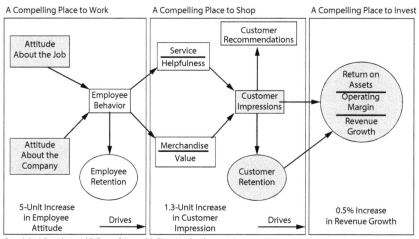

Figure 11.5 Relationship Between Attitudes and Profits [10].

These links between measures, often called the service-profit chain, offer a promising methodology for applying monetary values to hard-to-quantify measures.

In addition to this particular example, many other examples of this type of analysis have been developed over a period of time in all types of global organizations. For example, the Danish postal service developed a correlation between employee engagement and postal revenue per employee. Essentially, employees sold more postal products as they became more engaged. In Akzo Nobel in Amsterdam, a significant correlation between employee engagement and safety was noted. In other words, there are fewer accidents when employees are more engaged. At Lowe's home improvement stores in the United States, increased employee engagement resulted in increased sales [11]. As the employees are more engaged, they sell more products. At Southeast Corridor Bank, there was a correlation between engagement and employee turnover. As employees become more engaged, they are more likely to stay with the organization [12]. Lastly, for PolyWrighton, a plastics manufacturer, engagement was directly related to quality improvements. As employees become more engaged, they produced better quality work [13]. These examples are a small sample of the variety of data that is already available. Though the data was analyzed by other teams, it is available to show the linkage between a hard-to-value measure (such as engagement) and an easy-to-value measure (such as retention, quality, safety, or sales).

Using Estimates from Participants

In some cases, participants in the program should estimate the value of improvement. This technique is appropriate when participants are capable of providing estimates of the cost (or value) of the unit of measure that has improved as a result of the program. With this approach, participants should be provided with clear instructions, along with examples of the type of information needed. The advantage of this approach is that the individuals who are most closely connected to the improvement may be able to provide the most reliable estimates of its value. As with isolating program effects, when estimates are used to convert measures to monetary values, adjustments are made to reduce the error in those estimates.

Figure 11.6 shows a calculation for the cost of a sexual harassment complaint at a healthcare organization. Some of the data conversion was from the records and the other was from estimates made by the staff. When combined, the number is credible and was accepted by senior executives [14].

$$\text{Cost per complaint} \quad \frac{\$852,000}{35} = \$24,343$$

Figure 11.6 Converting Data Using Historical Costs and Staff Input.

Using Estimates from the Management Team

In some situations, participants in a program may be incapable of placing a value on the improvement. Their work may be so far removed from the ultimate value of the process that they cannot provide reliable estimates. In these cases, the team leaders, supervisors, or managers of participants may be able to provide estimates. Thus, they may be asked to provide a value for a unit of improvement linked to the program.

In other situations, managers are asked to review and approve participants' estimates and confirm, adjust, or reject those values. For example, a program involving customer service representatives was designed to reduce customer complaints on a train for a state-run railway in Europe. The program did result in a reduction in complaints, but the value of a single customer complaint had to be identified to determine the value of the improvement. Although customer service representatives had knowledge of certain issues surrounding customer complaints, their scope was limited; so their managers were asked to provide a value. These managers had a broader perspective of the impact of a customer complaint, including the damage to the brand.

Senior management can often provide estimates of the value of data. In this approach, senior managers concerned with the program are asked to place a value on the improvement based on their perception of its worth. This approach is used when calculating the value is difficult or when other sources of estimation are unavailable or unreliable.

Using Program Staff Estimates

The final strategy for converting data to monetary values is using program staff estimates. Using all available information and experience, the staff members most familiar with the situation provide estimates of the value. For example, a particular program for an international oil company was designed to reduce dispatcher absenteeism and address other performance problems. Unable to identify a value using the other strategies, the consulting staff estimated the cost of an absence to be $200. This value was then used in calculating the savings from the reduction in absenteeism that followed the program implementation. Although the program staff may be qualified to provide accurate estimates, this approach is sometimes perceived as biased. It should therefore be used only when other approaches are unavailable or inappropriate.

Selecting the Technique

With so many available, the challenge is selecting one or more techniques appropriate for the situation and available resources. Developing a list of techniques for the situation may be helpful. The guidelines that follow may aid in selecting a technique and finalizing the value.

Choose a Technique Appropriate for the Type of Data

Some techniques are designed specifically for hard data, whereas others are more appropriate for soft data. Thus, the type of data often dictates the strategy. Standard values are developed for most hard data items, and organization records and cost statements are used in the process. Soft data often involve the use of external databases, links with other measures, and estimates. Experts are used to convert both types of data to monetary values.

Move from Most Accurate to Least Accurate

The techniques in this chapter are presented in order of accuracy. Standard values are usually most accurate and therefore the most credible. But, as mentioned earlier, they are not always readily available. When standard values are not available, the following sequence of operational techniques should be tried:

- Calculate the value from historical costs from organization records (if available and there is enough time to do it)
- Use internal and external experts
- Search external databases
- Locate links with other measures
- Collect estimates

Each technique should be considered based on its feasibility and applicability to the situation. The technique associated with the highest accuracy is always preferred if the situation allows.

Consider Source Availability

Sometimes the availability of a particular source of data determines the method selection. For example, experts may be readily accessible. Some standard values are easy to find; others are more difficult. In other situations, the convenience of a technique is a major factor in the selection. The Internet, for example, has made external database searches more convenient.

As with other processes, keeping the time investment for this phase to a minimum is important so that the total effort directed to the ROI study does not become excessive. Some techniques can be implemented in much less time than others. Devoting too much time to the conversion process may dampen otherwise enthusiastic attitudes about the use of the methodology, plus drive up the costs of the evaluation.

> *"Time is more valuable that money. You can get more money, but you cannot get more time." – Jim Rohn*

Use the Source with the Broadest Perspective on the Issue

According to Guiding Principle 3 in Figure 4.8, the most credible data source must be used. The individual providing estimates must be knowledgeable of the processes and the issues surrounding the valuation of the data. For example, consider the estimation of the cost of a grievance in a manufacturing plant. Although a supervisor may have insight into what caused a particular grievance, he or she may have a limited perspective. A high-level manager may be able to grasp the overall impact of the grievance and how it will affect other areas. Thus, a high-level manager would be a more credible source in this situation.

Use Multiple Techniques When Feasible

The availability of more than one technique for obtaining values for the data is often beneficial. When appropriate, multiple sources should be used to provide a basis for comparison or for additional perspectives. The data must be integrated using the standards. The first consideration is credibility. If one stands out as more credible, it should be used, following Guiding Principle #3. If they are all similar, then the conservative approach of using the lowest value is used, following Guiding Principle 4 in Chapter 4. This applies only when the sources have equal or similar credibility.

Converting data to monetary values has its challenges. When the particular method has been selected and applied, several adjustments or tests are necessary to ensure the use of the most credible and appropriate value with the least amount of resources.

Apply the Credibility Test

The discussion of techniques in this chapter assumes that each data item collected and linked to a program can be converted to a monetary value. Highly subjective data, however, such as changes in staff attitudes or a reduction in the number of conflicts, are difficult to convert. Although estimates can be developed using one or more strategies, such estimates may lack credibility with the target audience, which can render their use in analysis questionable.

The issue of credibility in combination with resources is illustrated in Figure 11.7. This is a logical way to decide whether to convert data to monetary values or leave them intangible. Essentially, in the absence of standard values, many other ways are available to capture the data or convert them to monetary values. However, there is a question to be answered: can it be done with minimum resources? Some of the techniques mentioned in this chapter—such as searching records or maybe even searching the Internet—cannot be performed with minimal use of resources. However, an estimate obtained from a group or from a few individuals is available with minimal use of resources. Then we move to the next question: will the donor or executive client, who is interested in the program, buy into the monetary value assigned to the measure with a two-minute minimum explanation? If so, then it is credible enough to be included in the analysis; if not, then move it to the intangibles. The intangible benefits of a program are also important and are covered in much more detail in the next chapter.

Consider the Short-Term/Long-Term Issue

When data are converted to monetary values, usually one year's worth of data is included in the analysis for short-term solutions, following Guiding Principle 9 in Figure 4.8. The issue of whether a program is short term or long term depends on the time it takes to complete or implement it. If one group participating in the program and working through the process takes months or years to complete it, then it is probably not short term.

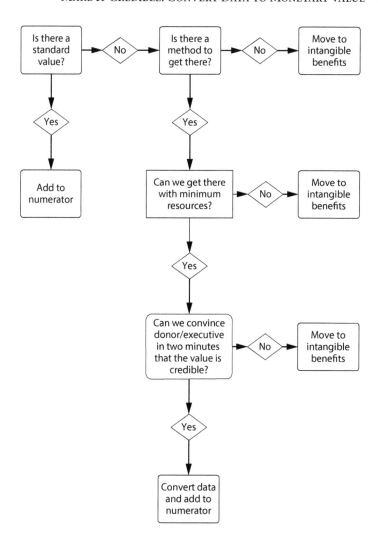

Figure 11.7 To Convert or Not to Convert.

In general, it is appropriate to consider a program short term when one individual takes one month or less to learn what needs to be done to make the program successful. When the lag between program implementation and the consequences is relatively brief, a short-term solution is also appropriate. When the development or acquisition costs are very high, this is usually when a long-term solution is appropriate. When a program is long term, no time limit for data inclusion is used, but the time value should be set before the program evaluation is undertaken. Input on the time value should be secured from all stakeholders, including the sponsor, donor, implementer, designer, and evaluator. After some discussion, the estimates of the time factor, the benefits stream, should be conservative and perhaps reviewed by finance and accounting. When a program is a long-term solution, extrapolation will need to be used to estimate multiple years of value. Few sponsors will wait several years to see if a program is successful.

In response to reports that the country has the second-highest percentage of obese people, relative to the size of the region's population, a Middle Eastern medical clinic decided to set up a Cardiology Centre of Excellence. The clinic is a privately owned acute care hospital. Currently, it is licensed for only a Diagnostic Catheter Lab and not for an Interventional Catheter Lab, authorized to insert stents and pacemakers. Patients requiring these services have to be transferred to other facilities. To achieve its goal of creating a Cardiology Centre of Excellence, the clinic needs to prepare a theater for open-heart surgery, acquire the license for an Interventional Catheter Lab, and have its staff learn and apply the appropriate skills for those procedures [15].

The cost of the new equipment for the Centre is high, and the clinic does not expect a positive ROI for the first three years. However, the clinic has set impact objectives for its new Centre's first year:

- Zero patient transfers to any other facility
- Increase revenue for the Cardiology Department by 20 percent
- Grow the number of patients for the Interventional Catheter Lab from 0 to 500 in the first six months

While this information will provide the clinic's managers with initial simple performance data, the benefit stream must be set. In a meeting involving the equipment supplier, the clinic manager, a representative from finance and accounting, and the evaluation team, a four-year payout was established after the impact is realized, six months in this case. The impacts are extrapolated for four years for the ROI calculation. This enabled the team to have an ROI calculation for the program in six months to make a decision on the success of this program. To control risk in this decision, the data would continue to be monitored for the four-year period.

Consider an Adjustment for the Time Value of Money

Since investment in a program is made in one time period and the return is realized at a later time, some organizations adjust program benefits to reflect the time value of money using discounted cash flow techniques. The actual monetary benefits of the program are adjusted for the time period. The amount of adjustment, however, is usually small compared with the typical benefits of programs.

Although this may not be an issue for every program, it should be considered for each program, and some standard discount rate should be used. Consider the following example of how this is calculated. Assume that a program costs $100,000, and it is expected to take two years for the full value of the estimate to be realized. This is a long-term solution spanning two years. Using a discount rate of 6 percent, the cost for the program for the first year would be $100,000 x 106% = $106,000. For the second year it is $106,000 x 106%, or $112,360. Thus, the program cost has been adjusted for a two-year value with a 6 percent discount rate. This assumes that the program sponsor could have invested the money in some other program and obtained at least a 6 percent return on that investment.

Final Thoughts

Showing the real money requires just that—money. Business impact data that have improved as a result of a program must be converted to money. Standard values make this process easier, but easy is not always an option, and other techniques must sometimes be used. Experts, internal or external, are usually available to provide a value based on their experience and expertise. External databases can be located, estimates can be provided, and the value can even be calculated using conservative principles. However, if a measure cannot be converted with minimum resources or with no assurance of credibility, the improvement in the measure should be reported as an intangible benefit.

After the data are converted to monetary values, the next step is collecting the program costs and calculating the ROI, detailed in Chapter 13. But first, let's address the intangibles, those measures not converted to money.

12

Make It Credible: Identify the Intangibles

A physician in a provincial health system in Canada was interested in making some changes in the procedures for colon cancer surgery. He had been reading about some successes with an innovative approach from the United Kingdom regarding changes in prep and aftercare with some important results and wanted to give this a try. However, he knew it would be a change for the system, which would require time and resources to implement it. This change had to generate enough improvements (cost saving or cost avoidance) to overcome the cost of the change. In essence, he needed to show a positive ROI.

Recognizing that it's difficult to secure funds to make this change, he wanted to experiment with a trial first. A small sample would represent minimal costs that could be absorbed by his particular hospital. With the assistance of ROI Institute and ROI Institute Canada, he set up the evaluation following the ROI Methodology. He had identified key impact measures that he wanted to influence: complications, infections, readmissions, and length of stay. This new approach should have improvements on all of these measures.

A group of 17 patients had the new procedures and their results compared with a control group of 17 other patients properly matched with the experimental group. The control group followed the routine procedure. To make this work with the experimental group, the staff had to be convinced that this procedure was good for patient care and necessary to control the cost of healthcare in the province (reaction). He also had to make sure that the staff knew how to properly take care of the prep and aftercare (learning). This involved off-the-job training and demonstrations on the job to make it work. He had to ensure that the staff were following the new process precisely to make sure that it was being applied properly (application). Finally, he would monitor the impacts of the two groups (impact).

The results were amazing. There were no complications, infections, or readmissions in the experimental group compared to numbers that ranged from 12–24 percent in the control group. The length of stay was reduced by three days as well. He presented these dramatic results to the senior team and asked for money for a larger sample. His thinking was that this was a small sample of 17 and it was not statistically significant to make an inference about the rest of the population. Each year, the province would have about 500 of these surgeries. Along with these results, there was an important measure that had to be addressed properly, the length of stay, which represented a reduction of three days. There was some debate on the value of reducing those days. Some would argue that since there is a waiting line for people to get into the healthcare system, saving a day off someone's stay doesn't actually save money. There's always someone to take the bed. The cynics would argue that the new patients arriving would have some extra initial costs of testing and that for a brief number of days it would probably cost more. Obviously, this is short-sighted thinking. There should be monetary value of that measure.

The finance and accounting team provided costs for improvement in complications, infections, and readmissions. They indicated that they could actually support a value for each day saved, in the length of stay calculation, but there would still be some debate on the value. Because of this potential debate, it was left as an intangible—and a very important one. Logic centered on this issue. The evaluation team didn't want to debate the monetary value of saving one day on a particular stay. A debate could derail the presentation. The team knew there was some monetary value in this intangible but would leave it as an intangible so that it became upside potential.

The good news is that this program produced a very positive ROI of 118 percent. When it was presented to the senior team, the results were so impressive that they were not interested in funding another group, but they decided to just change the entire procedure. As the CFO said in the meeting, "I see some definite cost savings that we can easily capture, particularly with readmission and infections and this is enough cost avoidance to cover the cost of this program and still some. I can see some money savings here that we could use for some other processes. The length of stay improvement is a plus."

This type of analysis on a new approach can make a big difference. It also underscores the power of intangibles, the measures that are not converted to money but are still very powerful in making the argument.

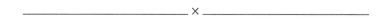

Almost all programs will generate results that include both tangible and intangible measures. By definition and based on the guiding principles of the ROI Methodology, an intangible benefit is a measure that is not converted to money, because the conversion cannot be accomplished with minimum resources and with credibility. These measures are usually identified at the beginning of the program and monitored after the program has been completed. Although not converted to monetary values, they are an important part of the evaluation process; for many programs, they are the most important outcome. In this chapter, we explore the role of intangibles, how to measure them, when to measure them, and how to report them.

Why Intangibles are Important

The range of intangible measures is almost limitless. This chapter emphasizes just a few common and desired outcomes of programs. Figure 12.1 highlights examples of these measures. Some measures make the list because of the difficulty in measuring them; others because of the difficulty in converting them to money. Still others are on the list for both reasons. Being labeled as intangible does not mean that these items can never be measured or converted to monetary values. In one study or another, each item on the list has been monitored and quantified in financial terms. However, in typical programs, these measures are considered intangible benefits because of the difficulty in converting them to monetary values.

Intangible measures are not new. Intangibles drive funding for major programs and drive the economy. Some organizations are built on them. In every direction we look, intangibles are not only important, but also critical to organizations. Here's a recap of why they have become so important.

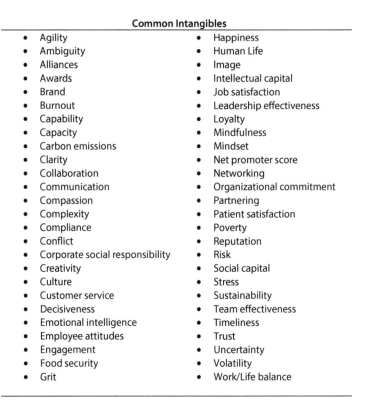

Figure 12.1 Common Intangibles.

Intangibles are the Invisible Advantage

When examining the reasons behind the success of organizations, intangibles are often found. A highly adaptive company continues to develop new and improved products. A government agency reinvents itself. A company with highly involved and engaged employees attracts and keeps talent. An organization shares knowledge with employees, providing a competitive advantage. Still another organization is able to develop strategic partners and alliances. These successes are often measured by what are considered to be intangibles. These intangibles do not often appear in cost statements and other record keeping, but they are there, and they make a huge difference.

Sometimes at work, we measure everything except what counts. Numbers are comforting— income, expenditures, crime, poverty, productivity, health status, staff retention—and create an illusion of control. But when we're confronted by spectacular success or failure, everyone from the top executive to the janitor points in the same direction: the culture. Beyond measure and sometimes apparently beyond comprehension, culture has become the secret sauce of organizational life: the thing that makes the difference but for which no one has the recipe [1].

According to Heffernan, the paradox of organizational culture lies in the fact that, while it makes a big difference, it is comprised of small actions, habits, and choices. The accumulation of these behaviors—coming from everywhere, from the top and the bottom of the hierarchy, from inside and outside the company itself—creates an organization's culture. It feels chaotic and yet, at the same time, exerts an influence on everything anyone does.

This represents both a curse and a blessing. For leaders, the curse lies in the sense that culture emerges of its own volition—not just beyond measure but also beyond their control. We may not be able to measure culture, but we can measure the high rate of failure for programs aiming at culture change; that stands at around 70 percent. So, the idea emerges that culture is elusive, hard to manage, impossible to command.

Trying to identify, measure, and react to intangibles may be difficult, but the ability to do so exists. Intangibles transform the way organizations work, the way employees are managed, the way products are designed, the way services are sold, and the way customers are treated. The implications are profound, and an organization's strategy must address them. Although invisible, the presence of intangibles is felt, and the results are concrete.

"Anything that is measured and watched, improves." – Bob Parsons

We are in the Intangible Economy

The intangible economy has evolved from basic changes that date to the Iron Age, which evolved into the Agricultural Age. In the late nineteenth century and during the early twentieth century, the world moved into the Industrial Age. From the 1950s forward, the world has moved into the Technology and Knowledge Age, and these moves translate into intangibles. During this time, a natural evolution of technology has occurred. During the Industrial Age, companies and individuals invested in tangible assets like plants and equipment. In the Technology and Knowledge Age, companies invest in intangible assets, like brands, systems, collaboration, culture, and image. The future holds more of the same, as intangibles continue to evolve into an important part of the overall economic system [2].

More Intangibles are Converted to Tangibles

The good news is that data, often regarded as intangible, are now being converted into monetary values. Because of this, classic intangibles are now accepted as tangible measures, and their value is more easily understood. Consider, for example, patient satisfaction. Just a decade ago, few healthcare organizations had a clue as to the monetary value of patient satisfaction. Now more healthcare organizations have taken the extra step to link patient satisfaction directly to patient revenues, recommendations, and other measures.

Over a decade ago, Jackson made progress to place a value on reputation [3]. More recently, Worline and Dutton concluded that compassion connects to the bottom line, fuels strategic advantage, motivates innovation, and drives service quality [4]. Through our work at ROI Institute, we have converted stress to money [5].

Tracy and Morin attempted to connect trust to the bottom line. Trust, they say, is the lubricant of society and the glue that holds societies together. When trust is present, when goals are relatively congruent, there is room for honest disagreement—an essential ingredient for innovation and growth. On the other hand, when trust is absent, innovation suffers and costs rise exponentially. Think of the games played with time logs, insurance claims, and expense accounts. No wonder economists are concerned about trust. It finds its way into all their calculations—whether the Gross National Product or the economics of the firm [6].

Organizations are seeing the tremendous value that can be derived from intangibles. As this chapter will illustrate, more data are being accumulated to show monetary values, moving some intangible measures into the tangible category.

Case Study

In her ROI case study, *TM at the St. Mary-Corwin Farm Stand Prescription Pantry*, Rev. Linda Stetter outlined the value of the farm stand prescription program at the St. Mary-Corwin Medical Center. As the Director of Mission Integration and Spiritual Care at this hospital in southeastern Colorado, Rev. Stetter charged herself with measuring and calculating the ROI of the prescription aspect of the farm stand. This program was developed to address high levels of morbidity due to obesity and diabetes in Pueblo County.

In her case study, Rev. Stetter discussed the importance of the farm stand program to those who benefit from it:

> "This is a population that has been so marginalized and so short-changed that they really don't know what questions to ask, or they don't feel comfortable asking questions or telling us what their needs are. They needed to know that they could trust us, that we would provide a safe environment throughout the course of the farm stand season, and that they could confide in us without any adverse consequences."

Rev. Stetter highlighted the case of one individual, identified as TM, as he and his family went through the farm stand prescription pantry program. Aside from providing the family of six with food, those managing the program also provided counseling and even helped TM avoid an unnecessary surgery that he had been told he needed. Based on one unnecessary surgery prevented, she calculated the ROI:

Scenario #3 (all costs)

$$ROI = \frac{10,235 - 1,277}{1,277} \times 100 = 701.5\%$$

Although the calculated ROI for this program, 701.5%, is very high and based only on one prevented surgery, she was able to get attention and make the point that even more value comes from the "priceless" intangibles Rev. Stetter identified. TM learned to trust the people associated with the farm stand, reframed "taking charity" into "paying it forward" through volunteering efforts the family is taking on, and became receptive to counseling.

Intangibles Drive Programs and Investments

Some programs are implemented because of the intangibles. For example, the need to have greater collaboration, partnering, branding, reputation, image, communication, teamwork, or service will drive programs. In the public sector, the need to reduce poverty, improve health status, lower the number of homeless, employ disadvantaged citizens, and save lives often drives programs. From the outset, the intangibles are the important drivers and become the most important measures. Consequently, more executives include a string of intangibles on their scorecards, such as key operating reports, key performance indicators, dashboards, and other routine reporting systems. In some cases, the intangibles represent nearly half of all measures that are monitored.

As a general rule, only about 15 percent of the value of a contemporary organization can be tied to such tangible assets as buildings and equipment. Intangible assets have become the dominant investment in businesses [7]. They are a growing force in the economy, and measuring their values poses challenges to managers and investors. They can no longer be ignored. They must be properly identified, selected, measured, reported, and (in some cases) converted to monetary values.

Measuring and Analyzing Intangibles

In some programs, intangibles are more important than monetary measures. Consequently, these measures should be monitored and reported as part of the program evaluation. In practice, every program, regardless of its nature, scope, and content, will produce intangible measures. The challenge is to identify them effectively and report them appropriately.

Measuring the Intangibles

From time to time, it is necessary to explore the issue of measuring the difficult to measure. Responses to this exploration usually occur in the form of comments instead of questions. "You can't measure it," is a typical response. This cannot be true, because anything can be measured. What the frustrated observer suggests by the comment is that the intangible is not something you can count, examine, or see in quantities, like items produced or products sold. In reality, a quantitative value can be assigned to or developed for any intangible. If it exists, it can be measured. Consider human intelligence for example. Although human intelligence is vastly complex and abstract with myriad facets and qualities, IQ scores are assigned to most people and most people seem to accept them.

The software engineering institute of Carnegie-Mellon University assigns software organizations a score of 1 to 5 to represent their maturity in software engineering. This score has enormous implications for the organizations' business development capabilities, yet the measure goes practically unchallenged [8]. Each year, *Fortune* magazine creates a list of the 100 Best Companies to Work For. Being on the list is a great recruiting tool and retention strategy [9].

Several approaches are available for measuring intangibles. Intangibles that can be counted include alliances, staff complaints, and conflicts. These can be recorded easily and constitute one of the most acceptable types of measures. Unfortunately, many intangibles are based on attitudes and perceptions that must be measured. The key is in the development of the instrument of measure. The instruments are usually developed around scales of 3, 5, and even 10 points to represent levels of perception. The instruments to measure intangibles consist of three basic varieties.

The first instrument lists the intangible items and asks respondents to agree or disagree on a five-point scale (where the midpoint represents a neutral opinion). Other instruments define various qualities of the intangible, such as its reputation. A five-point scale can easily be developed to describe degrees of reputation, ranging from the worst rating—a horrible reputation—to the best rating—an excellent reputation. Still other ratings are expressed as an assessment on a scale of 1 to 10, after respondents review a description of the intangible. Studies use these types of surveys routinely [10].

The second instrument to measure the intangible connects it, when possible, to a measure that is easier to measure or easier to value. For example, staff engagement is one of the most measured intangibles. Employee engagement often connects to productivity, retention, quality, and safety [11]. As shown in Figure 12.2, most hard-to-measure items are linked to an easy-to-measure item. In the classic situation, a soft measure (typically the intangible) is connected to a hard measure (typically the tangible). Although this link can be developed through logical deductions and conclusions, having some empirical evidence through a correlation analysis (as shown in the figure) and developing a significant correlation between

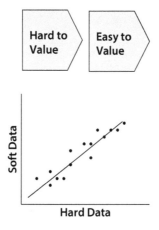

Figure 12.2 The Link Between Hard-to-Value and Easy-to-Value Items.

the items is the best approach. However, a detailed analysis would have to be conducted to ensure that a causal relationship exists. In other words, just because a correlation is apparent, does not mean that one caused the other. Consequently, additional analysis, other empirical evidence, and supporting data could pinpoint the actual causal effect.

A third instrument for measuring the intangible is the development of an index of different values. These could be a combination of both hard and soft data items that make up a particular index value. An index is a single score representing some complex factor that is constructed by aggregating the values of several different measures. Measures making up the index are sometimes weighted based on their importance to the abstract factor being measured. Some index measures are based strictly on hard data items. For example, the US poverty level is based on a family income amount equal to three times the money needed to feed a family as determined by the US Department of Agriculture, adjusted for inflation using the consumer price index. Sometimes an index is completely intangible, such as the customer satisfaction index developed by the University of Michigan.

Intangibles are often combined with a variety of tangibles to reflect the performance of a business unit, function, or program. Intangibles are also often associated with nonprofit, nongovernment, and public-sector organizations. Figure 12.3 shows the performance measures reflecting greatness at the Cleveland Orchestra. For the Cleveland Orchestra, intangibles include such items as comments from cab drivers; tangibles include ticket

Superior Performance	Distinctive Impact	Lasting Endurance
Emotional response of audience; increase in number of standing ovations	Cleveland's style of programming increasingly copied; becoming more influential	Excellence sustained across generations of conductors—from George Szellthrough, Pierre Boulez, Christoph von Dohnanyi, and Franz Wilser-Most
Wide technical range; can play any piece with excellence, no matter how difficult—from soothing and familiar classical pieces to difficult and unfamiliar modern pieces	A key point of civic pride; cab drivers say, "We're really proud of our orchestra."	
Increased demand for tickets; demand for more complex, imaginative programs in Cleveland, New York, and Europe	Orchestra leaders increasingly sought for leadership roles and perspectives in elite industry groups and gatherings	Supporters donate time and money; invest in long-term success of orchestra; endowment triples
Invited to Salzburg Festival (first time in 25 years), signifying elite status among top European orchestras		

Adapted from *Good to Great and the Social Sectors* by Jim Collins (Collins 2005)

Figure 12.3 Measuring Greatness at the Cleveland Orchestra.

sales. Collectively and regardless of how difficult they are to obtain, these data sets reflect the overall performance of the orchestra [12].

Converting to Money

Converting the hard to measure to monetary values is challenging, to say the least. Examples in this chapter show various attempts to convert these hard-to-value measures to monetary values. When working with intangibles, the interest in the monetary contribution expands considerably. Three major groups have an interest in the monetary value. First are the sponsors who fund a particular program. They almost always seek monetary values among the measures. Second, the public is involved in some way with many intangibles. Even private-sector organizations are trying to improve their image and reputation, and public confidence. These days, the public is interested in the financial impacts of these organizations. They are no longer willing to accept the notion that the intangibles are enough to fund programs, particularly if they are funded by tax dollars. Third, the individuals who are actively involved with and support the program often need, and sometimes demand, that the monetary value be developed.

Case Study

At Yale University, the most popular course these days is a course on happiness. It is taught to students who are sometimes struggling to find meaning and value in much of what they do and are involved in. The course has been, surprisingly, very popular to all types of students.

According to the *New York Times'* David Shimer, "The course, taught by Laurie Santos, a psychology professor and the head of one of Yale's residential colleges, tries to teach students how to lead a happier, more satisfying life in twice-weekly lectures. Dr. Santos speculated that Yale students are interested in the class because, in high school, they had to deprioritize their happiness to gain admission to the school, adopting harmful life habits that have led to what she called 'the mental health crises we're seeing at places like Yale.' A 2013 report by the Yale College Council found that more than half of undergraduates sought mental healthcare from the university during their time there [13]."

In this case, increased happiness could be linked to metal illness outcomes, such as healthcare costs, absenteeism, and productivity.

Happiness shows up everywhere. Many organizations measure happiness through job satisfaction, which has several components, such as satisfaction with pay, career, supervisor, and the work. Employee engagement focuses more on the fulfilling aspects of the work individuals are doing, such as being more responsible, involved in decisions, accountable for results, and willingness to share information. A person with these characteristics may be a good team member. Engagement has been connected to retention, productivity, and quality, which are all easily converted to money.

The United Nations has entered the happiness trend by having a happiness index, which measures six main components. According to a UN report, the six factors are GDP per capita, healthy years of life expectancy, social support (as measured by having someone to count on in times of trouble), trust (as measured by a perceived absence of corruption in government and business), perceived freedom to make life decisions, and generosity (as measured by three recent donations). The top 10 countries rank highly on all six of these factors. In 2017, Norway was at the top of the happiness index, while the United States ranked 12th [14].

Should you worry about the happiness index? If you're the Minister of Happiness, as in Dubai, you might want to see the monetary value. For example, the Roads and Transport Authority (RTA) in Dubai is interested in the monetary value of happiness because it has to show the ROI on projects. RTA builds additional roads, bridges, new lanes, transit systems, water taxis, and other kinds of transport processes to keep citizens happy. Until recently, there haven't been ROI studies for a new bridge, canal, or road lane addition. Instead, these changes were implemented because there was a need to eliminate road congestion, accidents, and driving times. Essentially, the RTA wants to make citizens happy with the transportation system.

In our work with RTA, we were surprised to find that there is a happiness department, nestled within this large organization, with some interesting data helpful for the project managers to determine the ROI of new projects. For example, this department found a correlation between happiness with transit and the amount of money citizens spend in the city. If they're happy with transit—it is reliable, takes a short amount of time to travel, and is safe—they're more likely to go to the mall and spend money, and citizens spending money ultimately helps the city.

In short, there is usually a way to develop the monetary value to happiness. We suspect that in Norway, the happiness index has brought in tourists to see what goes on there, as well as some who want to stay there for a long period of time, or even live there. Maybe there is a monetary value to the Happiness Index. The key issue is that it can be done and is being done…if it is needed.

The approaches to convert to monetary values were detailed in Chapter 11. The specific methods used in that chapter all represent approaches that may be used to convert the intangibles to monetary values. Although these methods will not be repeated here, showing the path most commonly used to capture values for the intangibles is helpful. Figure 12.4 shows the typical path of converting intangibles to monetary values, building on the methods in Chapter 11.

The first challenge is to locate existing data or measure the intangible item in some way, making sure the data are accurate and reliable. Next, an expert may be able to place a monetary value on the item based on experience, knowledge, credentials, and track record. Stakeholders may provide their input, although it should be factored for bias. Some stakeholders are biased in one way or the other—they want the value to be smaller or larger depending on their particular motives. This input may have to be adjusted or thrown out altogether.

Finally, the data are converted using the conservative processes described in Chapter 11, often adjusting for the error in the process. Unfortunately, no specific rule exists for converting each intangible to monetary value. By definition, an intangible is a measure that is not converted to money because the conversion cannot be accomplished with minimum resources, with credibility.

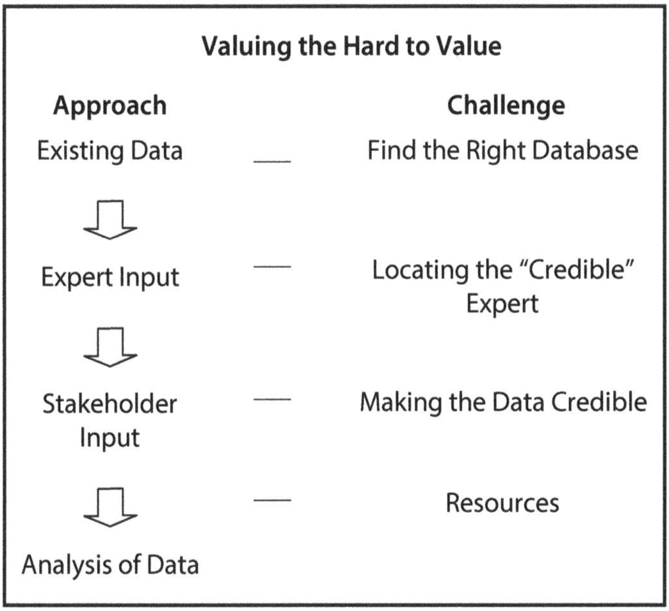

Figure 12.4 Valuing the Hard to Value.

Case Study

Workplace Conflict & How Business Can Harness It To Thrive, **CPP Global Human Capital Report.**

This graphic is impressive for getting your attention…but it may not be accurate. This is distributed by an organization that offers programs on conflict resolution. The critical parts of this monetary value are the assumptions and steps taken to calculate the value, which are contained in the reference. It's dated, conducted in 2008, although it was distributed in a marketing piece in 2018. Although the researchers asked 5,000 employees in nine countries (USA, Brazil, and seven European countries), the response rate is not provided. The critical parts of this monetary value are the assumptions and steps taken to calculate the value, which are contained in the reference. The money spent is based on the number of hours spent on conflict each week by American employees. If a conflict resolution program reduced conflicts and reduced the time spent on conflicts, the time saved could be claimed if the time saved is used on other productive work. Employees would have to be asked that follow-up question. Credibility of the data should be the concern throughout the analysis.

Identifying and Collecting Intangibles

Intangible measures can be taken from different sources and at different times during alignment and program life cycle, as depicted in Figure 12.5. They can be uncovered early in the process, during the needs assessment, and their collection can be planned for as part of the overall data collection strategy. For example, one program has several hard data measures linked to it. Stress, an intangible measure, is also identified and monitored with no plans to convert it to a monetary value. From the beginning, this measure is destined to be a nonmonetary, intangible benefit reported with the ROI results.

A second opportunity to identify intangible benefits is in the planning process, when clients or sponsors of the program agree on an evaluation plan. Key stakeholders can usually identify the intangible measures they expect to be influenced by the program. For example, a change management program in a large multinational company was conducted, and an ROI analysis was planned. Program leaders, participants, participants' managers, and experts identified potential intangible measures that were perceived to be influenced by the program, including collaboration, communication, and teamwork.

A third opportunity to collect intangible measures presents itself during data collection. Although the measure may not be anticipated in the initial program design, it may surface on a questionnaire, in an interview, or

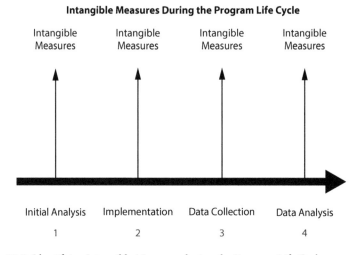

Figure 12.5 Identifying Intangible Measures during the Program Life Cycle.

during a focus group. Questions are often asked about other improvements linked to a program, and participants usually provide several intangible measures for which no plans are available to assign a value. For example, in the evaluation of a leadership development program at the World Bank Group, participants were asked what specifically had improved about their work and relationships with team members as a result of the program. Participants provided more than a dozen intangible measures that managers attributed to the program.

The fourth opportunity to identify intangible measures is during data analysis, while attempting to convert data to monetary values. If the conversion loses credibility, the measure should be reported as an intangible benefit. For example, in a program to reduce incidents of malaria, preventing deaths was identified early in the process as a measure of program success. A conversion to monetary values was considered, but lacked accuracy, credibility, and support. Consequently, saving human lives was reported as an intangible benefit.

Analyzing Intangibles

For each intangible measure identified, some evidence of its connection to the program must be shown. However, in many cases, no specific analysis is planned beyond tabulation of responses. Early attempts to quantify intangible data sometimes resulted in aborting the entire process, with no further data analysis being conducted. In some cases, isolating the effects of the program may be undertaken using one or more of the methods outlined in Chapter 10. This step is necessary when program leaders need to know the specific amount of change in the intangible measure that is linked to the program. Intangible data often reflect improvement. However, neither the precise amount of improvement nor the amount of improvement directly related to a program is always identified. Because the value of these data is not included in the ROI calculation, a detailed analysis is not necessary. Intangible benefits are often viewed as additional evidence of the program's success and are presented as supportive qualitative data.

After a measure is determined to be an intangible, a step must be taken to link it to the program. This can be easily accomplished with a single question using a five-point scale, as shown in Figure 12.6. The most credible source (usually the participants) provides input about the influence of

Please indicate the extent to which the program has influenced the following measures:

Intangible Measure	No Influence	Some Influence	Moderate Influence	Significant Influence	Very Significant Influence
Image	☐	☐	☐	☐	☐
Teamwork	☐	☐	☐	☐	☐
Brand	☐	☐	☐	☐	☐
Engagement	☐	☐	☐	☐	☐
Stress	☐	☐	☐	☐	☐
Patient Satisfaction	☐	☐	☐	☐	☐
Communications	☐	☐	☐	☐	☐
Engagement	☐	☐	☐	☐	☐

Figure 12.6 Connecting to Intangibles.

the program on the intangibles. The program evaluators must decide the box that must be checked to conclude that there was an influence. Usually, box three (moderate influence) is used as a minimum. Also, the evaluators must decide the minimum number of responses with three, four, or five to be included on the charts in the report. This is usually 10 percent to 20 percent of the sample being evaluated.

> *"Not everything that counts can be counted, and not everything that can be counted counts." – Albert Einstein*

Final Thoughts

Intangible measures are crucial to reflecting the success of a program. Although they may not carry the weight of measures expressed in monetary terms, they are nevertheless an important part of the overall evaluation. Intangible measures should be identified, explored, examined, and monitored for changes linked to programs. Collectively, they add a unique dimension to the final report because most, if not all, programs involve intangible variables. The range of intangible measures is practically limitless.

Now that we've identified intangible measures, we must capture the overall program costs and calculate the ROI. We'll discuss these two steps in the next chapter.

13

Make It Credible: Capture Costs of the Program and Calculate ROI

A publicly owned electrical utility serving several states in the United States was very interested in controlling costs for its 12 power-generating locations, ranging from coal fired to nuclear power. Top executives realized that the creative spirit often lay with the employees who knew where improvements could be made and could see innovative opportunities to reduce costs. They wanted to tap the creativity of the team and pay them for the ideas.

The approach taken is a classic suggestion system based on cost savings which has been implemented by many organizations, often with good success. Benchmarking data suggest that, if implemented properly, about 10 percent of the workforce would actually make suggestions. The general manager (GM) had requested an evaluation of the program at the ROI level.

As the Organization Effectiveness (OE) team implemented the suggestion system, they were very well aware of what was necessary to achieve this success. Using the ROI Methodology, they started with the end in mind with direct cost reduction or cost avoidance as the desired impact.

The evaluation team knew that the reaction would be easy to measure. For learning, it's important for the employees to know how to make a suggestion, how it's evaluated, when it's evaluated, who evaluates it, when they will be notified, and when they receive the money. These knowledge points are necessary for employees to see the value and timeliness of the system and, consequently, plan to makes suggestions. During meetings with all employees, the system was described with examples. At the end of the meeting, reaction data were collected with a brief feedback questionnaire. Learning data were captured with an anonymous and nonthreatening true/false quiz to make sure employees knew how it worked. After the meeting, employees were making the suggestions driven by an application objective of 10 percent (a minimum of 100 percent of employees will have suggestions).

Since the OE team perceived this system to be operational for several years and have long-term impact, the value stream for monetary benefits was set for two years. This time period was agreed to at the very beginning of the project before implementation, as part of the evaluation planning. This meant that two years of operating data would be captured and compared to the total cost of the program. The OE team had the luxury of waiting for this period of time. If there was pressure to see value sooner, the cost savings from projects accumulated up to that point would be extrapolated for a two-year period, assuming the same rate of idea submission and implementation.

From the beginning, the general manager was concerned about the cost of the program. Anticipating much activity, the suggestion system manager (a member of the OE team) staffed up for the new system, placing a full-time suggestion system administrator (SSA) in each of their 12 facilities and four in the headquarters office. These costs are significant, and the GM was anxiously awaiting an ROI study after two years of operation.

When a person makes a suggestion for cost savings and it was implemented, the anticipated life of that idea was established. Some suggestions would have a long life because a process was changed that would be operational for a long time. Others would simply be a one-time cost savings. The life value was established following conservative financial principles. The payout is based on the life of the suggestion and is paid as a lump sum amount. This approach was motivational for the employees because they could submit ideas that could have a five-year stream, and those employees would be paid for the total amount when their suggestions were implemented. Figure 13.1 explains how the chain of impact works for this system with the results at different levels.

Employee Suggestion System				
Type of Data	Data Collection Method	Data Source	Timing	Results
Reaction (Level 1)	Survey	Employees	At the end of the announcement meeting	4.3 out of 5 rating on motivational, satisfaction, and engaging
Learning (Level 2)	Quiz	Employees	At the end of the announcement meeting	7.5 out of 10 on the procedures, case documentation, award determination, and notification
Application and Implementation (Level 3)	Monitor Records	Employee Suggestion System	Routinely	10.4% participation rate
Business Impact (Level 4)	Monitor Business Performance	Employee Suggestion System	Routinely	$1.52 million in 2 years
Cost	Monitor Records	Cost Statements	Annually	$2.1 million cost in 2 years
ROI (Level 5)	—	—	—	−28%
Intangibles	Questionnaire	Sample of Employees	Annually	Increased cooperation, commitment to the organization, engagement, employee satisfaction, and teamwork

Figure 13.1 Types and Levels of Data.

The monetary savings generated for the program over a two-year period were a total of $1.52 million, an impressive number. Had the evaluation stopped at that point, the group would be celebrating this impressive milestone. However, the GM wanted to see comparison with the total cost, including the administrative cost, the salaries of the staff, their operating expenses, the actual payouts to employees, and any upfront development costs associated with the system. When the costs were tallied, the total cost for the two years was $2.1 million.

The ROI was a negative value because the total operational costs ($2.1 million) exceeded the monetary benefits during the same two-year period. ROI presents the ultimate accountability as the monetary benefits ($1.52 million) are compared to the cost ($2.1 million):

$$ROI = \frac{(\$1.52\text{million} - \$2.1\text{million})}{\$2.1\text{million}} \times 100 = -28\%$$

With these negative results, the team was very disappointed and suggested that perhaps it should be continued because important intangibles were connected to the system, such as teamwork, commitment, engagement, and satisfaction. While that logic may be feasible in some programs, the GM emphasized that it would not work with this project. Because the nature of this initiative was based on providing cost savings, it would not be suitable to spend more money on a cost-saving system than it was providing in cost reduction or cost avoidance. The GM asked, "How will this look in the newspaper? Because we're government and we're transparent with our programs and this evaluation, it will probably be in the newspaper." Incidentally, he reminded the team that they had an objective for a positive ROI, "Although we didn't set a precise amount for this objective, we wanted it to have more savings than it costs."

The good news is that the adjustment to make it positive was very obvious to the OE team. There were too many staff members. During data collection for the study, it appeared that the staff was only about 25 percent utilized in the operating plants. One person perhaps could cover two or more plants and that would not necessarily lower the outcomes.

Eight jobs were eliminated and the employees in those jobs were placed in open jobs so that no one actually lost his or her job but moved to an open position. This is important because without this action there's really no cost reduction for the utility for this system. Going forward with this reduction, a very positive ROI is generated.

This study highlights two important issues about ROI analysis. First, you don't see the ultimate accountability until you push the evaluation to the ROI level. The monetary value was impressive, but the costs were very high. Second, because the program is not working at the ROI level doesn't mean that it is discontinued. In fact, it's rare that programs are discontinued because of a negative ROI. The program is adjusted to deliver the value that it should be delivering.

———————————— × ————————————

This chapter explores the costs of programs and the ROI calculation. Specific costs that should be captured are identified, along with economical ways in which they can be developed. One of the primary challenges addressed in this chapter is deciding which costs should be captured or estimated. For major programs, some costs are hidden and rarely counted. The conservative philosophy of the ROI is to account for all costs, direct and indirect. Several checklists and guidelines are included. The monetary values for the benefits of a program are combined with program cost data to calculate the return on investment. In this chapter we explain the various techniques, processes, and issues involved in calculating and interpreting the ROI.

The Importance of Costs and ROI

One of the main reasons for monitoring costs is to create budgets for programs. The initial costs of most programs are usually estimated during the proposal process and are often based on previous programs. A clear understanding of costs is necessary so that they can be used to determine the costs of future programs and future budgets. To make this task easier, it is helpful to track them using different categories, as explained later in this chapter. Developing accurate costs by category builds a database for understanding and predicting costs in the future.

Costs should be monitored in an ongoing effort to control expenditures and keep the program within budget. Monitoring costs not only reveals the status of expenditures but also gives visibility to expenditures and encourages the program team to spend wisely. And, of course, monitoring costs in an ongoing process is much easier, more accurate, and more efficient than trying to reconstruct events to capture costs retrospectively.

Monitoring program costs is an essential step in developing the ROI calculation because it represents the denominator in the ROI formula. As described in the first four chapters, ROI has become a critical measure demanded by many stakeholders, including clients and senior executives. It is the ultimate level of evaluation, showing the actual payoff of the program, expressed as a percentage and based on the same formula as the evaluation for other types of investments.

"Diligence is the mother of good luck." – Benjamin Franklin

Fundamental Cost Issues

The first step in monitoring costs is to define and address issues relating to cost control. Several rules apply to tabulating costs. Consistency and standardization are necessary. A few guidelines follow:

- Monitor all costs, even if they are not needed now.
- Costs must be realistic and reasonable.
- Some costs will not be precise; estimates are okay.
- Disclose all costs.

Other key issues are detailed later in this section.

Fully Loaded Costs

During the Obama administration, investigators recovered a record-breaking $4.1 billion in healthcare fraud during 2011, a reflection of the Obama administration's increased focus on fighting fraud. At the time, *USA Today* noted that the federal government collected $7.20 for every dollar spent on fighting fraud, according to the Department of Health and Human Services (HHS) inspector general [1]. This ratio translates to an ROI calculation of 620 percent, representing an impressive return on investment of expenditures in tackling healthcare fraud. The officials attributed this progress to nine enforcement action teams in cities such as Chicago and Miami. The government increased funding to Senior Medicare Patrol teams from $9 million in 2010 to $18 million in 2011 in the form of Administration on Aging grants in fraud-heavy states such as California and Michigan.

With this impressive ROI came much scrutiny. Some of the critics of this program asked for an account of the benefits to see whether conservative assumptions were made in the analysis. The critics also wanted to understand whether all of the costs of the effort to capture the fraud were included, including costs with justice systems' time and direct expenses. Sometimes these factors are underestimated or omitted in calculations. Finally, they wanted to know whether other factors outside of these patrol teams could have reduced the expenditures. At the last count, the Justice Department and HHS had not provided clear answers to these questions.

This story underscores the importance of having credible analysis when the program culminates with an actual ROI calculation. ROI data are likely to be scrutinized. ROI is the one measure that is often emotional; if the measure is too high it becomes unbelievable, if the measure is too low or negative, top executives and administrators want to place blame and use the information in a punitive way, rather than as a process improvement tool.

"All money is a matter of belief." – Adam Smith

Because a conservative approach is used to calculate the ROI, costs should be fully loaded, which is Guiding Principle 10 (see Chapter 4). With this approach, all costs (direct and indirect) that can be identified and linked to a particular program are included. The philosophy is simple: for the denominator, "when in doubt, put it in" (i.e., if there is any question as to whether a cost should be included, include it, even if the cost guidelines for the organization do not require it). When an ROI is calculated and reported to target audiences, the process should withstand even the closest scrutiny to ensure its credibility. The only way to meet this test is to include all costs. Of course, from a realistic viewpoint, if the controller or chief financial officer insists on not using certain costs, then leaving them out or reporting them in an alternative way is appropriate.

Case Study

The World Health Organization (WHO) estimates that about 284 million people are visually impaired, worldwide, with 90 percent of them living in developing countries. Eighty percent of all visual impairment is treatable or preventable. The goals of an initiative in sub-Saharan Africa have been to eliminate the main causes of avoidable blindness for 100 million people by the year 2020. This is a joint program between WHO and the International Agency for the Prevention of Blindness. This program is one of the initiatives working towards achieving this goal, facilitated under an international board.

The program is a partnership initiative that seeks to link specialist or medical institutions in the United Kingdom with a training hospital or institution in the developing country to help build capacity for eye care in that country. The program receives contributions to its funding from two international eye-care NGOs but has to raise the rest. Therefore, it is imperative that it can show the true costs for each link as well as the impact of these investments.

The team established a standardized way of collecting data across each link. They identified that the full costs of each link included both direct costs (such as costs of administration and management travel, accommodation, evaluation cost, etc.) and indirect costs (salary of participating teams such as specialists and trainees, use of hospital facilities for training for both parties, etc.) [2].

Costs Reported without Benefits

A top administrator in the Ministry of Innovation asked about the success of all the design thinking workshops that had been conducted in organizations in this Southeast Asian country. The program team responded with the number of workshops, number of participants, and the total costs of the program. The minister was disappointed and asked for the outcomes.

Costs are the input to the program, not outcomes. Because costs can easily be collected, they are presented to management in many ingenious ways, such as in terms of the total cost of the program, cost per day, and cost per participant. While these may be helpful for efficiency comparisons, presenting them without identifying the corresponding benefits may be problematic. When most executives review program costs, a logical question is raised: what benefit was received from the program? This is a typical management reaction, particularly when costs are perceived to be very high.

Unfortunately, many organizations have fallen into this trap. For example, in one organization, all the costs associated with a major transformation program were tabulated and reported to the senior management team. From an executive perspective, the total figure exceeded the perceived value of the program, and the executive group's immediate reaction was to request a summary of (monetary and nonmonetary) benefits derived from the overall transformation. The conclusion was that few, if any, economic benefits were achieved from the program. Consequently, budgets for this and similar programs were drastically reduced in the future. While this may be an extreme example, it shows the danger of presenting only half the equation. Because of this, some organizations have developed a policy of not communicating cost data unless the benefits can be captured and presented along with the costs, even if the benefits are subjective and intangible. This helps maintain a balance between the two components.

Princess Al Anood Foundation, the largest foundation in Saudi Arabia and one of the largest in the Middle East, expressed concern over this issue when it comes to the charities and nonprofits they support in that region. Some of the recipients of the funds from the foundation report those funds (which are input) as a measure of success. This is disappointing and, in an attempt to change this thinking, the foundation organized an ROI for nonprofits conference in that country in 2018.

Develop and Use Cost Guidelines

When multiple programs are being evaluated, it may be helpful to detail the philosophy and policy on costs in the form of guidelines for the evaluators or others who monitor and report costs. Cost guidelines detail specifically which cost categories are included with programs, and how the data are captured, analyzed, and reported. Standards, unit cost guiding principles, and generally accepted values are included in the guidelines. Cost guidelines can range from a one-page brief to a 100-page document in a large, complex organization. The simpler approach is better. When fully developed, cost guidelines should be reviewed and approved by the finance and accounting staff. The final document serves as the guiding force for collecting, monitoring, and reporting costs. When the ROI is calculated and reported, costs are included in summary or table form, and the cost guidelines are usually referenced in a footnote or attached as an appendix.

Sources of Costs

It is sometimes helpful to first consider the sources of program costs. Four major categories of sources are illustrated in Figure 13.2. The charges and expenses from the program team represent the major segment of costs, and are usually transferred directly to the client, donor,

Source of Costs	Cost Reporting Issues
Project team fees and expenses	• Costs are usually accurate • Variable expenses are usually underestimated
Vendor/suppliers fees and expenses	• Costs are usually accurate • Variable expenses are usually underestimated
Client expenses, direct and indirect	• Direct expenses are usually not fully loaded • Indirect expenses are rarely included in costs • Sometimes understated
Equipment, services, and other expenses	• May lack accountability

Figure 13.2 Sources of Innovation Project Costs.

or sponsor for payment. These are often placed in subcategories under fees and expenses. A second major cost category relates to the vendors or suppliers who assist with the program. A variety of expenses, such as consulting or advisory fees, may fall in this category. A third major cost category is those expenses borne by the client organization, both direct and indirect. In many programs, these costs are not identified but nevertheless are part of the costs of the program. The final cost category involves expenses not covered in the other three categories. These include payments for equipment and services needed for the program. Finance and accounting records should track and reflect the costs from these different sources, and the process presented in this chapter can also help track these costs.

Prorated versus Direct Costs

Usually all costs related to a program are captured and expensed to that program. However, some costs are prorated over a longer period. Equipment purchases, software development and acquisitions, and the construction of facilities are all significant costs with a useful life that may extend beyond the program. Consequently, a portion of these costs should be prorated to the evaluation of a particular group of participants in the program. Under a conservative approach, the expected life of the program is fixed or estimated. Some organizations will assume a period of one year of operation for a simple program. Others may consider three to five years as appropriate. If a question is raised about the specific time period to be used in this calculation, the finance and accounting staff should be consulted, or appropriate guidelines should be developed and followed.

For example, an automobile company built a wellness and fitness center for employees at one of its large production plants in Tennessee. The building that houses the center is a capital expenditure and should have a long life. Twenty years would be common. The life of the wellness and fitness center may not be that long, and a shorter period was needed in an ROI study on the center. This study, involving 200 participants, tracked the impact of the center on healthcare costs, absenteeism, safety, productivity, and attraction and retention of employees. The cost of the building was included in the cost of the wellness and fitness program, but not all the costs. A ten-year life was used, which was approved by all stakeholders. This was considered very conservative because most buildings are usually depreciated for a 20-year period. The cost of the building was divided by the total anticipated number of employees served in a 10-year period. This was an estimate based on current operation. This yielded a facility cost per participant. To prorate this to the study, this number is multiplied by 200 and becomes a line item in the cost of the program.

Employee Benefits Factor

Employee time is valuable, and when time is required for a program, the costs for that time must be fully loaded, representing total compensation including employee benefits. This means that the employee benefits factor should be included. This number is usually well known in the organization and is used in other costing formulas. It represents the cost of all employee benefits expressed as a percentage of payroll. In some organizations, this value is as high as 50–60 percent. In others, it may be as low as 25–30 percent. The average in the United States is 32 percent [3].

Specific Costs to Include

Figure 13.3 shows the recommended cost categories for a fully loaded, conservative approach to estimating program costs. Consistency in capturing all these costs is essential, and standardization adds credibility. Each category is described in this section.

Cost Item	Prorated	Expensed
Initial analysis and assessment	✓	
Development of solutions	✓	
Acquisition of solutions	✓	
Implementation and application		
Salaries/benefits for program team time		✓
Salaries/benefits for coordination time		✓
Salaries/benefits for participant time (if appropriate)		✓
Program materials		✓
Hardware/software	✓	
Travel/lodging/meals		✓
Use of facilities		✓
Capital expenditures	✓	
Maintenance and monitoring		✓
Administrative support and overhead	✓	
Evaluation and reporting		✓

Figure 13.3 Project Cost Categories.

Initial Analysis and Assessment

One of the most underestimated items is the cost of conducting the initial analysis and assessment that leads to the need for the program. In a comprehensive program, this involves data collection, problem solving, assessment, and analysis. In some programs, this cost is near zero because the program is implemented without an initial assessment of need. However, as more program sponsors place attention on needs assessment and analysis in the future, this item will become a significant cost.

Development of Program Solutions

Also significant are the costs of designing and developing the program. These costs include time spent in both the design and development, and the purchase of supplies, technology, and other materials directly related to the solution. As with needs assessment costs, design and development costs are usually charged to the program. However, if the solution can be used in other programs, the major expenditures can be prorated.

Acquisition Costs

In lieu of development costs, some program leaders use acquisition costs connected to the purchasing of solutions from other sources, to use directly or in a modified format. The costs for these solutions include the purchase price, support materials, and licensing agreements. Some programs have both acquisition costs and solution development costs. Acquisition costs can be prorated if the acquired solutions can be used in other programs.

Implementation Costs

The largest cost segment in a program is associated with implementation and delivery. The time (salaries and benefits), travel, and other expenses of those involved in the program in any way should be included. These costs can be estimated using average or midpoint salary values for specific job groups. When a program is targeted for an ROI calculation, participants can provide their salaries directly in a confidential manner. This cost becomes an issue when employees in an organization are involved. For nonprofit programs, employees may not be involved because participants may not be "employees." Sometimes volunteers are involved, as highlighted in this case study.

Program materials, such as field journals, instructions, reference guides, case studies, surveys, and participant workbooks, should be included in the implementation costs, along with license fees, user fees, and royalty payments. Supporting hardware, software, and videos should also be included.

The cost for the use of facilities needed for the program should be included. For external meetings, this is the direct charge for the conference center, hotel, or motel. If the meetings are conducted internally, the conference room represents a cost for the organization, and the cost should be estimated and incorporated, even if it is uncommon to include facilities costs in other cost reporting. If a facility or building is constructed or purchased for the program, it is included as a capital expenditure, but is prorated. The same is true for the purchase of major hardware and software when they are considered capital expenditures.

Case Study

JobsNow! is a program designed to assist inner-city youth find a suitable job using volunteer mentors. The program is tackling the high unemployment rate for the under-25 age group, which hovers in the 20 to 30 percent range in major cities. Volunteers are recruited and screened as mentors and matched to one or more job seekers.

The impact measures for success are jobs secured and crime prevented (unemployed youth have high crime rates). Both measures are easily converted to money. The costs for the program include all direct and indirect categories. Because the mentors are volunteers, there is no direct costs apart from administrative expenses of recruiting, selection, and coordination.

To properly account for the value of mentors, the evaluation team used no salary for the mentors in the first ROI calculation. This is the actual ROI under the current system. Another ROI calculation is presented using an average salary for the mentors. A comparison of the two ROIs shows the value of volunteer effort. If the second ROI calculation is positive, the evaluation reveals that the program is successful from an economic perspective, even if mentors are paid for their services.

Maintenance and Monitoring

Maintenance and monitoring involve routine expenses necessary to maintain and operate the program. These are ongoing expenses that allow the new programs solution to continue. They may involve staff members and additional expenses, and they may be significant for some programs.

Support and Overhead

The cost of support and overhead includes the additional costs not directly charged to the program—any program cost not considered in the above calculations. Typical items are the cost of administrative and clerical support, telecommunication expenses, office expenses, salaries of client managers, and other fixed costs. Usually, this is provided in the form of an estimate allocated in some convenient way.

Evaluation and Reporting

The total evaluation cost completes the fully loaded costs. Activities under evaluation costs include developing the evaluation strategy, designing instruments, collecting data, analyzing data, preparing a report, and communicating the results. Cost categories include time, materials, purchased instruments, surveys, and any consulting fees.

Cost Tabulation in Action

It may be helpful to review an actual case study from the government sector. This agency offered a master's degree in information science to high potential employees from a prestigious university, all on agency time. The costs are varied and significant.

Problem and Solution

The Federal Information Agency provides various types of information to other government agencies and businesses as well as state and local organizations, agencies, and interested groups. Operating through a network across the globe, the work is performed by several hundred communication specialists with backgrounds in systems, computer science, electrical engineering, and information science. Almost all of the specialists have bachelor's degrees in one of these fields. The headquarters and operation center are in the Washington, D.C., area, where 1,500 of these specialists are employed [4].

FIA has recently experienced two problems that have senior agency officials concerned. The first problem is an unacceptable rate of employee turnover for this group of specialists—averaging 38 percent in the past year alone. This has placed a strain on the agency to recruit and train replacements. An analysis of exit interviews indicated that employees leave primarily for higher salaries. As a federal government agency, FIA is somewhat constrained in providing competitive salaries. It has become extremely difficult to compete with private sector for salaries and benefits. Although salary increases and adjustments in pay levels will be necessary to lower turnover, FIA is exploring other options in the interim.

The second problem concerns the need to continuously update the technical skills of the staff. While the vast majority of the 1,500 specialists have bachelor's degrees in various fields, only a few have master's degrees in their specialty. In this field, formal education is quickly outdated. The annual feedback survey with employees reflected a strong interest in an internal master's degree program in information science. Consequently, FIA explored the implementation of an in-house master's degree in information science conducted by the School of Engineering and Science at Regional State University (RSU). The master's degree program would be implemented at no cost to the participating employee and conducted on the agency's time during routine work hours. Designed to address both employee turnover and skill updates, the program would normally take three years for participants to complete.

Program Description

RSU was selected for the master's program because of its reputation and the match of its curriculum to FIA needs. The program allows participants to take one or two courses per semester. A two-course per semester schedule would take three years to complete. Both morning and afternoon classes were available, each representing three hours per week of class time. Participants were discouraged from taking more than two courses per term. Although a thesis option was normally available, FIA requested a graduate project be required for six hours of credit as a substitute for the thesis. A professor would supervise the project. Designed to add value, the project would be applied in the agency and would not be as rigorous as the thesis.

Classes were usually offered live with professors visiting the agency's center. Participants were asked to prepare for classroom activities on their own time but were allowed to attend classes on the agency's time. A typical three-year schedule is shown in Figure 13.4.

Senior management approved the M.S. curriculum, which represented a mix of courses normally offered in the program and others specially

	Year 1	Year 2	Year 3
Fall	2 Courses – 6 hours	2 Courses – 6 hours	2 Courses – 6 hours
Spring	2 Courses – 6 hours	2 Courses – 6 hours	2 Courses – 6 hours
Summer	1 Course – 3 hours	1 Course – 3 hours	

Graduate Project – 6 Hours

Total Semester Hours - 48

Figure 13.4 Typical 3-Year Schedule.

selected for FIA staff. Two new courses were designed by university faculty to be included in the curriculum. These two represented a slight modification of existing courses and were tailored to the communication requirements of the agency. Elective courses were not allowed for two reasons. First, it would complicate the offering to a certain extent, requiring additional courses, facilities, and professors—essentially adding cost to the program. Second, FIA wanted a prescribed, customized curriculum that would add value to the agency while still meeting the requirements of the university.

Selection Criteria

An important issue involved the selection of employees to attend the program. Most employees who voluntarily left the agency resigned within the first four years and were often considered to have high potential. With this in mind, the following criteria were established for identifying and selecting the employees to enroll in the program.

1. A candidate should have at least one year of service prior to beginning classes.
2. A candidate must meet the normal requirements to be accepted into the graduate school at the university.
3. A candidate must be willing to sign a commitment to stay with the agency for two years beyond program completion.
4. A candidate's immediate manager must nominate the employee for consideration.
5. A candidate must be considered "high potential" as rated by the immediate manager.

The management team was provided initial information on the program, kept informed of its development and progress prior to actual launch, and briefed as the program was described and selection criteria was finalized.

It was emphasized that the selection should be based on objective criteria, following the guidelines offered. At the same time, managers were asked to provide feedback as to the level of interest and specific issues surrounding the nomination of candidates.

A limit of 100 participants entering the program each year was established. This limit was based on two key issues:

1. The capability of the university in terms of staffing for the program—RSU could not effectively teach over 100 participants each semester.
2. This was an experiment that, if successful, could be modified or enhanced in the future.

Program Administration

Because of the magnitude of the anticipated enrollment, FIA appointed a full-time program administrator who was responsible for organizing and coordinating the program. The duties included registration of the participants, all correspondence and communication with the university and participants, facilities and logistics (including materials and books), and resolving problems as they occur. FIA absorbed the total cost of the coordinator. The university assigned an individual to serve as liaison with the agency. This individual was not additional staff; the university absorbed the cost as part of the tuition.

The Drivers of Evaluation

This program was selected for a comprehensive evaluation to show its impact on the agency using a four-year timeframe. Several influences created the need for this detailed accountability:

1. Senior administrators have requested detailed evaluations for certain programs considered to be strategic, highly visible, and designed to add value to the agency.
2. This program was perceived to be very expensive, demanding a higher level of accountability, including return on investment.
3. Because retention is such a critical issue for this agency, it was important to determine if this solution was the appropriate one. A detailed measurement and evaluation should reflect the success of the program.

The passage of federal legislation and other initiatives in the USA, aimed at bringing more accountability for taxpayers' funds, has created a shift in public sector accountability.

Consequently, the implementation team planned a detailed evaluation of this program beyond the traditional program evaluation processes. Along with tracking costs, the monetary payoff would be developed, including the ROI. Because this is a very complex and comprehensive solution, other important measures would be tracked to present an overall, balanced approach to the measurement.

Program Costs

The cost of the program was tabulated and monitored and reflected a fully loaded cost profile, which included all direct and indirect costs. One of the major costs was the tuition for the participants. The university charged the customary tuition, plus $100 per semester course per participant to offset the additional travel and faculty expense of conducting and coordinating the program. The tuition per semester hour was $200 ($600 per three-hour course).

The full-time administrator was an FIA employee, receiving an annual base salary of $37,000, with a 45 percent employee benefits upload factor. The administrator had expenses of approximately $15,000 per year. Salaries for the participants represented another significant cost category. The average salary of the job categories of the employees involved in the program was $47,800, with a 45 percent employee benefits factor. Salaries usually increase approximately 4 percent per year. Participants attended class a total of 18 hours for each semester hour of credit. Thus, a three-hour course represented 54 hours of off-the-job time in the classroom. The total hours needed for one participant to complete the program was 756 hours (14 × 54).

Another significant cost category was classroom facilities. For the 100 participants, four different courses were offered each semester and each course was repeated at a different time slot. With a class size of 25, eight separate semester courses were presented. Although the classrooms used for this program were those normally used for other training and education programs offered at the agency, the cost for providing the facilities was included. (Because of the unusual demand, an additional conference room was built to provide ample meeting space.) The estimate for the average cost of all meeting rooms was $40 per hour of use.

The cost for the initial assessment was also included in the cost profile. This charge, estimated to be approximately $5,000, included the turnover analysis and was prorated for the first three years. FIA's development costs for the program were estimated to be approximately $10,000 and were prorated for three years. Management time involved in the program was minimal but estimated to be approximately $9,000 over the three-year period. This consisted primarily of meetings and memos regarding the program. Finally, the evaluation costs, representing the cost to actually track the success of the program and report the results to management, were estimated to be $10,000. A summary of the costs is reported in Figure 13.5.

The ROI Calculation

The term return on investment is the ultimate accountability for a program and is desired by some sponsors and donors. Its use is growing, particularly for expensive, important, and high-profile programs, such as the previous example. Sometimes, we find a very broad definition for ROI that includes any benefit from the program. In this situation, ROI becomes a vague concept in which even subjective data linked to a program are included. In this book, the return on investment is defined more precisely and represents an actual value determined by comparing program costs to benefits. The

	Year 1	Year 2	Year 3	Total
Initial Analysis (Prorated)	$ 1,667	$ 1,667	$ 1,666	$ 5,000
Development (Prorated)	3,333	3,333	3,334	10,000
Tuition – Regular	300,000	342,000	273,000	915,000
Tuition – Premium	50,000	57,000	45,500	152,500
Salaries/Benefits (Participants)	899,697	888,900	708,426	2,497,023
Salaries/Benefits (Program Administrator)	53,650	55,796	58,028	167,474
Program Coordination	15,000	15,000	15,000	45,000
Facilities	43,200	43,200	34,560	120,960
Management Time	3,000	3,000	3,000	9,000
Evaluation	3,333	3,333	3,334	10,000
Total	$1,372,880	$1,413,229	$1,145,848	$3,931,957

Figure 13.5 Cost Summary.

two most common measures are the benefit/cost ratio (BCR) and the ROI formula. Both are presented along with other approaches to calculate the return or payback.

The formulas presented in this chapter use annualized values and the first-year impact is used for short-term programs. Using annualized values is an accepted practice for developing the ROI in organizations. This approach is a conservative way to develop the ROI since many short-term programs have added value in the second or third year. For long-term programs, longer timeframes should be used. For example, in an ROI analysis of a major software purchase at SAP, the world's largest business software vendors, a five-year timeframe was used. However, for short-term programs that take only a few weeks to implement (such as a stress reduction program for new parents or a family financial planning program), first-year values are appropriate.

When selecting the approach to measure ROI, the formula used, and the assumptions made in arriving at the decision to use this formula, should be communicated to the target audience. This helps prevent misunderstandings and confusion surrounding how the ROI value was developed. Although several approaches are described in this chapter, two stand out as preferred methods: the benefits/costs ratio and the basic ROI formula. These two approaches are described next.

Benefit/Cost Ratio

One of the original methods for evaluating programs is the benefits/costs ratio. Benefit cost analysis was developed by governments, and its history dates back several centuries. Benefit cost analysis allowed governments to make decisions about building roads, bridges, and canals. This method compares the benefits of the project with the costs, using a simple ratio. In formula form:

$$BCR = \frac{\text{Program Benefits}}{\text{Program Costs}}$$

In simple terms, the BCR compares the annual economic benefits of the program with the costs of the program. A BCR of 1 means that the benefits equal the costs. A BCR of 2, usually written as 2:1, indicates that for each dollar spent on the program, two dollars were returned in benefits. The following example illustrates the use of the BCR. A program on conflict resolution was implemented at an electric and gas utility. In a follow-up evaluation, action planning and business performance monitoring were used to capture the benefits. The first-year payoff for the program was $1,077,750. The total, fully loaded implementation costs were $215,500. Thus, the ratio was:

$$BCR = \frac{\$1,077,750}{\$215,500} = 5:1$$

For every dollar invested in the program, five dollars in benefits were realized.

ROI Formula

Perhaps the most appropriate formula for evaluating program investments is net program benefits divided by costs. This is the traditional financial ROI and is directly related to the BCR. The ROI ratio is usually expressed as a percentage where the fractional values are multiplied by 100. In formula form:

$$ROI = \frac{\text{Net Program Benefits}}{\text{Program Costs}} \times 100$$

Net program benefits are program monetary benefits minus costs. A shortcut to calculate ROI is to subtract 1 from the BCR and multiply by 100 to get to the ROI percentage. For example, a BCR of 2.45 is the same as an ROI value of 145 percent (1.45 × 100%). This formula is essentially the same as the ROI for capital investments. For example, when a firm builds a new plant, the ROI is developed by dividing annual earnings by the investment. The annual earnings are comparable to net benefits (annual benefits minus the cost). The investment is comparable to the fully loaded program costs.

An ROI of 50 percent means that the costs were recovered, and an additional 50 percent of the costs were returned. A program ROI of 150 percent indicates that the costs have been recovered, and an additional 1.5 times the costs are returned.

An example illustrates the ROI calculation. Public and private sector groups concerned about literacy have developed a variety of programs to address the issue. Magnavox Electronics Systems Company was involved in one unique literacy program that focused on language and math skills for entry-level electrical and mechanical assemblers. The results of the program were impressive. Productivity and quality alone yielded an annual value of $321,600.

The total, fully loaded costs for the program were just \$38,233. Thus, the return on investment was:

$$ROI = \frac{(\$321,600 - \$38,233)}{\$38,233} \times 100 = 741\%$$

For each dollar invested, Magnavox received \$7.41 in return after the costs of the program were recovered.

Investments in plants, equipment, subsidiaries, or other major items and capital expenditures are not usually evaluated using the ROI calculation. Using the ROI formula to calculate the return on noncapital investments, described in this book, essentially places these investments on a level playing field with capital investments whose valuation uses the same formula and similar concepts. The ROI calculation is easily understood by key management and financial executives who regularly work with investments and ROI.

Case Study

When SCL Health was made aware of four focus areas that offered opportunities to improve performance in Clinical Documentation Integrity (CDI), they jumped at the chance. These areas were people, process, tools and technology, and physician engagement, and together they represented a performance gap in CDI which, if closed, would be worth well over \$16 million annually. A program titled *Cracking the Code for Clinical Documentation Excellence* was developed to improve performance in these four areas. The purpose of this extensive program is to comprehensively train qualified acute clinical nurses on the processes and procedures of CDI within a timespan of 12 weeks.

Bette Kidane, director of Enterprise Learning and Personal Development at SCL Health, knew from the start how important it is to evaluate training. She knew that the ROI Methodology was the best way to credibly and accurately evaluate this new training program and its impact on the performance of the CDI department. Bette calculated the BCR and ROI of the program:

$$BCR = \frac{\$75,575}{\$182,097} = .42$$

$$ROI = \frac{\$75,575 - \$182,097}{\$182,097} \times 100 = -58\%$$

While the ROI was negative, Bette, her team, and CDI leadership stakeholders now have a better understanding of the causes of the negative ROI and what can be done to make it positive, as well as how long it will take for the program benefits to break even with the program costs. Because both tangible and intangible benefits were reported in the study, the CDI leadership stakeholders were able to validate that the training program was worth the significant investment, in spite of the negative ROI. Examining all of the benefits was helpful for this program because it provided a complete picture of the value CDI received in exchange for the funds spent on direct and indirect costs.

"What this study has taught me is that being able to show the value of the training helps people make the right decisions. Now I can say, do you understand the total cost of a program?" Bette said. "Moreover, evaluating the training, individual job performance and ROI data enabled us to identify consistent, high performers on the CDI team. Using this information, we can now define talent profiles based on the competencies and qualifications of those individuals. The talent profiles can be used going forward to identify successful individuals to hire into our CDI team. That individual performance data would not have been so easy to identify if we had not completed the ROI study."

Monetary Benefits

It is helpful to review the monetary benefits part of the equation. The monetary benefits are captured when the impact data are converted to monetary data, as explained in Chapter 11. The benefits are either cost savings (cost avoidance) or profits.

Profits can be generated through increased revenue from sales, memberships, tuition, or license fees. In practice, there are more opportunities for cost savings than for profits. Cost savings can be realized when accidents are prevented, convicted felons don't return to prison, time to graduate is reduced, or disease is prevented. In a review of almost 500 studies, the vast majority of them were based on cost savings.

Approximately 85 percent of the studies used benefits based on cost savings, cost reduction, or cost avoidance. The others used benefits based on sales increases, where the earnings were derived from the profit margin.

Nonprofits can have revenues and the concept of "profit" can apply. For example, a recruiting program for a university generates new students who pay tuition. The additional cost of one student is less than the tuition. The difference in a "marginal amount or reserve." This is similar to the profit. Cost savings are important for nonprofits and public-sector organizations, where opportunities for profit are often unavailable.

Misuse of ROI

The formula provided above should be used consistently throughout an organization. Deviations from or misuse of the formula can create confusion, not only among users but also among finance and accounting teams. The chief financial officer (CFO) and the finance and accounting staff should become partners in the implementation of the ROI Methodology. The program team must use the same financial terms as those used and expected by the CFO. Without the support, involvement, and commitment of these individuals, the wide-scale use of ROI will be unlikely.

Figure 13.6 shows some financial terms that are misused in literature. In the innovation field, terms such as return on ideas (or innovation),

Term	Misuse	CFO Definition
ROI	Return on ideas	Return on investment
	Return of impact	
	Return of information	
	Return on innovation	
	Return on inspiration	
	Return of intelligence	
ROE	Return on expectation	Return on equity
	Return on events	
	Return on exhibit	
	Return on engagement	
ROA	Return on anticipation	Return on assets
ROCE	Return on client expectation	Return on capital employed
ROP	Return on people	?
ROR	Return on resources	?
ROT	Return on technology	?
ROW	Return on web	?
ROM	Return on marketing	?
ROO	Return on objectives	?
ROQ	Return on quality	?
ROC	Return on character	?

Figure 13.6 Misused Financial Terms.

abbreviated as ROI, are used to describe the benefits of innovation without the financial calculation. This will confuse the CFO, who assumes that ROI refers to the return on investment described above. For meetings, the return on involvement (ROI) is used. NASA uses a term, return on inspiration (ROI) for students who are exposed to space and technology. Technology groups use return on information (ROI) or return on intelligence (ROI). These terms create confusion with executives. Sometimes return on expectations (ROE), return on anticipation (ROA), and return on client expectations (ROCE) are used, also confusing the CFO, who assumes the abbreviations refer to return on equity, return on assets, and return on capital employed, respectively. The events field uses return on event (ROE), return on exhibit (ROE), or return on engagement (ROE).

The use of these non-CFO-friendly terms for the benefits of a program will also confuse and perhaps lose the support of the finance and accounting staff. Other terms such as return on people, return on resources, return on technology, return on web, and return on marketing are used with almost no consistency in terms of financial calculations if they are provided at all. The bottom line: don't confuse the CFO. Consider this person an ally, and use the same terminology, processes, and concepts when applying financial returns for programs.

Social Return on Investment

SROI is the acronym for Social Return on Investment, a relatively new term for communicating the value of a nonprofit's impact on the community. The most credible calculation comes from the New Economics Foundation, which suggests that SROI "captures social value by translating outcomes into financial values [5]." SROI uses the general formula:

$$SROI = \frac{\text{Tangible+ Intangible Value to the Community}}{\text{Total Resource Investment}}$$

If all the tangible and intangible value is all the outcome data, then this represents the total benefits, based on cost avoidance. If the total resource investment is all the cost of the program, then this is the cost of the program. Therefore, this is actually the benefit cost ratio, which has been used by governments for centuries.

There are other variations of this concept. It has the advantage of being more "acceptable" to those individuals who are uncomfortable with the standard ROI calculation. The disadvantage is that the funders and executives may think that this concept and subsequent calculation is not credible.

ROI Objectives

Specific expectations for ROI should be developed before an evaluation study is undertaken. Although no generally accepted standards exist, four strategies have been used to establish a minimum expected ROI for the program.

The first approach is to set the ROI using the same values for investing in capital expenditures, such as equipment, facilities, and new companies. For North America, Western Europe, and most of the Asia-Pacific area, including Australia and New Zealand, the cost of capital is quite low, and the internal target for ROI is usually in the 13–18 percent range. Thus, using this strategy, organizations would set the minimum expected ROI for a project at the same value expected from other investments.

A second strategy is to use an ROI minimum target value that is above the percentage expected for other types of investments. The rationale behind this strategy is that the ROI process for programs in this noncapital area is still relatively new and often involves subjective input, including estimations. Because of this, a higher standard is suggested.

A third strategy is to set the ROI value at a breakeven point. A 0 percent ROI represents breakeven; this is equivalent to a BCR of 1. This approach is used when the goal is to recapture the cost of the program only. This is the ROI objective for many public-sector organizations, where much of the value and benefits from the program come through the intangible measures, which are not converted to monetary values. Thus, an organization will use a breakeven point for the ROI based on the reasoning that it is not attempting to make a profit from a particular program.

A fourth and often used strategy is to let the client or program sponsor set the minimum acceptable ROI value. In this scenario, the individual who initiates, approves, sponsors, funds, or supports the program establishes the acceptable ROI. Almost every program has a major sponsor, and that person may be willing to specify an acceptable value. This links the expectations for financial return directly to the expectations of the sponsor.

Whose ROI?

In some situations, it is helpful to understand the ROI from different perspectives. Because there are different stakeholders, the ROI calculation may be needed from the view of each stakeholder. To do this, the costs of each perspective is compared to the monetary benefits from each perspective.

Neighborhood Insurance has conducted an annual agents conference for many years. The conference requires about three days off the job and is not mandatory, but agents are encouraged to participate. Each agent is provided a marketing budget, out of which the conference travel expenses are taken. Otherwise, agents can use the money on other marketing activities. The conference focuses on new products, changes in current products, and new sales strategies and tools. It is considered by executives at least to be a valuable event. The senior executives have been concerned that 40 percent of agents do not attend. Apparently, these agents do not see enough value in the conference to spend the marketing money to attend—they think their ROI will be negative. The CEO asked the meeting and events staff to explore two issues:

1. Is this the proper solution to drive the business? If so, what is the ROI in this conference?
2. How can ROI results be used to drive attendance in the future?

The director of meetings and events, working with the analytics team, saw this issue as an opportunity to confirm the appropriateness of the solution. Through a series of meetings and actions, she revisited the reasons for the conference in an attempt to align this solution to the business and develop clear objectives for business measures. The review involved meetings with key executives and managers who are involved in and supported the conference. The review allowed the team to reflect on the business purpose of the conference, clarifying the specific actions needed by the agents and adjusting the conference learning agenda.

As part of this review, she developed specific objectives for reaction, learning, application, and impact levels. These objectives, approved by the executives, provided focus and direction to designers, developers, speakers, facilitators, agents, and sponsors. The result of the review was a revised version of the conference that properly aligns it with business measures.

To clearly understand the value of this conference, the ROI calculation is needed from two perspectives: the company's ROI and the agent's ROI. The company invests in the cost of developing and presenting the conference and must have enough monetary benefits to cover the cost of the conference, to have positive ROI. The agents must have enough commissions (from increased sales) to cover their costs of travel and their time away from the office to have a positive ROI.

Executives were convinced that the revised conference will drive the value needed from both perspectives. If it does drive the value anticipated, the results of the new solution (revised conference) will be used to convince the agents who are not attending that they should be there in the future because of their positive ROI. The good news is that the conference did just that [6].

Other ROI Measures

In addition to the traditional ROI formula, several other measures are occasionally used under the general heading of return on investment. These measures are designed primarily for evaluating other financial measures but sometimes work their way into program evaluations.

Payback Period (Breakeven Analysis)

The payback period is commonly used for evaluating capital expenditures. With this approach, the annual cash proceeds (savings) produced by an investment are compared against the original cash outlay for the investment to determine the multiple of cash proceeds that is equal to the original investment. Measurement is usually in terms of years and months. For example, if the cost savings generated from a program are constant each year, the payback period is determined by dividing the original cash investment (including development costs, expenses, etc.) by the expected or actual annual savings. The net savings are found by subtracting the program expenses.

To illustrate this calculation, assume that the initial cost of a program is $100,000, and the program has a three-year useful life. Annual net savings from the program are expected to be $40,000. Thus, the payback period is:

$$Payback\ period = \frac{Total\ investments}{Annual\ savings}$$

$$= \frac{\$100,000}{\$40,000} = 2.5\,years$$

In this case, the program will "pay back" the original investment in 2.5 years. The payback period method is simple to use but has the limitation of ignoring the time value of money.

Discounted Cash Flow

Discounted cash flow is a method of evaluating investment opportunities in which certain values are assigned to the timing of the proceeds from the investment. The assumption behind this approach is that a dollar earned today is more valuable than a dollar earned a year from now, based on the accrued interest possible from investing the dollar.

There are several ways of using the discounted cash flow concept to evaluate a program investment. The most common approach uses the net present value of an investment. The savings each year are compared with the outflow of cash required by the investment. The expected annual savings are discounted based on a selected interest rate, and the outflow of cash is discounted by the same interest rate. If the present value of the savings exceeds the present value of the outlays, after the two have been discounted by the common interest rate, the investment is usually considered acceptable by management. The discounted cash flow method has the advantage of ranking investments, but it requires calculations that can become difficult. Also, for the most part, it is subjective.

Internal Rate of Return

The internal rate of return (IRR) method determines the interest rate necessary to make the present value of the cash flow equal zero. This represents the maximum rate of interest that could be paid if all program funds were borrowed, and the organization was required to break even on the program. The IRR considers the time value of money and is unaffected by the scale of the program. It can be used to rank alternatives, and to accept or reject decisions when a minimum rate of return is specified. A major weakness of the IRR method is that it assumes all returns are reinvested at the same internal rate of return. This can make an investment alternative with a high rate of return look even better than it really is and make a program with a low rate of return look even worse. In practice, the IRR is rarely used to evaluate program investments.

Final Thoughts

ROI, the fifth and final outcome evaluation level, compares program costs with program monetary benefits. Costs are important and should be fully loaded in the ROI calculation using direct and indirect costs. From a practical standpoint, some costs may be optional, and depend on the organization's guidelines and philosophy. However, because of the scrutiny ROI calculations typically receive, all costs should be included, even if this goes beyond the requirements of the organization's policy. After the benefits are collected and converted to monetary values and the program costs are tabulated, the ROI calculation itself is easy. Plugging the values into the appropriate formula is the final step. Two basic approaches for calculating return were presented: the ROI formula and the benefit/cost ratio in this chapter. Each has its advantages and disadvantages. We also briefly discussed alternatives to the standard ROI determination.

Now that we have fully detailed the process, our next chapter details how to report the results, telling a compelling story.

14

Tell the Story: Communicate Results to Key Stakeholders

Joan Kravitz was a little nervous as she faced the top executive audience. She had been there a couple of times for other briefings, but never with this particular issue. As she scanned the room, she saw the senior executives who were interested in her briefing, and, more importantly, in the success of the Executive Leadership Program. She was confident that she knew the material and had a clear agenda. She had practiced this briefing with her own team, who gave her very candid feedback.

Joan's program was an ROI study on the company's executive leadership development program conducted by a very prestigious business school. It was very expensive and had been conducted for leaders in the company for five years. Although the program was supported by executives, pushing it to record levels of funding, the top executives offered an interesting challenge and request. They wanted to see the impact that this program was having on the organization, and, if possible, the financial ROI. Fortunately, Joan received this request in enough time to implement changes into the program to keep it focused on results and have the participants committed to showing the value of their individual and team programs. She had some very intriguing data. Yes, there were some bumps along the way, but there was still a good story to tell, and she was very proud of it.

As Joan scanned the audience, she knew the perspectives of the different audience members. The CEO was not there, but all the other senior team members were present. She was disappointed, because the CEO was the champion of this program, but an urgent schedule change prohibited him from being there. She would have a private session with him to cover the agenda. The CFO seemed to support the program, but he was really concerned about budgets, costs, and the value of every program, including this one. The operations executive VP saw the program as helpful but was still concerned about business value. The VP of design and engineering did not support the program and rarely nominated participants for it. The VP of marketing was a solid supporter of the program. The friendliest face in the group was the executive VP of HR, who was a very strong supporter of this program and actively involved in various parts of it. The remaining members of the group were largely neutral about the program.

Joan knew that there were two major issues that she had to address. Not only must she show the results and secure approval for any changes in the program, but she must show them the methodology she was using. Yes, they all thought they knew ROI, but not the way she was presenting it. Although this particular process used the same formula that the CFO would use for a capital investment, it was the way in which the data were collected that made it so interesting and credible. Conservative processes were used, which should agree with this group, but she had to explain it to them quickly, in a mere 30 minutes. She also had a little fear that, if they really liked this process, they might want to see this type of analysis for all programs. So, she also had to show them that this process should be used very selectively. All these things were racing through her mind as she opened the presentation.

The Presentation

"Good morning, colleagues," Joan began, "Thank you for coming and giving up your precious time to see the value of a program that you have supported for several years. We all know the Advanced Leadership Program, which has enjoyed a five-year history with this company, with over 200 individuals participating. We have some results to show you from the group that participated last year. While these results are very intriguing and impressive, they do point to some important changes we need to make, and I want to secure your approval for these changes."

Joan began to relax and get comfortable with her presentation, and she saw an engaged audience. There were no grumpy expressions or frowns at that point.

Joan quickly described the program and revealed the methods that were being used to show the value.

"Our method of choice to evaluate this program is the ROI Methodology, adopted by 5,000 organizations. It is the most-used evaluation system in the world, and it is ideal for measuring this type of program, because it captures reaction to the program, learning about the program content, application of the content, business impact, ROI, and intangibles.

"It operates with a system of logical processes that you see in front of you. It uses some very conservative standards that I know you will find to be most credible and convincing. Here are two standards as applied to this study. First, all the cost of the program was used in the calculation, including the executive's time away from work. Second, for individual programs, we claimed only one year of monetary value on the benefit side. We all know that if an executive changes behavior and implements changes for the team, there will be multiple years of benefits. For the team programs that are being implemented throughout the organization, a three-year payoff was used, which is very conservative. These timeframes were endorsed by finance and accounting. These two standards, which are number nine and 10 on the list in front of you, are only two of the 12 standards we followed in conducting this study."

Joan noticed quickly that the executives began to glance at the standards while trying to pay attention to her at the same time. This was what she wanted. She captured their interest with those two assumptions, and they began to look at some of the others. She felt she could only allocate about two minutes for this issue, because she had much more to present.

Reaction and Learning

"As I present the results, please feel free to ask questions at any time. We will keep this very interactive, and I promise you, we will keep it within 30 minutes. The first two levels of results, reaction and learning, are presented first. While these may not be of much interest to you, we know that the program could go astray if the participants don't see value in it. Also, if they didn't really learn anything about themselves, their team, or their own competencies, then there won't be any subsequent actions, behavior change, and impact. Fortunately, we have very positive reaction and learning results."

Joan took two minutes for coverage on Level 1 (reaction) and Level 2 (learning), and she quickly moved on to Level 3 (application).

Application

"Application describes the extent to which these executives are changing the way they work, changing their behavior from a leadership perspective. I'm sure that you are more interested in this." Joan spent three minutes describing the table with the application data. "At this point, it is appropriate to examine the barriers and enablers, the important issues that inhibit or enhance application. Here are the barriers for these executives to use this program. As you can see, they are not very strong, but it is good to know what they are. If this program had significant barriers, we would want to work on them quickly."

By then, Joan had taken a total of 10 minutes. Now she knew that the rest of the time would be focused on impact and ROI. Up to that point, there had been no questions, much to Joan's surprise. She thought that this group would always be engaged, but she knew the next section would get them involved.

Business Impact

"In terms of business impact, we examined three sets of data," Joan explained. "The first was individual programs that the participants took on, centered on an important business measure in their particular business unit. Using action plans, they made improvements with these measures. Your report will have a copy of the action plan and sample copies of completed ones. This chart shows a sampling of individual programs, highlighting the specific measures selected and the amount of money the improvements represent, as participants actually converted the improvements to money. These improvements, which were monitored six months after their action plans were initiated, were impressive. The chart also shows the basis for this conversion, and it addresses another important issue, isolating the effects of this program." This was where Joan began to have some anxieties, because she was concerned about the executives' reaction to this issue.

"As you know, when any improvement is made, there are multiple factors that can drive it. These executives selected measures that are often influenced by various factors, and sometimes we implement programs aimed at those improvements. So, we must sort out the impact of this program from other influences. Our best method for accomplishing this is an experimental versus control group arrangement, where one group of executives is involved in this program, and another is not. As you can imagine, this won't work here, because they all have different measures from different business units. And there are some other analytical techniques that, unfortunately, also won't work. So, we have to rely on the executives to provide this information. But the good news is that they are very credible. These are the individuals who have achieved the results, and we don't think there is any reason why they would attribute more results to this program than some other influence.

"This information was collected in a very nonthreatening, unbiased way, by having them list the other factors that have improved the results and then provide the percentage of improvement that should be attributed to this program. Because this is an estimate—and we don't like estimates—we asked them another question that serves as an error adjustment. We asked them, 'What is your confidence in the allocation that you have just provided, on a scale of 0–100 percent?' For example, if someone was 80 percent confident in an allocation to the program, that reflects 20 percent error. So, we would take out the 20 percent. This is achieved by multiplying by the 80 percent. Let me take you through an example."

Joan described one particular participant and followed the data through the chart to show the value. In the example, an executive reported an improvement with three other factors causing it. He or she allocated 25 percent to the leadership program and was 70 percent confident with that. In that case, 17.5 percent (25 percent × 70 percent) was allocated to the program.

As expected, this table attracted a lot of interest and many questions. Joan spent some time very confidently responding to those.

The CFO opened up, "If I want to see this particular measure, pointing to a particular individual, I could go to that business unit and find the measure and track what has changed."

Joan responded, "Yes, you can see the actual unit value of that measure, and we can provide you the business unit if you would like to. On the chart, we did not use specific names, because we did not want this to appear to be a performance evaluation for the executive. This should be process improvement; if this program doesn't work, we need to fix it and not necessarily go after the participant. So, we can provide to you the business units if you want to do that kind of audit."

The CFO added, "There is really no need to do that; I was just curious."

Joan continued, "Please remember that the groups took on team programs and that this particular group of people had four programs. Three of those programs have been implemented, and the other has not, at least at this point. So, we don't count any value for the fourth program. For the three programs implemented, we used a three-year payoff. These programs represented needed changes in the organization. Let me quickly describe the three programs."

Joan methodically described these programs, showing their monetary value, the assumptions that were made, and the isolation issue. This took about five minutes, but it attracted interest, as the executives asked a few questions about them.

Joan presented a summary of the money from individual programs and team programs to show the money saved or generated because of this leadership program. She reminded the audience that the amount claimed was connected to the leadership program, isolated from other influences.

Next, Joan presented the cost. She had previously reviewed the cost categories with finance and accounting, and they agreed with Joan. In fact, Joan invited Brenda, her finance and accounting representative, to the meeting, and she was there. After showing the detailed cost table, with a quick cost summary discussion, she noted that all cost was included. Joan turned to Brenda and asked for her assessment of the categories of cost that were included. Brenda confirmed that all costs seemed to be covered, and some items were included that might not be necessary. For example, the time away from work probably should not be included, because these executives got their jobs done anyway. Joan added, "We wanted to be consistent and credible, so we have included all the cost." Joan quickly looked at the CFO and could see he was really intrigued and pleased with this brief part of the presentation.

ROI

Finally, Joan showed the ROI calculation, and she presented it two ways. The first ROI was based on individual programs alone, and this generated an ROI of 48 percent. Joan added, "We have a standard that if someone doesn't provide you with data, then you assume it had no value. Of the 30 people in this session, six did not provide us data, perhaps for good reason. Because it was not there, we included zero for them. This is guiding principle number six," Joan added. "When the team programs are included, the number is staggering, with 831 percent ROI. Please remember, the data on these programs have been approved by the executives involved in the program. Only a portion of the program that is connected directly to this program is used in the calculation, recognizing that other factors could have influenced these particular data sets. So, this is a huge value add from the program."

Intangibles

Joan moved on to the intangibles. She had asked the participants about the extent to which this program was influencing certain measures that were largely intangibles; a chart in the report listed the key intangibles. This attracted some interest from the executives as Joan described how the table was constructed. The CFO asked about connecting these measures to monetary values. "They have not been converted to money in our organization," Joan replied, "but some organizations have done so, and we recommend that we pursue more of those types of conversions. The trend these days," added Joan, "is to convert more of the classic intangibles to money. This would be a good time to focus on this task." The CFO agreed.

Conclusion and Recommendations

Joan quickly concluded with a summary and some recommendations that she wanted to make, based on the comments from participants. The team program seemed to be a bit cumbersome. It generated a lot of frustration with the participants. Maybe the individual program should be enough, they suggested. Also, since this program had been operating for some time, many of the really challenging and necessary team programs had already been addressed. Although new ones were generated, this could be an optional part of the process. Joan's recommended change was to make the team program optional.

After some discussion among the group, the executives concluded that the team programs should be a part of the process, with administrative support provided to help these executives with the work. Joan added that some support had been provided, and it was accounted for in the cost of the program but having more support available would certainly be helpful.

So, the change that Joan recommended to be approved, wasn't. The decision did underscore the support for this program and the results that she had presented. Joan concluded the conversation by asking if there were any other major programs that should be evaluated at this level. But she cautioned that this level of evaluation took resources for the team to conduct the study plus the cost of having it reviewed by an external expert. Executives discussed the topic and identified two other programs that they wanted to see evaluated at this level.

The CFO indicated this was a good presentation and that he certainly appreciated the effort. Joan was pleased when the executives left the room. The HR executive was elated. "This was exactly what we need to be doing, Joan," she said, "You have done an amazing job."

Reflection

Walking back to her office, Joan was relieved. She felt good about her presentation and the support from executives. She was very pleased that she was able to show the results of an important soft program in a tangible, credible way. The presentation was challenging, but it was not too difficult. She had methodically followed the guidelines shown later in Figure 14.9.

The Importance of Communicating Results

Now that we have the results in hand, what's next? Do we tell a story? If so, how should it be structured? Should we use the results to modify the program, change the process, demonstrate the contribution, justify new programs, gain additional support, or build goodwill? How should the data be presented? The worst course of action is to do nothing. Achieving results without communicating them is like planting seeds and failing to fertilize and cultivate the seedlings—the yield will be less than optimal. This chapter provides useful information for presenting evaluation data to your various audiences in the form of both oral and written reports.

Communicating results is critical to program success. The results achieved must be conveyed to stakeholders not just at program completion, but throughout the duration of the program. Continuous communication maintains the flow of information so that adjustments can be made, and all stakeholders are kept up to date on the status of the program.

Mark Twain once said, "Collecting data is like collecting garbage—pretty soon we will have to do something with it." Measuring program success and collecting evaluation data mean nothing unless the findings are communicated promptly to the appropriate audiences, so that they are apprised of the results and can take action in response if necessary. Communication is important for many reasons, and here are four of those reasons.

Communication is Necessary to Make Improvements

Information is collected at different points during the process and providing feedback to involved groups enables them to take action and make adjustments if needed. Thus, the quality and timeliness of communication are critical to making improvements. Even after the program is completed, communication is necessary to make sure the target audience fully understands the results achieved, and how the results may be enhanced in future programs, or in the current program if it is still operational. Communication is the key to making important adjustments at all phases of the program.

Communication is Necessary to Explain the Contribution

The overall contribution of the program, as determined from the six major types of measures, is unclear at best. The different target audiences will each need a thorough explanation of the results. The communication strategy— including techniques, media, and the overall process— will determine the extent to which each group understands the contribution. Communicating results, particularly in terms of business impact and ROI, can quickly overwhelm even the most sophisticated target audiences. Communication must be planned and implemented with the goal of making sure the respective audiences understand the full contribution.

Communication is a Politically Sensitive Issue

Communication is one of those issues that can cause major problems. Because the results of a program may be closely linked to political issues within an organization, communicating the results can upset some individuals while pleasing others. If certain individuals do not receive the information, or if it is delivered inconsistently between groups, problems can quickly surface. Not only must the information be understood, but issues relating to fairness, quality, and political correctness make it crucial that the communication be constructed and delivered effectively to all key individuals.

Different Audiences Need Different Information

With so many potential target audiences requiring communication on the success of a program, the communication must be individually tailored to their needs. A varied audience has varied needs. Planning and effort are necessary to ensure that each audience receives all the information it needs, in the proper format, at the proper time. A single report for presentation to all audiences is inappropriate. The scope, the format, and even the content of the information will vary significantly from one group to another. Thus, the target audience is the key to determining the appropriate method of communication.

Communication is a critical need for the reasons just cited, although it is often overlooked or underfunded in programs. This chapter presents a variety of techniques for accomplishing communication of all types for various target audiences.

Case Study

Hewlett-Packard Corporation (HP), like many global technology firms, is concerned about talent retention—a considerable issue, given its workforce of 330,000 employees. In some areas, HP was facing higher-than-expected talent departure. By the time the departure occurred, it was too late to respond. An earlier intervention perhaps could have kept the employee from leaving. Predicting a potential flight risk ahead of time poses a challenge. Working with a specific group of 300 specialists, HP developed a model to predict the flight risk of an individual based on his or her job, pay raises, job performance ratings, rotational assignments, and salaries. Not included in the predictors was a promotion, unless the promotion resulted in a significant pay increase [1].

With this model, HP developed a flight risk score, much like a score for credit risk. In theory, this score would enable managers to intervene in the case of a departure risk. In the beginning, HP was concerned about how the model would be used and the fact that it would be controversial. It could easily be abused if not addressed properly. HP worked diligently with the management team, communicating the model and the flight risk score. The company outlined precise procedures for using these data properly, including a report delivery system.

With this approach, only a select few high-level managers may view individual employee scores—and only scores for employees under them. These managers were trained in interpreting flight risk scores and understanding their limitations, ramifications, and confidentiality. In fact, if unauthorized parties got their hands on the report itself, they would find no names or identifying elements for the employees listed there—only cryptic identifiers, which the authorized manager has the key to unscramble and match to real names. All security systems have vulnerabilities, but this one is fairly bulletproof.

For the team of 300 employees, only three managers see these results. A tool displays the flight risk scores in a user-friendly, nontechnical view that delivers supporting contextual information about each score in order to help explain why it is high or low. These managers are trained in advance to understand the flight risk scores in terms of their accompanying explanations—the factors about the employee that contributed to the score—so that these numbers aren't deferred to as a forceful authority or overly trusted in lieu of other considerations.

The results were impressive. Staff attrition rates that were above 20 percent in some regions decreased to 15 percent and continued to trend downward. This success is credited in large part to the impact of flight risk reports and their well-crafted delivery.

This study illustrates the importance of communicating and using data appropriately so that they are not misused, and they drive intended improvement and desired success. The alternative is misused data that never help an organization achieve the intended improvement.

Principles of Communicating Results

The skills needed to communicate results effectively are almost as sensitive and sophisticated as those needed for obtaining results. The style of the communication is as important as the substance. Regardless of the message, audience, or medium, a few general principles apply.

> *"Leadership is a way of thinking, a way of acting and, most importantly, a way of communicating." – Simon Sinek*

Communication Must be Timely

In general, program results should be communicated as soon as they become known. From a practical standpoint, however, it is sometimes best to delay the communication until a convenient time, such as the publication of the next client newsletter or the next general management meeting. Several questions are relevant to the timing decision. Is the audience ready for the results in view of other issues that may have developed? Is the audience expecting results? When will the delivery have the maximum impact on the audience? Do circumstances dictate a change in the timing of the communication?

Communications Should be Targeted to Specific Audiences

As stated earlier, communication is usually more effective if it is designed for the specific group being addressed. The message should be tailored to the interests, needs, and expectations of the target audience. The results of the program should reflect outcomes at all levels, including the six types of data presented in this book. Some of the data are developed earlier in the program and communicated during the implementation of the program. Other data are collected after program implementation and communicated in a follow-up study. The results, in their broadest sense, may incorporate early feedback in qualitative form all the way to ROI values expressed in varying quantitative terms.

Media Should be Carefully Selected

Certain media may be more appropriate for a particular group than others. Face-to-face meetings may be preferable to special bulletins. A memo distributed exclusively to top executives may be a more effective outlet than the company newsletter. The proper format of communication can determine the effectiveness of the process.

Communication Should be Unbiased and Modest in Tone

For communication to be effective, facts must be separated from fiction, and accurate statements distinguished from opinions. Some audiences may approach the communication with skepticism, anticipating the presence of biased opinions. Boastful statements can turn off recipients, and most of the content will be lost. Observable phenomena and credible statements carry much more weight than extreme or sensational claims, which often detract from the importance of the results.

Communication Must be Consistent

The timing and content of the communication should be consistent with past practices. A special presentation at an unusual time during the course of the program may provoke suspicion. Also, if a particular group, such as top management, regularly receives communication on outcomes, it should continue receiving communication even if the results are not positive. Omitting unfavorable results leaves the impression that only positive results will be reported.

Make the Message Clear

The communication must be clear and precise. In short, it must be well written. Harold Evans, one of the greatest editors of our time, offers timeless advice for making meaning clearer: "Refresh your writing. Unravel convoluted sales talk written to deceive. See through campaigns erected on a tower of falsehoods. Billions of words come at us every day with unimaginable velocity and shriveled meaning, in social media posts, bloated marketing, incomprehensible contracts, and political language designed to make lies sound truthful. The digital era has had unfortunate effects on understanding. Ugly words and phrases are picked up by the unwary and passed on like a virus. Cryptic assertion supplants explanation and reasoned argument. Muddle and contradiction suffocate meaning [2]."

Testimonials Must Come from Respected Individuals

Opinions are strongly influenced by other people, particularly those who are respected and trusted. Testimonials about program results, when solicited from individuals who are respected within the organization, can influence the effectiveness of the message. This respect may be related to leadership ability, position, special skills, or knowledge. A testimonial from an individual who commands little respect and is regarded as a substandard performer can have a negative impact on the message.

The Audience's Bias of the Program Will Influence the Communication Strategy

Opinions are difficult to change, and a negative opinion toward a program or program team may not change with the mere presentation of facts. However, the presentation of facts alone may strengthen the opinions held by those who already support the program. Presentation of the results reinforces their position and provides them with a defense in discussions with others. A program team with a high level of credibility and respect may have a relatively easy time communicating results. Low credibility can create problems when one is trying to be persuasive.

The Process for Communicating Results

The communication of program results must be systematic, timely, and well planned, and the process must include seven components in a precise sequence, as illustrated in Figure 14.1. The first step is critical and consists of an analysis of the need to communicate the results from a program. Possibly, a lack of support for the program was identified, or perhaps the need for adjusting or maintaining the funding for the program was uncovered. Instilling confidence or building credibility for the program may be necessary. It is important first of all to outline the specific reasons for communicating the results.

The second step focuses on the plan for communication. Planning should include numerous agenda items to be addressed in all communications about the program. Planning also covers the actual communication, detailing the specific types of data to be communicated, and when and to which groups the communication will be presented.

The third step involves selecting the target audiences for communication. Audiences range from top management to past participants, and each audience has its own special needs. All groups should be considered in the communication strategy. An artfully crafted, targeted delivery may be necessary to win the approval of a specific group.

The fourth step is developing a report, the written material explaining program results. This can encompass a wide variety of possibilities, from a brief summary of the results to a detailed research document on the evaluation effort. Usually, a complete report is developed, and selected parts or summaries from the report are used for different media.

Media selection is the fifth step. Some groups respond more favorably to certain methods of communication. A variety of approaches, both oral and written, are available to the program leaders.

Deliver the message in the form of appropriate information, represents the sixth step. The communication is delivered with the utmost care, confidence, and professionalism.

The seventh and last step, but certainly not the least significant, is analyzing reactions to the communication. An informal analysis may be appropriate for many situations. For an extensive and more involved communication effort, a formal, structured feedback process may be necessary. The nature of the reactions could trigger an adjustment to the subsequent

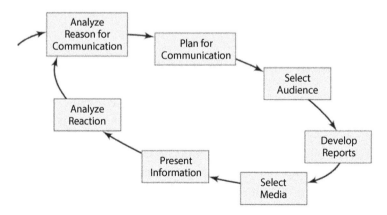

Figure 14.1 A Communications Model for Results.

communication of results for the same program or provide input for adapting future program communications.

The seven steps are discussed further in the following sections.

Step 1: Analyze Reason for Communication

Because there may be various reasons for communicating results, a list should be tailored to the organization and adjusted as necessary. The reasons for communicating results depend on the specific program, the setting, and the unique needs of each party. Some of the most common reasons are:

- Securing approval for the program and the allocation of time and money
- Gaining support for the program and its objectives
- Securing agreement on the issues, solutions, and resources
- Enhancing the credibility of the program leader
- Reinforcing the processes used in the program
- Driving action for improvement in the program
- Preparing participants for the program
- Optimizing results throughout the program and the quality of future feedback
- Showing the complete results of the program
- Underscoring the importance of measuring results
- Explaining techniques used to measure results
- Motivating participants to become involved in the program
- Demonstrating accountability for expenditures
- Marketing future programs

There may be other reasons for communicating results, so the list should be tailored to the needs of each organization.

Step 2: Plan for Communication

Any activity must be carefully planned to achieve maximum results. This is a critical part of communicating the results of the program. The actual planning of the communication is important to ensure that each audience receives the proper information at the right time, and that necessary actions are taken. Several issues are crucial in planning the communication of results:

- What will be communicated?
- When will the data be communicated?
- How will the information be communicated?
- Where will the information be communicated?
- Who will communicate the information?
- Who is the target audience?
- What are the specific actions required or desired?

For example, in a stress management program for teams working in a high-stress environment, an ROI study was conducted to show the value of the program to current and prospective participants. Figure 14.2 outlines this strategy. Three separate documents were developed to communicate with the different target groups in a variety of ways [3].

The communication plan is usually developed when the program is approved. This plan details how specific information is to be developed and communicated to various groups, and the expected actions. In addition, this plan details how the overall results will be communicated, the time frame for communication, and the appropriate groups to receive the information. The program leader, key managers, and stakeholders need to agree on the degree of detail in the plan.

Step 3: Select Audience

The following questions should be asked about each potential audience for communication of program results:

- Are they interested in the program?
- Do they really want to receive the information?

Communication Document	Communication Target	Distribution
Complete report with appendices (75 pages)	• Organization development team • Safety and health staff • Team manager	Distributed and discussed in a special meeting
Executive Summary (8 pages)	• Senior management in the business units • Senior corporate management	Distributed and discussed in routine meeting
General interest overview and summary without the actual ROI calculation (10 pages)	• Program participants	Email
Brochure highlighting program, objectives, and specific results	• Prospective team leaders	Included with program descriptions

Figure 14.2 Communications Strategies.

- Has a commitment been made to include them in the communications?
- Is the timing right for this audience?
- Are they familiar with the program?
- How do they prefer to have results communicated?
- Do they know the program leader? The program team?
- Are they likely to find the results threatening?
- Which medium will be most convincing to this group?

For each target audience, three steps are necessary. To the greatest extent possible, the program leader should get to know and understand the target audience. Also, the program leader should find out what information is needed and why. Each group will have its own required amount of information; some will want detailed information, while others will prefer a brief overview. Rely on the input from others to determine the audience's needs. Finally, the program leaders should take into account audience bias. Some audiences will immediately support the results, others may oppose them, and still others will be neutral. The staff should be empathetic and try to understand the basis for the differing views. Given this understanding, communications can be tailored to each group. This is critical when the potential exists for the audience to react negatively to the results.

The target audiences for information on program results are varied in terms of roles and responsibilities. Determining which groups will receive a particular item of communication requires careful thought, because problems can arise when a group receives inappropriate information or is overlooked altogether. A sound basis for audience selection is to analyze the reason for the communication, as discussed earlier. Figure 14.3 identifies common target audiences and the basis for audience selection. Several audiences stand out as critical. Perhaps the most important audience is the client (group or individual) who initiates the program, arranges funding, usually selects the program leader, and makes the decisions based on the recommendations from the program. Another important target audience is top executives. This group is responsible for allocating resources to the program and needs information to help them justify expenditures and gauge the effectiveness of the efforts. In some cases, this group is the client.

Participants need feedback on the overall success of the effort. Some individuals may not have been as successful as others in achieving the desired results. Communicating the results creates additional subtle pressure to implement the program effectively and improve results in the

Primary Target Audience	Reason for Communication
Client	• To secure approval for the program
Managers	• To gain support for the program
Participants	• To secure agreement with the issues
Top Executives	• To enhance the credibility of the program leader • To improve the results and quality of future feedback
Immediate Managers	• To reinforce the processes used in the program • To prepare participants for the program
Program Team	• To drive action for improvement • To create the desire for a participant to be involved
Key Stakeholders	• To show the complete results of the program
Support Staff	• To explain the techniques used to measure results
All Employees	• To demonstrate accountability for expenditures
Prospective Participants	• To market future programs

Figure 14.3 Common Target Audiences.

future. For those achieving excellent results, the communication will serve as reinforcement.

Communication of results to program participants is often overlooked, with the assumption that once the program is completed, they do not need to be informed of its success.

Communicating with the participants' immediate managers (or significant others) is essential. In many cases, these managers must encourage participants to implement the program. Also, they are key in supporting and reinforcing the objectives of the program. An appropriate return on investment strengthens the commitment to program and enhances the credibility of the program team.

The program team must receive information about program results. Whether for small programs in which team members receive a program update, or for larger programs where a complete team is involved, those who design, develop, facilitate, and implement the program require information on the program's effectiveness. Evaluation data are necessary so that adjustments can be made if the program is not as effective as it was projected to be.

Step 4: Develop Reports

The type of formal evaluation report to be issued depends on the degree of detail in the information presented to the various target audiences. Brief summaries of program results with appropriate charts may be sufficient for some communication efforts. In other situations, particularly those involving major programs requiring extensive funding, a detailed evaluation report is crucial. A complete and comprehensive impact study report is usually necessary. This report can then be used as the basis for more streamlined information aimed at specific audiences and using various media. One possible outline for an ROI/impact study report is presented in Figure 14.4.

A brief one-page summary may be possible for an audience who understands the basic concepts of the ROI Methodology. Figure 14.5 presents an example of a one-page summary for a leadership programs for first-level leaders.

While the impact study report is an effective, professional way to present ROI data, several cautions are in order. Since this report documents the success of a program involving a group of participants, credit for the success must go completely to the participants and their immediate leaders or significant others. Their performance generated the success. Also, it is important to avoid boasting about results. Grand claims of overwhelming success can quickly turn off an audience and interfere with the delivery of the desired message.

The methodology should be clearly explained, along with the assumptions made in the analysis. The reader should easily see how the values were developed, and how specific steps were followed to make the process more conservative, credible, and accurate. Detailed statistical analyses should be placed in an appendix.

Step 5: Select Media

Many options are available for the dissemination of program results. In addition to the impact study report, commonly used media are meetings, interim and progress reports, organization publications, and case studies. Figure 14.6 lists a variety of options to develop the content and the message.

Meetings

If used properly, meetings are fertile ground for the communication of program results. All organizations hold a variety of meetings, and some may

1. General information
    - Background
    - Objectives of study
2. Methodology for impact study
    - Levels of evaluation
    - ROI process
    - Collecting data
    - Isolating the effects of the program
    - Converting data to monetary values
3. Data collection analysis issues
4. Results: General information
    - Response profile
    - Success with objectives
5. Results: Reaction
    - Data sources
    - Key issues
6. Results: Learning
    - Data sources
    - Key Issues
7. Results: Application and implementation
    - Data sources
    - Key issues
8. Results: Impact
    - Data sources
    - Isolating the effects of the program
    - Key issues
9. Results: ROI
    - Converting data to money
    - Project costs
    - ROI and its meaning
10. Results: Intangible measures
11. Barriers and enablers
    - Barriers
    - Enablers
12. Conclusions
13. Recommendations
14. Exhibits

Figure 14.4 Outline for an Impact Study Report.

provide the proper context to convey program results. Along the chain of command, staff meetings are held to review progress, discuss current problems, and distribute information. These meetings can be an excellent forum for discussing the results achieved in a program that relates to the group's activities. Program results can be sent to executives for use in a staff meeting, or a member of the program team can attend the meeting to make the presentation.

Regular meetings with management groups are a common practice. Typically, discussions will focus on items that might be of help to work

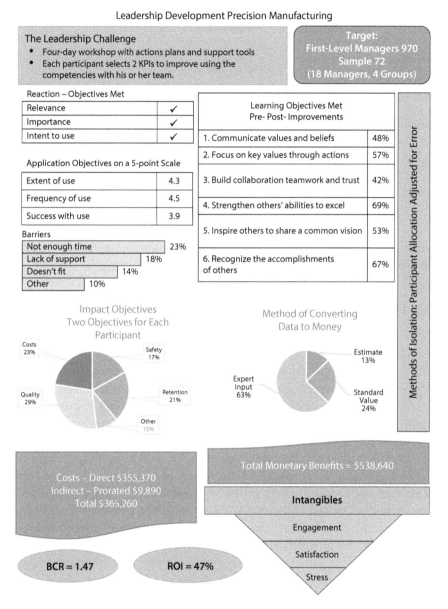

Figure 14.5 Example of a One-Page Summary.

units. The discussion of a program and its results can be integrated into the regular meeting format. A few organizations have initiated the use of periodic meetings for all key stakeholders, where the program leader reviews progress and discusses next steps. A few highlights from interim program

Meetings	Detailed Reports	Brief Reports	Electronic Reporting	Mass Publications
Executives	Impact Study	Executive Summary	Website	Announcements
Management	Case Study (Internal)	Slide Overview	E-mail	Bulletins
Stakeholders	Case Study (External)	One-Page Summary	Blog/Social Media	Newsletters
Staff	Major Articles	Brochure	Video	Brief Articles

Figure 14.6 Options for Communicating Results.

results can be helpful in building interest, commitment, and support for the program.

Interim and Progress Reports

Although usually limited to large programs, a highly visible way to communicate results is the use of interim and routine memos and reports. Published or disseminated by e-mail on a periodic basis, they are designed to inform management about the status of the program, to communicate interim results of the program, and to spur needed changes and improvements.

A secondary reason for the interim report is to enlist additional support and commitment from the management group, and to keep the program intact. This report is produced by the program team and distributed to a select group of stakeholders in the organization. The report may vary considerably in format and scope and may include a schedule of planned steps or activities, a brief summary of reaction evaluations, initial results achieved from the program, and various spotlights recognizing team members or participants. Other topics may also be appropriate. When produced in a professional manner, the interim report can boost management support and commitment.

Routine Communication Tools

To reach a wide audience, the program leader can use internal, routine publications. Whether a newsletter, magazine, newspaper, or electronic file, these media usually reach all employees or stakeholders. The content can have a significant impact if communicated appropriately. The scope should be limited to general-interest articles, announcements, and interviews.

Results communicated through these types of media must be important enough to arouse general interest. For example, a story with the headline "New Program Helps Reduce Teen Suicide" will catch the attention of many readers because it is likely they can appreciate the magnitude and relevance of the study. Reports on the accomplishments of a group of participants may not generate interest if the audience cannot relate to the accomplishments.

For many programs, results are not achieved until weeks or even months after the program is completed. Participants need reinforcement from many sources. Communicating results to a general audience may lead to additional pressure to continue the program or introduce similar ones in the future.

Stories about participants involved in a program and the results they have achieved can help create a favorable image. Participants are made aware that the organization is investing time and money to improve performance and prepare for the future. This type of story provides information about a program that employees otherwise may be unfamiliar with, and it sometimes creates a desire in others to participate if given the opportunity.

General-audience communication can bring recognition to program participants, particularly those who excel in some aspect of the program. Public recognition of participants who deliver exceptional performance can enhance their self-esteem, and their drive to continue to excel. A program can generate many human-interest stories. A rigorous program with difficult challenges can provide the basis for an interesting story on participants who made the extra effort.

Here is an example of general audience communication involving program results for four initiatives to assist convicted felons [4].

Case Study

Officials connected with business and government in Etowah County say programs aimed at employed rehabilitated felons are working, turning offenders into gainfully employed taxpayers.

Heather New, president of the Chamber of Gadsden & Etowah County, said interest is growing among employers in several programs that take one-time felons and put them to work.

"We're heard nothing but a positive response since we started holding information sessions about these programs," New said.

Another event will be scheduled within the next four to six weeks, she said.

A criminal record can reduce the chances a job applicant gets a call-back by 50 percent, according to Etowah County Circuit Judge David Kimberly. But tax credits of up to $9,000 are available to any company hiring a felon, New said. There are also federal tax incentives available to employers of repatriated felons.

According to Neon Workforce Technologies, of more than 162,000 arrests in Alabama in 2015, only 22,279 were for violent crimes.

"There is an untapped resource for our workforce pipeline," New said.

What are the programs?

There's Community Corrections, which provides transportation and drug testing for those on probation or in diversion programs. Dominique Langdon, director of Etowah County Community Corrections, said it serves about 1,000.

Formed in 1998, the program was created to provide alternatives to jail time that reduce costs, offer drug rehab and hopefully end in a productive citizen. Graduates pay for their participation in drug court, and outpatient counseling is not paid by the taxpayer.

The county's Substance Abuse Program, or SAP, provides job-training assistance along with drug counseling. Scott Hassell, chief deputy of corrections with the Etowah County Sheriff's Office, said SAP has been good for the county.

"Every school and government building in the area has been renovated or had maintenance by a SAP participant," he said. "When you give them an opportunity to work, they feel like a man or woman again."

Work release, which has about 30 people employed as of last month, is eligible to nonviolent offenders who receive extensive counseling, treatment and training.

Etowah County Circuit Judge David Kimberly said without treatment and employment, about two-thirds of the offenders return to jail.

"With treatment, upon release it improves by 68.5 percent," he said. "If employed more than six months, it drops to almost zero percent."

There's also the Fatherhood Initiative. Pastor Willie J. Simmons said participants of this program may have had convictions for violent crimes but have to show continuous involvement in the program as well as 18 months of intensive counseling and training.

"They have everything to lose," he said. "You're not going to find a more dedicated employee."

New said the Chamber is trying to connect resources for both employers and those who are trying to rebuild their lives.

"There are opportunities that are not having their needs met, and needs that are not finding their opportunities," she said.

Email and Electronic Media

Internal and external Internet pages, company-wide intranets, and emails are excellent vehicles for releasing results, promoting ideas, and informing employees and other target groups of program results. Email, in particular, provides a virtually instantaneous means of communicating results to and soliciting responses from large groups of people. For major programs, some organizations create blogs to present results and elicit reactions, feedback, and suggestions.

Program Brochures and Pamphlets

A brochure might be appropriate for a program conducted on a continuing basis, or where the audience is large and continuously changing. The brochure should be attractive and present a complete description of the program, with a major section devoted to results obtained with previous participants, if available. Figure 14.7 shows an infographic of results that would be ideal for a brochure for potential donors. Measurable results and reactions from participants, or even direct quotes from individuals, can add spice to an otherwise dull brochure [5].

For example, the executive education division of the Indian School of Business conducted ROI studies on several of their popular executive education courses. With the successful evaluation and positive ROI, the brochures were updated to include how participants applied what they learned, the impact of the program, and actual ROI data. This positions the messaging from location, learning, and facilitators to application, impact, and ROI, underscoring the results of the program.

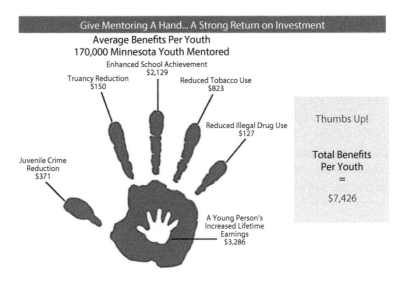

Figure 14.7 Infographic on Mentoring.

Case Studies

Case studies represent an effective way to communicate the results of a program. A typical case study describes the situation, provides appropriate background information (including the events that led to the program), presents the techniques and strategies used to develop the study, and highlights the key issues in the program. Case studies tell an interesting story of how the program was implemented and the evaluation was developed, including the problems and concerns identified along the way.

For example, the Ministry of Education (MOE) in the Sultanate of Oman has developed a book of ROI case studies of key programs for teachers, principals, and administrators. This book makes a powerful statement about the results delivered by the MOE.

Step 6: Present Information

The key to delivering the message is to understand the audience and their perspective, and then show what's in it for them. Regardless of the form of communication (briefing, meeting, webinar, blog, one-page summary, article, or case study), the challenge is to drive home the message and persuade the audience. Darlene Price, communications expert, provides her advice for delivering the message:

- Stop worrying about perfecting your communication and start connecting with your audience
- Organize your presentation with persuasive logic and an effective structure
- Ensure a dynamic, confident delivery every time with live presentations
- Engage and involve your audience when possible to make your message meaningful and memorable
- Use PowerPoint more effectively to reinforce your message and optimize impact
- Manage nervousness and create a great first impression in live and recorded presentations
- Cultivate a variety of image enhancers that will subtly lend power to your presentation—and much more

Being able to communicate to a group of decision makers and positively influence their thinking is a sure path to success [6].

Routine Feedback on Program Progress

A primary reason for collecting reaction and learning data is to provide feedback, so that adjustments can be made throughout the program. For most programs, data are routinely collected and quickly communicated to a variety of groups. A feedback action plan designed to provide information to several audiences using a variety of media may be an option. These feedback sessions may point out specific actions that need to be taken. This process becomes complex and must be managed in a very proactive manner. The following steps are recommended for providing feedback and managing the overall process. Some of the steps and concepts are based on the recommendations of Peter Block in his successful book *Flawless Consulting* [7].

- *Communicate quickly.* Whether the news is good news or bad, it should be passed on to individuals involved in the program as soon as possible. The recommended time for providing feedback is usually a matter of days, and certainly no longer than a week or two after the results become known.
- *Simplify the data.* Condense the data into an easily understandable, concise presentation. This is not the appropriate situation for detailed explanations and analysis.
- *Examine the role of the program team and the client in the feedback process.* The program leader is often the judge, jury,

prosecutor, defendant, and/or witness. On the other hand, sometimes the client fills these roles. These respective functions must be examined in terms of reactions to the data and the actions that are called for.

- *Use negative data in a constructive way.* Some of the data will show that things are not going so well, and the fault may rest with the program leader or the client. In this case, the story basically changes from "Let's look at the success we've achieved" to "Now we know which areas to change."

- *Use positive data in a cautious way.* Positive data can be misleading, and if they are communicated too enthusiastically, they may create expectations that exceed what finally materializes. Positive data should be presented in a cautious way—almost in a discounting manner.

- *Choose the language of the meeting and the communication carefully.* The language used should be descriptive, focused, specific, short, and simple. Language that is too judgmental, macro, stereotypical, lengthy, or complex should be avoided.

- *Ask the client for reactions to the data.* After all, the client is the number one customer, and it is most important that the client be pleased with the program.

- *Ask the client for recommendations.* The client may have some good suggestions for what needs to be changed to keep a program on track, or to put it back on track should it derail.

- *Use support and confrontation carefully.* These two actions are not mutually exclusive. At times, support and confrontation are both needed for a particular group. The client may need support and yet be confronted for lack of improvement or sponsorship. The program team may be confronted regarding the problem areas that have developed but may need support as well.

- *React to and act on the data.* The different alternatives and possibilities should be weighed carefully to arrive at the adjustments that will be necessary.

- *Secure agreement from all key stakeholders.* It is essential to ensure that everyone is willing to make any changes that may be necessary.

- *Keep the feedback process short.* Allowing the process to become bogged down in long, drawn-out meetings or lengthy documents is a bad idea. If this occurs, stakeholders will avoid the process instead of being willing participants.

Following these steps will help move the program forward and generate useful feedback, often ensuring that adjustments are supported and can be executed.

Storytelling

Numbers cannot tell the whole story and other means of communication are required to define and articulate the results. Stories are uniquely useful in their ability to bring people onto the same page and to organize information and present it in an efficient and accessible manner.

Stories foster empathy and connectedness, as they prioritize information and objectives. They provide a clear beginning, middle, and end. The narrative structure of a story is a teaching tool that can make complex data or relationships more easily accessible to an audience. Because the important ideas are set in a metaphor that people can easily understand, both storytellers and listeners can move past arcane details and focus on the problem at hand. The immediacy of the story helps people track the important relationships while empathizing with the subject. This allows for a richer experience and fosters greater insight into the nature of the program, its place in the organization, and how the choices of the participants contribute to its success [8].

The simple rationale for telling stories is that they work. Here are eight of Paul Smith's 10 most compelling reasons to tell stories, and he has much evidence to back them up:

1. Storytelling is simple.
2. Storytelling is timeless.
3. Stories are contagious.
4. Stories are easier to remember.
5. Stories inspire.
6. Stories appeal to all types of audiences.
7. Stories fit in the workplace where most of the work happens.
8. Telling stories shows respect for the audience [9].

A logical structure is helpful to develop stories. Although the structure can vary, Figure 14.8 presents an efficient checklist appropriate for most stories from a storytelling expert.

Another storytelling expert, Carmine Gallo, offers 10 storytelling secrets [10]:

1. Make stories at least 65 percent of your presentation.
2. Use simple words and analogies to hide complexity.

Hook
- Why should I listen to this story?

Content
- Where and when did it happen?
- Who is the hero? (Are they relatable?)
- What do they want? (Is that worthy?)

Challenge
- What is the problem/opportunity? (Relevant?)

Conflict
- What did the hero do about it? (Honest struggle?)

Resolution
- How did it turn out in the end?

Lesson
- What did you learn?

Recommended Action
- What do you want me to do?

Figure 14.8 Story Structure Checklist.

3. Enrich your story with specific and relevant details.
4. Deliver serious topics with a side of humor.
5. Tell authentic and personal stories tailored to your audience.
6. Be succinct; use a few well-chosen words.
7. Use pictures to illustrate your story.
8. Wrap data in stories to make a personal connection.
9. Take every opportunity to hone your presentation skills.
10. Don't make your story good; make it great.

"Storytelling is not something we do. Storytelling is who we are."
– Carmine Gallo

Presentation of Results to Senior Management

Perhaps one of the most challenging and stressful types of communication is presenting an impact and ROI study to the senior management team, which also serves as the client for a program. The challenge is convincing this highly skeptical and critical group that outstanding results have been achieved (assuming they have) in a very reasonable timeframe, addressing the salient points, and making sure the managers understand the process. Two potential reactions can create problems. First, if the results are very impressive, making the managers accept the data may be difficult. On the other extreme, if the data are negative, ensuring that managers don't over-react to the results and look for someone to blame is important. Several guidelines can help ensure that this process is planned and executed properly.

Arrange a face-to-face meeting with senior team members to review the results. If they are unfamiliar with the ROI Methodology, this meeting is necessary to make sure they understand the process. The good news is that they will probably attend the meeting because they have never seen ROI data developed for this type of program. The bad news is that it takes pre-cious executive time, usually about an hour, for this presentation. After the meeting with a couple of presentations, an executive summary may suffice. At this point, the senior members will understand the process, so a short-ened version may be appropriate. When a particular audience is familiar with the process, a brief version may be developed, presented earlier.

The results should not be disseminated before the initial presentation or even during the session but should be saved until the end of the session. This will allow enough time to present the process and collect reactions to it before the target audience sees the ROI calculation. Present the ROI Methodology step by step, showing how the data were collected, when they were collected, who provided them, how the effect of the program was iso-lated from other influences, and how data were converted to monetary val-ues. The various assumptions, adjustments, and conservative approaches are presented along with the total cost of the program, so that the target audience will begin to buy into the process of developing the ROI.

When the data are actually presented, the results are revealed one level at a time, starting with Level 1, moving through Level 5, and ending with the intangibles. This allows the audience to observe the reaction, learning, application and implementation, business impact, and ROI procedures. After some discussion of the meaning of the ROI, the intangible measures are pre-sented. Allocate time for each level as appropriate for the audience. This helps to defuse potential emotional reactions to a very positive or negative ROI.

Show the consequences of additional accuracy if this is an issue. The trade-off for more accuracy and validity often is more expense. Address this issue when necessary, agreeing to add more data if they are required. Collect concerns, reactions, and issues involving the process and make adjustments accordingly for the next presentation.

Collectively, these steps will help in the preparation and presentation of one of the most important meetings in the ROI Methodology. Figure 14.9 shows the recommended approach to an important meeting with the sponsor.

Purpose of the Meeting:
- Create awareness and understanding of ROI.
- Build support for the ROI Methodology.
- Communicate results of study.
- Drive improvement from results.
- Cultivate effective use of the ROI Methodology.

Use These Ground Rules:
- Do not distribute the impact study until the end of the meeting.
- Be precise and to the point.
- Avoid jargon and unfamiliar terms.
- Spend less time on the lower levels of evaluation data.
- Present the data with a strategy in mind.

Follow This Presentation Sequence:
1. Describe the program and explain why it is being evaluated.
2. Present the methodology process.
3. Present the reaction and learning data.
4. Present the application data.
5. List the barriers and enablers to success.
6. Address the business impact.
7. Show the costs.
8. Present the ROI.
9. Show the intangibles.
10. Review the credibility of the data.
11. Summarize the conclusions.
12. Present the recommendations.

Figure 14.9 Guidelines for the Executive Briefing.

Case Study

Paul Smith, former P&G executive, shares an interesting story about presenting results to top executives:

"I've had the opportunity to deliver a presentation to the then-CEO of Procter & Gamble (P&G) A.G. Lafley four or five times in the decade he held that position. The first time was unforgettable. That day I learned a valuable lesson—the hard way—about how not to present to the CEO.

"I'd been given 20 minutes on the agenda of the Executive Global Leadership Council meeting. This group included the CEO and a dozen or so of the top officials in the company. They met weekly in a special room on P&G's executive floor designed just for them. It was a perfectly round room with modern features, centered on a perfectly round table. Even the doors were curved so as not to stray from the round motif. My presentation was the first item on the agenda that day, so I arrived 30 minutes early to set up my computer and make sure all the audiovisual equipment worked properly. I was, after all, making my first presentation to the CEO. I wanted to make sure everything went smoothly.

"The executives began filing into the room at the appointed time and taking up seats around the table. After half of them had arrived, Mr. Lafley entered the room. He walked almost completely around the table, saying hello to each of his team members and, to my horror, sat down in the seat immediately underneath the projection screen—with his back to it!

"This was not good. 'He'll be constantly turning around in his seat to see the presentation,' I thought, 'and he'll probably hurt his neck. Then he'll be in a bad mood, and he might not agree to my recommendation.' But I wasn't going to tell the boss where to sit, so I started my presentation.

"About five minutes in, I realized Mr. Lafley hadn't turned around even once to see the slides. I stopped being worried about his neck and started worrying that he wasn't going to understand my presentation. And if he didn't understand it, he certainly wouldn't agree to my recommendation. But again, I wasn't going to tell the CEO what to do. So, I just kept going.

"At ten minutes into the presentation—halfway through my allotted time—I noticed that he still hadn't turned around once to look at my slides. At that point, I stopped being worried and just got confused. He was looking right at me and was clearly engaged in the conversation. So why wasn't he looking at my slides?

"When 20 minutes had expired, I was done with my presentation, and the CEO hadn't ever bothered to look at my slides. But he did agree to my recommendation. Despite the success, as I was walking back to my office, I couldn't help but feel like I'd failed somehow. I debriefed the whole event in my head, wondering what I had done wrong. Was I boring? Did I not make my points very clear? Was he distracted with some billion-dollar decision far more important than whatever I was talking about?

"But then it occurred to me. He wasn't looking at my slides because he knew something that I didn't know until that moment. He knew if I had anything important to say, I would say it. It would come out of my mouth, not from that screen. He knew those slides were there more for my benefit than for his.

"As CEO, Mr. Lafley probably spent most of his day reading dry memos and financial reports with detailed charts and graphs. He was probably looking forward to that meeting as a break from that tedium and as an opportunity to engage someone in dialogue—to have someone tell him what was happening on the front lines of the business, to share a brilliant idea, and to ask for his help. In short, he was hoping for someone to tell him a story. Someone like me. That was my job during those 20 minutes. I just didn't know it yet.

"Looking back, I realize it was probably no accident Mr. Lafley chose the seat he did. There were certainly others he could have chosen. That position kept him from being distracted by the words on the screen and allowed him to focus on the presenter and on the discussion [11]."

Step 7: Analyze Reaction

The best indicator of how effectively the results of a program have been communicated is the level of commitment and support from the managers, executives, and sponsors. The allocation of requested resources and voiced commitment from top management are strong evidence of management's positive perception of the results. In addition to this macro-level reaction, a few techniques can also be helpful in measuring the effectiveness of the communication effort.

When results are communicated, the reactions of the target audiences can be monitored. These reactions may include nonverbal gestures, oral remarks, written comments, or indirect actions that reveal how the communication was received. Usually, when results are presented in a meeting, the presenter will have some indication of how they were received by the group. Usually, the interest and attitudes of the audience can be quickly evaluated. Comments about the results, formal or informal, should be noted and tabulated.

Program team meetings are an excellent arena for discussing the reaction to the communicated results. Comments can come from many sources depending on the particular target audience. When major program results are communicated, a brief feedback questionnaire may be administered to the entire audience or a sample of the audience. The purpose of the questionnaire is to determine the extent to which the audience learned and believed the information presented. This is practical only when the effectiveness of the communication will have a significant impact on future actions by the program team.

Final Thoughts

Communicating results is a crucial step in the overall evaluation process. If not executed adequately, the full impact of the results will not be recognized, and the evaluation study may be a waste of time. We began the chapter with general principles and seven steps for communicating program results. These can serve as a guide for any significant communication effort. We then discussed the various target audiences, with emphasis on the executive group because of its importance. We also suggested a format for a detailed evaluation report. Additionally, we presented the most commonly used media for communicating program results, including meetings, client publications, and electronic media. The executive briefing is the most challenging and important method of communicating results to clients and top executives. The chapter opened with a best practice example for communicating results to senior executives.

These general principles are vital to the overall success of the communication effort. They should serve as a checklist for the program team planning the dissemination of program results. The last step, optimize results, is presented in the next chapter.

15

Optimize Results: Use Black Box Thinking to Increase Funding

Many industries have been decimated in the United States as the manufacturing facilities have moved offshore. Manufacturing industries such as tires, textiles, and steel have relocated to India, China, and other countries. The pulp and paper manufacturing sector has experienced this offshoring, and it's a somewhat perplexing situation. The United States has an ample supply of timber available to facilitate manufacturing of pulp and paper to be used in a variety of different products, construction materials, and consumer products. But the cost of producing paper in US paper mills became so high that it was cheaper for some organizations to cut down the trees, ship the lumber to China and have the pulp processed there. The finished product is then shipped back to the United States directly from China.

The industry pointed to many factors causing this problem, but one critical factor was the talent available to run the paper mills. The organizations needed a large number of capable and skilled plant operators, which was simply not available in these local areas. Recognizing this need,

Alabama Southern College joined forces with a group of community colleges to form a National Pulp and Paper Technology Consortium with the objective of training skilled paper operators for these plants. Funding was received from the National Science Foundation to create these programs to supply skilled employees to this industry. This was implemented with the plan that this would make a difference in offshoring any additional manufacturing in this critical area.

Four centers were identified for these programs offering two-year degree programs serving four geographic areas where there are heavy forest industries. These were in the Southeast, Midwest, Northwest, and Northeast. Community colleges in those areas provided the programs for two-year degrees in pulp and paper technology. The local employers would hire these graduates who could work at a reasonable wage rate for the employers, so labor costs were not so high, but at the same time, a wage that was much better than the local talent in the community could obtain in other places.

Employers were involved in the program, supporting it in a variety of ways, including offering scholarships for participants to complete the program. Part of the strategy from the National Science Foundation was for the program to be funded by the industry in the future. The initial foundation grant would get it started, but ultimately, the industry had to pay for it. In doing so, the proposal had the component to measure the ROI of this program from the perspective of the employer.

Before this program was implemented, employers had to pay high wages for this capability, or they developed their own training programs to develop this capability. Both options were expensive for the industry and therefore created the need for this program. As the program was offered and became operational, the employers hired the graduates. They began to deliver impressive value to the employers. The analysis in the ROI study showed that the investment the companies were making was quite low, but the value they were receiving was quite high— their ROI was very positive. The results, when presented to the employers, made a great case for the employers to support the program more. Eventually, they picked up more of the cost through scholarship programs. This ultimately led to more absorption of the program by the industry [1].

---------- × ----------

This study illustrates how ROI data can be used for important decision making for funding when the results are reported to the right audiences. Program evaluators must use business evaluation for maximum value. This means results are used to make improvements. If a program is not as successful as it needs to be, the data usually collected indicate what must change to make it better. If it is successful, the data also show what can be changed to make it more successful. Optimizing results is the goal, particularly when the results include business impact and ROI data. Optimization increases the ROI, which helps funders and decision makers decide where to invest in the future, such as allocating more of the budget to a particular area. The challenge is making continuous improvements that lead to optimization that leads to allocation.

Process Improvement is the Key: Black Box Thinking

With the intense competition for resources, it is important to show key funders and supporters the value of programs. Very credible and unmistakable results make a great case for maintaining or increasing funding. However, it starts with the issue of process improvement, as data are collected and used to make changes to improve the program. Whether the program is delivering the desired results or not, the challenge is to make it even better, using the results and increasing the ROI. Even with competitive funding situations, you can keep or improve your budget. Figure 15.1 shows this connection between the evaluation and allocation of funds.

Unfortunately, most programs fail to deliver the desired results. The reason for the failure must be uncovered, and adjustments must be made, much like the use of black boxes on airplanes. We can learn much from black box thinking, and Matthew Syed's book *Black Box Thinking: Why Most People Never Learn from Their Mistakes—But Some Do* brings into focus the power and payoff of learning from failure [2].

Failure is something we all have to endure from time to time, whether it is missing a deadline, flunking an examination, or even a neighborhood softball team losing a game. Sometimes, failure can be far more serious. For doctors and others working in safety-critical industries, getting it wrong can have deadly consequences. Let's explore two contrasting industries to see what we can learn about failure: aviation and healthcare.

Figure 15.1 Optimize Results.

The Aviation Industry

In the aviation industry, the attitude toward failure is striking and unusual. Every aircraft is equipped with two almost-indestructible black boxes, one of which records instructions sent to the onboard electronic systems and another that records the conversations and sounds in the cockpit. If there is an accident, the boxes are opened, the data are analyzed, and the reason for the accident pinpointed. This ensures that procedures can be changed so that the same error never happens again. Through this method, aviation has attained an impressive safety record.

In 2013, there were 36.4 million commercial flights worldwide carrying more than three billion passengers, according to the International Air Transport Association. Only 210 people died. For every one million flights on Western-built jets, there were 0.41 accidents—a rate of one accident per 2.4 million flights [3].

In 2014, the number of fatalities increased to 641, in part because of the crash of Malaysia Airlines Flight 370, where 239 people died. Most investigators believe that this was not a conventional accident but an act of deliberate sabotage. But even if we include this in the analysis, the jet accident rate per million takeoffs fell to a historic low of 0.23 in 2014 [4]. For members of the International Air Transport Association, many of whom have the most robust procedures to learn from error, the rate was 0.12 (one accident for every 8.3 million takeoffs) [5].

Aviation grapples with many safety issues. New challenges arise almost every week. In March 2015, the Germanwings suicide plane crash in the French Alps brought pilot mental health into the spotlight. Industry experts promise that they will always strive to learn from adverse events so that failures are not repeated. After all, that is what aviation safety ultimately means.

Perhaps the efforts of those industry experts are paying off—2017 has been declared the safest year on record for commercial passenger air travel by the Aviation Safety Network. There has been a steady decrease in aviation deaths over the last 20 years [6]. The method of failure analyzation used by those in the aviation industry to improve airline safety has proved itself invaluable.

The Healthcare Industry

In healthcare, however, things are very different. In 1999, the American Institute of Medicine published a landmark investigation called "To Err Is Human." It reported that between 44,000 and 98,000 Americans die each year as a result of preventable medical errors [7]. In a separate investigation, Lucian Leape, a Harvard University professor, put the overall numbers higher. In a comprehensive study, he estimated that a million patients are injured by errors during hospital treatment and that 120,000 die each year in America alone [8].

But these statistics, while shocking, almost certainly underestimate the true scale of the problem. In 2013, a study published in the *Journal of Patient Safety* [9] put the number of premature deaths associated with preventable harm at more than 400,000 per year. (Categories of avoidable harm include: misdiagnosis, dispensing the wrong drugs, injuring the patient during surgery, operating on the wrong part of the body, improper transfusions, falls, burns, pressure ulcers, and postoperative complications.) Testifying to a Senate hearing in the summer of 2014, Peter J. Pronovost, MD, professor at the Johns Hopkins University School of Medicine and one of the most respected clinicians in the world, made a startling comparison.

"What these numbers say is that every day, a 747, two of them are crashing. Every two months, 9/11 is occurring," he said. "We would not tolerate that degree of preventable harm in any other forum [10]." These figures place preventable medical error in hospitals as the third-biggest killer in the United States—behind only heart disease and cancer.

These numbers are not complete because they do not include fatalities caused in nursing homes or in outpatient settings, such as pharmacies, care centers, and private offices, where oversight is less rigorous. According to Joe Graedon, adjunct assistant professor in the Division of Pharmacy Practice and Experiential Education at the University of North Carolina, the full death toll due to avoidable error in American healthcare is more than half a million people per year [11].

Medical errors follow a normal bell-shaped distribution [12]. They occur most often when physicians and clinicians are going about their business with the diligence and concern you would expect from the medical profession. But there is also something deeper at work, something that has little to do with resources and everything to do with culture. It turns out that many of the errors committed in hospitals have subtle but predictable patterns. With open reporting and honest evaluation, these errors could be spotted, and reforms put in place to stop them from happening again, as in the aviation industry. Unfortunately, they are not always reported.

Failure to learn from mistakes has been one of the single greatest obstacles to human progress. Healthcare is just one strand in a long, rich story of evasion. Confronting this could transform not only healthcare but business, politics, and much else. A progressive attitude to failure turns out to be a cornerstone of success for any institution.

We find it difficult to accept our own failures. When failure is related to something important in our lives—our job, our role as a parent, our wider status—it is taken to a different level altogether. When our professionalism is threatened, we put up defenses. We don't want to think of ourselves as incompetent or inept. We don't want our credibility to be undermined in the eyes of our colleagues. For senior doctors, who have spent years in training and reached the top of their profession, being open about mistakes can be almost traumatic.

Society as a whole has a deeply contradictory attitude toward failure. Even as we find excuses for our own failings, we are quick to blame others who mess up. We have a deep instinct to find scapegoats. We are so keen to conceal our own mistakes partly because we are so willing to blame others for theirs. We anticipate, with remarkable clarity, how people will react, how they will point the finger, how little time they will take to put themselves in the tough, high-pressure situation in which the error occurred. The net effect is simple: it destroys openness and creates cover-ups. It hides the vital information we need in order to learn.

Failures in Programs

When examining all types of programs, we know:

1. More than half of programs are wasted (not used or implemented, although we want them to be used). The culprit: failure in the system.
2. Most program evaluators do not measure success at the levels desired by top executives (Levels 4 and 5). The culprit: fear of results (perceived failure) [13].

The failure of programs (or the fear of failure) is serious, although it may seem trivial. After all, what will it hurt if participants:

- Are involved in a program when they are not in a role or situation to make the program successful?
- Are not interested in the program content, information, or concepts and are not motivated to use it?
- Choose not to learn how to make the program successful?
- Fail to take action to make the program successful?

This is not so important unless you examine the numbers from all types of programs in governments, NGOs, nonprofits, and businesses. For example, we have six clients at ROI Institute with more than $1 billion each in their learning and talent development budgets alone. If 50 percent of participants do not use what they learn, this is a waste of over $3 billion in these six organizations alone. Now it becomes important.

We cover up mistakes, not only to protect ourselves from others but to protect us from ourselves. Experiments have demonstrated that we all have a sophisticated ability to delete failures from memory. Far from learning from mistakes, we edit them out of the official autobiographies we keep in our own heads.

This basic perspective—that failure is profoundly negative, something to be ashamed of in ourselves and judgmental about in others—has deep cultural and psychological roots. According to Sidney Dekker, a psychologist and systems expert at Griffith University, Australia, the tendency to stigmatize errors is at least two-and-a-half thousand years old [14].

We need to redefine our relationship with failure, as individuals and as organizations. This is the most important step on the journey to very successful programs. Only by redefining failure will we unleash progress, creativity, and resilience.

Making Adjustments in Programs

The good news is that the causes of failure (or disappointing results) can be identified, and adjustments can be made at different points in the cycle. These adjustments are all aimed at making the program or project more successful and essentially moving it from mediocre or negative results to delivering very positive results. Even if the results are positive, adjustments can still make improvements. This helps to improve funding, but it will also address other important issues, such as increased support, commitment, respect, and involvement.

"Never confuse a single defeat with a final defeat." – F. Scott Fitzgerald

The Fear of Results

As discussed earlier, the greatest barrier to evaluating programs at the impact and ROI levels is a fear of the results. Stakeholders with ownership of the program are concerned that disappointing results may reflect unfavorably on them and their individual performance. Some fear this outcome would lead to budget cuts or maybe a decision to discontinue the program.

This is not necessarily the case. The issue is the reason for the ROI evaluation. If you wait for the funder, sponsor, or top executive to ask for the results, then you are at a disadvantage, with a short timeline. The program may not be properly aligned and designed to achieve the desired results, and you will have missed the opportunity to make the needed adjustments to deliver the results. In addition, the request places you on the defensive, and that's not a good place to be.

You always want to be on the offensive, be proactive, and drive accountability. This positions you in a much better situation for sponsors to react to negative data. In this scenario, you are initiating the evaluation of the program to ensure that it is delivering results. If it's not, adjustments are made. The continuous process of evaluating and improving programs is the best way to overcome the fear of negative results.

You Can Always Make it Better

The design thinking process, emphasized in this book, focuses on results at each step in the program cycle. If the results are not there, adjustments are made. It is extremely rare for a program to be perfect, delivering maximum results in the first attempt. Instead, there will be barriers and difficulties through the chain of value. Hopefully, these obstacles will be minimal, but they could be major. Either way, it's an opportunity for improvement and making the program better—that's your goal.

When you follow the processes in this book, negative outcomes are minimized because of the focus on results in the beginning and adjustments throughout the cycle to deliver those results. Using the ROI Methodology with design thinking creates a high probability of a positive ROI, essentially guaranteeing positive results. This helps to reduce the fear and anxiety of delivering undesirable outcomes.

When Do You Discontinue the Program?

Although rare, there are times when the program needs to be discontinued. (If the steps described in this book are followed properly, then that should not happen.) In some cases, the right audience is not involved, the wrong solution is implemented, or the program is not aligned to business measures. When this happens, the appropriate action may be to discontinue the program. If there is no way that the program can be adjusted or modified to deliver positive results (yet positive results are needed), then it is best to eliminate the program.

In one large telecom organization, a program was requested by a senior executive. When the program evaluation team attempted to link the program to the business measures provided by the executive, the connection was weak at best. When questioned if this was the right solution to deliver, the executive asked them to implement the program. He was not interested in discussions about "the right solution." When the program was implemented, the results at Level 1 were unfavorable, prompting a discussion with this executive to examine if, perhaps, this was the wrong solution. The participants said this program was not relevant to their work or important to their success, and they didn't intend to use it. Obviously, with that reaction, it will be difficult or impossible to have business success.

The executive refused to believe the data and suggested that it should be successful on the job. A follow-up evaluation conducted later validated what the team suspected. The participants did not use the content, because it wasn't helpful to them, it was not needed, and there was no support from their management team. Consequently, the business measure that was allegedly connected to the program did not improve. When confronted with this data, the executive reluctantly agreed to discontinue the program.

Further analysis of the situation revealed that there was a close relationship between this executive and the supplier for the program that biased his ability to be objective. You must have the courage to discontinue a program when it is not working and cannot be successful.

In our work at ROI Institute, we have the opportunity to see many program evaluations that are negative, with as many as 40 to 50 percent of programs being negative on the first evaluation. However, a negative study will usually lead to improvements. Our estimate is that approximately 10 percent of negative programs are actually discontinued, making it less than 5 percent of ROI-evaluated programs overall that are discontinued because of lack of results. They are discontinued because it is the wrong solution for the participants involved or because the business measure desired cannot be influenced by this solution, which is the right thing to do under those scenarios.

This is an important issue, because there is a concern among some program owners and evaluators that almost all programs will be negative. A further concern is that almost all negative studies will lead to program cancellation. Fortunately, these are myths. When the process described in this book is followed correctly, the chances of a negative study are diminished dramatically, and the chance of discontinuing the program is very low.

The Timing of Changes

Changes are made at different points in the cycle, even in the initial processes of selecting the proper solution and understanding the environment where the participants reside. This step attempts to explore whether the solution will be effective in that environment. If a significant barrier exists, it may be necessary to stop the process and address the barrier by trying to minimize, remove, or go around it. After this analysis and assessment phase, as the chain of value unfolds, each level presents an opportunity for making adjustments.

Level 0, Input

As discussed earlier, at Level 0, it is important to have the right people in the program at the right time. This issue focuses on should be involved, or the target audience for the program. They must have an opportunity to use what they are learning to make the program successful.

Early in the process, the target audience must be clearly identified. If participants are not in the target group or not in a position to make the program successful, they should be not allowed to participate, unless there is some other reason for having them involved, such as future opportunities.

The other key concern at Level 0 is the timing. Ideally, participants should be involved in the program just as they need to use the concepts and information to make the program work. For example, you don't want to start a diet and exercise program just before the holiday season. This is not always a perfect match, but it needs to be as close as possible. If it's too early, participants will forget what to do to make the program successful. If it's late, bad habits may evolve that will have to be changed. Ideally, participants should be able to use the content immediately.

Level 1, Reaction Measures

Reaction data is another predictor of success; participants must see the program as something that they will use and make successful. If they see it as not relevant, not important to their success, or not necessary, they may not use it. When reaction is captured and does not meet these objectives, it is best to make adjustments. If participants do not see value, more communication or more information about the program may be required. Adjustments are minimized if reaction objectives are developed that clearly define the desired reaction. This issue was described in detail in Chapter 8, *Make it Matter: Design for Input, Reaction, and Learning.*

Level 2, Learning Measures

Sometimes, participants are not learning what is necessary to make the program successful. As mentioned in Chapter 8, there are various ways to measure learning, ranging from informal self-assessment processes to very structured objective tests, demonstrations, and simulations. If participants are not successful in meeting the learning objectives, adjustments will need to be made in the program. The flow of information, the way content is presented, or the time devoted to learning could influence the level of learning. The activities, discussions, or focus of the learning modules may need to be adjusted for more learning. The important issue in learning design is to make sure the participants have the knowledge or skills and to make adjustments along the way if they don't. The concern is that if participants are not learning, there will be no application from this program, and without application, there is no impact. This is the logic model, the Chain of Value.

> *"An organization's ability to learn, and translate the learning into action rapidly, is the ultimate competitive advantage." – Jack Welch*

Level 3, Application Measures

Level 3 (application) is where the chain of value most likely breaks: Participants just don't use what they have learned in the program. This disappointment is usually a result of the tremendous number of barriers that often exist to keep the participant from taking action to make the program successful. This area of concern has been discussed several times in this book, with almost an entire chapter devoted to it (Chapter 9). Changes are usually made in three situations within the data collection process.

In the first situation, data collection reveals a gap where individuals are not using what they've learned, compared to what should be occurring from the application objectives. Comments are usually provided that can indicate the reason for the gap. This gap might deserve more attention, particularly if the problem is occurring at just one part of the process.

The second situation is to identify the barriers to application with a direct question to participants. Whether they are labeled impediments, inhibitors, or obstacles, the barriers are those items that kept the participants from using the content to the extent that they could or should. If there are huge barriers, a program may be devastated. Unfortunately, this occurs more often than expected. Each barrier identifies what should be adjusted, and these are often issues that must be changed with assistance from others.

A third situation is the identification of enablers, those items that have enhanced results. The enablers, collected directly from the participants, should be present for every program and may be unique to the individuals. What some participants found to be an enabler, may not have enabled others. Just like barriers, enablers are powerful for making improvements. Ideally, enablers are there for everyone.

Level 4, Impact Measures

For some program evaluations, the impact measures have not improved, and the challenge is to find out what happened. Three issues can cause this. The first issue is that there is a misalignment in the beginning, and the specific business measure monitored is not the right measure for this program. The business measure may be correctly targeted as the one that needs to be changed, but this program will not improve it. A second issue is that the program is having an adverse effect on another business measure that wasn't anticipated, and adjustments must be made. This situation is common. For example, a program is designed to reduce the cost of healthcare may decrease patient satisfaction. The related variables need to be monitored for this adverse effect and adjustments made to correct it.

Other factors actually influencing the measure may be a third reason for having disappointing results. The program may be moving the measure in the right direction, but something else is pushing it in the opposite direction. For example, a program designed to reduce youth unemployment fails to show an improvement because jobs disappeared, sparked by a mild recession. These influences should clearly be identified in the isolation process (described in Chapter 10), where a particular step is taken to isolate the effects of the program on the data.

Making the Adjustments

When adjustments need to be made, some will be obvious and should be made as quickly as they are uncovered, particularly at Levels 0, 1, and 2. Other stakeholders outside of the program evaluation team may need to be involved. Sometimes, input will be needed from the participants' managers or significant others. This is particularly true for Level 0, when the wrong participants are involved at the wrong time. Also, when Level 3 evaluation reveals that participants are not making the program successful, the reason must be identified. Whether it is manager (or significant other) support or some other obstacle in the system, this will need to be changed. Finally, still other adjustments may involve executives, including the sponsors.

For example, when there is a mismatch with the business measures, this will require a discussion with the sponsor. When groups face serious challenges or barriers in the program area, adjustments must be addressed by the executives.

It is helpful to show the impact these changes will make. For example, at Level 3, the changes can be dramatic, and a brief analysis can show how they will affect the impact and ROI. That's a great way to secure support for the changes, particularly when a significant effort is needed from managers or executives. The key is to implement the changes as soon as possible, involve others as necessary, and stick with the determination to make it work.

"If you fell down yesterday, stand up today." – H.G. Wells

Increasing ROI

Fundamentally, ROI is increased by either increasing the monetary benefits of the program (the numerator of the equation) or by decreasing the cost of the program (the denominator). Sometimes, both are necessary.

Addressing Costs

The cost seems a logical place for action, as costs are easily understood. Is there a way to reduce the cost of the program? Some cost reductions are easier to spot than others. The opening story in Chapter 13 revealed how costs can sometimes be excessive.

The Healthy Living Group at Alberta Health Services in Canada conducts a variety of smoking cessation programs. If a person under the age of 35 stops smoking, a significant healthcare cost can be avoided. Some programs cost more than others. By conducting ROI studies on several programs, the evaluators can see which programs yield the highest ROI. For example, if two programs yield the same impact but one has less cost, it has a higher ROI. This analysis shows the efficient use of funds.

Cost reduction possibilities for programs often spark discussions about converting classroom learning to eLearning, online learning, blended learning, or mobile learning. Sometimes, this is the right thing to do, and other times, it is not. During the global recession, learning departments witnessed a shift to eLearning as executives were cutting costs, including training costs and travel costs. Facilitator-led learning converted to eLearning looked like a great way to address both of these cost categories by dramatically lowering training costs (the facility and facilitator) and lowering the travel costs of participants. Unfortunately, some of this was implemented without enough thought about the impact that the program was actually delivering.

We observed one dramatic shift in a major computer company as it examined the learning needs for the sales team to sell new products and product upgrades. Each year, the marketing team at a global computer company launches over 100 new products, services, or upgrades. The challenge is to prepare the sales team to sell them. In the past, facilitator-led new-product training was offered regionally, on a monthly basis. Then, an eLearning module was developed for each product or upgrade. For every module, Level 3 (application) and Level 4 (impact) objectives were developed.

Early in the transition to eLearning, a comparison was made between facilitator-led and eLearning training. For one product, a Level 4 objective was for 80 percent of participants to sell the product in two weeks and meet a specific revenue target in three months. For the classroom version, this would mean that 20 participants out of 25 would sell the product in the first two weeks. The group met the revenue target, and a 150 percent ROI was delivered.

For the eLearning version, only 20 percent achieved a sale in two weeks, with a lower revenue realized. This would mean that 5 of the 25 participants would sell the product in the first two weeks. However, because of the low cost of eLearning, the ROI was about 450 percent.

As you can see from this example, eLearning can produce a higher ROI because of the lower cost, but it does not provide the same impact that executives want to see. The executives wanted to make sure that technology-based learning delivered the same impact as its facilitator-led counterpart. When this occurs, lowering the cost of the program increases the ROI significantly.

Cheaper is not always the right answer. We see this with major programs, even classroom-designed programs. There is a misconception that if the costs are lowered, the ROI will improve—always. Consider this situation: an organization is interested in building the capability and expertise of the learning and talent development team. They want a certified professional designation for the staff. They examine the certification from ATD program, Certified Professional in Learning and Performance (CPLP), and think it is too expensive [15].

Instead, they select and purchase another certification program that is available from the Strategic Management Institute. This certification is only $200 per person, whereas the ATD certification is almost $2,000 per person.

A subsequent analysis of the impact of this certification shows no impact on the team. By definition, if there is no impact, yet they absorbed the cost of the program, the calculation is a negative 100 percent. Unfortunately, taking the less-expensive option didn't work for this organization. Another study, conducted for ATD by an independent organization, revealed a very positive ROI for the ATD program. The conclusion: a cheaper program doesn't necessarily deliver a higher ROI.

Addressing the Monetary Benefits

When the monetary value isn't what you thought it would be, it could be that the measure or measures that are being influenced, when converted to money, are not at the level that was expected. This may require a review of the data conversion process to make sure it is accurate. Also, it could be that there are other measures influenced, or the intangibles that were not converted to money may need to be converted in the future. The challenge is to increase the monetary value credibly.

In one program in a restaurant chain, the impact of a performance management program for store managers was based on improving unplanned absenteeism. When the ROI was calculated, it was less than expected. However, it appeared that the number produced by the method to convert data to money might be unusually low, using a value of only $41.00 for an absence. Although that number was the accepted standard value, comparing that value to similar absenteeism studies in the literature suggested that it was an understatement of results. The value should have been about one and a half to two times the daily wage rate. The executives agreed. The value was adjusted going forward to be more accurate, and the standard was changed to reflect this new value [16].

Timing of Assessments

As this chapter underscores, the adjustments should start early in the process, and making changes along the way in dynamic format ensures that programs deliver the monetary value expected. Even at the program's conclusion, it is sometimes helpful to review the process to see what else could be changed to increase the monetary benefits. Unfortunately, adjustments are usually made at the end of the program because many organizations are not designing for results. A program is not effective when the impact measures at Level 4, when converted to monetary value, don't yield enough monetary benefit to calculate a positive ROI. The adjustments described earlier can be significant and hold many opportunities. Figure 15.2

Adjustment Possibilities		
Issue	Level	Opportunity
Audience	0	Moderate
Timing	0	Low
Importance	1	High
Motivation	1	High
Relevance	1,2	High
Appropriateness	1,2	Low
Usability	1,2,3	High
Design	2,3,4	High
Process	3	Moderate
Support	3	High
Transfer Barriers	3	High
Alignment	4	High
Focus	1,2,3,4	High

Figure 15.2 Opportunities for Adjustments.

summarizes some of the adjustments with some comments about possibilities. Sensitivity analysis can be used to see how these various impacts may play out in the calculation. The key is to make adjustments, and if these changes are significant, to measure the success again and calculate the new ROI.

Influencing Allocation

The theme of this book is that an important goal of evaluation is to have an influence on the funding for programs. Whether the objective is to minimize the reductions in the budget, maintain the current budget, or increase the budget, this is probably the most important outcome of this results-based approach. We witnessed some organizations actually increasing program budgets during the Great Recession, when budgets were being cut in other places. This is moving beyond avoiding budget cuts or maintaining existing budgets to increasing budgets in the face of reductions in other areas. This is powerful, and it is a culmination of designing for value through the process.

Investment versus Cost

It's helpful to revisit the concept of cost and investments. An organization has many activities that represent costs, and the perception of executives and administrators about these costs becomes critical. If executives see the activity as an investment with a positive ROI, then there is a reluctance to minimize or reduce it. When the activity has no apparent impact, or there are no credible data to show its effects, then there is often a desire to reduce, minimize, control, or even eliminate it.

We witnessed an important example of this in 2015, when two very successful and wealthy investors bought two important global brands, Kraft and Heinz, and merged them. Warren Buffett, in the United States, with Berkshire Hathaway, and Carlos Alberto Sicupira, from Brazil, teamed up for this purchase. When the merger was announced, Carlos was interviewed by the *Financial Times* in London and was asked about the value he saw in this merger. He responded, "When I examine these two organizations, I see costs. Costs are like fingernails, they have to be cut constantly [17]."

Carlos has a reputation for cutting costs, and that is still playing out now as those two companies have merged; the process, as expected, is brutal. If a particular staff support function or process is not able to show the impact and maybe ROI for their expenditures, then they are at a disadvantage and often suffer significant cost reductions. This is very dramatic, and it has had a devastating effect on those "soft" functions that had very little impact and ROI data.

We saw an interesting example of this in Bombardier, a maker of regional jet aircraft in Canada. Bombardier was developing a new larger aircraft to compete with Airbus and Boeing. Although the company was not necessarily struggling, it was limiting costs to fund this new aircraft. In a move to conserve cash, the CFO sent a memo to all employees, which was reported in *The Globe and Mail,* a Canadian newspaper. Essentially, the memo said that the company needed to conserve cash to fund development of the new model, and in doing so, unnecessary expenses should be eliminated or reduced. The memo added that, effective immediately, all training, recruiting, external consultants, and off-site meetings were suspended. Apparently, the CFO had concluded that those expenses produced little, if any, results. It was easy to cut them, and that was what he was doing, or at least postponing them for a while. Figure 15.3 summarizes the cost versus investment issue. It's a simple but powerful concept.

An important exercise is to think about how top executives, who provide funding for programs, see these programs in your organization. Do they see them as an investment or as an expense? If it is not perceived as an investment, you could easily see ups and downs in funding, where budgets are cut during tough times and increased during lean times, often wreaking havoc with programs that are tracking important issues. To convince

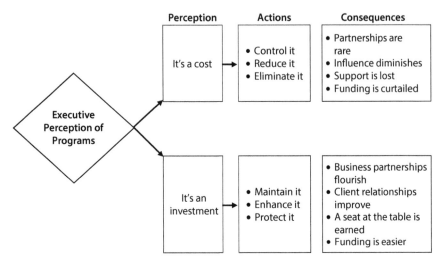

Figure 15.3 Costs Versus Investment Perception.

executives that your programs are an investment, you must show an impact or ROI evaluation for a few of the major programs.

Competition for Funding

The competition for funds is fierce. The budget for your program is often desired by others in the organization. When funding becomes significant, with many staff members, then it really becomes a target for others who want your budget. Although they may have significant budgets, they might want to claim part of your budget.

From the top executive perspective, there is a dilemma. For example, IT and marketing typically show the ROI of major programs. HR and learning and talent development rarely show the value of what they are doing, and this creates a problem. As a recent article in *Harvard Business Review* suggested, "Few HR departments have felt compelled to make the case that any of their practices could drive profits. Many don't calculate ROI, even though other functions have been expected to do so for at least a generation. That just feeds into business leaders' view of HR as a cost center where the goal is always to cut, cut, cut [18]."

Program leaders must make sure there is some mechanism to convince executives that this is a good investment, and this is accomplished with data. You do it with impact and ROI, not with Levels 3, 2, or 1 data, and certainly not with Level 0. You must have convincing data that you are making a difference and that your proposed budget contributes to that. The more credible and specific the data, in terms of impact and ROI, the more convincing your story and the more likely that you'll get your budget approved.

> *"In the budget approval process, you get what you can sell. These days, it's easier to sell impact and ROI." – Jac Fitz-enz*

Anxiety and Downturns Translate into Cost Reduction

When there is a downturn in the economy, executives look for budgets that they can easily cut. If they see it as an expense or cost, it's easy to cut. If they see it as an investment, they may not cut it. You want them to resist the temptation to cut your budget. Also, as we have noticed in the global economy, when there is uncertainty, anxiety, or volatility with wars, politics, and terrorism, there is a tendency to prepare for the unknown by having a tighter ship and leaner budget. This translates into significant budget controls and sometimes budget cuts. We even have witnessed companies with record profits still cutting budgets because of the uncertain future. What they are doing is trimming the parts they think do not necessarily add value, those items that are, perhaps, "nice-to-do" instead of "absolute must-dos." Without data that shows your programs make a difference, it is difficult even to argue to keep the budget.

The Great Recession of 2008–2009 had a lasting effect on many organizations, not only in terms of keeping budgets in check but in demanding up-front accountability before new programs are implemented. The concept of forecasting ROI is now common in many organizations. We have had several program managers say that they cannot implement a major program now unless they provide an ROI forecast. This is a tremendous change from what we have experienced previously and is fully explained in the next chapter [19].

The good news is that a program will be funded if an executive thinks that it is a good investment, one that is going to generate a positive return. We see this routinely. For example, Jack Phillips was involved in the banking industry in the 1990s recession in the United States. He was president of the bank's retail division and general manager of the bank's mortgage company. Because of the recession, the bank staff was reduced by about 20 percent. This was because there were fewer people coming to the branch to make deposits, make loans, or purchase other products, so the existing staffing levels were not needed. At the same time, HR budgets were increased by roughly the same percentage. The rationale was that this was the time to have the best people with the best skill sets, perhaps multi-tasking to accomplish the work of others. This was a time when people needed to be at their best, so it was time to invest more. The board of directors and the other operating executives would not have agreed to this if they hadn't been convinced that these programs were investments and that these investments would reap a positive ROI. Over a period of years before the research, Jack was able to convince his executives with multiple studies demonstrating that investing in people produces a positive ROI. Without that perception, that investment would not have continued.

Final Thoughts

This chapter shows how the results of an evaluation is used to improve programs to optimize the ROI. With this increased ROI, the allocation of funds can be influenced. Ultimately, you need to influence the funding for your program, but you can only do this with credible data to show that you have made a difference and are delivering a positive ROI for major programs.

This chapter is also the capstone of the results-based philosophy of the book. Although Step 1 started with *why* and details why we are tackling a different program, this step shows why we are even concerned about the evaluation in the beginning. It details why a serious approach to evaluation is needed. You have serious budgets, serious challenges, and serious consequences. You have to show the value, and this can be achieved. The approach is not to measure your way to a positive ROI but to design the entire process to deliver ROI. That's what is needed, and that is what the book will do. The next chapter shows how to forecast ROI before the program is implemented.

16

Forecast the ROI

Lars Rienhold, CEO, is proud of the accomplishments of Family Mutual Health and Life Insurance Company (FMI), which has enjoyed a rich history of serving families throughout North America for almost 80 years. With a focus on health and life insurance products, FMI is regarded as a very innovative and low-cost health insurance provider. Top executives are proud of their cost control efforts and the low prices they can offer. Company advertisements regularly highlight their low-cost approach, quality of service and ethical practices [1].

Lars is a man of considerable and contagious personality, continually trying to offer affordable health and life insurance policies, provide excellent customer service, and be a responsible citizen. As part of this effort, Lars wanted to ensure that FMI was doing all it could to help the environment. While FMI's carbon footprint was relatively low compared to manufacturing companies, its headquarters was located in a congested area where employees had long commute times. This was having an impact on employees and the environment.

During a recent trip to Calgary, Canada, he saw a television report about a local company that had implemented a work-at-home program. The report presented the actual amount of carbon emissions that had been prevented with this program. Lars thought that FMI should be able to implement a similar program, with the possibility of employees working from home. He brought this idea to Melissa Lufkin, executive vice president of human resources. The message was short. "I want us to make a difference. I think this is the way to do it. But we can't just let people work from home. We have to make an office at home look, feel, and function like the office at headquarters." Lars added that this was a major change in policy and could be quite expensive. He added, "Let's consider this for a few job groups but forecast the ROI before we proceed. This must add business value for us to sustain it."

Melissa began her investigation by discussing the issue with the operations chief. Although there was some resistance, John Speegle, executive vice president of operations, was interested in exploring the idea. John was concerned about the lack of a productivity increase in the past three years with the largest segment of employees, the claims processors and the claims examiners. That should be the target. About 950 employees were involved in processing or examining claims submitted by customers or healthcare providers. Claims examiners reviewed claims that were disputed or when an audit sparked a review of a particular claim. These job groups had grown to the point that the office space they occupied in Building 2 was overflowing, impeding productivity. Given the company's continued growth, it was likely that a new building space or perhaps a new facility was needed to manage the growth.

John was very interested in lowering the real estate cost of new office space, which averaged about $17,000 per person per year and improving productivity, which was at a rate of 33.2 claims processed and 20.7 claims examined per day.

Melissa discussed the issue with Linda Green, vice president of claims, to hear her concerns about processors and examiners working at home. Linda was supportive but raised some concerns. "Some of our managers want to keep tabs on what is going on and they think employees need to be in the building to see that everyone is working and busy. I'm afraid it is a matter of control, which they may have a hard time giving up if people work remotely." Linda added, "I realize that the right approach might make their jobs easier, but right now they may not be at that point."

Next, Melissa met with the IT department and discussed how they could equip workstations at home with the latest technology. She found a supportive audience in Tim Holleman, senior vice president and chief information officer, who thought that employees could be set up with adequate security and technology to work at home in the same manner as they were working on-site. Tim added, "They can have full access to all databases and they could be using high-speed processes. It would cost FMI a substantial amount the first year but may not represent a very significant cost in the long run."

Melissa then contacted Anne Burson, executive vice president of sales and marketing, to uncover any customer service issues that might arise. Anne was in favor of the move as long as customer service would not suffer. The claims examiners were in direct contact with the customers and she wanted to make sure that acceptable customer service was maintained. Also, many of the processors had to make routine direct telephone or email contact with healthcare suppliers, as well as patients, and they wanted to maintain these contacts at an acceptable level.

Finally, Melissa met with the chief financial officer, Rodrick Harper, to discuss the program and the plan to measure its success. Melissa was eager to show the value of the innovation program and had challenged her staff to measure success, even using ROI. Rod's interest was really piqued. He said, "Let's make sure this is very credible analysis and that it is very conservative. Frankly, I think we want to be involved when you discuss ROI. I think it's proper that we use a standard approach to analysis and we would like to be involved in this every step of the way, if you don't mind." Melissa was pleased with the support, but somewhat anxious about working with the finance and accounting team to evaluate a program that she ultimately would own.

Melissa and her HR staff explored the anticipated reaction of the employees to determine how they would perceive a work-at-home program. She was not sure how many would take advantage of the opportunity. The staff conservatively estimated that at least a third would opt to participate in the program. For many in this group, working at home would be a huge motivator and would make a difference in retaining them at FMI. Current annualized turnover of the two groups is 22.3 percent.

With the approval of the key team, Melissa and her team got busy developing the forecast. The first step was to pinpoint the objectives. Figure 16.1 shows the objectives for the program by different levels, ranging from reaction to ROI. Melissa secured agreement on the objectives from those stakeholders involved.

With a clear understanding of the proposed program and the connection to the business impact measures, a forecast was now possible. Assuming that about one-third of employees would sign up for this program, the forecast was based on 317 participating employees (one-third of 950). Based on the percentage makeup of the two groups, this translated into 237 and 80, respectively, for processors and examiners.

After implementing this program:
Reaction
•   Employees should see the work-at-home program as satisfying, important, rewarding, and motivational. •   Managers must see this program as necessary, appropriate, and important to FMI.
Learning
•   Employees must know the realities of working at home, the conditions, roles, and regulations. •   Employees must have the discipline and tenacity to work at home. •   Managers must be able to explain company policy and regulations for working at home. •   Managers must be able to manage remotely.
Application
•   Managers should conduct a meeting with direct reports to discuss policy, expected behavior, and next steps. •   At least 30 percent of eligible employees should volunteer for at-home assignments within one month. •   At-home offices should be built and should be properly equipped. •   Work-at-home employees should work effectively at home. •   The at-home workplace should be free from distractions and conflicting demands. •   Managers should properly administer the company's policy. •   Managers should manage the remote employees effectively.
Impact
For those involved in the program:
•   Commute time should be reduced to an average of 15 minutes per day. •   Office expense per person should reduce by 20 percent in six months. •   Productivity should increase by five percent in six months. •   Employee turnover should reduce to 12 percent in six months. •   Unplanned absenteeism should be reduced. •   Stress should be reduced. •   Carbon emissions should be reduced. •   The company's image as a green company should be enhanced. •   Employee job satisfaction should improve.
ROI
•   The company should achieve a 25 percent return on investment.

Figure 16.1 Detailed Objectives.

Figure 16.2 shows the development of the monetary forecast, following estimated improvement in business measures. The estimated business impact was obtained directly from the chief of operations and the vice president of claims. The monetary value of a claim also was obtained by these stakeholders, estimated to be $10 cost for processing a claim and $12 for review of a claim. The office expenses were estimated to be $17,000 and the cost of a turnover taken directly from a similar study (where the cost of turnover was pegged as a percentage of annual pay) was provided at $25,400. With this in mind, the calculations are listed below:

Anticipated Participation
• Target Group: 950 • Predicted Enrollment: 1/3 • 950 x 33 1/3% = 317 • Allocation: 237 processors   80 examiners
Estimated Impact

• Productivity: 1 additional claim processed
  1 additional claim examined
• Office expense: 20% reduction
  $17,000 x 20% = $3,400
• Turnover reduction: 22.3% to 12% = 10.3% improvement

Converting Productivity to Money
• Value of one claim = $10.00 • Value of one disputed claim = $12.00 • Daily improvement = 1 claim per day • Daily improvement = 1 disputed claim per day • Annual value = 237 x 220 work days x 1 x 10.00 = $521,400 • Annual value = 80 x 220 days x 1 x 12.00 = $211,200
Office Expense Reduction
• Office expenses in company office: $17,000 annually per person • Office expenses at home office: $13,600 first year per person • Net improvement: $3,400, first year • Total annual value = 317 x 3,400 = $1,077,800
Converting Turnover Reduction to Money
• Value of one turnover statistic = $25,400 • Annual improvement related to program = 10.3% • Turnover prevention: 317 x 10.3% = 33 turnovers prevented • Annual value = $25,400 x 33 = $838,200

Figure 16.2 Forecast of Monetary Benefits.

The costs of the program were estimated to be about $1 million. This estimate is the total cost including the amount of the initial analysis to determine whether this was the proper solution and the development of that solution. The majority of the charges were in the IT support and maintenance, administrative and coordination categories. When the monetary benefits are combined with the cost, the ROI forecast is developed, as shown in Figure 16.3.

Although this number is quite impressive, in her presentation to the senior executives, Melissa stressed that there were significant intangibles, such as the contribution to the environment, which is not included in this calculation.

Total Forecasted Monetary Benefits		
Benefits =	$521,400	Processor Productivity
	211,200	Examiner Productivity
	1,077,800	Office Costs
	838,200	Turnover Reduction
	$2,648,600	
Costs =	$1,000,000	
BCR =	$\dfrac{\$2,648,600}{\$1,000,000} = 2.65$	
ROI =	$\dfrac{\$2,648,600 - 1,000,000}{\$1,000,000} \times 100 = 165\%$	

Figure 16.3 Forecasted ROI.

Other factors such as job satisfaction, job engagement, stress reduction and image were huge intangibles that should be directly influenced from this. However, because these programs need to be based on good business decisions, the ROI forecast is credible and conservative and based on only one year of value. Much more value will be realized after the first year, because most of the office setup expenses will occur in the first year. The top executives felt comfortable with the analysis and gave the go ahead for the program.

———————————— × ————————————

This case study reveals the power of an ROI forecast before the program or project is implemented. It also illustrates the type of analysis for developing the forecast. Although critical for the go/no-go decision, the forecast makes it a better program. The rest of the evaluation study is available in the reference.

Confusion sometimes exists about when to develop the ROI. The traditional approach, which we described in previous chapters, is to base ROI calculations on business impact obtained after the project or program is implemented, using business impact measures converted to monetary values. With this chapter, we illustrate that ROI can be calculated at earlier stages—even before it is initiated.

The Importance of Forecasting ROI

Although ROI calculations based on post-program data are the most accurate, sometimes it is important to know the forecast before the program is initiated, or before final results are tabulated. Certain critical issues drive the need for a forecast before the program is completed, or even pursued. This is more of an issue in the private sector but is now moving to the public sector. Some governments, NGOs, and nonprofits are beginning to require forecasts. Having a credible forecast might be the best way to attract a donor's attention.

Expensive Programs

In addition to reducing uncertainty, forecasting may be appropriate for costly programs. In these cases, implementation is not practical until the program has been analyzed to determine the potential ROI. For example, if the program involves a significant amount of effort in design, development, and implementation, a sponsor or donor may not want to expend the resources, not even for a pilot test, unless some assurance of a positive ROI can be given. In another example, an expensive technology purchase may be necessary to launch a process or system. An ROI may be necessary before purchase, to ensure that the monetary value of the outcomes outweigh the cost of technology and implementation. While there may be trade-offs in deploying a lower-profile, lower-cost pilot, the pre-program ROI is still important, and may prompt some sponsors to stand firm until an ROI forecast is produced.

> *"A penny saved is a penny earned." – Benjamin Franklin*

> *"A penny saved is, well, a penny." – Quicken Loans Onboarding Guide*

High Risks and Uncertainty

Sponsors want to remove as much uncertainty as possible from the program, and act on the best data available. This concern sometimes pushes the program to a forecast ROI, even before any resources are expended to design and implement it. Some programs are high-risk opportunities or solutions. In addition to being expensive, they may represent critical initiatives that can make or break an organization. Or the situation may be one where failure would be disastrous, and where there is only one chance to get it right. In these cases, the decision maker must have the best data possible, and the best data possible often include a forecast ROI.

The opening story in this chapter represents a program that is expensive with high risks and uncertainty. The cost for a pilot is $1 million. If the program doesn't work, it would be difficult to reverse it. Because of this, executives asked for a forecast.

In another example, a fine dining restaurant chain wanted to eliminate the waiters. Customers would be handed a tablet when they arrived. They perused the menu and wine list, made their order, and the food and wine were delivered by the kitchen staff. At the end of the meal, the bill would be settled online with the tablet. Because of the program's high stakes and uncertainty, company executives requested a forecast before pursuing the program. They needed to know not only whether this program would be worthwhile financially, but also what would change with customer satisfaction, image, and brand, and how the program would unfold. This required a comprehensive forecast involving various levels of data, up to and including the ROI.

Sometimes, a forecast can help to attract donors. The following article is a plea for funding to fight AIDS in the southern parts of the United States.

Case Study

Over the past 30 years, the landscape of HIV in the United States has changed dramatically, shifting away from the coastal and urban centers where it first emerged and establishing a new foothold in the southern United States. In 2015, the South accounted for an estimated 38 percent of the total U.S. population, according to the U.S. Census Bureau. However, as estimated half of all new HIV diagnoses occurred in the South. Not only are Southerners more likely to contract HIV, they are dying at higher rates of complications for AIDS as well.

Our response to HIV must include the struggle against inequality, discrimination and stigma in the South. These forces conspire to stop people from knowing their status, accessing care and preventing new infections. Simply put, we cannot achieve our national goals for HIV if we do not focus on the epidemic in the South.

AIDS United has sought to end illness and death from HIV in the decade it has spent investing in the South. And it is this vision that motivated Funders Concerned Against AIDS to convene five of the nation's leading funders of HIV programs to launch the new collaborative Southern HIV Impact Fund.

The Fund will support organizations across the South in formulating a coordinated, more effective response to the disproportionate impact

HIV has in the region. Our partners will work to tackle the very issues at the root of the epidemic's persistent toll. Fighting these will turn the tide of the epidemic.

Putting an end to HIV and fighting to preserve our nation's health is a fight that will take all of us to win, and win it we must. I urge you to join us in this struggle. An AIDS-free South and an AIDS-free America are possible [2].

More detail in terms of some type of forecast would be helpful. A potential donor might want to know more about the strategy with specific details, such as:

1. What specific perceptions about HIV/AIDS are we changing (Level 1)?
2. What information will be provided to various audiences (Level 2)?
3. What specific actions will be taken by the target groups to avoid contracting HIV/AIDS (Level 3)?
4. What specific actions will be taken by those individuals infected by HIV/AIDS (Level 3)?
5. What will be the reduction in incidents of HIV/AIDS, given a target funding level (Level 4)?
6. What will be the reduction in deaths due to HIV/AIDS, given a target funding level (Level 4)?

This level of detail, based on a credible analysis, just might make a difference with a donor.

Post-Program Comparison

An important reason for forecasting ROI is to see how well the forecast holds up under the scrutiny of post-program analysis. Whenever a plan is in place to collect data on a program's success, comparing actual results to a forecast is helpful. In an ideal world, a forecast ROI would have a defined relationship with the actual ROI—or at least one would lead to the other, after adjustments. The forecast is often an inexpensive process because it involves estimates and assumptions. If the forecast becomes a reliable predictor of the post-program analysis, then the forecast ROI might substitute for the actual ROI. This could save money on the use of post-program analysis.

The Federal Information Agency (FIA), visited in Chapter 14, faced an annual turnover rate of employees that was perceived to be quite high in the category of communication specialist. These individuals were engaged in a variety of telecommunications services and activities that required a college degree, often in computer science, information science, or electrical engineering [3].

The first step of the analysis was to clearly understand the definition of *turnover*. Technically, any employee leaving is considered turnover. Even if that person is involved in a fatal traffic accident, it is recorded as a turnover. Most managers think of turnover as voluntary turnover, counting those people who leave the organization voluntarily. Others prefer the definition of *avoidable turnover*, suggesting that it's not just those who leave of their own volition, but also those who were forced to leave but could have been retained with proper counseling or with a better match of the individual and the organization. Still others prefer the definition of *regrettable turnover*, which suggests that some lesser-performing employees leave voluntarily but their departures don't pose a problem. At the costlier end of the scale is the departure of high-potential employees; turnover for this particular group is regrettable.

At FIA, the discussion led to defining turnover as the departure of high potentials (which was regrettable turnover). Further analysis of exit interview data indicated that the turnover of high potentials was occurring during the first five years of employment. The rate of departure of these high-potential employees was 29 percent. So, the specific definition of the problem for FIA was a 29 percent rate of turnover of high-potential employees during the first five years of employment. Further analysis found that the cost of this turnover was twice the annual salary for each turnover statistic. Based on initial analysis describing the situation, it was obvious FIA had a problem worth solving.

A brief forecast confirmed this. A total of 1,500 specialists were in this job group. The proposed solution could reduce the turnover to about 10 percent, a change of 19 percent. This would represent 1,500 x 19 percent = 285 turnovers prevented. The average salary is $69,310. The cost of one turnover is $138,620. If the solution is successful, the total cost of turnover avoided is $138,620 x 285 = $39,506,700. If the solution costs less than this amount, it is a positive ROI. A follow-up evaluation confirmed this.

Compliance

More than ever, organizations are requiring a forecast ROI before they undertake major programs. For example, one organization requires any program with a budget exceeding \$500,000 to have a forecast ROI before it grants program approval. Some units of government have enacted legislation that requires program forecasts. With increasing frequency, formal policy and legal structures are reasons to develop ROI forecasts.

Major NGOs, such as the World Bank Group, require value for money for major expenditures, administered through the procurement department. Sometimes this is required before a program is implemented. Collectively, these reasons are leading more organizations to develop ROI forecasts so their sponsors and donors will have an estimate of programs' expected payoff.

The Trade-Offs of Forecasting

The ROI can be developed at different times and with different levels of data. Unfortunately, the ease, convenience, and costs involved in capturing a forecast ROI create trade-offs in accuracy and credibility. As shown in Figure 16.4, there are five distinct time intervals during a program when the ROI can be developed. The relationship between the timing of the ROI and the factors of credibility, accuracy, cost, and difficulty is also shown in this table.

- A pre-program forecast can be developed using estimates of the impact of the program. This approach lacks credibility and accuracy but is the least expensive and least difficult to calculate. Because of the interest in pre-program forecasting, this scenario is expanded in the next section of this chapter.

ROI with	Data Collection Timing (Relative to Project)	Credibility	Accuracy	Cost to Develop	Difficulty
1. Pre-Program Data	Before program	Can have low credibility	Can be inaccurate	Inexpensive	Not difficult
2. Reaction Data	During program				
3. Learning Data	During program				
4. Application Data	After program				
5. Business Impact Data	After program	Very credible	Very accurate	Expensive	Very difficult

Figure 16.4 Time Intervals When ROI can be Developed.

- Reaction data can be extended to develop an anticipated impact, including the ROI. In this case, participants anticipate the chain of impact as a program is implemented and drives specific business measures. This forecast is completed after the program has begun. The estimates of impact come from individuals who now know about the program and its possibilities. While accuracy and credibility increase from the pre-program basis, this approach lacks the credibility and accuracy desired in many situations. However, it is easily accomplished and is a low-cost option and is discussed in more detail here.
- In programs where there is a substantial learning component, learning data can be used to forecast the ROI. This approach is applicable only when formal testing shows a relationship between test scores and subsequent performance in the organization or field. When this correlation is available (it is usually developed to validate the test), test data can be used to forecast subsequent performance. If performance can be converted to monetary value, the ROI can be developed. This has less potential as a forecasting tool and is not discussed in more detail [4].
- When frequency of skills or use of knowledge is critical, the application and implementation of those skills or knowledge can be converted to a value using a concept called utility analysis. While this is particularly helpful in situations where competencies are being developed and values are placed on improving competencies, it has limited applications in most programs and is not discussed in more detail [5].
- Finally, the ROI can be developed from business impact data converted directly to monetary values and compared to the cost of the program. This is not a forecast, but is a post-program evaluation, and the basis for the ROI calculations in this book. It is the preferred approach, but because of the pressures outlined above, examining ROI calculations at other times and with other levels is sometimes necessary.

The following sections in this chapter review in detail pre-program ROI forecasting, and ROI forecasting based on reaction.

Pre-Program ROI Forecasting

Perhaps one of the most useful ways to convince a sponsor that a program is beneficial is to forecast the ROI for the program. The process is similar to the post-program analysis, except that the extent of the impact must be estimated along with the program costs.

Basic Model

Figure 16.5 shows the basic model for capturing the data necessary for a pre-program forecast. This is a modified version of the post-program ROI process model presented in Chapter 4. In the pre-program forecast, the program outcomes are estimated, rather than being collected after program implementation. Data collection is kept simple, and relies on interviews, focus groups, or surveys of experts. Tapping into benchmarking studies or locating previous studies may also be helpful [6].

Beginning at the reaction level, anticipated or estimated reactions are captured. Next, the anticipated learning that must occur is developed, followed by the anticipated application and implementation data. Here, the estimates focus on what must be accomplished for the program to be successful. These items may be based on the objectives at each of these levels. Finally, the impact data are estimated by experts. These experts may include experts, specialists, suppliers, or potential participants in the program. In this model, the levels build on each other. Having data estimated at Levels 1, 2, and 3 enhances the quality of the estimated data at Level 4 (impact), which is needed for the analysis.

The model shows that there is no need to isolate the effects of a program as in the post-program model. The individual experts providing the

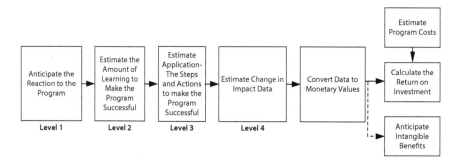

Figure 16.5 Pre-Project Forecasting Model.

impact data are asked the following question: "How much will the impact measure change as a result of the program?" This question ties the anticipated change in the measure directly to the program; thus, isolation is not needed.

This approach makes this process easier than the post-evaluation model, where isolating program impact is always required.

Converting data to money is straightforward using the techniques described in Chapter 11. Locating a standard value or finding an expert to make the estimate is the logical choice. Analyzing records and searching databases is a possibility. The monetary benefits are inserted in the numerator. The estimated cost of the program is inserted as the denominator. The projected cost-benefit analysis can be developed along with the ROI. The specific steps to develop the forecast are detailed next.

Basic Steps to Forecast ROI

Eighteen detailed steps are necessary to develop a credible pre-program ROI forecast using expert input:

1. **Understand the situation.** Individuals providing input to the forecast and conducting the forecast must have a good understanding of the present situation. This is typically a requirement for selecting the experts.

2. **Predict the present.** The program is sometimes initiated because a particular impact measure is not doing well. However, many of those measures often lag the present situation; they may be based on data taken several months ago. Also, these measures are based on dynamic influences that may change dramatically and quickly. It may be beneficial to estimate where the measure is now, based on assumptions and current trends. Although this appears to be a lot of work, it is not a new responsibility for most of the experts, who are often concerned about the present situation. Market share data, for example, are often several months old. Trending market share data and examining other influences driving market share can help organizations understand the current situation.

3. **Observe warnings.** Closely tied to predicting the present is making sure that warning signs are observed. Red flags signal that something is going against the measure in question, causing it to go in an undesired direction or otherwise not

move as it should. These often raise concerns that lead to new programs. These are early warnings that things may get worse; they must be factored into the situation as forecasts are made.

4. **Describe the new process, project, program, or solution.** The program must be completely and clearly described to the experts so they fully understand the mechanics of what will be implemented. The description should include the program scope, the individuals involved, time factors, and whatever else is necessary to express the magnitude of the program and the profile of the solution.

5. **Develop specific objectives.** These objectives should mirror the levels of evaluation, and should include reaction objectives, learning objectives, application objectives, and impact objectives. Although these may be difficult to develop, they are developed as part of the upfront analysis described in Chapter 7. Objectives provide clear direction toward the program's end. The cascading levels represent the anticipated chain of impact that will occur as the program is implemented.

6. **Estimate how participants will perceive the program.** In this step, the experts are trying to understand participants' reaction. Will they support the program? How will they support it? What may cause participants to become unsupportive? The response is important because a negative reaction can cause a program to fail.

7. **Estimate what the participants will learn.** To some extent, every program will involve learning, and the experts will estimate what learning will occur. Using the learning objectives, the experts will define what the participants will learn as they become involved in the program, identifying specific knowledge, skills, and information the participants must acquire or enhance during the program.

8. **Anticipate what participants should do because of the program.** Building on the application objectives, the experts will identify what actions will be taken as the program is implemented successfully. This step details specific actions taken, tasks, followed processes implemented, and technology used by the individuals. Steps 6, 7, and 8—based on reaction, learning, and application—provide important information that serves as the basis for the next step, estimating improvement in business impact data.

9. **Estimate the improvement in business impact data.** This is a critical step because the impact data generated are needed for the financial forecast. The experts will provide the estimate, in either absolute numbers or percentages, about the monetary change in the business impact measure (ΔP). While accuracy is important, it is also important to remember that a forecast is no more than an estimate based on the best data available at a given point. This is why the next step is included.

10. **Apply the confidence estimate.** Because the estimate attained in the previous step is not very accurate, an error adjustment is needed. This is developed by deriving a confidence estimate on the value identified in Step #9. The experts are asked to indicate the confidence they have in the previous data. The confidence level is expressed as a percentage, with 0 percent indicating "no confidence" and 100 percent indicating "certainty." This becomes a discount factor in the analysis, c.

11. **Convert the business impact data to monetary values.** Using one or more methods described in Chapter 11, the data are converted to money. If the impact measure is a desired improvement such as output, the value represents the gain obtained by having one more unit of the measure. If it is a measure that the organization is trying to reduce—like downtime, mistakes, or complaints—the value is the cost that the organization incurs as a result of one incident. For example, the cost of product returns may be 5 percent of sales. This value is noted with the letter V.

12. **Develop the estimated annual impact of each measure.** The estimated annual impact is the first-year improvement directly related to the program. In formula form, this is expressed as $\Delta I = \Delta Pc \times V \times 12$ (where ΔI = annual change in monetary value, ΔP = annual change in performance of the measure, c is the confidence factor – error adjustment - and V = the value of that measure). If the measure is weekly or monthly, it must be converted to an annual amount. For example, if three lost-time accidents will be prevented each month, the time saved represents a total of 36.

13. **Factor additional years into the analysis for programs that will have a significant useful life beyond the first year.** For these programs, the factor should reflect the diminished

benefit of subsequent years. The client or sponsor of the program should provide some indication of the amount of the reduction, and the values developed for the second, third, and successive years. It is important to be conservative by using the smallest numbers possible.

14. **Estimate the fully loaded program costs.** In this step, use all the cost categories described in Chapter 13, and denote the value as C when including it in the ROI equation. Include all direct and indirect costs in the calculation.

15. **Calculate the forecast ROI.** Using the total projected benefits and the estimated costs in the standard ROI formula. Calculate the forecast ROI as follows:

$$ROI(\%) = \frac{\Delta I - C}{C} \times 100$$

16. **Show variation.** Use sensitivity analysis to develop several potential ROI values with different levels of improvement (ΔP). When more than one measure is changing, the analysis may take the form of a spreadsheet showing various output scenarios and the subsequent ROI forecasts. The breakeven point will be identified.

17. **Identify potential intangible benefits.** Anticipate intangible benefits using input from those most knowledgeable about the situation, on the basis of assumptions from their experience with similar programs. Remember, the intangible benefits are those benefits not converted to monetary values, but possessing value nonetheless.

18. **Communicate the ROI forecast and anticipated intangibles with caution.** The target audience must clearly understand that the forecast is based on several assumptions (clearly defined), and that although the values are the best possible estimates, they may include a degree of error.

Following these 18 steps will enable an individual to forecast the ROI.

Sources of Expert Input

Everyone would benefit from seeing further into the future, whether buying new technology, crafting policy, launching a new product, or simply planning a customer event. Good forecasting doesn't require powerful computers or arcane methods. It involves gathering evidence from a variety of sources, thinking probabilistically, working in teams, keeping score, and being willing to admit error and change course [7].

Several sources of expert input are available for estimating improvement in impact data when the program is implemented. Ideally, experience with similar programs in the organization will help form the basis of the estimates the experts make. The experts may include:

- Clients and/or sponsors
- Donors
- Members of program team
- Professors/researchers
- Prospective participants
- Subject matter experts
- External experts
- Advocates (who can champion the program)
- Finance and accounting staff
- Analysts (if one is involved with the program)
- Executives and/or managers
- Customers, if appropriate

Collectively, these sources provide an appropriate array of possibilities for helping estimate the value of an improvement. Because errors may develop, ask for a confidence measure when using estimates from any source.

Securing Input

With the experts clearly identified, data must be collected from the individuals listed as experts. If the number of individuals is small (for example, one person from each of the expert groups involved), a short interview may suffice. During interviews, it is critical to avoid bias and to ask clear, succinct questions that are not leading. Questions should be framed in a balanced way to capture what may occur as well as what may not. If groups are involved, using focus groups may be suitable. For large numbers, surveys or questionnaires may be appropriate.

When the groups are diverse and scattered, the Delphi technique may be appropriate. This technique, originally developed by the Rand Corporation in the 1950s, has been used in forecasting and decision making in a variety of disciplines. The Delphi technique was originally devised to help experts achieve better forecasts than they might obtain through traditional group meetings, by allowing access to the group without in-person contact. Necessary features of a Delphi procedure are anonymity, continuous iteration, controlled feedback to participants, and a physical summary of responses. Anonymity is achieved by means of a questionnaire that allows group members to express their opinions and judgments privately. Between all iterations of the questionnaire, the facilitator informs the participants of the opinions of their anonymous colleagues. Typically, this feedback is presented as a simple statistical summary using a mean or median value. The facilitator takes the group judgment as the statistical average in the final round [8].

In some cases, benchmarking data may be available and can be considered as a source of input for this process. The success of previous studies may provide input essential to the program as well. It may include an extensive search of databases using a variety of search engines. The important point is to understand, as much as possible, the potential impact of the program.

Conversion to Money

The impact measures, forecasted by the experts, must be converted to monetary values for one, two, three, or more years depending on the nature and scope of the program. Standard values are available for many of these measures. Considering the importance of these measures, someone has probably placed monetary values on them. If not, experts are often available to convert the data to monetary values. Otherwise, existing records or databases may be appropriate sources. Another option is to ask stakeholders, perhaps some of the experts listed above, to provide these values for the forecast. This step is the only means of showing the money made from the program. Chapter 11 covered these techniques in more detail.

Estimate Program Costs

Program cost estimates are based on the most reliable information available, and include the typical categories outlined in Chapter 13. The estimates can be based on previous programs. Although the costs are unknown, this task is often relatively easy to accomplish because of its similarity to budgeting, a process that is usually routine with programs. Dividing costs into categories representing the functional processes of the program provides additional insight into program costs. Areas often not given enough attention include analysis, assessment, evaluation, and reporting. If these elements are not properly addressed, much of the value of the program may be missed. With these costs and monetary benefits, the forecast can be made using the ROI calculations presented in Chapter 13.

Case Study

The programs in the opening stories in the first four chapters could have been forecasted. However, it wasn't requested by the funder or pursued by the program owner. Most forecasting is in the business sector, although it is moving to the public sector now. The following case study is taken from the business sector.

Global Financial Services (GFS) wanted a better way for sales relationship managers to track routine correspondence and communication with customers. A needs assessment and initial analysis determined that customer contact management software was needed to assist with this task. The program would involve further detailing software requirements, selecting an appropriate software package, and implementing the software with appropriate job aids, support tools, and training. However, before pursuing the program and purchasing the software, a forecast ROI was needed. Following the steps previously outlined, it was determined that four business impact measures would be influenced by implementation of this program:

1. Increase in sales to existing customers
2. Reduction in customer complaints caused by missed deadlines, late responses, and failure to complete transactions
3. Reduction in response time for customer inquiries and requests
4. Increase in the customer satisfaction composite survey index

Several individuals provided input in examining the potential problem. With comprehensive customer contact management software in place, relationship managers should benefit from quick and effective customer communication and have easy access to customer databases. The software should also provide the functionality to develop calendars, to-do lists, and action plans. Relationship managers should further benefit from features such as built-in contact management, calendar sharing, and the fact that the software is Internet-ready. To determine the extent to which the four measures would change, input was collected from six sources:

1. Internal software developers with expertise in various soft-ware applications provided input on expected changes in each of the measures.
2. Marketing analysts supplied information on sales cycles, customer needs, and customer care issues.
3. Relationship managers provided input on expected changes in the impacts if the software was used regularly.
4. The analyst who confirmed the initial need for the software provided supplemental data.
5. The sponsor provided input on what could be expected from the program.
6. The proposed vendor provided input based on previous experience.

When input is based on estimates, the actual results will usually differ significantly. However, GFS was interested in a forecast based on analysis that, although very limited, would be strengthened with the best easily available expert opinion. Input was adjusted for the confidence of the estimates (this is the error adjustment) and other information to assess its credibility. After discussing the availability of data and examining the techniques to convert it to monetary values, the following conclusions were reached:

- The increase in sales could easily be converted to a monetary value, as the average margin for sales increase is applied directly.
- The cost of a customer complaint could be based on an internal value currently in use, providing a generally accepted cost.
- Customer response time was not tracked accurately, and the
- value of this measure was not readily available, making it an intangible benefit.
- No generally accepted value for increasing customer satisfaction was available, so customer satisfaction impact data would be listed as an intangible benefit.

The forecast ROI calculation was developed from combined input based on the estimates. The increase in sales was easily converted to monetary values using the margin rates, and the reduction in customer complaints was easily converted using the discounted value of a customer complaint. The costs for the program could easily be estimated based on input from those who briefly examined the situation. The total costs included development costs, materials, software, equipment, facilitators, facilities, and lost time for learning activities, coordination, and evaluation. This fully loaded projected cost, compared to the benefits, yielded a range of expected ROI values. Figure 16.6 shows possible scenarios based on payoffs of the two measures, as assessed by six experts. The ROI values range from a low of 12 percent to a high of 180 percent. The breakeven point could be developed with different scenarios. With these values in hand, the decision to move forward was easy: even the worst-case scenarios were positive, and the best case was expected to yield more than 10 times the ROI of the worst. As this example illustrates, the process must be simple, and must use the most credible resources available to quickly arrive at estimates.

Expert	Potential Sales Increase	Basis	Potential Complaint Reduction (Monthly Reduction)	Basis	Expected ROI	Credibility Rating (5 = highest 1 = lowest)
Relationship. mgr.	3.5%	Sales opportunity	3	Lower response time	60%	3
District mgr.	4%	Customer satisfaction	4	Lower response time	90%	4
Marketing analyst	3%	Missed opportunity	5	Quicker response	120%	4
Project sponsor	5%	Customer services	4	Quicker response	77%	4
Vendor	10%	Customer loyalty	12	Higher priority	180%	2
IT Analyst	2%	Customer relationships	3	Faster response	12%	2

Figure 16.6 Expected ROI values for Different Outputs.

Forecasting with a Pilot Program

Because of inaccuracies inherent in a pre-program forecast, a better approach is to develop a small-scale pilot program, with the ROI based on post-program data. This involves the following steps:

1. As in the previous process, develop Level 1, 2, 3, and 4 objectives.
2. Implement the program with a small-scale sample as a pilot program, excluding all the bells and whistles. (This keeps the program costs low without sacrificing integrity.)

3. Fully implement the program with one or more of the groups who can benefit from the initiative.
4. Develop the ROI using the ROI process model for post-program analysis as outlined in previous chapters.
5. Based on the results of the pilot program, decide whether to implement the program throughout the organization. Data can be developed using all six of the measures outlined in this book: reaction, learning, application, impact, ROI, and intangibles.

Evaluating a pilot program and withholding full implementation until its results can be developed provides less risk than developing an ROI forecast. For example, Walmart uses this method to evaluate pilot programs before implementing them throughout its chain of 5,000 US stores. Using pilot groups of 18–30 stores called "flights", the decision to implement a program throughout the system is based on six types of post-program data (reaction, learning, application, impact, ROI, and intangibles).

> *"The most reliable way to forecast the future is to try to understand the present." – John Naisbitt*

ROI Forecasting with Reaction Data

Another possibility is to develop a forecast based on reaction data after the participants are involved in the program. The reaction data are collected after participants are introduced to the program, learn what to do to make it successful, and know what is expected of them.

To forecast ROI at this level, participants are asked to state specifically how they plan to use the program, and what results they expect to achieve. They are asked to convert their planned accomplishments into monetary values and show the basis for developing the values. Participants can adjust their responses with a confidence factor to make the data more credible. Next, estimates are adjusted for confidence level. When tabulating data, participants multiply the confidence levels by annual monetary values. This produces a conservative estimate for use in data analysis. For example, if a participant estimated the monetary impact of the program at $10,000 but was only 50 percent confident in his or her estimate, a $5,000 value would be used in the ROI forecast calculations.

To develop a summary of the expected benefits, discard any data that are incomplete, unusable, extreme, or unrealistic. Then total the individual data items. Finally, as an optional exercise, adjust the total value again by a factor that reflects the unknowns in the process, and the possibility that participants will not achieve the results they anticipate.

When participants are exposed to, and learn about, a new process, there is a sense of excitement about the possibilities—this reaction ignores the barriers to implementation. This adjustment factor can be estimated by the program team, not participants. In one organization, the benefits are divided by two to develop a number to use in the calculation, based on a comparison with actuals follow-up in several studies.

Case Study

This process can best be described using an actual case. Global Engineering and Construction Company (GEC) designs and builds large commercial facilities like plants, paper mills, and municipal water systems. Safety is always a critical matter at GEC and commands much management attention. To improve safety performance, a safety leadership program was initiated for program engineers and construction superintendents. The program solution involved policy changes, audits, and training. Facilitated sessions focused on safety leadership, safety planning, safety inspections, safety meetings, accident investigation, safety policies and procedures, safety standards, and workers' compensation, all covered in a two-day session. Safety engineers and superintendents (the participants) were expected to improve the safety performance of their individual construction programs [9].

A dozen safety performance measures used in the company were discussed and analyzed in the two-day session. At the end of the session, participants completed a feedback questionnaire that probed specific action items planned as a result of the safety leadership program and provided estimated monetary values of the planned actions. In addition, participants explained the basis for estimates and placed a confidence level on their estimates. Figure 16.7 presents data provided by the participants. Only 19 of the 25 participants supplied data. (Experience has shown that approximately 70–80 percent of participants will provide usable data on this series of questions.) The estimated cost of the program, including participants' salaries for the time devoted to the program, was $358,900.

Some of the monetary values of the planned improvements were extremely high, reflecting the participants' optimism and enthusiasm at the beginning of an important program. As a first step in the analysis, extreme data items were omitted (one of the Guiding Principles of the ROI Methodology). Data such as "millions," "unlimited," and "$4 million" were discarded, and each remaining value was multiplied by the confidence value and totaled. This adjustment is one way of reducing highly subjective estimates. The resulting tabulations yielded a total improvement of $990,125 (rounded to $990,000). The projected ROI, which was based on the feedback questionnaire at end of the two-day session, is:

$$ROI = \frac{(\$990,000 - \$358,900)}{\$358,900} \times 100 = 176\%$$

Although these projected values are subjective, the results were generated by program participants who should be aware of what they could accomplish. A follow-up study would determine the actual results delivered by the group.

Participant No.	Estimated Value	Basis	Confidence Level	Adjusted
1	$80,000	Reduction in lost-time accidents	90%	$72,000
2	91,200	OSHA reportable injuries	80%	72,960
3	55,000	Accident reduction	90%	49,500
4	10,000	First-aid visits/visits to doctor	70%	7,000
5	150,000	Reduction in lost-time injuries	95%	142,500
6	Millions	Total accident cost	100%	—
7	74,800	Worker's compensation	80%	59,840
8	7,500	OSHA citations	75%	5,625
9	50,000	Reduction in accidents	75%	37,500
10	36,000	Worker's compensation	80%	28,800
11	150,000	Reduction in total accident costs	90%	135,000
12	22,000	OSHA fines/citations	70%	15,400
13	140,000	Accident reductions	80%	112,000
14	4 million	Total cost of safety	95%	—
15	65,000	Total worker's compensation	50%	32,500
16	Unlimited	Accidents	100%	—
17	20,000	Visits to doctor	95%	19,000
18	45,000	Injuries	90%	40,500
19	200,000	Lost-time injuries	80%	160,000
				Total $990,125

Figure 16.7 Level 1 Data for ROI Forecast Calculations.

Use of the Data

This type of analysis should be reserved for programs where the participants are very knowledgeable of their situation and have access to data and experts to help them be successful.

Caution is required when using a forecast ROI. The calculations are highly subjective and may not reflect the extent to which participants will achieve results. A variety of influences in the environment and setting can enhance or inhibit the attainment of impact goals. Having high expectations at the beginning of a program is no guarantee that those expectations will be met.

Although the process is subjective and possibly unreliable, it does have value:

1. **This data has more value than typical reaction data.** If the evaluation must stop at this point, this analysis provides more insight into the value of the program than data from typical reaction input, which report attitudes and feelings about a program. Sponsors and managers usually find this information more useful than a report stating that "40 percent of program team participants rated the program above average," or that "the participants are happy with the program."

2. **These data can form a basis for comparing different programs of the same type (e.g., smoking cessation programs).** If one program forecast results in an ROI of 300 percent and a similar program forecast results in a 30 percent ROI, it would appear that one program may be more effective. The participants in the first program have more confidence in the planned implementation of the program.

3. **Collecting these types of data focus increased attention on program outcomes.** Participants will know that specific actions are expected, which produce impact results for the program. The data collection helps participants plan the implementation of what they have learned to make the program successful. This issue becomes clear to participants, as they anticipate impact results and convert (or attempt to convert) them to monetary values. Even if the forecast is ignored, the exercise is productive because of the important message it sends to participants.

4. **The data can be used to secure support for a follow-up evaluation.** A skeptical administrator or executive may

challenge the data, and this challenge can be converted into support for a follow-up to see whether the forecast holds true. We have been challenged with this data with the comment "I don't believe this data." We always respond, "We don't believe it either, but it is coming from the participants who can make it happen. Let's follow up to see if it works." The only way to know whether these results will materialize is to conduct a post-program evaluation.

5. **If a follow-up evaluation of the program is planned, the post-program results can be compared to the ROI forecast.** Comparisons of forecast and follow-up data are helpful. If there is a defined relationship between the two, the forecast may be substituted for the more expensive follow-up. Also, when a follow-up evaluation is planned, participants are usually more conservative with their projected estimates.

The use of ROI forecasting with reaction data is increasing, and some organizations have based many of their ROI forecast calculations on this type of data. For example, one of the largest banks in the United States routinely develops ROI forecasts with reaction data. Although they may be subjective, the calculations do add value, particularly if they are part of a comprehensive evaluation system.

Forecasting Guidelines

The enterprise of the future, based on empiricism and analytical decision making, will indeed be considerably different from today's enterprise. In the future, even more than today, businesses will be expected to possess the talent, tools, processes, and capabilities to enable their organizations to implement and utilize continuous analysis of past business performance and events to gain forward-looking insight to drive business decisions and actions [10].

With the different forecasting timeframes outlined in this chapter, it may help to follow a few guidelines known to drive the forecasting possibilities within an organization. These guidelines are based on our experiences in forecasting in a variety of projects and programs [11].

1. **If you must forecast, forecast frequently.** Forecasting is an art and a science. Users can build comfort, experience, and history with the process by using it frequently.
2. **Make forecasting an essential part of the evaluation mix.** This chapter began with a list of essential reasons for

forecasting. The use of forecasting is increasingly being demanded by many organizations. It can be an effective and useful tool when used properly and in conjunction with other types of evaluation data. Some organizations have targets for the use of forecasting (e.g., if a program exceeds a certain cost, it will always require a pre-program forecast). Others will target a certain number of programs for a forecast based on reaction data and use those data in the manner described in this chapter. It is important to plan for the forecast and let it be a part of the evaluation mix, using it regularly.

3. **Forecast different types of data.** Although most of this chapter focuses on how to develop a forecast ROI using impact data, forecasting the value of the other types of data is important as well. A useable, helpful forecast will include predictions about reaction and perceived value, the extent of learning, and the extent of application and implementation. These types of data are very important in anticipating movements and shifts, based on the program that is planned. It assists in developing the overall forecast and helps the program team understand the total anticipated impact.

4. **Secure input from those who know the process best.** As forecasts are developed, it is essential to secure input from individuals who understand the dynamics of the environment, setting, and the measures being influenced by the program. Using these experts will increase not only the accuracy of the forecast, but also the credibility of the results. In some situations, it may be the analysts who are aware of the major influences in the setting and the dynamics of proposed actions.

5. **Long-term forecasts will usually be inaccurate.** Forecasting works better when it covers a short timeframe. Most short-term scenarios afford a better grasp of the influences that might drive the measures. In the long term, a variety of new influences, unforeseen now, could enter the process and drastically change the impact measures. If a long-term forecast is needed, it should be updated regularly.

6. **Expect forecasts to be biased.** Forecasts will sometimes have data from those who have an interest in the issue. This may be unavoidable. Some will want the forecast to be optimistic;

others will have a pessimistic view. Almost all input is biased in some way. Every attempt should be made to minimize the bias, adjust for the bias, or adjust for the uncertainty in the process. Still, the audience should recognize the forecast could be a biased prediction.

7. **Serious forecasting is hard work.** The value of forecasting often depends on the amount of effort put into the process. High-stake programs need a serious approach, collecting all possible data, examining different scenarios, and making the best prediction available. It is in these situations that mathematical tools and modeling can be valuable.

8. **Review the success of forecasting routinely.** As forecasts are made, it is imperative to revisit the forecast with post-program data to check its accuracy. This can aid in the continuous improvement of the processes. Some sources could prove to be more or less credible, specific input may be more or less biased, and certain analyses may be more appropriate than others. It is important to constantly improve the methods and approaches for forecasting.

9. **The assumptions are the most serious error in forecasting.** Of all the variables that can enter the process, the assumptions offer the greatest opportunity for error. It is important for the assumptions to be clearly detailed and communicated. When multiple input items are solicited, each forecaster should use the same set of assumptions, if possible.

10. **Utility is the most important characteristic of forecasting.** The most important use of forecasting is providing information and input for the decision maker. Forecasting is a tool for those attempting to make decisions about program implementation. It is not a process intended to maximize the output or minimize any particular variable. It is not a process undertaken to dramatically change the way a program is implemented. It is a process to provide data for decisions.

Final Thoughts

In this chapter, we illustrated that ROI calculations can be developed at different times and at different evaluation levels. Although most program leaders focus only on impact data for ROI calculations. In a follow-up scenario, there is a growing need to forecast impact and ROI earlier in the process. ROI forecasts developed before a program begins can be useful to the sponsor and are sometimes necessary before the program can be approved. Forecasts made during program implementation can be useful to management and participants and can focus participants' attention on the economic impact of the program. Using ROI estimates before or during the program will require a focus on accuracy.

As expected, pre-program ROI forecasts have the image of low credibility and accuracy, yet have the advantage of being inexpensive and relatively easy to develop. However, ROI forecasts using estimates of impact data can be more credible and accurate using the guidelines in this chapter. The reality is that forecasting is an important part of the measurement mix. It should be pursued routinely and used regularly in decision making.

Whether you have completed a forecast ROI or a post-program ROI, the results must be reported to stakeholders. In the next chapter, we detail how and when results are communicated, and to whom they are communicated. Storytelling will be a part of the communication process.

17

Make It Work: Sustaining the Change to a Results-Based Process

The commandant of the New Jersey State Police Academy, Captain Coyne, wanted results-based thinking to permeate the academy from analysis and assessment to design, development, delivery, evaluation, and reporting. He wanted all the members of the academy to understand how business results are driven. Yes, the police academy had business measures (output, quality, cost, and time). His philosophy was to ensure programs began with the proper alignment (start with why), beginning with the end in mind. He also wanted to make sure that proper solutions were selected, objectives were developed, programs were designed with results in mind, and programs delivered the desired results.

Team members should deliver powerful content, ensuring that it transfers to the job and that it has impact. He wanted to evaluate all programs, but he wanted to examine only a few at the impact level. His concern, most importantly, was that all members understand what causes results and what they could do to drive those results. He needed a results-based approach to clearly show the business value for learning. He required each member of the police academy, a team of about 75 individuals, to be involved in the ROI Certification. An important part of the certification is five days of intensive training.

Severe and challenging weather conditions occurred during the week of training for one cohort. A large snowstorm struck the Jersey shore during that January session. Normally, the faculty members of the academy would assume other assignments to help address many of the issues and problems brought on by such a storm. In this case, Captain Coyne received permission to allow the 25 people attending the certification to remain in the course. The academy remained open, even though it was delayed two hours on one of the days. He insisted that everyone attend, and even offered to allow any member of the class to spend the night at the academy if they desired; some did. As a result, everyone was in attendance, even on the largest snow day.

This demonstration of unwavering commitment to the results-based process left an important impression on the participants. Clearly, this is not just a "nice-to-know" process, but as the captain stated, "This is essential for our work in the future."

———————————— × ————————————

Developing ROI capability and implementing ROI throughout the organization must be a high priority for the senior leader of the organization. This cannot be implemented on an "as-we-have-time" basis or when other priorities have been addressed. It *must* receive priority and commitment.

Even the best-designed process or model is of little value unless it is effectively and efficiently integrated into the organization. This is not difficult, but it requires that all stakeholders change a few things about what they do....and change will be resisted. Some of this resistance to change is based on fear and misunderstanding. Some is real, based on actual barriers and obstacles. Although the methodology presented in this book is a step-by-step, logical, and simple process, it can fail if it is not properly integrated, fully accepted, and adequately supported by those who must make it work within the organization. This final chapter focuses on some of the most effective means of overcoming resistance to implementing a results-based method.

"The question is not, 'when will things get back to normal?' The question is, 'what will the new normal look like?'" – Gary Marx

Overcoming Resistance

The task is to shift the responsibility for driving business impact to all stakeholders, with each individual altering his or her efforts. The entire team is designing for and expecting results. Although some would argue that the changes should have been there earlier, they are not in place in most organizations.

Resistance to this type of change appears in a variety of ways, including comments, remarks, actions, or behaviors. Figure 17.1 provides typical comments that indicate an open resistance to increased accountability:

"We have met the enemy and he is us." – Pogo, Cartoon Character

Each comment signals an issue that must be resolved or addressed in some way. A few are based on realistic barriers, but others are based on myths that must be dispelled. Resistance to the process may reflect underlying concerns. For example, owners of programs may fear losing control, while others may feel vulnerable to whatever actions may follow if the program is not successful. Still others may be concerned about any process that brings change or requires additional effort. It may take evidence of tangible and intangible benefits to convince participants that it is in their best interest to make the program successful. Although most program owners want to see the results of a program, they may have concerns about the information that's needed and whether their personal performance is being judged while the program is undergoing evaluation. Participants may express the same fears.

The challenge is to implement the methodology systematically and consistently so that it becomes a normal task, part of a routine, and a standard process built into programs. The implementation necessary to overcome resistance covers a variety of areas. Figure 17.2 shows the actions outlined in this chapter, which are presented as building blocks to overcoming resistance. They are all necessary to construct the proper base or framework to dispel myths and remove or minimize barriers. The remainder of this

• It costs too much.	• This is not necessary.
• It takes too much time.	• How can we be consistent with this?
• Who is asking for this?	• Our administrators don't want this.
• This is not part of my responsibilities.	• Our team leaders will not support this.
• I did not have input on this.	• This is not easy.
• I do not understand this.	• This is not practical.
• What happens when the results are negative?	• The results will be misused.

Figure 17.1 Typical Resistance to Increased Accountability.

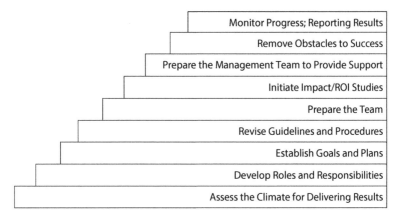

Figure 17.2 Building Blocks for Overcoming Resistance.

chapter presents specific strategies and techniques devoted to each building block.

Assess the Climate

Some organizations assess the current climate for achieving results as a first step toward implementation. One way to do this is to develop a survey to determine the current perspectives of the program team. A special instrument is available for this at ROI Institute (www.roiinstitute.net), and it is also attached as Appendix A. Conducting interviews with key stakeholders to determine their willingness to follow the program through to ROI is another way. With an awareness of the current status, the program implementation team can plan for significant changes and pinpoint particular issues that need support as the results-based model is implemented.

Develop Roles and Responsibilities

Defining specific roles and responsibilities for different stakeholders addresses many of the resistance factors and helps pave a smooth path for implementation.

Identifying a Champion

As an early step in the process, designate one or more individuals as the internal leaders for driving business results. In most change efforts, someone (or a group) must take responsibility for ensuring that the process is implemented successfully. This is someone (or a group) who has a passion for measuring success, enjoys solving problems, understands the organization's operation, and possesses excellent written and oral communications. This leader serves as the champion and is usually the one who understands the process best and sees vast potential for its contribution. More importantly, this leader is willing to teach others and will work to sustain sponsorship.

The champion may be the program evaluator, if there is one. For larger organizations, the director of program evaluation may be the champion. The entire team may serve as the champions. Some organizations have a section or department to manage the process. For example, the Ministry of Education in the Sultanate of Oman created an ROI department to implement the results-based process. The entire team served as champions.

Developing the Champion

In preparation for this assignment, individuals usually receive special training that builds specific skills in and knowledge of the assessment, evaluation, and design thinking. The role of the implementation leader is quite broad and includes many specialized duties. In some organizations, the implementation leader can take on many roles, ranging from diagnostician to problem solver to communicator.

Leading the process is a difficult and challenging assignment that requires unique skills. Fortunately, programs are available to teach these skills. For example, ROI Institute offers a program that is designed to certify individuals who will be assuming leadership roles in the implementation of the ROI Methodology. This certification is built around 10 specific skill sets linked to successful ROI implementation, focusing on the critical areas of data collection, isolating the effects of the program, converting data to monetary value, presenting evaluation data, and building capability. This process is quite comprehensive but may be necessary to build the skills needed for taking on this challenging assignment [1].

Establishing a Task Force

Making the process work well may require the use of a task force, which usually comprises a group of individuals from different parts of the program or client team who are willing to develop a results-based approach and implement it in the organization. Selecting the task force may involve volunteers, or participation may be mandatory according to specific job responsibilities. The task force should represent the cross section necessary for accomplishing any stated goals. Task forces have the additional advantage of bringing more people into the process and developing more ownership of and support for the results-based process.

Assigning Responsibilities

Determining specific responsibilities is critical, because confusion can arise when stakeholders are unclear about their particular assignments in the process. Responsibilities apply to two areas. The first is the assessment, measurement, and evaluation responsibility of the entire team. Everyone involved in the process will have some responsibility, including all the stakeholders listed in Figure 17.3. Typical key roles necessary to drive business results are listed for each stakeholder group.

When there is an evaluation team (or team of champions), several responsibilities exist for the team. These responsibilities may include providing input on designing instruments, planning specific evaluations, analyzing data, and interpreting the results. General duties include:

- Ensuring that the initial analysis or diagnosis for the program includes specific business impact measures
- Developing specific application and business impact objectives for the program
- Keeping the organization or team members focused on application and impact objectives
- Communicating the rationale for evaluation
- Assisting in follow-up activities to capture application and business impact data
- Providing assistance for collection, analysis, and reporting of data
- Communicating results, and
- Driving improvements and optimizing ROI

Assigning responsibilities for results requires attention throughout the process. Although the team must be assigned specific responsibilities for delivery, requiring others to serve in support functions is not unusual.

Establish Goals and Plans

Establishing goals, targets, and objectives is critical to implementation, particularly when several goals are planned. Establishing goals also includes detailed planning documents for individuals and for the overall process.

Stakeholders	Key Roles
Analysts	• Align with the business • Select proper solution • Develop objectives at four levels
Designers	• Design for the proper audience • Design for the proper convenience • Design for cost • Design for time
Developers	• Design for application • Design for impact
Facilitators	• Teach to application • Teach to impact • Expect success • Coordinate evaluation
Program owners/coordinators	• Expect success • Coordinate evaluation • Communicate results
Sponsors	• Expect success • Require business results • Support process • Use results
Participants	• Use content • Drive impact • Provide data
Managers of participants (Significant others)	• Expect success • Require business results • Encourage application
Evaluators	• Expect success • Collect data • Measure results • Communicate results • Drive improvement • Optimize ROI

Figure 17.3 Key Roles.

Setting Evaluation Targets

Establishing specific targets for evaluation levels is an important way to make progress with measurement and evaluation. As emphasized throughout this book, not every program should be evaluated to the ROI level. Knowing in advance to which level the program will be evaluated helps in

Level	Target*
Level 1, Reaction	100%
Level 2, Learning	80%
Level 3, Application and Implementation	40%
Level 4, Business Impact	25%
Level 5, ROI	10%

*Percent of programs evaluated at this level.

Figure 17.4 Evaluation Targets at Scripps Health.

planning what measures will be needed and how detailed the evaluation must be at each level. Figure 17.4 presents an example of the targets set for evaluation at each level from Scripps Health. Targets should be set early in the process, with the full support of the entire team. If practical and feasible, the targets should also have the approval of key managers—particularly the senior management team.

Developing a Plan for Implementation

An important part of implementation of the results-based process is establishing a timetable. This document becomes a master plan for completion of the different elements presented earlier. Beginning with forming a team and concluding with meeting the targets previously described, this schedule is a program plan for transitioning from the present situation to the desired future situation. Items on the schedule include developing specific ROI programs, building staff skills, developing policy, and teaching managers the process. Figure 17.5 shows an example of a plan for implementing the results-based process for the World Food Programme, a large NGO. The more detailed the document, the more useful it becomes. The program plan is a living, long-range document that should be reviewed frequently and adjusted as necessary. More importantly, those engaged in delivering business results should always be familiar with it.

Revise Guidelines and Procedures

Another part of planning is revising or developing the organization's policy or guidelines on measurement and evaluation. The guidelines document contains information developed specifically for the process. It is created with input from the team and key managers or stakeholders. This

Figure 17.5 ROI Implementation Plan for a Large NGO.

	J	F	M	A	M	J	J	A	S	O	N	D	J	F	M	A	M	J	J	A
Team formed	▓																			
Responsibilities defined		▓																		
Policy developed			▓	▓																
Targets set		▓																		
Capability developed					▓	▓														
ROI Program (A)						▓	▓	▓												
ROI Program (B)							▓	▓	▓											
ROI Program (C)												▓	▓	▓	▓					
ROI Program (D)											▓	▓	▓	▓	▓	▓				
Communications/Improvement																	▓	▓	▓	▓
Managers/Administrators trained																▓	▓	▓	▓	▓
Support tools developed					▓	▓														
Guidelines developed		▓	▓	▓																

document addresses critical matters that will influence the effectiveness of the process. These may include adopting the five-level framework presented in this book, requiring Level 3 and 4 objectives for some or all programs, and defining responsibilities for the participants.

Guidelines provide structure and direction for the team and others who work closely with the process. Guidelines also provide an opportunity to communicate basic requirements and fundamentals of performance and accountability. More than anything, they serve as tools to teach others, especially when they are developed collaboratively. If guidelines are developed in isolation, the team and management will be denied their sense of ownership, rendering the guidelines neither effective nor useful.

Procedures for assessment, measurement, and evaluation are important for showing how to use the tools and techniques, guide the design process, provide consistency, ensure that appropriate methods are used, and place the proper emphasis on each of the areas. Procedures are more technical than guidelines and often include detailed steps showing how the process is undertaken and developed. They frequently involve specific forms, instruments, and tools necessary to facilitate the process.

Prepare the Team

Program implementation team members may see this process as an unnecessary intrusion into their normal responsibilities that absorbs precious time and stifles creative freedom. Several issues must be addressed when preparing the team for implementation.

Involving the Team

For each key issue or major decision regarding implementation, involve the team in the process. Team input is essential as evaluation guidelines are prepared and procedures are developed. It will be more difficult for the team to resist if they helped design and develop the process. Use meetings, brainstorming sessions, and task forces to involve the team in every phase of developing the framework and the supporting documents.

Teaching the Team

Team members may have inadequate skills in assessment, measurement, and evaluation, because these areas are not always a formal part of the team's or evaluator's job preparation. Consequently, the champion must learn the eight steps in this book and teach them to the entire team. Teaching materials are available from www.roiinstitute.net.

Initiate ROI Studies

Sarah McCullough was the head of HR for a national bank in the Middle East. She was a very successful and effective HR executive. She wanted to show the executives that, in this bank, both HR and learning and talent development are connected to the business and that they drive success with their projects and programs. She asked for the leaders of the different programs, projects, and functional sections within HR to attend the ROI Certification program to develop assessment, measurement, and evaluation skills. In total, 35 attended.

Recognizing that some leaders would be apprehensive about measuring the success of their programs, perhaps even frightened of the outcomes, Sarah wanted to remove that anxiety. She did this by conducting a one-hour session in the workshop to discuss her vision of how they would be accountable and connect to the business. She also mentioned that she wanted a minimum of seven ROI studies on major programs from this group. She went on to say that it is best to select the programs that are high profile, very expensive, and very important to the organization, and that command the attention of top executives. For those individuals who selected a program to evaluate at this level, she would think more favorably about their performance. For the next performance review, this action would be a plus, even if the ROI is negative.

She asked for volunteers to evaluate their particular programs and, as expected, most of them volunteered. Then it was a matter of selecting which programs were the best for this level of evaluation. In all, there were seven programs, five people per team, and they all became CRPs. She removed the fear of results.

The first tangible evidence of the value of using the results-based process may be seen at the initiation of the first program for which an ROI calculation is planned. Because of this, it is important to identify appropriate programs and keep them on track. Selecting appropriate programs for ROI analysis is critical. Only certain types of programs qualify for comprehensive, detailed analysis. The example above shows how to tackle this issue.

Prepare the Management Team

The head of learning and development for Garanti Bank, one of Turkey's most profitable and successful banks, was very determined to make sure that the learning and development team focused on results. Following assignments in a variety of field operations roles, she took on the role of head of learning and development with a mandate to add value to the organization. After searching for ways and processes, she focused on the ROI Methodology as the tool to show the impact of programs and also improve current programs.

After attending a two-day ROI workshop in Istanbul, she decided that she wanted several of the team members to become Certified ROI Professionals (CRPs), available from ROI Institute. She offered ROI Certification to the group on a voluntary basis. She asked for volunteers to take a greater role in accountability and measurement and to become experts in the process. To do so meant that each had to complete an ROI study, evaluating a program all the way through to ROI, and then use the information from that study to make improvements and communicate the results to the top executives. To her surprise, almost 30 individuals volunteered. Showing her full support, she participated in the certification at every step in the process, constantly reinforcing what the executives wanted from the learning team, providing examples, and offering encouragement. As a tribute to her, all who volunteered for the certification eventually became CRPs.

After the certification program, she continued to support the team by providing assistance and rewarding them for achieving this designation. The image and influence of the learning and talent development team increased. Based on the success of their programs, Garanti Bank won an award from ATD, the largest organization of learning and talent development professionals in the world.

She followed up with a second group, two years later, and again, all volunteered to be involved in the process. As part of the introduction to the second group, she said, "You have volunteered for this program, and we want you to be successful with it. Being successful means you have to become a CRP. Doing nothing with what you have learned is not an option. You must follow through and complete this assignment. If you accomplish this, we will properly recognize and reward you for your good efforts."

Perhaps no group is more important to the results-based process than the management team, who must allocate resources for learning and talent development programs and then support them. In addition, the management team often provides input into and assistance for the results-based process. Preparing, training, and developing the management team should be carefully planned and executed.

Conducting a briefing is one effective approach to prepare executives and managers for the process. Varying in duration from one hour to half a day, this type of practical briefing can provide critical information and enhance support for the results-based process. Managers leave these briefings with greater appreciation of ROI and its potential impact on programs as well as a clearer understanding of their role in the process. More importantly, they often renew their commitment to react to and use the data collected in the results-based process.

A strong, dynamic relationship between the learning and talent development team and key managers is essential for successful implementation. There must be a productive partnership that requires each party to understand the concerns, problems, and opportunities of the other. Developing a beneficial relationship is a long-term process that must be deliberately planned for and initiated by key employee program team members. The decision to commit resources and support a solution may be based on the effectiveness of this relationship.

Remove Obstacles

As this process is implemented, obstacles to its progress will inevitably crop up. The obstacles are based on concerns discussed in this chapter, some of which may be valid, but others of which may be based on unrealistic fears or misunderstandings.

Dispelling Myths

As part of the implementation, attempts should be made to dispel the myths and remove or minimize the barriers or obstacles. Much of the controversy regarding impact, ROI, and additional accountability comes from misunderstandings about what the process can and cannot do and how it can or should be implemented in an organization. Some of the biggest misunderstandings include:

- This is too complex for most users.
- This is expensive and consumes too many critical resources.
- If senior management does not require impact and ROI, there is no need to pursue it.
- This is a passing fad.
- ROI is only one type of data.
- Impact and ROI analysis is not future-oriented; it only reflects past performance.

- ROI is rarely used by organizations.
- The impact and ROI analysis cannot be easily replicated.
- Impact and ROI analysis is not a credible process; it is too subjective.
- Impact and ROI cannot be used with soft programs.
- Isolating the influence of other factors is not always possible.
- This is only appropriate for large organizations.
- No standards exist for the ROI Methodology.

These are all myths. A variety of learning initiatives and reinforcement processes are needed with the team to dispel these myths and misunderstandings. Appendix B presents a brief quiz on many of these issues. The answers are in Appendix C.

Delivering Bad News

Receiving inadequate, insufficient, or disappointing news is one of the most difficult obstacles for a team to overcome. The time to think about bad news is early in the process, but this must be done without losing sight of its value. You should look for red flags along the way and make adjustments if possible. You should lower expectations with key stakeholders throughout the process. In essence, bad news means that things can change, they need to change, and the situation can improve. The team simply needs to be convinced that good news can be found in a bad-news situation. Here is some advice to follow when delivering bad news:

- Never fail to recognize the power to learn and improve with a negative study.
- Never alter the standards.
- Remain objective throughout the process.
- Prepare the team for the bad news.
- Consider different scenarios.
- Find out what went wrong.
- Adjust the story line to: "Now we have data that show how to make this program more successful." In an odd way, this puts a positive spin on data that are less than positive.

Using the Data

It is unfortunately too often the case that programs are evaluated and significant data are collected, but no action is taken. Failure to use data is a

Use of Evaluation Data	Appropriate Level of Data				
	1	2	3	4	5
Adjust program design.	✓	✓	✓		
Improve implementation.	✓	✓	✓	✓	
Influence application and program impact.			✓	✓	
Improve management support for the program.			✓	✓	
Improve stakeholder satisfaction.			✓	✓	✓
Recognize and reward participants.		✓	✓	✓	
Justify or enhance budget.				✓	✓
Reduce costs.		✓	✓	✓	✓
Market programs in the future.	✓		✓	✓	✓
Optimize ROI.				✓	✓

Figure 17.6 Use of Evaluation Data.

tremendous obstacle because the team has a tendency to move on to the next program or issue and focus on other priorities. Figure 17.6 shows how the different levels of data can be used to improve programs. It is critical that the data be used—the data were essentially the justification for undertaking the evaluation in the first place. Failure to use the data may mean that the entire evaluation was a waste.

There are many reasons for using the results after collection. These will become actions items for the team to ensure that changes and adjustments are made. In addition, the client or sponsor must act to ensure that the uses of data are appropriately addressed.

Monitor Progress

A final element of the implementation process is monitoring the overall progress made and communicating that progress. Although often overlooked, an effective communication plan can help keep the implementation on target and let others know what the process is accomplishing.

The initial schedule for implementation is based on key events or milestones. Routine progress reports should be developed to communicate the status of these events or milestones. Reports are usually developed at six-month intervals, but they may be more frequent for short-term programs. Two target audiences, the learning and talent development team and the senior managers, are critical for progress reporting. All team members should be kept informed of progress, and senior managers should know the extent to which the results-based process is being implemented and how it is working within the organization.

Final Thoughts

Even the best model or process will fail if it is not used and sustained. This final chapter explores the implementation of the results-based process. If not approached in a systematic, logical, and planned way, the process will not be an integral part of program implementation, and accountability will suffer, support will diminish, and funding may be reduced. This chapter presents the different building blocks that must be considered and issues that must be addressed to ensure that implementation is smooth and uneventful, and sustained. Smooth implementation is the most effective means of overcoming resistance to designing, delivering, and measuring business results. The outcome is a complete integration of business results as a mainstream component of major programs.

> *"The test of a first-rate intelligence is the ability to hold two opposed ideas in the mind at the same time, and still retain the ability to function. One should, for example, be able to see that things are hopeless and yet be determined to make them otherwise." – F. Scott Fitzgerald*

This book outlines the relevant steps necessary to deliver results, optimize the ROI, and use the results to influence the budget in the future. The focus is shifted from value capture to value creation. If done properly, it will transform your programs from a nice-to-have (and necessary) function to a business-driving process. It is possible and worth it! Good luck.

> *"Change is inevitable. Progress is optional." – Gary Marx*

References

Preface

1. TechWrite, Inc. "Dr. John H. White, TechWrite President." http://www.tech-writeinc.com/jhwhiteDT.htm

Chapter 1

1. GBHEM.org. "Communicating Organizational Relevance through an ROI Methodology." July 28, 2017.
2. D. Nickson and S. Siddons. *Project Disasters and How to Survive Them*. London, UK: Kogan Page. 2005.
3. W. Bogdanich and M. Forsyth. "How McKinsey Lost Its Way in South Africa". New York Times. June 26, 2018. https://www.nytimes.com/2018/06/26/world/africa/mckinsey-south-africa-eskom.html.
4. T. Jackson. *Prosperity Without Growth: Foundations for the Economy of Tomorrow*, 2nd edition. New York, NY: Routledge. 2017.
5. About FedEx. Corporation Fact Sheet. 2017. http://about.van.fedex.com/our-story/company-structure/corporate-fact-sheet/
6. G. Colvin. "The FedEx Edge." *Fortune*. April 3, 2006. 49.

7. J. Saul. *The End of Fundraising: Raise More Money by Selling Your Impact.* San Francisco, CA: Jossey-Bass. 2011.
8. B. Gates and M. Gates. "Dear Warren: Our 2017 Annual Letter." February 14, 2017. https://www.gatesnotes.com/2017-Annual-Letter?WT.mc_id=02_14_2017_02AL2017GFO_GF-GFO_&WT.tsrc=GFGFO
9. H. Van der Berg. *International Economics: A Heterodox Approach,* 3rd edition. New York, NY: Routledge. 2017.
10. Project Management Institute. "About Us." https://www.pmi.org/about
11. J. Pfeffer and R.I. Sutton. *Hard Facts, Dangerous Half-Truths and Total Nonsense: Profiting from Evidence-Based Management.* Boston, MA: Harvard Business School. 2006.
12. J.M. Jones. "Congressional Job Approval Ties Historic Low of 13%." Gallup. August 16, 2011. http://news.gallup.com/poll/149009/congressional-job-approval-ties-historic-low.aspx
13. D. Pallotta. *Charity Case: How the Nonprofit Community Can Stand Up for Itself and Really Change the World.* San Francisco, CA: Jossey-Bass. 2012.
14. D. Pallotta. *Charity Case: How the Nonprofit Community Can Stand Up for Itself and Really Change the World.* San Francisco, CA: Jossey-Bass. 2012.
15. J. Pfeffer and R.I. Sutton. *Hard Facts, Dangerous Half-Truths and Total Nonsense: Profiting from Evidence-Based Management.* Boston, MA: Harvard Business School. 2006.

Chapter 2

1. This is an actual case. The name of the individual and the location has been disguised at the request of the parties involved. For more information on this case, please contact ROI Institute.
2. J. Saul. *The End of Fundraising: Raise More Money by Selling Your Impact.* San Francisco, CA: Jossey – Bass. 2011.
3. J.J. Phillips and P.P. Phillips. *Handbook of Training Evaluation and Measurement Methods,* 4th edition. London, UK: Routledge. 2016.
4. K. Miller. *We Don't Make Widgets: Overcoming the Myths That Keep Government from Radically Improving.* Washington, DC: Governing Books. 2006.

Chapter 3

1. C.R. Covey. *The 7 Habits of Highly Effective People: Restoring the Character Ethic.* New York, NY: Simon & Schuster. 1989.
2. S.R. Covey, S. Covey, M. Summers, and D.K. Hatch. *The Leader in Me: How Schools Around the World Are Inspiring Greatness, One Child at a Time.* New York, NY: Simon & Schuster. 2014.

3. Wikipedia. "Logic model." https://en.wikipedia.org/wiki/Logic_model

4. L.W. Knowlton and C.C. Phillips. *The Logic Model Guidebook: Better Strategies for Great Results*. Thousand Oaks, CA: SAGE Publications. 2013.

5. L.W. Knowlton and C.C. Phillips. *The Logic Model Guidebook: Better Strategies for Great Results*. Thousand Oaks, CA: SAGE Publications. 2013.

6. D.L. Stufflebeam and G. Zhang. *The CIPP Evaluation Model: How to Evaluate for Improvement and Accountability*. New York, NY: The Guilford Press. 2017.

7. D.L. Stufflebeam. "Stufflebeam's improvement-oriented evaluation." In D.L. Stufflebeam and A.J. Shinkfield, *Systematic Evaluation*. Norwell, MA: Kluwer. 1985. 151 – 207.

8. D.T. Campbell and J.C. Stanley. "Experimental and quasi-experimental designs for research on teaching." In N.L. Gage (Ed.), *Handbook of Research on Teaching*. Chicago, IL: Rand McNally. 1963. 171 – 246.

9. E.R. House and K.R. Howe. "Deliberative democratic evaluation." In K.E. Ryan and L. DeStefano (Eds.), *Evaluation as a Democratic Process: Promoting Inclusion, Dialogue, and Deliberation* (New Directions for Evaluation, no. 85). San Francisco, CA: Jossey-Bass. 2000. 3 – 12.

10. M.N. Provus. *Discrepancy Evaluation Model*. Pittsburgh, PA: Pittsburgh Public Schools. 1969.

11. E.W. Eisner. "Educational connoisseurship and criticism: Their form and functions in educational evaluation." In G.F. Madaus, M. Scriven, and D.L. Stufflebeam (Eds.), *Evaluation Models: Viewpoints on Educational and Human Services Evaluation*. Norwell, MA: Kluwer. 1983. 335 – 348.

12. R.L. Hammond. *Evaluation at the Local Level*. Tucson, AZ: EPIC Evaluation Center. 1972.

13. M.S. Scriven. "Goal-free evaluation." In E.R. House (Ed.), *School Evaluation: The Politics and Process*. Berkeley, CA: McCutchan. 1973. 319 – 328.

14. E.G. Guba. *Toward a Methodology of Naturalistic Inquiry in Educational Evaluation*. Los Angeles, CA: University of California, Center for the Study of Evaluation. 1978.

15. R.E. Stake. "A theoretical statement of responsive evaluation." *Studies in Educational Evaluation, 2*. 1976. 19 – 22.

16. R.O. Brinkerhoff. *The Success Case Method: Find Out Quickly What's Working and What's Not*. San Francisco, CA: Barrett-Koehler. 2003.

17. M.Q. Patton. *Utilization-Focused Evaluation*, 4th ed. Thousand Oaks, CA: SAGE Publications. 2008.

Chapter 4

1. H. Wolfson. "Program Reduces Blood Infections in Alabama Hospitals." *The Birmingham News*. October 25, 2011.

2. T. Brown. *Change By Design: How Design Thinking Transforms Organizations and Inspires Innovation*. New York, NY: Harper Business. 2009.

3. I. Mootee. *Design Thinking for Strategic Innovation: What They Can't Teach You at Business or Design School.* Hoboken, NJ: Wiley. 2013.
4. P.P. Phillips and J.J. Phillips. *Business Case For Learning: Using Design Thinking to Deliver Business Results and Increase the Investment in Talent Development.* Alexandria, VA: HRDQ and ATD. 2017.
5. J.J. Phillips and P.P. Phillips. *Show Me the Money: How to Determine ROI in People, Projects, and Programs.* San Francisco, CA: Berrett-Koehler. 2007.

Chapter 5

1. "Bloomberg Businessweek Names Harvard #1 U.S. Business School in 2017 MBA Ranking." Bloomberg. November 16, 2017. https://www.bloombergmedia.com/press/bloomberg-businessweek-2017-best-business-schools/
2. M. Korn. "College Funding with A Catch." *Wall Street Journal.* March 13, 2017.
3. "Georgia State University." *U.S. News & World Report.* 2018. https://www.usnews.com/best-colleges/georgia-state-1574
4. E. Shapiro. *Fad Surfing in the Boardroom: Managing in the Age of Instant Answers.* Cambridge, MA: Perseus Book Group. 1996.
5. S. Calvert. "Police Overtime Is Getting a Closer Look." *Wall Street Journal.* March 13, 2017. A3.
6. J.J. Phillips and P.P. Phillips. *The Consultant's Guide to Results-Driven Business Proposals: How to Write Proposals That Forecast Impact and ROI.* New York, NY: McGraw-Hill. 2010.

Chapter 6

1. D. McSwain. "Street Population Soars After SD Ups Homeless Spending." *San Diego Union-Tribune.* October 25, 2016. A-14.
2. A. Parker. "Stakeholders Must Collaborate." *San Diego Union-Tribune.* October 22, 2017. B-8, B-10.
3. D.G. Robinson, J.C. Robinson, J.J. Phillips, P.P. Phillips, and D. Handshaw. *Performance Consulting: A Strategic Process to Improve, Measure, and Sustain Organizational Results,* 3rd ed. San Francisco, CA: Berrett-Koehler. 2015.
4. W. Rothwell, C.K. Hohne, and S.B. King. *Human Performance Improvement,* 2nd ed. New York, NY: Routledge, 2017.

Chapter 7

1. P.P. Phillips and J.J. Phillips. *Value for Money: Measuring the Return on Non-Capital Investments (Chapter 13: Measuring ROI in Business Coaching, Nations Hotel).* Birmingham, AL: ROI Institute, Inc. 2018.

2. P.P. Phillips and J.J. Phillips. *The Business Case for Learning: Using Design Thinking to Deliver Business Results and Increase the Investment in Talent Development*. Alexandria, VA: ATD and HRDQ. 2017.
3. J.J. Phillips and P.P. Phillips. *Beyond Learning Objectives: Develop Measurable Objectives That Link to the Bottom Line*. Alexandria, VA: ATD. 2008.
4. R.F. Mager. *Preparing Instructional Objectives*. Belmont, CA: Fearon Publishers. 1962.
5. B.S. Bloom. *Taxonomy of Educational Objectives*. New York, NY: David McKay Co, Inc. 1956.
6. P.P. Phillips and J.J. Phillips. *Value for Money: Measuring the Return on Non-Capital Investments (Chapter 10: Measuring ROI in an Absenteeism Reduction Program, Metro Transit Authority)*. Birmingham, AL: ROI Institute, Inc. 2018.
7. J.J. Phillips, W. Brantley, and P.P. Phillips. *Project Management ROI: A Step-by-Step Guide for Measuring the Impact and ROI for Projects*. Hoboken, NJ: Wiley. 2011.

Chapter 8

1. S. Mautz. *Make it Matter: How Managers Can Motivate by Creating Meaning*. New York, NY: AMACOM. 2015.
2. P.P. Phillips and J.J. Phillips. *Value for Money: Measuring the Return on Non-Capital Investments*. Birmingham, AL: ROI Institute, Inc. 2018.
3. M.W. Allen. *Michael Allen's Guide to e-Learning: Building Interactive, Fun, and Effective Learning Programs for Any Company*, 2nd edition. Hoboken, NJ: Wiley. 2016.
4. Gram Vikas. http://www.gramvikas.org/
5. C. Seelos and J. Mair, *Innovation and Scaling for Impact: How Effective Social Enterprises Do It*. Stanford, CA: Stanford Business Books. 2017.
6. P.P. Phillips and J.J. Phillips. *Value for Money: Measuring the Return on Non-Capital Investments*. BWE Press, Birmingham, AL: ROI Institute, Inc. 2018.
7. P.P. Phillips, J.J. Phillips, and B.C. Aaron. *Survey Basics*. Alexandria, VA: ASTD Press. 2013.
8. J.J. Phillips and P.P. Phillips. *Handbook of Training Evaluation and Measurement Methods*, 4th edition. London, UK: Routledge. 2016.
9. P.P. Phillips and J.J. Phillips. *Value for Money: Measuring the Return on Non-Capital Investments (Chapter 9: Measuring ROI in a Masters Degree Program, Federal Information Agency)*. Birmingham, AL: ROI Institute, Inc. 2018.

Chapter 9

1. J. Walker, "Wearable maker Jawbone insolvent, two years after $3bn valuation." *Technology*. July 7, 2017. http://www.digitaljournal.com/tech-and-science/

technology/once-innovative-wearable-brand-jawbone-goes-into-liquidation/article/497066#ixzz5CHhMWycX

2. L. Entis. "What Comes Next For Fitness Trackers?" *Fortune*. July 24, 2017. http://fortune.com/2017/07/24/fitness-trackers-wont-make-you-fit-can-they-make-you-well/

3. J.M. Jakicic, K.K. Davis, and R.J. Rogers. "Effect of Wearable Technology Combined With a Lifestyle Intervention on Long-Term Weight Loss." *JAMA*. 2016.

4. P.P. Phillips, J.J. Phillips, and B.C. Aaron. *Survey Basics*. Alexandria, VA: ASTD Press. 2013.

5. S.R. Covey. *The 7 Habits of Highly Effective People: Restoring the Character Ethic*. New York, NY: Simon & Schuster. 1989.

6. W. Bowen. *A Complaint Free World: How to Stop Complaining and Start Enjoying the Life You Always Wanted*. New York, NY: Harmony. 2013.

7. L. Freifeld, ed. "Top 10 Hall of Fame Outstanding Training Initiatives." *Training Magazine*. September/October 2016.

8. E. Weber, P.P. Phillips, and J.J. Phillips. *Making Change Work: How to Create Behavioural Change in Organizations to Drive Impact and ROI*. London: Kogan Page. 2016.

9. P.P. Phillips and J.J. Phillips. *Value for Money: Measuring the Return on Non-Capital Investments (Measuring ROI in a Career Development Initiative: A Global Computer Company, by H. Burkett)*. Birmingham, AL: ROI Institute, Inc. 2018.

Chapter 10

1. S.D. Levitt and S.J. Dubner. *Freakonomics: A Rogue Economist Explores the Hidden Side of Everything*. New York, NY: William Morrow. 2005.

2. P.P. Phillips, J.J. Phillips, and R. Ray. *Measuring the Success of Employee Engagement*. Alexandria, VA: ATD Press. 2016.

3. T.L. Strome. *Healthcare Analytics for Quality and Performance Improvement*. Hoboken, NJ: Wiley. 2013.

4. J. Surowieki. *The Wisdom of Crowds: Why the Many Are Smarter Than the Few and How Collective Wisdom Shapes Businesses, Economics, Societies and Nations*. New York, NY: Doubleday. 2004.

Chapter 11

1. M.C. O'Guin. *The Complete Guide to Activity-Based Costing*. Upper Saddle River, NJ: Prentic Hall. 1991.

2. A. Parker. "Stakeholders Must Collaborate." *San Diego Union-Tribune*. October 22, 2017. B-8, B-10.

3. Best College Values. "What is the Value of a College Degree?" 2018. http://www.bestcollegevalues.org/what-is-the-value-of-a-college-degree/.
4. P.W. Farris, N.T. Bendle, P.E. Pfiefer, and D.J. Ribstein. *Marketing Metrics: 50+ Metrics Every Executive Should Master.* Upper Saddle River, NJ: Wharton School Publishing. 2006.
5. Adapted from *Marketing Metrics: 50+ Metrics Every Executive Should Master* by Paul W. Farris, Neil T. Bendle, Phillip E. Pfeifer, and David J. Ribstein, Upper Saddle River, NJ: Wharton School Publishing, 2006, p. 46–47.
6. J. Campanella, ed. *Principles of Quality Costs*, 3rd edition. Milwaukee, WI: American Society for Quality. 1999.
7. Watch Blog: Following the Federal Dollar. U.S. Government Accountability Office. "How Much Does Crime Cost?" November 29, 2017. https://blog.gao.gov/2017/11/29/how-much-does-crime-cost/.
8. Cost of Crime Calculator. RAND Corporation. https://www.rand.org/jie/justice-policy/centers/quality-policing/cost-of-crime.html.
9. P.P. Phillips and J.J. Phillips. *Value for Money: Measuring the Return on Non-Capital Investments (Chapter 10: Measuring ROI in an Absenteeism Reduction Program, Metro Transit Authority).* Birmingham, AL: ROI Institute, Inc. 2018.
10. President and Fellows of Harvard College. *Relationship Between Attitudes and Profits.* 1998.
11. C.T. Coco. "From Employed…To Engaged." *T+D Magazine.* November 2009. 40 – 43.
12. P.P. Phillips and J.J. Phillips. *Value for Money: Measuring the Return on Non-Capital Investments (Chapter 8: Measuring ROI in Engagement Linked to Retention Improvement, Southeast Corridor Bank).* Birmingham, AL: ROI Institute, Inc. 2018.
13. P.P. Phillips and J.J. Phillips. *Value for Money: Measuring the Return on Non-Capital Investments (Chapter 21: Measuring ROI in a Blended Learning Solution for Engagement, PolyWrighton).* Birmingham, AL: ROI Institute, Inc. 2018.
14. P.P. Phillips and J.J. Phillips. *Value for Money: Measuring the Return on Non-Capital Investments (Chapter 1: Measuring ROI in Sexual Harassment Prevention, Healthcare).* Birmingham, AL: ROI Institute, Inc. 2018.
15. J. Massey and J. Harrison. *Evaluating Human Capital Projects: Improve, Prove, Predict.* London, UK: Routledge. 2014.

Chapter 12

1. M. Heffernan. *Beyond Measure: The Big Impact of Small Changes.* New York, NY: TED Books, Simon & Schuster. 2015.
2. R.E.S. Boulton, B.D. Libert, and S.M. Samek. *Cracking the Value Code.* New York, NY: Harper Business. 2000.
3. K. T. Jackson. *Building Reputational Capital: Strategies for Integrity and Fair Play That Improve the Bottom Line.* Oxford, UK: Oxford University Press. 2004.

4. M.C. Worline and J.E. Dutton. *Awakening Compassion at Work: The Quiet Power That Elevates People and Organizations*. San Francisco, CA: Berrett-Koehler. 2017.

5. P.P. Phillips and J.J. Phillips. *Value for Money: Measuring the Return on Non-Capital Investments*. Birmingham, AL: BWE Press. 2018.

6. D. Tracy and W.J. Morin. *Truth, Trust, and the Bottom Line: 7 Steps to Trust-Based Management*. Chicago, IL: Dearborn Trade. 2001.

7. The Federal Reserve. www.FederalReserve.Gov

8. J. Alden. "Measuring the 'Unmeasurable.'" *Performance Improvement*. May/June 2006. 7.

9. *Fortune*. 100 Best Companies to Work For. 2018. http://fortune.com/best-companies/.

10. T. Bradberry and J. Greaves. *Emotional Intelligence 2.0*. San Diego, CA: TalentSmart. 2009.

11. P.P. Phillips, J.J. Phillips, and R. Ray. *Measuring the Success of Employee Engagement*. Alexandria, VA: ATD Press. 2016.

12. J. Collins. *Good to Great and the Social Sectors*. New York, NY: Harper Collins, 2005.

13. D. Shimer. "Yale's Most Popular Class Ever: Happiness." *The New York Times*. January 26, 2018. https://www.nytimes.com/2018/01/26/nyregion/at-yale-class-on-happiness-draws-huge-crowd-laurie-santos.html

14. World Happiness Report 2017. http://worldhappiness.report/

Chapter 13

1. K. Kennedy. "Fight Against Health Care Fraud Recovers $4.1B." *USA Today*. February 14, 2012. 4A. https://usatoday30.usatoday.com/news/washington/story/2012-02-14/sebelius-holder-announce-health-care-fraud-money/53097474/1

2. J. Massey and J. Harrison. *Evaluating Human Capital Projects: Improve, Prove, Predict*. London, UK: Routledge. 2014.

3. "2017 Employee Benefits: Remaining Competitive in a Challenging Talent Marketplace." *SHRM*. June 2017.

4. P.P. Phillips and J.J. Phillips. *Value for Money: Measuring the Return on Non-Capital Investments (Chapter 9: Measuring ROI in a Masters Degree Program, Federal Information Agency)*. Birmingham, AL: ROI Institute, Inc. 2018. – Although we have permission to use the real name of this organization, we prefer to keep the name private in print because of the nature and sensitivity of the organization. We would be happy to reveal the name in a conversation and discuss the case in detail.

5. H. Strombaugh. "How to Prove Your Nonprofit's Impact with SROI." *The Balance*. December 27, 2017. https://www.thebalance.com/using-sroi-to-show-your-nonprofit-s-impact-2501977

6. P.P. Phillips and J.J. Phillips. *Proving the Value of HR: ROI Case Studies.* Alexandria, VA: SHRM. 2010.

Chapter 14

1. T. Davenport and. E. Siegel. *Predictive Analytics: The Power to Predict Who Will Click, Buy, Lie, or Die.* Hoboken, NJ: Wiley. 2013.
2. H. Evans. *Do I Make Myself Clear? Why Writing Well Matters.* New York, NY: Little, Brown and Company. 2017.
3. P.P. Phillips and J.J. Phillips. *Value for Money: Measuring the Return on Non-Capital Investments (Chapter 3: Measuring ROI in Stress Management, Midwest Electric, Inc.).* Birmingham, AL: ROI Institute, Inc. 2018.
4. W. Thornton. "Workforce programs help rehabilitated felons." *The Birmingham News.* July 19, 2017.
5. Based on conservative assumptions and outcomes and valuations, a representative program returns benefits of $2.72 for every dollar of resources used (dollars spent plus volunteer time). A program returns $1.87 of public benefits (public cost savings and increased tax revenues) for every dollar spent on the program. *Reference: P.A. Anton (Wilder Research) and Prof. J. Temple (University of Minnesota). *Social Return on Investment in Youth Mentoring Programs.* 2007.
6. D. Price. *Well Said! Presentations and Conversations that Get Results.* New York, NY: AMACOM. 2012.
7. P. Block. *Flawless Consulting,* 3rd edition. San Diego, CA: Pfeiffer. 2011.
8. I. Mootee. *Design Thinking for Strategic Innovation: What They Can't Teach You at Business or Design School.* Hoboken, NJ: Jon Wiley. 2013.
9. P. Smith. *Lead with a Story: A Guide to Crafting Business Narratives That Captivate, Convince, and Inspire.* New York, NY: AMACOM. 2012. Used with permission.
10. C. Gallo. *The Storyteller's Secret: From TED Speakers to Business Legends, Why Some Ideas Catch On and Others Don't.* New York, NY: St. Martin's Press. 2016.
11. P. Smith. *Lead with a Story: A Guide to Crafting Business Narratives That Captivate, Convince, and Inspire.* New York, NY: AMACOM. 2012. Used with permission.

Chapter 15

1. This study was conducted by ROI Institute, Inc. For a copy of this study, please contact info@roiinstitute.net.
2. M. Syed. *Black Box Thinking: Why Most People Never Learn from Their Mistakes—But Some Do.* New York, NY: Portfolio. 2015.
3. IATA. http://www.iata.org/publications/Documents/iata-safety-report-2013.pdf

4. IATA. http://www.iata.rg/pressroom/pr/Pages?2015-03-09-01.aspx

5. Members of the IATA. http://www.iata.org/pressroom/facts_figures/facts_sheets/Documents/safety-fact-sheet.pdf

6. D. Shepardson. "2017 Safest Year on Record for Commercial Passenger Air Travel: Groups." *Reuters.* January 1, 2018. https://www.reuters.com/article/us-aviation-safety/2017-safest-year-on-record-for-commercial-passenger-air-travel-groups-idUSKBN1EQ17L

7. The Institute of Medicine. "To Err Is Human," https://www.iom.edu/~/media/Files/Report%20Files/1999/To-Err-is-Human/To%20Err%20is%20Human%201999%20 %20report%20brief.pdf

8. P.I. Buerhaus. "Lucian Leape on the Causes and Prevention of Errors and Adverse Events in Health Care." *Journal of Nursing Scholarship.* June 2007.

9. J.T. James. *A New, Evidence-based Estimate of Patient Harms Associated with Hospital Care.* http://journals.lww.com/journalpatientsafety/Fulltext/2013/09000/A_New_Evi-dence_based_Estimate_of_Patient_Harms.2.aspx

10. C-SPAN. http://www.c-span.org/video/?320495-1/hearing-patient-safety

11. J. Graedon and T. Graedon. *Top Screwups Doctors Make and How to Avoid Them.* New York, NY: Harmony. 2012.

12. M. Syed. *Black Box Thinking: Why Most People Never Learn from Their Mistakes—But Some Do.* New York, NY: Portfolio. 2015.

13. P.P. Phillips and J.J. Phillips. *The Business Case for Learning: Using Design Thinking to Deliver Business Results and Increase the Investment in Talent Development.* Alexandria, VA: ATD and HRDQ. 2017.

14. S. Dekker. Lecture in Brisbane: https://vimeo.com/102167635

15. ATD. *Certification Institute.* https://www.td.org/certification.

16. P.P. Phillips and J.J. Phillips. *Value for Money: Measuring the Return on Non-Capital Investments (Chapter 6: Measuring ROI in Performance Management Training, Cracker Box, Inc.).* Birmingham, AL: ROI Institute, Inc. 2018.

17. S. Daneshkhu, L. Whipp, and J. Fontanella-Khan. "The Lean and Mean Approach of 3G Capital." *Financial Times.* May 7, 2017.

18. P. Cappelli. "Why We Love to Hate HR...and What HR Can Do About It." *Harvard Business Review.* July-August 2015.

19. J.J. Phillips and P.P. Phillips. *The Consultant's Guide to Results-Driven Business Proposals: How to Write Proposals That Forecast Impact and ROI.* New York, NY: McGraw-Hill. 2010.

Chapter 16

1. P.P. Phillips and J.J. Phillips. *Value for Money: Measuring the Return on Non-Capital Investments (Chapter 20: Measuring ROI in a Work-at-Home Program, Family Mutual Health and Life Insurance Company (FMI)).* Birmingham, AL: ROI Institute, Inc. 2018. The name of the organization and individuals have been disguised at the request of the organization.

2. J. Milan Jr. "Ending HIV/AIDS in the South Is Key for Ending It Everywhere." *MediaPlanet*. December 2017.

3. P.P. Phillips and J.J. Phillips. *Value for Money: Measuring the Return on Non-Capital Investments (Chapter 9: Measuring ROI in a Masters Degree Program, Federal Information Agency)*. Birmingham, AL: ROI Institute, Inc. 2018.

4. S.A. Shrock and W.C. Coscarelli. *Criterion – Reference Test Development: Technical and Legal Guidelines for Corporate Training*. Hoboken, NJ: Wiley. 2008.

5. J.J. Phillips and P.P. Phillips. *Handbook of Training Evaluation and Measurement Methods*, 4th edition. London, UK: Routledge. 2016.

6. J.J. Phillips and P.P. Phillips. *The Consultant's Guide to Results-Driven Business Proposals*. New York, NY: McGraw Hill. 2010.

7. P.E. Tetlock and D. Gerdner. *Superforecasting: The Art and Science of Prediction*. New York, NY: Crown Publishers. 2016.

8. S.J. Armstrong. *Principles of Forecasting: A Handbook for Researchers and Practitioners*. Boston, MA: Kluwer Academic Publishers. 2001.

9. P.P. Phillips and J.J. Phillips. *Value for Money: Measuring the Return on Non-Capital Investments (Chapter 10: Measuring ROI in Safety Leadership, Global Engineering and Construction Company)*. Birmingham, AL: ROI Institute, Inc. 2018.

10. L.S. Maisel and G. Cokins. *Predictive Business Analytics: Forward-Looking Capabilities to Improve Business Performance*. Hoboken, NJ: Wiley. 2014

11. D.A. Bowers. *Forecasting for Control and Profit*. Menlo Park, CA: Crisp Publications. 1997.

Chapter 17

1. ROI Institute. www.roiinstitute.net.

Appendix A

How Results-Based Are Your Projects and Programs?

Instructions: For each of the following statements, please circle the response that best matches the extent to which programs at your organization deliver business results. Select only one choice. Please be candid with your responses. All organizations deliver business results. These are impact measures of output (students graduated, jobs secured), quality (AIDS infections, homicides), time (prison time, response time), and costs (healthcare costs, disability payments).

1. The direction of our programs:
   a. Shifts with requests, problems, and changes as they occur.
   b. Is determined by top executives and leaders and adjusted as needed.
   c. Is based on a mission and a strategic plan for the organization or the community.

2. The primary rationale for our programs is:
   a. To respond to requests by managers and community leaders to deliver programs and services.
   b. To help management and community leaders react to crisis situations and reach solutions through programs and services.
   c. To implement many programs in collaboration with clients and leaders to prevent problems and crisis situations.

3. The goals of our programs are:
   a. Set by the program teams based on perceived demand for programs.
   b. Developed consistent with the organization's plans and goals.
   c. Developed to integrate with operating goals and strategic plans of the organization or the community.

4. Most new programs are initiated:
   a. By request of top leaders and administrators.
   b. When a program appears to be successful in another organization.
   c. After a needs assessment has indicated that the program is needed.

5. The proper solution, driven by our program is:
   a. Obvious.
   b. Part of the request for the program.
   c. Derived from a performance analysis.

6. To define learning plans to support programs:
   a. Program teams are asked to choose learning from a list of existing courses.
   b. Participants are asked about their learning needs.
   c. Needs are systematically derived from a thorough analysis of performance problems.

7. The responsibility for results from programs:
   a. Rests primarily with the program team.
   b. Is a responsibility of the learning staff and designers, developers, and facilitators who jointly ensure that results are obtained.
   c. Is a shared responsibility of the program team, participants, designers, facilitators, managers, and significant others with all working together to ensure business success.

8. Objectives for each program are set at
   a. The reaction and learning levels, to create expected reactions and learning to make the program successful.
   b. The application level to define what participants must do to make the program successful.
   c. The reaction, learning, application, and impact levels.

9. Systematic, objective evaluation, designed to ensure that participants are successful:
   a. Is never accomplished; the only evaluations are during the program, and they focus on how much the participants enjoyed the program.
   b. Is occasionally accomplished; participants are asked if the learning was effective on the job.
   c. Is frequently and systematically pursued; implementation is evaluated after learning is completed.

10. New programs are designed and developed:
   a. Internally; a staff of designers and specialists is used.
   b. By suppliers; we usually purchase programs modified to meet the our needs.
   c. By using internal staff and suppliers; this is accomplished in the most economical and practical way to meet deadlines and cost objectives.

11. Costs for our program are accumulated:
   a. On a total aggregate basis only.
   b. On a program-by-program basis.
   c. By specific process components such as design, development, and delivery, in addition to a specific program.

12. Steps are taken to improve programs:
    a. Occasionally.
    b. When a problem is identified.
    c. Routinely at each step in the process.

13. To ensure that the program is properly implemented, we:
    a. Encourage participants to apply what they have learned and report results.
    b. Ask managers and significant others to support and reinforce and report results.
    c. Utilize a variety of strategies appropriate for each situation.

14. The program team's interaction with operating and field management is:
    a. Rare; issues are almost never discussed with them.
    b. Occasional; issues are discussed during activities such as needs analysis or program coordination.
    c. Regular; communication is used to build relationships as well as to develop and deliver programs.

15. A method to show the attribution of major programs on impact measures:
    a. Is never pursued.
    b. Is sometimes discussed and implemented.
    c. Is always implemented.

16. Most clients or funders view your programs as:
    a. Questionable - they waste too much time.
    b. Necessary activities that probably cannot be eliminated.
    c. Important resources that can improve organizations, communities, and individuals.

17. Programs are:
    a. Activity-oriented (all parents attend the "Stress Reduction for New Parents Workshop").
    b. Individual–results based (the participant will stop smoking).
    c. Organizational and community–results based (the youth unemployment rate will decrease by 25 percent).

18. The return on investment in our programs is measured primarily by:
    a. Subjective opinions.
    b. Observations by management and reactions from participants.
    c. Tracking productivity, cost savings, quality, or time measures.

19. New programs are implemented at my organization without some formal method of evaluation:
    a. Regularly
    b. Seldom
    c. Never

20. Programs are initiated when a very specific:
    a. Awareness need is identified
    b. Behavioral need is identified
    c. Business need is identified

21. The results of programs are communicated:
    a. When requested; to those who have a need to know.
    b. Occasionally; to members of management only.
    c. Routinely; to a variety of selected target audiences.

22. Management (or significant other) involvement in program evaluation:
    a. Is minor; no specific responsibilities and few requests.
    b. Is moderate; consists of informal responsibilities for evaluation, with some non-routine requests.
    c. Is very specific; all managers and significant others have some responsibilities in evaluation.

23. The results of our programs are used to:
    a. Validate the need of the program.
    b. Reward those who made it successful.
    c. To secure more funds for programs in the future.

24. During a business decline at me organization or in our community, our programs will:
    a. Be the first to have its staff reduced.
    b. Be retained at the same staffing level.
    c. Go untouched in staff reductions, and possibly be beefed up.

25. We provide funders (or donors) with:
    a. Participation data to show who is involved.
    b. Data about success with program completion.
    c. Impact data defining the specific contribution of the program.

26. Budgeting for our programs is based on:
    a. Last year's budget.
    b. Whatever the manager can "sell."
    c. A zero-based system built around need and feasibility of proposed programs.

27. The principal group that ultimately approves program expenditures is:
    a. The program leader.
    b. A top executive.
    c. The funders or donors.

28. Over the last two years, the budget for our program has:
    a. Decreased.
    b. Remained stable.
    c. Increased.

29. Top leader's involvement in the implementation of programs:
    a. Is limited to sending invitations, extending congratulations, awarding certificates, etc.
    b. Includes monitoring progress, opening/closing presentations, providing presentations on the importance of the program, etc.
    c. Includes program participation to see what's involved, conducting/administering segments of the program, requiring key managers to be involved, etc.

30. When a participant is involved in a program, his or her manager (or significant other) is likely to:
    a. Make no reference to the program.
    b. Ask questions about the program and encourage the use of the program content or material.
    c. Require use of the program material and provide rewards when the program is successful.

Score the assessment instrument as follows. Allow:

- 1 point for each (a) response.
- 3 points for each (b) response.
- 5 points for each (c) response.

The total will be between 30 and 150 points.

The interpretation of scoring is provided below. The explanation is based on the input from hundreds of organizations and program evaluators.

Score range	Analysis of score
120–150	*Outstanding Environment* for achieving results with your programs. Great management support. A truly successful example of results-based programs.
90–119	*Above Average* in achieving results with your programs. Good management support. A solid and methodical approach to results-based programs.
60–89	*Needs Improvement* to achieve desired results your programs. Management support is ineffective. Programs do not usually focus on results.
30–59	*Serious Problems* with the success and status of your programs. Management support is nonexistent. Programs are not producing or showing the value of the program to funders, sponsors, and donors.

Appendix B

ROI Quiz

True or False? Please choose the answer you feel is most correct

	T	F
1. The ROI Methodology collects or generates just one data item, expressed as a percentage.	○	○
2. A program with monetary benefits of $200,000 and costs of $100,000 translates into a 200% ROI.	○	○
3. The ROI Methodology is a tool to strengthen and improve programs, projects, and processes.	○	○
4. After reviewing a detailed ROI impact study, senior executives will usually require ROI studies on all programs.	○	○
5. ROI studies should be conducted very selectively, usually involving 5–10% of programs.	○	○
6. While it may be a rough estimate, it is always possible to isolate the effects of a program on impact data.	○	○
7. A program costing $100 per participant, designed to support 100 participants, is an ideal program for an ROI study.	○	○
8. Data can always be credibly converted to monetary value.	○	○
9. The ROI Methodology contains too many complicated formulas.	○	○
10. The ROI Methodology can be implemented for about 3–5% of my budget.	○	○
11. ROI is not future oriented; it only reflects past performance.	○	○
12. ROI is not possible for soft programs.	○	○
13. A negative ROI will kill my program.	○	○
14. The best time to consider an ROI evaluation is three months after the program is completed.	○	○
15. In the early stages of implementation, the ROI Methodology is a process improvement tool and not a performance evaluation tool for the program team.	○	○
16. If senior executives and donors are not asking for ROI, there is no need to pursue the ROI Methodology.	○	○

So, how did you do?

The answers are contained in Appendix C. Now that the answers to the quiz have been provided, see how you fared. Tally your scores. Based on the interpretations below, what is your ROI acumen?

No. of correct responses	Interpretation
14–16	You could be an ROI consultant
10–13	You could be a speaker at the next ROI Conference
7–9	You need a copy of a thick ROI book
4–6	You need to attend a two-day ROI workshop
1–3	You need to attend the ROI certification

Appendix C

Answers to the Quiz in Appendix B

1. F
2. F
3. T
4. F
5. T
6. T
7. F
8. F
9. F
10. T
11. F
12. F
13. F
14. F
15. T
16. F

If you have questions about the answers, we would be delighted to discuss them with you. Please contact us at info@roiinstitute.net.

Index

Action planning, 53
Action plans, 211–217
  collect action plans, 215
  confidence level for estimates, 215
  data and ROI, 215–217
  effects of program, 214–215
  goals and targets, setting, 212
  implementation, 214
  monetary value, 214
  unit of measure, 212–214
Alignment model, 98–99
Align programs with business, 93–118
  alignment model, 98–99
  beginning with the end in mind, 97
  business measure, identifying, 110–112
  business needs, 109–118
  challenge, 97
  change, 97–98
  consequences of inaction, 117
  costs of problem, 105–107
  discipline and determination, 98
  forecast and, 108–109
  impact data, sources of, 115–116
  impact measures, critical, 96
  key questions to ask, 102
  measures, identifying, 116
  new programs, reasons for, 104–105
  obvious *versus* not-so-obvious payoffs, 102–104
  opportunity, determining, 109
  paralysis by analysis, 98
  payoff needs, 99–102
  tangible *versus* intangible, better approach, 115

value of opportunity, 107–108
Allocation, influencing, 396–400
  anxiety and downturns, cost reduction, 399–400
  competition for funding, 398–399
  investment *versus* cost, 396–398
Analysis investment, 126
Appropriate method selection, 222–224
  additional method, utility of, 224
  cost of method, 223
  data input, manager (or significant other) time, 223
  data input, participants' time, 222–223
  data type, 222
  method accuracy, 223
  normal work activities, disruption, 223
Attribution, lack of emphasis, 49

Benefit-cost analysis, 47–49, 74
Benefit-cost ratio (BCR), 47, 85
Black box thinking, funding, 381–400
  adjustments in programs, 387–389
  allocation, influencing, 396–400
  aviation industry, 384
  discontinue the program, 388–389
  failures in programs, 386–387
  fear of results, 387–388
  healthcare industry, 384–386
  opportunity for improvement, 388
  process improvement, 383–387
  ROI, increasing, 393–396
  timing of changes, 390–393

Budget constraints, 9
Built-in application tools, 226–229
　application tools/templates, 227
　job aids, 227–228
　plans and guides, improvement, 227
Business measure, identifying,
　　110–112
　cost, 110–112
　output, 110
　quality, 110
　time, 112
Business need, defining, 113–115
　client service, 114
　employee development/
　　advancement, 114
　image/reputation, 115
　initiative/innovation, 114
　leadership, 114
　work climate/satisfaction, 114
Business performance data
　existing performance measures,
　　219–220
　monitoring, 219–221
　new measures, developing, 221
Businessweek magazine, 93

Capitalism, 5
Cause-and-effect relationship, 127
Chain of value, focus, 50–51
Chaplaincy groups, 3
Chaplains, 54
Chief financial officer (CFO), 56, 57
Chronicle of Philanthropy, 15
CIPP evaluation model, 45
Civility ordinances, 119
Communications, program, 174–176
　announcements, 175
　brochures, 175
　correspondence, 176
　workbooks and participant guides,
　　176
Connectivity, 63
Conservative nature, 63
Cost-effective approach, 30–31

Cost reduction, 33
Costs of program, 315–344
　classroom facilities, 332
　cost tabulation in action, 328–333
　FIA's development costs, 333
　importance of, 319
　specific costs, 325–328
Cost tabulation in action, 328–333
　criteria, selection, 330–331
　drivers of evaluation, 331–332
　problem and solution, 328–329
　program administration, 331
　program description, 329–330
Counseling program, 25
Counseling services, 21
Cybersecurity, 31

Data, types, 61–62, 70–75
　application and implementation,
　　73–74
　impact, 74
　input, 70–72
　learning, 73
　reaction and planned action, 72–73
　return on investment, 74–75
Data categories types, 26
Data collection
　action plans, 211–217
　for application and impact, 204–218
　application data, collecting,
　　224–225
　collecting at periodic intervals,
　　198–199
　cultural bias for, 224
　early, detailed feedback, 198
　focus groups, 210
　impact data, collecting, 225–226
　for input, reaction, and learning,
　　194–197
　interviews, 209
　measuring with simulation, 196–197
　measuring with tests, 196
　observations, 210–211
　performance contract, 217–218

pre-program, 198
programs with multiple parts, 199
questionnaires and surveys,
    194–196, 204–209
timing of, 197–199, 224–226
unclear timing, 51–52
Data to monetary value, conversion,
    265–295
annual amount of change, 271
annual value of improvement, 271
budgeting, 268–269
change in performance data, 271
estimates, management team, 289
estimates from participants,
    288–289
historical costs from records,
    282–284
input from experts, 284–285
key steps in, 270–272
linking with other measures,
    286–288
program staff estimates, 289–290
technique, selection, 290–295
unit of measure, focus on, 270
value of each unit, 270–271
values from external databases,
    285–286
Decision-making, 18, 138, 269, 382,
    418, 427, 430
Designing, basis of levels, 149–152
application, 150
empathy, use, 151–152
impact of program, 150
input, 149–150
learning, 150
reaction, 150
ROI, 151
Design thinking, 78, 388
Diagnostic tools, 126
Disabling frequency rate (DFR), 250
Disengaged talent, 31
Domestic violence law (DVL), 250
Donors, 10–11
Dynamic adjustments, 62

Effective evaluation model, criteria, 60
Effects of program, isolation, 237–264
experimental design, 246–249
impact of other factors, 253–254
mathematical modeling, 252–253
method, selection, 263–264
myths, 240–242
other factors, identify, 243–244
preliminary issues, 242–244
qualitative isolation methods,
    254–263
quantitative and research isolation,
    244–254
reality, 240
review chain of impact, 242–243
trend line analysis, 249–252
eLearning investment, 56
Enhanced logic model, 39–67
Evaluation
capital expenditures, 61
managing resources, 57–58
plan, 52
profile of, 35
Evaluation, planning, 166–172
data collection plan, 167
evaluation purpose, 166
outcome evaluations, feasibility, 167
project plan, 171–172
ROI analysis plan, 167–171
Expectations, 29
Expectations, creating, 178–181
identifying impact measures, 179
involving managers, 181

Feasibility, right solution selection,
    119–140
analysis techniques, 125–127
forecasting ROI, 138
implementation, time needed, 138
learning needs, 131–134
matching solutions to needs,
    135–136
matrix diagram, 136–137
mismatches, avoiding, 139

multiple solutions, tackling, 140
performance dialogue, 122–125
performance needs, 122
preference needs, 134–135
short-term *versus* long-term costs, 138
solutions for maximum payoff, 138–140
verify the match, 139
Fitbit, 203
Forecasting, ROI, 401–430
basic steps, 414–417
compliance, 410–411
expensive programs, 407
guidelines, 427–429
high risks and uncertainty, 407–409
importance of, 407–411
pilot program, 422–423
post-program comparison, 409–410
reaction data, 423–425
trade-offs of, 411–412
use of data, 426–427
Freakonomics, 239
Fundamental cost issues, 320–325
cost guidelines, develop and use, 323–325
costs without benefits, 322
employee benefits factor, 325
fully loaded costs, 320–321
prorated *versus* direct costs, 324–325
sources of costs, 323–324

General Board of Higher Education and Ministry (GBHEM), 1
Generally Accepted Accounting Principles (GAAP), 61
Global Finance Organization (GFO), 141, 142
Global reporting initiative (GRI), 5
Graduation rates, 94

Homeless, 79, 119, 120, 121, 220, 277

Impact objectives, 53
Improved behaviors payoff, 29–30
Incarceration, 21
Input, design, 183–187
motivation, 186
need, 184–185
readiness, 186
target audience, 183–184
timing and duration, 185–186
Intangibles, identifying, 297–313
analyzing, 312–313
converted to tangibles, 302–303
converting to money, 307–308
identifying and collecting, 311–312
importance of, 299–300
intangible economy, 301
invisible advantage, 300–301
measuring, 304–307
programs and investments, driving, 303–304
Internal Revenue Service (IRS), 27
Investment, inability to influence, 59
Investment, optimization, 59

King Khalid University, 56

Language of business, 3
Leadership development workshop, 3
Learning, design, 193–194
activities, 194
learning style, 194
sequencing and time, 194
Learning needs, 131–134
demonstrations, 132
job and task analysis, 131–132
management assessment, 133
observations, 132
subject-matter experts (SMEs), 131
tests, 132–133
Length of stay (LOS), 252, 253
Logic models, 42, 49
components of, 43
elements, 44–45

Make it credible concept, 237–264
Make it matter concept, 173–199
Making it stick, step, 201–235
Measurement process, 63, 64
Measurement systems, 63, 64, 94
Media, selection, 356, 363–370
 case studies, 370
 email and electronic media, 369
 interim and progress reports, 366
 meetings, 363–366
 program brochures and pamphlets, 369
 routine communication tools, 366–369
Monetary benefits, 32
Monetary values, 5, 33, 267
 executive appetite for, 16
 importance of, 6, 267–270
 money, impressive impact, 268
 understand problems and cost data, 269–270
 value equals money, 267–268
 vital to organizational operations, 269

Needs assessments *versus* activities, 52
Neighborhood insurance, 340
Noncapital investments, 48
Nongovernment organizations (NGOs), 25
Nonprofits, 31, 33, 35

Objectives at multiple levels, 152–159
 application objectives, 155–156
 impact objectives, 157
 learning objectives, 154–155
 reaction objectives, 153–154
 return on investment (ROI) objectives, 158–159
Operating budget, 35
Organization for the Prohibition of Chemical Weapons (OPCW), 55

Participants' manager, 230–234
 most influential group, 230–231
 post-program activities, 232
 pre-program activities, 231
 during program activities, 232
 reinforcement tools, 232–233
Participants role, changing, 177–178
 necessity, 177
 roles, defining, 177–178
 roles, documenting, 178
Patient satisfaction, 54
Payoff needs, 99–102
Performance contract, 217–218
Performance dialogue, 122–125
 benchmarking, 124
 data and records, 123
 disasters, discussion, 125
 discussion, initiating, 123
 evaluation, use, 124–125
 high-profile donor, 125
Pilot group, 246
Placement rates, 94
Planto Reduce Turnover, 137
Potential payoff, 122
Power and politics, 18
Power of expectations, 144–147
Preference needs, 134–135
 key issues, 134–135
Pre-program ROI forecasting, 413–422
 basic model, 413–414
 conversion to money, 419
 expert input sources, 417–418
 program cost estimates, 419–422
 securing input, 418–419
Process improvement, lack of focus, 58–59
Program Action Logic Model, 43
Program costs, 9–10
Program evaluation model, 46
Program failures, 8–9
Programs, basis of value, 31
Project costs, 9–10

Qualitative isolation methods, 254–263
customer estimates, program impact, 260
internal or external expert estimates, 260–261
manager's estimate, impact, 259–260
participants' estimate, impact, 255–259
wisdom of crowds, 261
Quality measures, 27, 33

Reaction, design, 187–193
forecasting ROI, 192–193
measuring, 191
reaction data, using, 192
topics to measure, 188–189
Real money, 34
Results-based process, sustaining change, 431–446
bad news, delivering, 444
champion, developing, 435
champion, identifying, 434–435
climate, assess, 434
data, using, 444–445
evaluation targets, setting, 437–438
goals and plans, establishing, 436–438
guidelines and procedures, revising, 438–440
initiate ROI studies, 441
management team, preparing, 442–443
myths, dispelling, 443–444
obstacles, removing, 443
plan for implementation, 438
progress, monitoring, 445
resistance, overcoming, 433–434
responsibilities, assigning, 436
task force, establishing, 435–436
team, involving, 440
team, preparing, 440
team, teaching, 440–441
Return on expectations (ROE), 18

Return on investment (ROI)
calculation, 27–28, 38, 312, 333–343
benefit/cost ratio, 334–335
discounted cash flow, 342–343
internal rate of return (IRR), 343
misuse of ROI, 338–339
monetary benefits, 337–338
payback period (breakeven analysis), 342
ROI formula, 335–337
ROI objectives, 340
Return on investment (ROI) methodology, 1, 2, 8, 22–24, 36, 41, 47, 48, 64, 65–66, 69–91, 143, 181–183, 297, 299, 382, 383, 406
actions to take, 183
aligning with business, 89
align programs with business, 78–81
application and impact, design for, 83
applications, 4, 5
benefits-costs ratio (BCR), 85
black box thinking, 86–87
capture costs of projects, 85
certification process, 64
certification program, 23
certification workshop, 25
costs, addressing, 393–395
data, analyzing, 83–86
data, types of, 70–75
data collection, 82–83
data to monetary value, conversion, 84
design thinking, 77–78
effects of program, 83–84
evaluation, plan, 78–82
fear of, 17
feasibility, 81
forecasting, 401–430
image and building respect, enhancing, 90
impacts and intangibles, 28–29

implementing and sustaining process, 87–88

importance of, 319

improving processes, 89

improving support, 90

increasing, 393–396

initial analysis, 75–77

initiate, studies, 441

input, reaction, and learning, design for, 82

intangible benefits, 84–85

justifying or enhancing budgets, 90–91

key stakeholders, use of storytelling, 86

making it stick, 203

monetary benefits, addressing, 395

negative value, 318

operating standards and philosophy, 87

preparation and skills, 17

process model, 78–83

productive partnerships, building, 91

profits and, 33–34

projects, solutions and participants, 66–67

public sector and, 34–35

requirements, 64

ROI review, 182

success, expecting, 81–82

sustainability, 19

timing of assessments, 395–396

value proposition, validating, 89

Safe operations practice (SOP) program, 249

Seven habits, 40, 41

"Show me" generation, 6–7

Simplicity, 63

Smoking cessation program, 34

Social return on investment (SROI), 18, 339

Social security administration, 32

Soft data, 113–115

Specific costs, 325–328

acquisition costs, 326

evaluation and reporting, 328

implementation costs, 326–327

initial analysis and assessment, 326

maintenance and monitoring, 327–328

program solutions development, 326

support and overhead, 328

Stakeholders, tell the story, 345–379

analyze reaction, 378–379

analyze reason for communication, 359

application, 348

audience, selection, 360–362

audiences, information, 353–355

audience's bias, communication strategy, 357

business impact, 348–350

clear and precise, message, 356–357

communicating, importance of, 352–355

communicating results, principles, 355–357

communicating results, process, 357–359

communication, politically sensitive issue, 353

communication to explain contribution, 353

communication to make improvements, 352–353

consistent communication, 356

intangibles, 351

media, selection, 356, 363–370

plan for communication, 359–360

presentation, 346–347

present information, 370–371

reaction and learning, 347–348

recommendations, 351

reflection, 352

reports, developing, 363

ROI calculation, 350

routine feedback, program progress, 371–373
senior management, results presentation, 374–378
specific audiences, communication, 355–356
storytelling, 373–374
testimonials about program, 357
timely communication, 355
unbiased and modest, communication, 356
Standard monetary values, 272–290
cost of inadequate quality, 276–278
employee time savings, compensation, 279–281
finding, 281
non availability of, 281–290
output data to money, converting, 273–275
Student success, 94
Success, expecting, 141–172
analysts, 163
application/impact objectives, design and development, 160
application/impact objectives, evaluation, 161–162
application/impact objectives, facilitation, 160–161
application/impact objectives, participants, 161
application/impact objectives drive programs, 160
designer role, 163
designing, basis of levels, 149–152
developer, 163
evaluation, planning, 166–172
evaluator, 165
facilitator's role, 164
impact objectives, sponsors and donors, 161
objectives at multiple levels, 152–159
objectives levels, stakeholders, 162
other stakeholders, 165–166

participants, 164–165
participants/significant others, managers, 165
power of expectations, 144–147
power of objectives, 160–162
program owner, 164
roles and responsibilities, defining, 162–166
sponsor or donor, 165
success of programs, defining, 147–149

Technique, selection
appropriate for data type, 290
credibility test, 292
most to least accurate, 290–291
multiple techniques, feasibility, 291–292
short-term/long-term issue, 292–294
source availability, 291
source with broadest perspective, 291
time value of money, adjustment for, 294–295
Time commitment, 17–18
Timing of changes, 390–393
application measures, 391–392
impact measures, 392
input, 390
learning measures, 391
making adjustments, 392–393
reaction measures, 390

United Methodist Church, 1
United Methodist Endorsing Agency (UMEA), 1
University Cooperative Extension Programs, 43

Value evolution, 1–19
benchmarking limitations, 15–16
evidence-based/fact-based management, 14

globalization, 13–14
impact level, measurement, 11
institutions, mistrust, 15
managers' new business focus, 12
process improvements, 12
project management growth, 14

Values
    definition of, 7–8
    shift, 4–16
    types of, 5–6

Wikipedia, 42
Workplace, 174